# Family Communication:

## Cohesion and Change
## Fourth Edition

# Family Communication:
## Cohesion and Change
## Fourth Edition

**Kathleen M. Galvin**
Northwestern University

**Bernard J. Brommel**
Northeastern Illinois University

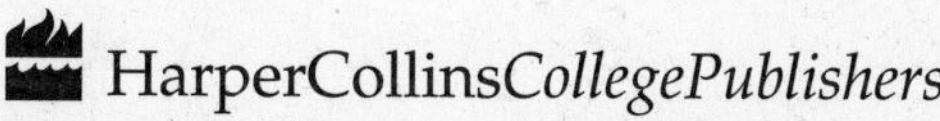

Acquisitions Editor: Cynthia Biron
Project Coordination, Text and Cover Designer: Ruttle Graphics, Inc.
Cover Photographs: Comstock, Inc.
Art Studio: Ruttle Graphics, Inc.
Photo Researcher: Kelly Mountain
Electronic Production Manager: Angel Gonzalez Jr.
Manufacturing Manager: Willie Lane
Electronic Page Makeup: Ruttle Graphics, Inc.
Printer and Binder: R.R. Donnelly & Sons Company
Cover Printer: The Lehigh Press, Inc.



**FAMILY COMMUNICATION: COHESION AND CHANGE, FOURTH EDITION**



Library of Congress Cataloging-in-Publication Data
Galvin, Kathleen M.
Family communication: cohesion and change/Kathleen M. Galvin, Bernard J. Brommel. — 4th ed.
p. cm.
Includes bibliographical references and index.
ISBN 0-0673-99628-X
1. Communication in the family—United States. 2. Interpersonal communication—United States. I. Brommel, Bernard J., 1930- . II. Title.
HQ734.G19 1996 95-3972
306.87—dc20 CIP

95 96 97 98 9 8 7 6 5 4 3 2 1

*To my family: The Galvins, Wilkinsons, Nicholsens, and Sullivans, plus the special friends I consider as my family.*

*KMG*

*To my children and grandchildren; with thanks to Joseph De Vito, Pete Tortorello, Vic Silvestri, and Terry Cozad. I dedicate my part of this edition to the memory of my sister Florence Cairo, and my friends Randy Treff and Phil Davitt. Their dying gave new meanings to my sense of the importance of family.*

*BJB*

# Contents

# Preface

It is a pleasure to introduce the fourth edition of *Family Communication: Cohesion and Change,* the first textbook to address the family from a communication perspective. The earlier editions have been used by students and teachers of family-related courses in communication, psychology, sociology, counseling and home economics.

Historically, family interaction received attention solely within medical and therapeutic perspectives focusing on families with an ill or dysfunctional member. Only recently have scholars turned their attention to interaction within functional families. The past fifteen years have witnessed growing interest in ordinary family interaction processes within all of the social sciences. Current thinking places strong emphasis on theories and perspectives which value methodological diversity and recognize the diversity of family experience. Increasing numbers of communication scholars are researching specific aspects of family communication and these studies increasingly fill pages of the text.

The basic premise of this book is that communication processes serve to constitute as well as reflect families. Relying on symbolic interaction and systems theories, we consider, the communication processes within the family as well as the extent to which they affect and are affected by larger social systems.

The focus of the text remains descriptive rather than prescriptive, because we believe that description provides the understanding necessary to the eventual development of valuable approaches and strategies. We examine how family members typically perform primary family functions—regulating cohesion and adaptability—and secondary family functions—developing appropriate family images, themes, boundaries, and biosocial beliefs.

The first four chapters establish the foundation of the text. Chapter one presents basic communication and family concepts and an overview of rapidly changing family demographics. Chapter two details a framework for analyzing family communication relying on primary and secondary functions and the dialectical struggle which undergirds family relationships over time. Chapter three establishes the systems perspective. The fourth chapter provides an explanation of how family meanings develop and illustrates the influential role of multigenerational communication patterns on current family functioning. Later chapters explore communication issues related to basic family interactions: relationship development, intimacy, roles, power, conflict, developmental stages, and adjustment to unpredictable crises. The final chapters focus on the psychological, physical, and temporal contexts for family communication patterns and discusses perspectives on well family functioning plus approaches to improving family communication.

With each edition we have attempted to reflect the constantly changing family experience and the rapidly expanding research. In this edition we focus extensively on diverse family forms, with special attention to gender and ethnicity, all critical issues to contemporary family scholars. We attempt to articulate more explicitly our underlying theoretical structures, to emphasize dialectal thinking, to include more qualitative studies and to emphasize psychological as well as physical contexts. Whereas in the early editions we relied heavily on research in related areas, we believe this edition synthesizes the best of current related research in communication as well as across the social sciences.

Throughout the book we present first-person examples (names and identifying data have been changed) that complement the content. In this edition we have linked these more directly to the text to illustrate the direct application of concepts.

Many persons contributed to the completion of the fourth edition. We received valuable feedback on manuscript drafts from Gail Whitchurch, Indiana University/Purdue University, Indianapolis; Glen Stamp, Ball State University.

We are grateful to Cynthia Biron and Michael Gibbons and the Harper Collins editorial staff for their supportive encouragement and guidance. Our students and clients provided insightful commentaries and examples. Frances Pearcy and Marilyn Mueller typed the manuscript while Katie King and Andrea Spitz provided research support. Charles Wilkinson supplied numerous examples from his family practice.

Our own families have grown and changed over the past fifteen years, a process that has taught us a great deal more about family life and family communication. To our family members we express our gratitude for their exceptional patience, moral support and unwitting examples.

Finally, this book comes from our own commitment to, and enthusiasm for, teaching family communication. Unlike most other academic courses, students bring their personal experiences to the course content and, thus, start with considerable insight and knowledge of the subject. From them, and through our practice and research, we continue to learn about how families interact and what it means to be a member of a family system.

Kathleen M. Galvin

Bernard J. Brommel

# 1

# Introduction to the Family

Families: We are born into a family, mature in a family, form new families, and leave them at our deaths. Family life is a universal human experience. Yet, no two people share the exact same experience, partly because of the unique communication patterns in each family system. Because the family is such a powerful influence on our lives, we need to examine family interaction patterns to understand ourselves better as members of one of the most complex and important parts of society. These communication patterns serve to construct as well as reflect familial experience. In short, we create our families just as we are created by these families.

As you read this book, you will examine a subject you already know something about, since you have spent your life in some type or types of family arrangements. Yet, since you have lived in only one or a small number of families, your experience is limited compared to the range of possible family experiences. Your reading should expand your understanding of many types of families and their communication patterns. You should find similarities and differences from your experiences.

This book presents a framework for examining communication within families. By the end of the text, you should be able to apply this model to an unknown family and understand it as a communication system. We also hope that you will apply what you learn to your own family or to the family you will eventually form, in order to understand the communication dynamics of this important group.

Throughout this book, you will find some material written in the first person and set off from the text. These selections, some direct quotes and some reconstructions provided by friends, students, and clients, illustrate many of the concepts discussed in the text. These statements should enable you to understand the concepts more completely. Some material will remind you specifically of your own family experiences, while other material will seem quite different from your background, since people relate to each other very differently within a family.

As family members, teachers, and family therapists, we hold certain basic beliefs which undergird the words on the following pages. Our backgrounds have given us particular perspectives which affect how we view families and their communication. Our perspectives may be very similar, or they may be quite different from yours. Because our backgrounds influence our thinking and writing, we wish to share these with you to establish a context for understanding.

1. There is no "right" way to be a family. Family life is as diverse as the types of persons who create families. There are many types of families and numerous ways to relate within each family type. Families are human systems created by ordinary people; the "perfect" family does not exist. Each family must struggle to create its own identity as it experiences good times and stressful times. All families are influenced by the larger context in which they exist.

2. Communication serves to constitute as well as reflect family life. It is through talk that persons define their identities and negotiate their relationships with each other and the rest of the world. This talk also serves to indicate the state of family relationships.

3. Communication is the process by which family members work out and share their meanings with each other. Members create a relational culture, or a shared universe which may be viewed as a unique communication system.

4. Families are part of multigenerational communication patterns. Family members are influenced by the patterns of previous generations as they create their own patterns which will influence generations to come. The family serves as each person's first classroom in communication.

5. Well-functioning families work at managing their communication patterns. Developing and maintaining relationships takes work. Such families develop the capacity to adapt and to create change, to share intimacy and to manage conflict. Well-functioning families are self-aware; they value the goal of effective communication, understanding this may be achieved in various ways depending on the people involved. Yet, these family members consciously work at maintaining or improving their relationships through their communication.

This text attempts to introduce you to the diverse world of families and their complex communication patterns and to develop your observational and analytical skills. It will not present prescriptive solutions for family problems. We hope your increased understanding of family communication will be accompanied by an increased appreciation for complexities and change inherent in this area of study. We also hope you will find the area of family communication as fascinating and challenging as we do.

As an introduction to the family, this chapter will discuss definitional issues and family status. The next section establishes an understanding of the concept of the family which will be used throughout the rest of the book.

## FAMILIES: DEFINITIONAL ISSUES

What comes to your mind when you hear the word *family*? How would you define the term? Although *family* is a word used frequently, reaching agreement on its meaning is much more difficult than you might suspect. In the following section, you will see the variations implied in the simple term *family*.

### Family Types

There is no single, widely agreed-upon definition of the term *family*. Traditionally, blood and legal connections described families. Families have been viewed according to blood or consanguine ties and conjugal or marital ties, and described as networks of persons who live together over periods of time, and have ties of marriage and kinship to one another (Laing 1973). In their attempt to find the essence of family, Fitzpatrick and Badzinski (1985) suggest the only universal family type is a small, kinship-structured group whose primary function is the nurturing socialization of newborn children. This position describes a *family realm* which is created by the birth process and the establishment of ties across generations (Beutler et al. 1988), the core aspect being the "biological, emotional, social and developmental processes that are inherent in procreation and the nurturing of dependent children." This definition includes both intergenerational issues and alternative family forms.

In contrast, a family may be viewed more broadly as a group of people with a past history, a present reality, and a future expectation of interconnected mutually influencing relationships. Members often (but not necessarily) are bound together by heredity, legal marital ties, adoption, or a common living arrangement at some point in their

A two parent biological family is no longer the most common family form.

lifetime (Kramer 1980). As early as 1926, sociologist Burgess described the family as a "unity of interacting personalities existing chiefly for the development and mutual gratification of its members ... held together by internal cohesion rather than external pressures." In their recent work, Fitzpatrick and Badzinski (1994) express support for a broad understanding of family. They support the work of Wamboldt and Reiss (1989), who developed an actional process definition of the family as "a group of intimates who generate a sense of home and group identity; complete with strong ties of loyalty and emotion, and experience history and future" (728). Clearly, these definitions emphasize the personal, voluntarily connected relationships among family members, instead of relying solely on blood ties or legal agreements as the basis for a family.

As we talk about families in this book, we will take a broad, inclusive view. Therefore, if the members consider themselves to be a family, we accept their self-definition. Generally, we will refer to family as networks of people who share their lives over long periods of time bound by ties of marriage, blood, or commitment, legal or otherwise, who consider themselves as family and who share a significant history and anticipated future of functioning in a family relationship.

Such a definition encompasses countless variations of family forms and numerous types of interaction patterns.

In contemporary society, family diversity abounds. One indication of the complexities of today's families may be found in a review of current literature, which includes such categories as large, extended, blood-related groups, formal and informal communal groups, stepfamilies, single-parent families, and gay and lesbian partnerships. These families reflect multiple cultural and socioeconomic situations (Cherlin 1992; Heaton and Jacobson 1994). Your authors represent two very different family orientations. One grew up on an Iowa farm in a German-Irish family of nine children, married, fathered six children, divorced, and is now a grandfather of seven. The other grew up in New York City as an only child of Irish immigrants. After her parents died, she acquired an adopted Norwegian-German family with three siblings. Currently, she is married and raising three children, one of whom is adopted from Korea. Although blood relatives are important to each author, both have friends who are considered to be family members.

You may have grown up in a small family, or a four-generation household. Your brothers and sisters may be blood related, step, or adopted. Some of you may be single parents, stepparents, or foster parents. Whereas some of you may have experienced one long, committed marriage, others may have experienced divorce, death, and remarriage or a committed partnership. No simple pattern exists.

There are many categories of families. We will use a simple category system encompassing the following styles of family formation: the two-parent biological family, single-parent family, blended family, extended family, and committed partners. These are not discrete categories; some families may belong to more than one.

A two-parent biological family consists of parents and the children who are from the union of these parents. Thus, blood ties and the original marriage bond characterize this type. Although frequently thought of as "typical," this type of family no longer represents the most common family form.

A single-parent family consists of one parent and one or more children. This formation may include: an unmarried man or woman and his or her offspring; a man or a woman who lost his or her partner through death, divorce, or desertion, and the children of that union; a single parent and his or her adopted or foster children. When two parents are still involved in child care, the term "primary parent" may be used.

The blended family consists of two adults and their children, all of whom may not be from the union of their relationship. Most are families blended through remarriage, a situation that brings two previous systems into new family ties. You may have witnessed the com-

Many children spend part of their lives in a single parent family.

mon pattern in which a two-parent biological family becomes a single-parent family for a period of time, after which certain members become part of a stepfamily. Families may also be blended through the addition of adopted or foster children.

Although an extended family traditionally refers to that group of relatives living within a nearby area, it may be more narrowly understood as the addition of blood relatives, other than the parents, to the everyday life of a child unit. For example, this may take a cross-generational form, including grandparents who live with a parent-child system or who take on exclusive parenting roles for grandchildren:

---

*I grew up in an extended family. My great-grandparents were the dominant figures. Most of us lived with our grandparents at one time or another. There were six different households in the neighborhood I grew up in. My great-grandmother, referred to as "Mother," babysat for all the kids while our parents were at work.*

*There are also people who were informally adopted in my family. My mother and one of my cousins were raised by their grandmother, even though their parents did not live there. In my family no one is considered half or step. You are a member of the family, and that is that.*

---

Another variation of the extended family is the voluntaristic family, a couple or a group of people, some of whom are unrelated, who share a commitment to each other, live together, and consider themselves to be a family. Formal examples of these family types are found in communal situations such as a kibbutz or in a religious organization. Other extended families are informally formed around friendship or common interests or commitments. Two families may share so many experiences that, over time, both sets of children and parents begin to talk of each other as "part of the family."

Committed partners may include married couples without children, lesbian and gay partners, and cohabiting heterosexual couples. Although we often think of families as having children, partners may form their own familial unit as an outgrowth of their original families. Although their numbers are small, some married couples choose to remain child free, while others remain childless due to infertility. Homosexual partners may also be included in this category, as long as the partners consider each other family. Partners without children continue to serve as children to the previous generation and as siblings and extended family members to other generations, while at the same time providing loyalty and affection to one another.

Most people experience family life in an evolutionary manner, moving through different family forms over time, experiencing changes due to aging and unpredictable stresses.

In addition, most persons experience life with one or more biological, adopted, or stepsiblings, the longest lasting family relationships due to age similarity. Sibling relationships are significant sources of information on communication patterns, as this respondent notes:

---

*Because I have very close relationships with my two brothers and my sister, we know which buttons to push when we go home as adults. I find myself adding words back to my vocabulary that haven't been there in years, words such as "jerk," "brat," and "stupid." It is amazing how when I am with my family, we all revert to roles that we were in when we were children. Since I am the oldest, I find myself wanting to take charge.*

---

It is important to distinguish between two types of family experiences—current families and families-of-origin. Families in combination beget families through the evolutionary cycles of coming together and separating. Each person may experience life in different families starting with his or her family-of-origin. *Family-of-origin* refers to the family or families in which a person is raised. Noted family therapist Virginia Satir (1988) stresses the importance of the family-of-origin as the blueprint for peoplemaking. She suggests: "Blueprints vary from family to family. I believe some blueprints result in nurturing families, some result in troubled ones" (210). Multigenerational patterns, those of more than two generations, are considered as part of the blueprint (Hooper 1987). As you will discover, family-of-origin and multigenerational experiences are crucial in the development of communication patterns in current families.

## Family Systems

The systems perspective provides one way to gain insight in family functioning and family communication. This perspective holds that no individual exists in a vacuum. Rather, individuals are linked in ways that make them interdependent on others. Each individual is part of an overall *family system,* affecting and being affected by that system. Therefore, you cannot fully understand a person without knowing something about his or her family. An individual's behavior becomes more comprehensible when viewed within the context of the human system within which he or she functions. For example, one individual's behavior may appear strange to an outsider, but if you understand the whole family context, your perceptions may change. What may be viewed as problematic behavior in one setting may be functional in another context.

Within a system, the parts and the relationship between them form the whole; changes in one part will result in changes in the others. So, too, in families. Satir describes a family as a mobile (1988, 137). Picture a mobile that hangs over a child's crib, with people instead of elephants or sailboats on it. As events touch one member of the family, other members reverberate in relationship to the change in the affected member. Thus, if a family member loses a job, flunks out of school, wins the state basketball championship, marries, or becomes ill, such an event affects the entire family system, depending on each person's current relationship with that individual. In addition, because family members are human beings, not elephants or sailboats on a mobile, they can "pull their own strings," or make their own moves. At some point, a family member may choose to withdraw from the family and, by pulling away, forces other members into closer relationships. Thus, as members move toward or away from each other, all members are affected. Holding a systems perspective implies you will always observe and analyze families by paying attention to the relationships among members as opposed to paying attention only to one individual. From a communication perspective, it means being concerned with the patterns created between and among family members rather than paying attention to what individuals say.

## FAMILIES: CURRENT STATUS

### Demographics

The contemporary family exists in a world of constant change. In order to understand family interaction fully, it is necessary to examine the current status of family life in America. No matter how old you are, you have lived long enough to witness major changes in your family or in the families around you. These changes reflect pieces of an evolving national picture. In 1955, for example, 60 percent of all households in the United States consisted of an intact marriage, a working father, a homemaker mother, and two or more school-aged children. Today, only 7 percent of all households fit the traditional family image. At this point, there are more married couples without children than with children. Approximately 37 percent of American families are married with children under 18. American families reflect greater ethnic and racial diversity than they did earlier in this century. Many families face issues of poverty and anxiety. More families are constructing voluntary family links. Although research figures shift constantly and various sources provide slightly different numerical data, the overall point is clear; the American family has undergone dramatic changes in the twentieth century. Reports of census data attest to the scope of such change (Current Population Reports March, 1992).

The impact of recent decades of family change may be demonstrated by the current reality for children. The normal childhood experience of 61 percent of today's youth is to live with only one parent sometime before reaching age 18 (Single Parents 1992, 14). Children have fewer siblings than in previous times; the number of children in a family is slightly over two. Each year, approximately 50,000 children are adopted.

Current trends indicate that first marriages are taking place later. For example, the median age for women was 21 in 1975, 23 in 1985, and 24 in 1992. For men it was 26.5 in 1992, the highest since 1900. The average length of a first marriage ending in divorce ranged from 7.3 years in 1975 to 6.9 years in 1980 and went back up to 7.5 years in 1985. Often one partner is remarrying while the other is marrying for the first time. Almost half of all marriages now involve at least one partner remarrying.

Incidence of divorce has risen rapidly throughout this century, up 700 percent since 1900. This figure also reflects the longevity of persons in today's society. In earlier times, when more people died at a younger age, many unsatisfactory marriages were ended by death rather than divorce. Family historian Coontz (1992) emphasizes this point by saying:

> It is important to remember that the 50 percent divorce rate estimates are calculated in terms of a forty-year period and that many marriages in the past were terminated well before the death of one partner. Historian Lawrence Stone suggests that divorce has become a functional substitute for death. (16)

Recently, the divorce rate has remained relatively constant after the significant rise during the 1970s. Clearly this population shifts as over 70 percent of divorced persons remarry. The incidence of redivorce continues to rise.

At this time, remarriage rates are high and most divorced individuals will form a new partnership. About five out of six men and three out of four women remarry after divorce. About half of these remarriages occur within three years of divorce.

Approximately three-fourths of women who divorce eventually remarry, although the proportion seems to be declining. Childless divorced women under 30 are most likely to remarry, followed by divorced women with children under age 30. Older women are the least likely to remarry. Coontz generalizes about this experience saying, "About 50 percent of first marriages and 60 percent of second ones can be expected to end in divorce" (182).

Americans are witnessing the continuing rise of single-parent systems. In 1970, 11 percent of children under age 18 lived with their mothers, 1 percent with their fathers, and 85 percent with two parents. In 1982, 20 percent of children under 18 lived with their mothers, 2 percent with their fathers, and 75 percent with two parents. The remainder were cared for in institutional settings. The single-parent rates are rising because more children are entering life as part of a single-parent system. Whereas in 1960 approximately 5 percent of births occurred to unmarried women, by 1992 that figure had risen to over 25 percent (Single Parents 1992).

Today, single-parent families account for 9 percent of American households, or 26 percent of households with children. These figures do not include young, single-parents living with their parents. Men head close to 20 percent of single-parent households (Single Parents 1992, 15). Divorce accounts for about 46 percent of single parent households—out-of-wedlock births account for approximately 26 percent. 21 percent are due to marital separation and 7 percent due to death (Single Parents 1992, 15).

The stepfamily remains a vital family form although census figures are difficult to justify because of variations in custodial arrangements. One out of every three Americans is now a stepparent, a stepchild, a stepsibling, or some other member of a stepfamily (Larson 1992). This figure is predicted to rise to almost 50 percent by the turn of the century. Most children in remarried households live with their biological mother and stepfather.

Recent census data indicate the number of unmarried couple households is growing rapidly. Such households are defined as "two unrelated adults of the opposite sex sharing living quarters with or without children present." In 1988 there were 2.6 million unmarried couple households, nearly a third with children. This figure represents more than four times the number in 1970, and represents 5 percent of the couples in U.S. households. There were 1,891,000 unmarried couple households in 1983—more than three times the number in 1970. Although during the 1970s this type grew rapidly, the amount of growth since has been comparatively small.

Census figures on gay-male and lesbian couples are not available. Blumstein and Schwartz (1983) were the first to include such couples as a significant part of their study of couple types. They suggest that, until the 1970s, gay males and lesbians were a fairly invisible part of the American population. Studies in the 1970s and 1980s point toward the desire for couple relationships within the gay-male or lesbian community (McWhirter and Mattison 1984; Bozett 1987). A small percentage of gay men and lesbians have formed committed partnerships and consider themselves to be family and are finding varying levels of legal and institutional recognition of this union as a family type. Recently Laird (1993) used the terms "gay family" and "lesbian family" to refer to same-sex couples and to families with children headed by a lesbian or gay couple or solo parent (282).

Throughout the past decade the attention to gay and lesbian parenting has increased. The homosexual parent may be legally joined with a spouse of the opposite sex and have one or more biological or adopted children. It is estimated that there are more than 2 million gay parents (Coontz 182; Coleman 1992a). Likewise, some gay men and lesbians may become parents through adoption, foster care, or alternative fertilization (Bozett 1987).

All these changes are occurring against a backdrop of longer life expectancy. Persons born in 1960 have a life expectancy of 69.7 years, while those born in 1990 have an expectancy of 75.4 years, although gender differences exist. Men born in 1990 have a life expectancy of 71.8 years, while women have an expectancy of 78.8

years. The longevity results in an increase in four generation households. Increasing numbers (1.2 million) of children are living in grandparent headed households with or without a parent. Considering that most people marry first during their twenties, a continuous marriage might well be expected to last forty to sixty years. The number of married couples without children continues to rise as people live longer and women bear a small number of children in the early years of marriage. This is a new "era" for American couples aged 45–65. On a more somber note, widowhood has become an expectant life event for most older women. Over age 65, the ratio of widows to widowers is approximately 6:1. Siblings may become the core family experience for many older Americans.

The family descriptors do not capture fully the voluntaristic family commitments made by individuals or groups which are not recorded in census or related data. These include informal adoption, certain steprelations, and informal adult commitments to function as siblings or other types of family members.

## Economic Issues

All these changes are intertwined with economic and ethnic realities. Today, only 7 percent of households in the U.S. fit the traditional description of a family with a working father and a mother at home. Working mothers are commonplace. From 1970–1990, the number of working married women with children under age 6 increased from 30 percent to 58 percent. In those with children ages 6–17, it increased from 49 percent to 73 percent (Married with Children 1992). These figures will increase in the coming decades because young two-career couples are becoming a larger segment of the twenty to thirty-year old age group and dual income is seen as necessary if not desirable by most couples. Over 70 percent of single mothers are working. Most have little choice but to work. Due to these changes, the United States is witnessing a phenomenon of "latchkey children" who return from school hours before a parent returns from work and are expected to contribute to the successful running of the household. Young children may spend many of their waking hours with babysitters or in day-care centers, encountering their parents only a few hours a day.

Another economic reality which impacts directly on family life is poverty (Heaton and Jacobson 1994). One third of the homeless are families with children, a figure which is rising rapidly. Although a large number of poor families contain two parents, the female single parent family is five times more likely to live in poverty than the two parent family. In 1990, the poverty rate for all U.S. children under three was 24 percent; the poverty rate for African American children was 52 percent, 42 percent for Hispanic children, 21 percent for other ethnic/minority groups and 15 percent for white children (National Center for Children in Poverty 1993). The economic pressures add significant stress to the lives of these family members and this stress affects the ways family members relate to each other.

This is a difficult period for many families which are facing economic and safety concerns as well as worries about their children's futures. "In the late 20th century, at least one quarter of all Americans live in distressed communities—that is, neighborhoods that lack good schools, and good jobs at decent wages. The families in these communities demonstrate similar kinds of adaptive strategies in their struggles to resist the despair and demoralization that threaten to engulf them" (Jones 1993). Although all families report worrying about their children, poor minority parents are more likely to indicate extreme and frequent fear about their children's safety and well-being. Between 40–50 percent of urban poor parents worry that their children may get shot, drop out of school, get pregnant, or get a girl pregnant. Their children worry about being hurt or abused. (National Opinion Research Project 1991). These pressures have left many mothers severely depressed and have created a group of young children that witness violence and killing, which results in a *lost childhood* (Coleman 1992b). Such families face great odds as they struggle to adapt. In some cases, children are raised in a series of foster homes, but since these options are limited, there is talk of re-establishing a version of orphanages as well as establishing public boarding schools to protect students.

## Ethnic Issues

No examination of family status is complete without a discussion of the effect of ethnicity on family functioning. Within the past decades, two forces have combined to bring ethnic issues to the attention of family scholars. First, the overall ethnic composition of U.S. families is changing as the number of African American, Hispanic, and Asian families increased. Second, scholars are recognizing the long-term effect of ethnic heritage on family functioning.

American society represents a rapidly changing and diverse set of ethnic and cultural groups. In recent figures, the 1990 U.S. population was: Anglo 76 percent, African American 12 percent, Latino 9 percent, and Asian 3 percent. Non-white and Hispanic Americans will represent 28 percent of the total U.S. population in 2000, but the share of minorities will be 36 percent among children under 18. Minorities will be approaching over half the U.S. population as early as 2050 (Sandor 1994), when it is estimated the population will be: Anglo 52 percent; African American 16 percent; Latino 22 percent; and Asian 10 percent.

Families of varying ethnic/cultural backgrounds differ slightly in size. Whereas the general population averages 2.67 members per household, African American families average 2.90 members and Latino families average 2.43 members per household. Hispanic families are growing at the fastest rate. Whereas 21 percent of white families had children under 15, 28 percent of African American and 30 percent of Hispanic families reported young children. Traditionally these families report strong grandparent and extended family ties. Rates of marriage, divorce, and remarriage vary according to ethnic background (Cherlin 1992; Heaton and Jacobson 1994).

In general, classification systems are becoming less useful as people marry and adapt across cultures. For example, the number of African American and white interracial married couples has increased 78 percent since 1980. In 1990, more than 3 percent of births were to interracial couples (Sandor, 39). Currently over 4 percent of all children are of mixed race.

Although generalizations about cultural groups must always be accompanied by an indication of their many exceptions, a consideration of family ethnicity provides one more perspective from which to examine communication patterns. This perspective will receive increased attention. By the middle of the 21st century, Americans of European ancestry will be in the minority. This shift will influence underlying assumptions about how families work.

It is important to consider ethnicity in families because, contrary to popular myth, Americans have not become homogenized in a "melting pot"; instead, various cultural/ethnic heritages are maintained across generations. In her overview of studies in family ethnicity, McGoldrick (1993b, 342) points to the increasing evidence that ethnic values and identification are retained for many generations after immigration and play a significant role in family life and personal development throughout the life cycle. She maintains that second-, third-, and even fourth-generation Americans reflect their original cultural heritage in life-style and behavior.

---

*My parents' marriage reflected an uneasy blend of Italian and Norwegian cultures. My mother included her Italian relatives in on many issues my father considered private. He was overwhelmed by her family's style of arguing and making up and would retreat to the porch during big celebrations. I came to realize that cultural tension was reflected in many of their differences including their childrearing patterns. I carry pieces of those conflicting patterns within me today.*

---

Ethnicity may affect family life through its traditions, celebrations, occupations, values, and problem solving strategies. There are strong variations across cultures and familial issues such as age at first marriage, single parenthood, older marriages, changing marital partners, and male/female roles (Dilworth-Anderson and McAdoo 1988; McGoldrick 1993b). The definition of the concept *family* may differ across ethnic groups. For example, whereas the majority "White Anglo-Saxon" definition focuses on the intact nuclear unit, African American families focus on a wide kinship network, and Italians function with a large, intergenerational, tightly knit family which includes godparents and old friends. The Chinese are likely to include all ancestors and descendants in the concept of family. Each of these views has an impact on communication within the family.

Changes in family forms accompanied by economic and cultural variations have implications for the ways family members communicate with each other. For example, the rise of two career families alters the amount of time parents and children are in direct contact. Economic stress frequently results in escalating family stress. The high divorce rate increases the chances that family members of all ages will undergo major transitions including changes in their communication patterns. The growth in single parent systems and dual career couples increases a child's interpersonal contact with a network of extended family or professional caregivers. Most children in stepfamilies function within two different family systems, each with its own communication patterns. The family is no longer taken for granted as having one fixed form (Cheal 1993; Lewis, J. 1993). As American families reflect greater ethnic diversity, family life will be characterized by a wider range of communication patterns.

## Functional Families

At this point, it is important to forecast the types of families to be discussed in the upcoming chapters. Historically, most literature on family interaction has focused on dysfunctional or pathological families. Early studies examined families with a severely troubled or handicapped member, a trend that was followed by attempts to characterize "normal" families. As you may imagine from the previous description of the definitions and the status of families, there is little agreement on what is "normal." In recent years, attention has shifted to understanding the workings of the well-functioning, or "normal" family.

Early writers (Offer and Sabshin) provided four concepts for viewing normality—health, average, utopia, and process. Walsh (1993, 5–7) reworked these concepts into four perspectives.

1. *Normal Families as Asymptomatic Family Functioning.* This approach implies there are no major symptoms of psychopathology among family members.

2. *Normal Families as Average.* This approach identifies families that appear typical or seem to fit common patterns.

3. *Normal Families as Optimal.* This approach stresses positive or ideal characteristics often based on members' accomplishments.

4. *Normal Family Processes.* This approach stresses a systems perspective focusing on adaptation over the life cycle and adaptation to stresses and contexts.

The first three quickly proved limiting or unworkable because of the static nature of the definition. The transitional perspective provided a sense of variation and adaptation which captured the dynamic nature of family experience.

Studies of well-functioning families highlight the tremendous diversity of families that appear to be functioning adequately at a particular point in time (Kantor and Lehr 1976; Lewis et al. 1976; Reiss 1981; Olson, McCubbin, and Associates 1983; Fitzpatrick 1988; Walsh 1993).

In this text, we will focus on communication within the functional family, since this constitutes the primary experience for most of you. This book will attempt to dispel two myths: (1) there is one right way to be a family, and (2) there is one right way to communicate within a family. Throughout the following pages, you will encounter a wide variety of descriptions of family life and communication behavior. Our purpose is to help increase your understanding of the dynamics of family communication, not to suggest solutions to family problems. Hence, we will take a descriptive, rather than a prescriptive, approach.

We hope there is some personal, rather than just academic, gain from reading these pages. Most of you come from families that have their share of pain and problems as well as joy and comfort. It is our hope that you will gain a new insight into the people with whom you share your lives. As you go through this text, think about your own family or other real or fictional families with which you are familiar. We hope you choose to apply what you learn to your own family, although it may be difficult at times. The words of one of our students describes this process better than we can:

> *Analyzing my own family has not been an easy process. As I began, my entire soul cried out, "How do I begin to unravel the web of rules, roles and strategies that make up our system?" I do not claim to have all possible answers; certainly my opinions and attitudes are different from those of the others in my family. I also do not claim to have the answers to all our problems. But I have tried to provide answers to my own confusion and to provide some synthesis to the change and crises that I have experienced. And I have grown from the process.*

## CONCLUSION

This chapter provided an overview of what it means to be a family and the diversity of family life. We shared our basic beliefs about families and communication and moved on to an examination of family definitions and ethnic consideration of the family as a system. We examined the current status of the American family, touching on issues of trends in marriage, divorce and remarriage, the rise of dual career couples and single parent systems, increased life expectancy, economic pressures, and cultural diversity. Finally, we examined issues related to normal family functioning indicating this text would be descriptive rather than prescriptive in its approach.

## IN REVIEW

1. At this point in your personal and academic life, what is your definition of a family?
2. To what extent do you agree with the family categories described earlier? Describe how you would alter these categories, giving reasons for your choices.
3. Using a real or literary example, demonstrate the basic systems concept by describing how a change in one member of a family affected the other members.

4. Identify the family systems of four friends and describe them in terms of category types as well as socioeconomic and ethnic status. If possible, elaborate on how these factors appear to have affected members' interactions.

5. At this point in your personal and academic life, how would you describe a well-functioning family?

# 2

# Framework for Family Communication

Families repeat themselves within and across generations. Members become caught up in predictable and often unexamined life patterns which are created, in part, through their interactions with others. This text explores the family as a communication system, concentrating on the mutual influence between communication and family development or how communication patterns serve to create and reflect family relationships. Within the framework of common cultural communication patterns, each family has the capacity to develop its own communication code based on the experiences of individual members and the collective family experience. Most individuals develop their communication skills within the family context, learning both the general cultural language and the specific familial communication code. Since most people take their own backgrounds for granted, you may not be aware of the context your family provided for learning communication. For example, as a child you learned acceptable ways of expressing intimacy and conflict, how to relate to other family members, and how to share information outside the family. People in other families may have learned these things differently.

In order to understand the family as an interactive system, you need to explore key communication concepts and how they can be applied to the family. You also need to understand how family communication may be viewed through the dual lenses of symbolic interaction theory and systems theory, since these form the theoretical bases on which this approach is constructed.

This chapter will: (1) provide an overview of the communication process including the development of interpersonal meaning, (2) present a set of primary and secondary family functions which influence communication, and (3) establish a framework for examining family communication.

## THE COMMUNICATION PROCESS

*Communication* may be viewed as a *symbolic, transactional process*, or to put it more simply, the *process of creating and sharing meanings*. Saying that communication is symbolic means that symbols are used to create meaning and messages. Words or verbal behavior are the most commonly used symbols, but the whole range of nonverbal behavior, including facial expressions, eye contact, gestures, movement, posture, appearance, and spatial distance, is also used symbolically. Symbols may represent things, feelings, or ideas. They may also represent ideas or feelings that cannot be visualized such as anger or honesty. Families may use kisses, special food, teasing, or poems as symbols of love. Although symbols allow you to share your thoughts on the widest range of possible subjects, the symbols must be mutually understood for the meanings to be shared. For example, if family members do not agree on what activities are "fun," how much is "a lot" of money, or how to express and recognize anger, there will be confusion. If meanings are not mutually shared, messages may not be understood and the following type of misunderstanding may result:

*In my first marriage, my wife and I often discovered that we had very different meanings for the same words. For example, we agreed we wanted a "large" family but I meant three children and she meant seven or eight. I thought "regular" sex meant once a day and she thought it meant once a week. I thought spending a "lot of money" meant spending over three hundred dollars; she thought it meant spending over fifty dollars. In my second marriage, we talk very frequently about what our words mean so we don't have so many disagreements.*

To say that communication is transactional means that when people communicate, they have a mutual impact on each other. In short, you participate in communication; thus, in communicative relationships, participants are both affecting and being affected by the others simultaneously. It does not matter how much more talking one person appears to do; the mutual impact remains the same. The focus is placed on the relationship, not on the individual participants. Participation in an intimate relationship transforms fundamental reality definitions for both partners and in so doing transforms the partners themselves (Stephen and Enholm 1987).

A transactional view of communication and a systems perspective of the family complement each other, since both focus on relationships. Within these views, relationships take precedence over individuals. A communication perspective focuses on the interaction between two or more persons. Accordingly, from a systems perspective it is nonproductive to analyze each individual separately. Each individual communicates within an interpersonal context, and each communication act reflects the nature of those relationships. As two people interact, each creates a context for the other and relates to the other within that context. For example, you may perceive a brother-in-law as distant and relate to him in a very polite but restrained manner. In turn, he may perceive your politeness as formal and relate to you in an even more reserved manner. A similar situation is demonstrated by the following example:

---

*My father and brother had a very difficult relationship with each other for many years, although both of them had an excellent relationship with everyone else in the family. Dan saw Dad as repressive and demanding, although I would characterize him as serious and concerned. Dad saw Dan as careless and uncommitted, although no one else saw him that way. Whenever they tried to talk to each other, each responded to the person he created, and it was a continual battle.*

---

In the previous example, knowing Dan or his father separately does not account for their conflictual behavior when they are together. Both influence the other's interaction. Both create a context for the other and relate within the context. It is as if one says to the other, "You are sensitive," or "You are repressive," or "You are shiftless," and "that's how I will relate to you." The content and style of the messages vary according to how each sees himself or herself and how each predicts the other will react. As well as taking the environment or context into account, the transactional view stresses the importance of the communicators' perceptions and actions in determining the outcome of interactions.

Thus, the relationship patterns, not one or another specific act, become the focal point. One's perception of another and one's subsequent behavior can actually change the behavior of the other person. A mother who constantly praises her son for his thoughtfulness and sensitivity and notices the good things in his efforts may change her son's perception of himself and his subsequent behavior with her and other people. On the other hand, a husband who constantly complains about his wife's parenting behavior may lower her self-esteem and change her subsequent behavior toward him and the children. Thus, in relationships, each person (1) creates a context for the other,

Family members negotiate meanings in a variety of family activities.

(2) simultaneously creates and interprets messages, and, therefore, (3) simultaneously affects and is affected by the other.

To say that communication is a process implies it is continuously changing. Communication is not static; it does not switch on and off but, rather, develops over time. Process implies change. Relationships, no matter how committed, change continuously, and communication both affects and reflects these changes. The passage of time brings with it predictable and unpredictable crises, which take their toll on family regularity and stability. Yet, everyday moods, minor pleasures, or irritations may shift the communication patterns on a day-to-day basis.

As each day passes, family members subtly renegotiate their relationships. Today, you may be in a bad mood and people respond to that. Tomorrow, adaptations may need to be made around your brother's great report card. Next week a major job change may affect all your relationships. Over time, families change as they pass through stages of growth; members are born, age, leave, and die. As you will see in the chapters on family development and change, communication patterns reflect these developments in family life.

As indicated earlier, communication may be viewed as a symbolic, transactional process of creating and sharing meanings. Communication serves to create a family's social reality. Successful communication depends on the partners shared reality, or sets of meanings. (Bochner and Eisenberg 1987).

## Meanings and Messages

How often do people in close and committed relationships find themselves saying "That's not what I mean" or "What do you mean by that?" According to Stephen (1986), even in the most mundane interchanges, participants' messages imply their visions of the nature of social and physical reality as well as their values, beliefs, and attitudes. These are referred to as their meanings. Communication involves the negotiation of shared meanings; if meanings are not held in common, confusion or misunderstanding is likely to occur. A primary task of families is "meaning making," or the "co-creation of meanings." In their classic work, Berger and Kellner (1964) capture the sense of creating meanings within a marriage suggesting "Each partner's definition of reality must be continually correlated with the definitions of the other" (224). Such correlation requires regular communication. As indicated earlier, symbolic interaction is one lens through which family communication will be viewed. This theory is concerned with meaning and holds communication to be central to the process of creating a family's social reality. The meaning-making tasks of family members serve to create a relational culture or worldview which characterizes the family system.

***Development of Meanings*** How does a person develop a set of meanings? Basically, your views of the world result from your perceptual filter systems. For example, imagine each person has lenses, or filters, through which he or she views the world. Everyone views the world within the context of age, race, gender, religion, and culture. In addition, someone's view of reality will be affected by sibling position and family history with its myths, party lines, and traditions across generations (Lerner 1989, 71). These and other factors combine uniquely for each individual and determine how that person perceives and interacts with the world in general, and more specifically with the surrounding family system. Although this sounds like a very individualistic process, remember the transactional perspective. Each communicator constantly affects and is affected by the other; thus perceptions are co-created within the context of a relational system and are constantly influenced by that system.

Meanings emerge as information passes through a person's filter system. The physical state based on human sensory systems—sight, hearing, touch, taste, and smell—constitutes the first set of filters. Perceptions are also filtered through the social system or the way a person uses language, a person's accepted ways of viewing things, his or her cultural and class status, and all the socially agreed-upon conventions that characterize parts of his or her world. Eventually a person shares common meanings for certain verbal and nonverbal symbols with those around him or her. A person may share some very general experiences with many people and much more specific experiences with a smaller group of people. For example, with some acquaintances a person may share only general experiences, such as cultural background, including language, geographic area, customs, beliefs, and attitudes. With others, they may also share the specific and narrow experiences of living together in the house on 6945 Osceola Street and learning to understand each other's idiosyncracies.

Social experiences frame your world. The language you speak limits and shapes your meanings. For example, the current pressure to find new language to discuss stepfamilies reflects a belief that "step" terms are generally negative. Stepmothers in particular, face negative images of themselves due to the historically "wicked" word association. Proponents of change believe perceptions of stepfamilies will be altered by the use of language such as "remarried," "reconstituted," or "blended." Current terminology limits easy discussion of certain new family relationships such as "my stepmother's sister" or "my half brother's grandfather on his mother's side." Yet, although language may limit meanings, we are capable of broadening such perspectives by learning new terminology, opening ourselves to new experiences.

Thus, the overall culture affects perceptions and meaning, but the immediate groups to which one belongs exert a strong influence on an individual's perceptual set. The family group provides contextual meaning and influences the way meaning is given to sense data. If giving a handmade gift is considered a special sign of caring, a knitted scarf may be valued, while an expensive necklace may not. Being a member of the Thurman family, a farmer, a square dance caller, a volunteer fireman, or a church elder provides context for giving meaning to the world for the individual and for a small segment of people who surround that person. Although physical and social systems provide the basic general filters, specific constraints and experiences influence an individual's meanings. Individual constraints refer to the interpretations you create for your meanings based on your own personal histories. Although some of you may have similar histories, each person develops a unique way of dealing with sensory information and, thus, an individual way of seeing the world and relating to others in it. This concept is captured in the expression "No two children grow up in the same family."

Two members of the Thurman family may share being farmers, square dance callers, firemen, and church elders, yet they will respond differently to many situations. For example, many brothers and sisters disagree on the kind of family life they experienced together. One declares, "I had a very happy childhood" versus a sibling's statement, "I would never want to go through those years again." For each of you, specific events and people affect your meanings. Aunt Mary may have influenced your view of the world but not your sister's. Hoopes and Harper (1987) suggest that no two siblings really grow up in the "same family." Each experiences it differently, as indicated in the following example:

---

*In our house, my sister Diane was considered the "problem child." As far as experts can determine, her emotional difficulties stem from an unknown trauma when she was three, when they suggest she was rejected by my parents at a time when she needed love. The reality was that Diane functioned as a scapegoat for all of us. Although Diane and I are very close in age, we had different experiences in our family because of the way she perceived the family and was perceived by its members.*

---

Over time, communication or the symbolic transactional process permits individuals to negotiate shared meanings. After each encounter with a person or object, you become better able to deal with similar situations, and your behavior takes on certain patterns. The greater the repetition, the greater the probability of the assigned meaning.

Enduring relationships are characterized by agreements between members as to the meaning of things. These persons develop a relationship worldview reflecting the members' symbolic interdependence (Stephen 1986). Often people in families develop this worldview even though it may include agreements not to discuss certain topics.

After you have functioned within a family system, you become comfortable with the symbols, mainly because you are able to interpret them on all levels and feel that you really understand them. As a child, when you heard your mother yell "Jonathan" or "Elizabeth-Marie," you were able to tell from her tone of voice just what to expect. Today, you can sit at dinner and hear your younger sister say, "I just hate that Ernie Masters" and know that she has just found a new boyfriend.

***Levels of Meaning and Metacommunication*** Communication of meaning occurs on two levels: the content level and the relationship level. The content level contains the information, while the relationship level indicates how the information should be interpreted or understood. The relationship level is more likely to involve nonverbal messages. When your mother says, "When are you going to pick up those clothes?" she is asking an informational question, but there may be another level of meaning. It is up to you to determine if, by her tone of voice, she is really questioning at what time of day you will remove the dirty socks and jeans, or if she is telling you to get them out of there in the next thirty seconds. Relational pairs develop their own interpretation of symbols. When a father puts his arm on his daughter's shoulder, it may mean "I support you" or "slow down, relax." Usually the daughter will understand the intended message although she may misread the symbolic gesture and interpret it as "Let me take care of it."

*Metacommunication* occurs when people communicate about their communication, for example, when they give verbal and nonverbal instructions about how their messages should be understood. Such remarks as "I was only kidding," "This is important," or "Talking about this makes me uncomfortable" are signals to another on how to make certain comments, as do facial expressions, gestures, or vocal tones. On a deeper level, many couples or family members have spent countless hours talking about the way they fight or the way they express affection. Metacommunication serves an important function within families, because it allows members to state their needs, clarify confusion, and plan new and more constructive ways of relating to one another. As you will recognize, meanings serve a central function in all family communication processes.

## Dialectical Tensions

Significant relationships are not formed and maintained easily. Most long-term intimate relationships are built on a history of struggle as well as pleasure. A fable told by philosopher Arthur Schopenhauer captures the struggles humans have developing significant relationships.

> One wintry day a couple of chilled porcupines huddled together for warmth. They found that they pricked each other with their quills; they moved apart and were again cold. After much experimentation, the porcupines found the distance at which they gave each other some warmth without too much sting.

Sociologist Bellak (1970, 3) refers to this as the "porcupine dilemma," which raises the questions "How close can we get without interfering with each other? How much closeness do we need? How can we live together without hurting each other too much?" These questions are indicators of the tensions all relationships face. They are called *dialectical tensions* and are managed through communication. The term *dialectic* implies opposition, polarity, and, finally, interconnection. According to Montgomery (1992), relationships take place in the interplay of conflicting and interconnected forces. As people come together in relationships, they encounter tensions and struggles in managing the relationship. A dialectal approach focuses on competing and opposite possibilities that exist in a relationship (Brown, Altman, and Werner 1994). It recognizes the tension between partners as they negotiate and renegotiate what it means to be in a functioning relationship.

Communication scholars identify a range of possible interactional dialectical tensions including: autonomy–connection, openness–closeness, and predictability–novelty (Baxter 1990) as well as freedom to be independent—freedom to be dependent, affection–instrumentality, judgment–acceptance, expressiveness–protectiveness (Rawlins 1992). The primary dialectical concerns of autonomy–connection and predictability–novelty will be developed as part of the underlying framework for examining families.

Clearly dialectical tensions forcefully affect family life. According to Sabourin (1992), "The qualities of dialectical tensions—contradiction, interconnection, and change are inherent in the family's interaction." The process of coping with these relational paradoxes is called *dialectical management;* it is accomplished through communication. Family members regularly struggle with interpersonal stresses as partners try to simultaneously maintain stability while developing new individual interests. A child and parent may revisit the issue of autonomy or independence versus family connectedness throughout adolescence. Even an entire family may experience dialectical tensions with persons or groups outside the system. A drug arrest or school truancy may raise issues of family privacy versus a societal push for openness and access. The constant underlying dialectical tensions which confronts every relationship will continue as a theme throughout each chapter.

The ways in which people exchange messages influence the form and content of their relationships. Communication among family members shapes the structure of the family system and provides a family with its own set of meanings. Although we have used many family examples in describing the communication process, we have not explored the role of communication within the family. The following section examines the role communication plays in forming, maintaining, and changing family systems as families perform core functions.

## COMMUNICATION PATTERNS AND FAMILY FUNCTIONS

When you come into contact with other families, you may notice how their communication differs from that of the families in which you have lived. Everyday ways of relating, making decisions, sharing feelings, and handling conflict may vary slightly or greatly from your own personal experiences. Each family's unique message system provides the means of dealing with the major functions that give shape to family life. In other words, communication provides form and content to a family's life as members engage in family-related functions. We may define a function simply as something a system must do to avoid a breakdown (Cushman and Craig 1976). We will examine two primary family functions and four supporting functions that affect and are affected by communication and which taken together form a family's collective identity.

### Primary Functions

In their attempt to integrate the numerous concepts related to marital and family interaction, researchers Olson, Sprenkle, and Russell have developed what is known as the circumplex model of marital and family systems (Olson, Sprenkle, and Russell 1979; Olson, Russell, and Sprenkle 1983; Lavee and Olson 1991), an attempt to bridge family theory, research, and practice. Two central dimensions of family behavior are at the core of the model: family cohesion and family adaptability. Each of these dimensions are divided into four levels matched on a grid to create 16 possible combinations. The four types in the center of the grid are called balance; the four extremes are seen as dysfunctional. The theorists suggest moderate scores represent reasonable functioning whereas the extreme scores represent family dysfunction.

Over the past decade, the model has evolved to include three dimensions: (1) cohesion, (2) adaptability, and (3) communication. The two central dimensions are family cohesion and family adaptability, which are perceived as the intersecting lines of an axis. The third dimension is family communication, a facilitating dimension that enables couples and families to move along the cohesion and adaptability dimension (Olson, McCubbin, and Associates 1983). In recent writings, only the two dimensions of cohesion and adaptability are mentioned (Thomas and Olson 1994).

There have been questions raised about the entire use of the concept of adaptability (Beavers and Voeller 1983) and the use of supporting research scales and the curvilinear nature of cohesion (Farrell and Barnes 1993) Although we do not rely on the full circumplex model, we do establish the dimensions of cohesion and adaptability or change, as primary family functions.

In this text, the concepts of cohesion and change form a background against which to view communication within various types of families. From this perspective, two primary family functions involve:

1. Establishing a pattern of cohesion, or separateness and connectedness.

2. Establishing a pattern of adaptability, or change.

These functions vary with regularity as families experience the tensions inherent in a relational life.

***Cohesion*** From the moment you were born, you have been learning how to handle distance or closeness within your family system. You were taught directly or subtly how to be connected to, or separated from, other family members. Cohesion implies "the emotional bonding members have with one another and the degree of individual autonomy a person experiences in the family system" (Olson, Sprenkle, and Russell, 5). In other words, a family attempts to deal with the extent to which closeness is encouraged or discouraged.

Although different terminology is used, the issue of cohesion has been identified by scholars from various fields as central to the understanding of family life (Bochner and Eisenberg). Family researchers Kantor and Lehr (1976) view "distance regulation" as a major family function; family therapist Minuchin et al. (1967) talks about "enmeshed and disengaged" families; sociologists Hess and Handel (1959) describe the family's need to "establish a pattern of separateness and connectedness." There are four levels of cohesion ranging from extremely low cohesion (disengaged) to moderate (low to high) to extremely high cohesion (enmeshed) (Thomas and Olson 1994).

It is through communication that family members are able to develop and maintain or change their patterns of cohesion. A father may decide that it is inappropriate to continue the physical closeness he has experienced with his daughter now that she has become a teenager, and he may limit his touching or playful roughhousing. These nonverbal messages may be confusing or hurtful to his daughter. She may become angry, find new ways of being close, develop more outside friendships, or attempt to force her father back into the old patterns. A husband may demand more intimacy from his wife as he ages. He may ask for more serious conversation, make more sexual advances, or share more of his feelings. His wife may ignore this new behavior or engage in more intimate behaviors herself.

Families with extremely high cohesion are often referred to as "enmeshed"; members are so closely bonded and over-involved that individuals experience little autonomy or fulfillment of personal needs and goals. Family members appear fused or joined so tightly that personal identities do not develop appropriately. Enmeshed persons do not experience life as individuals, as indicated by the following example:

---

*My mother and I are the same person. She was always protective of me, knew everything about me, told me how to act, and how to answer questions. None of this was done in a bad way or had detrimental effects, but the reality is that she was and still is somewhat overbearing. If someone asked me a question, I typically answered, "Please direct all questions to my mother. She knows what to say."*

---

"Disengaged" refers to families at the other end of the continuum in which members experience very little closeness or family solidarity, yet each member has high autonomy and individuality. There is a strong sense of emotional separation or divorce. Members experience little or no sense of connectedness to each other as shown in Figure 2.1.

As you examine cohesion in families you may wish to look at indicators such as "emotional bonding, independence, boundaries, time, space, friends, decision making, and interests and recreation" (Olson, Sprenkle, and Russell, 6). Throughout this book, we will look at ways families deal with issues of coming together or staying apart and how they use communication in an attempt to manage their separateness and togetherness. Families do not remain permanently at one point on the cohesion continuum. Members do not come together and stay the same, as is evident from the previous examples. Because there are widely varying cultural norms for moderate or extremes of cohesion, what seems balanced for one family may be quite distant for another. For example, Latino families may find bal-

**FIGURE 2.1**

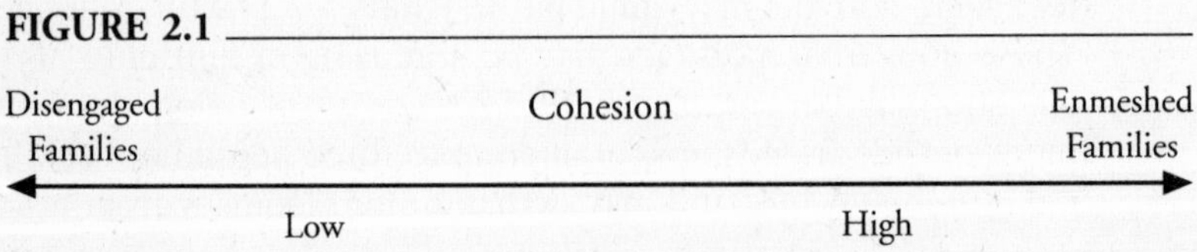

anced cohesion at a point that is too close for families with a Northern European background.

***Adaptability*** When you think of the changes in your own family over the past five or ten years, you may be amazed at how different the system and its members are at this point. A family experiences changes as it goes through its own developmental stages and deals with stresses that arise in everyday life, such as adapting to an illness or a job transfer of one of its members. Even everyday living involves relational tensions with which family members struggle.

Adaptability may be viewed as "the ability of a marital/family system to change its power structure, role relationships, and relationship rules in response to situational and developmental stress" (Olson, Sprenkle, and Russell 1983, 70). The researchers see family power structure, negotiation styles, role relationships, relationship rules, and feedback as central to the concept of adaptability. There are four levels of adaptability ranging from extremely low adaptability (rigid) to moderate (low to high) to extremely high adaptability (chaotic) (Thomas and Olson 1994) as shown in Figure 2.2.

Each human system has both stability–promoting processes (morphostasis, or form maintaining) and change–promoting processes (morphogenesis, or form creating). Such systems need periods of stability and change in order to function. Families that regularly experience extensive change may be considered chaotic. Due to total unpredictability and stress, they have little opportunity to develop relationships and establish common meanings. On the other extreme, rigidity characterizes families that repress change and growth.

Recently questions have been raised about the view of extreme flexibility as chaos, and therefore seen in a negative light, as opposed to seeing it as desirable (Lee, C. 1988). Although most scholars consider an excess or a paucity of change to be dysfunctional, they see the ability of a system to change its structure as generally necessary and desirable. Again issues of ethnicity and socioeconomic status impact a family's experience of change. For example, families which deal with poverty and rely on social welfare agencies often experience life as more chaotic than those for whom a solid economic situation reduces outside stresses.

Family systems constantly restructure themselves as they pass through predictable developmental stages. Marriage, pregnancy,

**FIGURE 2.2**

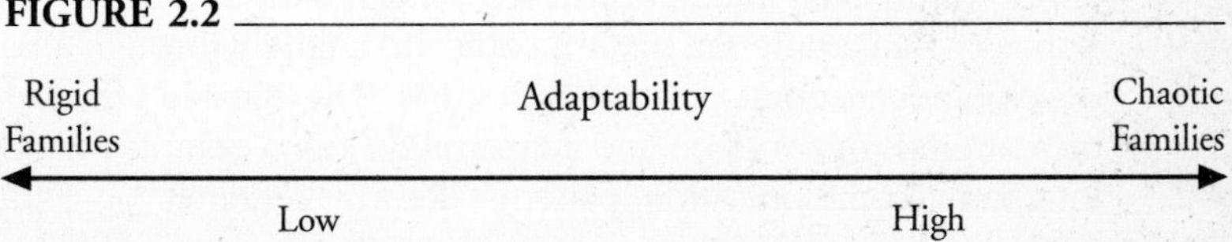

birth, parenting, and the return to the original couple all represent major familial changes. Likewise, when positive or negative stresses arise involving such issues as money, illness, or divorce, families must adapt. Finally, family systems must adapt both structurally and functionally to the demands of other social institutions as well as to the needs of their own members, as evidenced in the following example:

---

*My son and daughter-in-law adopted an older child and had to adapt their communication patterns to accommodate her. Although lying was forbidden in their family when they adopted Shirley, they had to reassess this position, because she had learned to lie for most of her life. My son and daughter-in-law had to learn to be more tolerant of this behavior, particularly when she first joined the family, or they would have had to send her back to the agency.*

---

Communication is central to the adaptive function of a family. Any effective adaptation relies on shared meanings gained through the family message system. Through communication, families make it clear to their members how much adaptation is allowed within the system while regulating the adaptive behaviors of their members and the system as a whole. Variables that affect this family function include: family power structure (assertiveness and control), negotiation styles, role relationships, and relationship rules and feedback (positive and negative). Olson et al. hypothesize that where there is a balance between change and stability within families, there will be more mutually assertive communication styles, shared leadership, successful negotiation, role sharing, and open rule making and sharing (13). The functions of cohesion and adaptability combine to create the two major functions family members continuously manage.

Adapting the work of Olson and his colleagues, you can visualize the mutual interaction of adaptability and cohesion within families by placing them on an axis (Figure 2.3a). By adding the extremes of cohesion (disengagement and enmeshment) and adaptability (rigidity and chaos), you can picture where more or less functional families would appear on the axis (Figure 2.3b).

The central area represents balanced or moderate levels of adaptability and cohesion, seen as a highly workable communication pattern for individual and family development, although there may be instances when a different pattern could aid a family through a particular developmental point or through a crisis. The outside areas represent the extremes of cohesion and adaptability, less workable for consistent long-term communication patterns. Recent research by Farrell and Barnes (1994) begins to question the curvilinear nature of cohesion.

**FIGURE 2.3**
**Family Cohesion/Adaptability Axes**

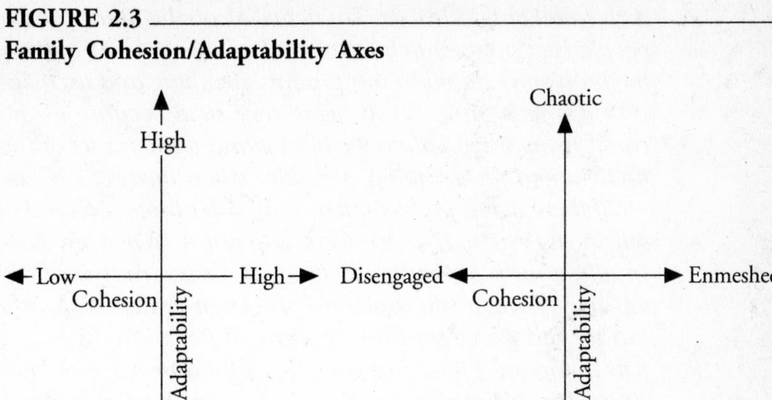


Most well-functioning families are found short of the extremes, except when they are under high levels of stress. In those situations, placement at the extreme may serve a purpose. This concept, based on the work of Lavee and Olson (1991), will be developed in Chapter 11. If a family is faced with the loss of a member through death, a highly cohesive communication pattern may be critical for mourning purposes. At the time of a family death, members may find themselves at point Y (Figure 2.4a). Such a family may be experiencing extreme closeness among remaining members but chaos in terms of dealing with the changes in roles or in everyday activities.

As another example, a family with an acting-out teenager may find itself shifting from point X to point Z on the axis, as the adolescent demands greater freedom and less connectedness from the family and forces changes upon the system (Figure 2.4b).

The situation in the following quotation may be graphed as three moves (Figure 2.4c):

**FIGURE 2.4**
**Application of Family Cohesion/Adaptability**

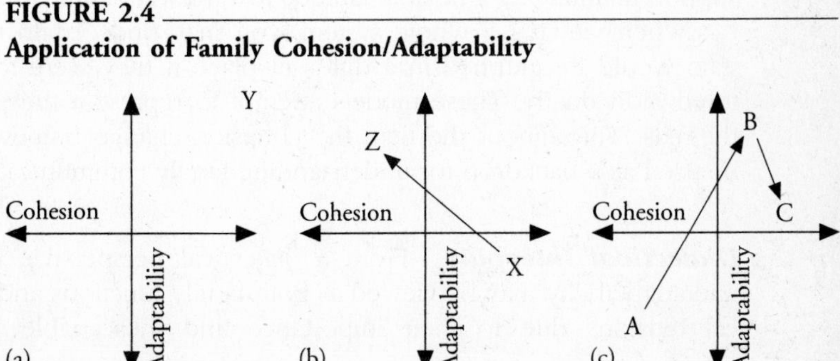

---

*As a small child I lived in an active alcoholic family in which people kept pretty much to themselves. We did not talk about the problems caused by our parents' drinking and we acted as if things were fine. Yet we were very rigid because we never could bring anyone into the house, and we never let outsiders know about the drinking. My older sister always took care of me if there was a problem, while my older brother locked himself in his room. Thus we were at point A. When my parents finally went into treatment, the house was crazy in a different way for a while, since no one knew exactly how to act, but we did get closer and we were all forced to discuss what was going on. I guess we got closer and almost too flexible or unpredictable (point B). Now, five years later, I'm the only child left at home and my sober parents and I have a relatively close and flexible relationship (point C).*

---

If you think about stages in your family life, you should be able to envision how the family shifted from one point to another on the cohesion–adaptability axis.

Olson, McCubbin, and Associates (1983) have indicated that families at different stages of development seem to function better in different areas of the model. For example, young couples without babies function best in either the upper right or lower left quadrants. Adolescents function best in the central, or balanced, area; older couples relate best in the lower right quadrant. Adolescents function best when they have average cohesion, being neither enmeshed with parents or disengaged, and when their adaptability is midway between rigidity and chaos. Obviously, these results indicate adolescents' need for a family system without threats or rigid rules. Older couples function best when cohesion is high but adaptability is low—more rigid. Possible explanations for these findings will become more clear in the chapters on developmental changes. Although results may differ for families from particular backgrounds or ethnic origins, these findings support maintaining a flexible attitude toward well-family functioning.

When viewing a whole system, you may find certain members who would be graphed in a different place if they were to be pictured individually. These models attempt to represent the group on the axis. Throughout the text, the cohesion/change framework will be used as a backdrop for understanding family communication.

***Dialectical Interplay*** From a dialectical perspective, cohesion and adaptability may be viewed as both family functions and dialectical tensions due to their importance and inescapable presence within the family. In discussing the cohesion function Sabourin (1992) suggests:

> The dialectical perspective is useful in explaining how difficult achieving balance can be. It is a contradiction to need both autonomy and connection with others … The dialectical perspective incorporates both … Hence some families emphasize togetherness at the expense of developing personal identities. (5)

Most families find they struggle over time with the issues of closeness and distance both between members and between the family system and outside persons or groups.

Thus, there is an opposing pull as members express needs for stability and variation and for novelty or predictability. The dialectical perspective reminds us of how members continuously experience tension as one member wants spontaneity and excitement while another values predictability and ease. Although these dialectical tensions related to cohesion and change will appear more apparent in the early stages of a relationship, real tensions must be managed throughout the life of a relationship.

Although the issues related to cohesion and adaptability/change are viewed as the primary functions, these functions do not provide a complete picture. There are additional family functions—supporting functions—that contribute to the understanding of family interaction.

## Supporting Functions

There are four supporting functions which, in conjunction with cohesion and adaptability, give shape to family life. Hess and Handel identify five processes, or family functions, which interact with the development of a family's message system. Because one of these processes relates to cohesion, we will list only the remaining four. The supporting family functions include:

> 1. Establishing a satisfactory congruence of images.
>
> 2. Evolving modes of interaction into central family themes.
>
> 3. Establishing the boundaries of the family's world of experience.
>
> 4. Dealing with significant biosocial issues of family life, such as gender, age, power, and roles. (4)

Each of these processes interacts with a family's point on the cohesion/adaptability axis and influences a family's communication pattern. Each is based on principles of symbolic interaction (LaRossa and Reitzes 1993), since their underlying thread is the role of subjective meanings.

***Family Images*** Relationship patterns can be viewed as metaphors. If you had to create a mental image or a metaphor for your family, what would it be? Do you see your family as a nest, a broken wagon wheel, a corporation, a spaceship, or a schoolroom? Every family operates as an image-making mechanism. Each member develops images of what the family unit and other family members are like; these images determine his or her patterns of interaction with the others. Patterns of the marital relationship, which often cannot be communicated through literal language, are explained metaphorically (Norton 1989). A person's image of his or her family embodies what is expected from it, what is given to it, and how important it is (Hess and Handel). Thus, the image has both realistic and idealized components that reflect both the imaged and the imaginer.

The following extended image conveys a good deal of information about this two parent family with five adolescent children:

---

*Picture a rock-and-roll band, complete with a lead singer, back-ups, and a variety of instrumentalists. My mother is definitely the lead singer, the star of the show, providing the cues for the members of her band. She sets the tempo for the performance and coordinates the sound. My father plays the bass guitar. Though not "in charge" of the show he provides the underlying beat that is constant. This bass beat often goes unnoticed, though it is crucial to the unity of the music. Each child has a distinct personality that is represented by his or her position in the band. I, as the oldest and only female child, sing back-up to my mother. I echo her voice when she is in need of support and highlight her notes. We share the spotlight at times, joining voices for added strength and effectiveness. Russ, as the oldest male child plays guitar alongside Dad. He is most like Dad, named after that side of the family, and following in Dad's professional footsteps. Therefore, the two play variations of the same instrument. The rest of my siblings, Zack (16), Edwin (12), and Bennett (11), play their own instruments. They vary according to personality and are integral parts of the overall sound.*

*At times, a band member loses touch with the others and goes awry. The result can be dissonance or noise. When all*

> *the instruments are in tune and are playing together, however, the result is pure melody.*

---

Less complex examples include:

---

> *My parents and the six kids are fighter planes in formation. My parents are the two fighter planes in front and the six children are in formation behind. We all go off in slightly different directions yet always remain behind the parent planes, always remain at full speed ahead, and always remain in some sort of formation. Occasionally one fighter plane may lose his place in the formation and become lost. Although no one slows down, help is extended over the radio, or, in desperate situations, one parent plane goes after the lost plane, bringing it back into formation.*

---

---

> *My family is a team, with my dad as a player-coach. We all work together for the survival of our team, and we all contribute. Each one of us has strengths and weaknesses, yet there is always that force driving us to achieve more together. As the player-coach, my dad has the responsibility of overseeing our performances.*

---

A family's conception of itself affects its orientation to areas such as cooperation versus competition and reaching out versus withdrawal, and affects communication. According to Jones (1982), the verbal and nonverbal behaviors of the family members are, in part, determined by this imagistic view of their relationship with each other and with the external environment. One dual career couple described their family as a "seesaw," saying, "We are able to balance each other well and be flexible in allowing the kids to move between us. But if a crisis hits and we have to move in new patterns, such as sideways, we run into problems."

If you think about metaphors within interactive systems of interaction, individual behaviors and relationships may be seen as metaphors. One set of siblings may be seen as "two peas in a pod"; another set may be "oil and water." If the persons involved hold very different images of their relationship to each other, the differences will be reflected in communication patterns. If two people's images of each other are congruent and consistent for a period of time, a predictable pattern of communication may emerge in which both are comfortable. For example, if a mother sees her son as a helpless and dependent creature, she may exhibit many protective behaviors, such as keeping bad news from him. If the son's image of his mother is as a protector, the congruence of the images will allow harmonious communication, but if the child sees his mother as a jailer, conflict may emerge. If one child sees the mother as a jailer and the other sees her as an angel, the lack of consistent images held by family members may result in strong alliances among those with congruent images. A husband and wife are likely to experience conflict if one sees the family as a "nest" involving nurturing, emotion, and protection, while the other sees it as a corporation involving a strong power structure and good organization. Yet, since complete consensus is improbable and change inevitable, the patterns will never become totally predictable. The level of congruence relates to the effectiveness of communication within the family. The family metaphor acts as a perceptual filter, an indicator of a family's collective identity, and serves as an impetus for future thought and action (Jones, T., 9).

***Family Themes*** As well as having images for the family and for every member, each family shares themes—or takes positions in relationship to the outer world that affect every aspect of its functioning. A theme may be viewed as a pattern of feelings, motives, fantasies, and conventionalized understandings grouped around a particular locus of concern, which has a particular form in the personalities of individual members (Hess and Handel, 11).

Themes represent a fundamental view of reality and a way of dealing with this view. Through its theme, a family responds to the questions, "Who are we?", "What do we do about it?", and "How do we invest our energies?" Themes may represent a family's attempt to deal with dialectical tensions by "taking a stand." For example, themes may emerge from predictable areas of contraction, independence-dependence, openness-closedness, predictability-novelty. Sample theme issues which some families value include: physical security, strength, dependability, inclusion, and separation. To demonstrate the viability of themes in a family, we view them as statements that actualize the values and collective identity:

The Nielsens play to win.

We have responsibilities for those less fortunate than us.

You can sleep when you die.

If God gives much, much is expected in return.

You can only depend on your family.

You can always depend on your family.

The Simons never quit.

You can always do better.

Seize the moment.

Be happy with what you have.

Take a chance.

Money is basic to life.

Respect La Via Vecchia (the old way).

The Logans welcome challenges.

We are survivors.

Do unto others as best you can.

We do not raise homing pigeons.

Themes relate directly to family actions, thereby allowing us to surmise a family's themes by watching its actions. Living according to a theme necessitates the development of various patterns of behavior, which affect: how members interact with the outside world, how they interact with each other, and how they develop personally. For example, a family with the theme "We have responsibility for those less fortunate than we are" might be a flexible system open to helping non-family members. They may give to charity, raise foster children, or work with the homeless. Yet, it may be difficult for such a family to accept help from an outside source because of its own self-definition as "helper." Members may tend to put themselves second as they deal with outside problems. Following the classic line of the shoemaker's children without shoes, a mother who lives according to this theme may spend hours working at an adolescent drop-in center for the community and be unaware of the problems her own teenage children are experiencing. Young members may grow up learning to minimize their problems and may not have much experience expressing painful feelings. Yet, they may learn to willingly sacrifice for those less fortunate and may be very empathetic and attuned to the needs of others. Family themes undergird everyday life, as the following portrays:

---

*I grew up with a family theme of "You can sleep when you die." Ours is a family which values action above all else, especially action pointed toward reaching goals or winning in competition. The task or the goal is the focus, not the person doing the task or reaching the goal. We were expected to be busy. Sitting around and chatting, or hanging out with*

(continued on page 40)

*friends was viewed as non-productive. I learned to hold conversations while cooking, exercising, doing chores, and practicing a musical instrument. Finding that interpersonal time was important to me.*

---

Family themes may be complex and subtle, involving worldviews that are not immediately obvious. It is important to identify a family's main theme(s) in order to fully understand the meanings and communication behavior of its members.

***Boundaries*** As well as developing images and themes, families create boundaries. The *boundary* of a system is what separates it from its environment, as well as from all that is nonsystem. In short, the boundary defines the system as an entity by allowing it to create a permeable separation between its interior elements and its environment (Broderick 1993; Constantine 1986). We can imagine boundaries as physical or psychological limits which regulate access to people, places, ideas, and values. All families establish some boundaries as they restrict their members from encountering certain physical and psychological forces. Most frequently, family boundaries regulate access to people, places, ideas, and values.

Some family boundaries are permeable, or flexible, and allow movement across them. Others resist movement and are rigid and inflexible (Figure 2.5). Finally, others are so invisible or diffuse that they are almost nonexistent.

External boundaries distinguish family members from the rest of the world; while internal boundaries help keep family members appropriately placed in relationship to each other. Let's look first at how external boundaries function.

Certain families permit or encourage their children to make many different kinds of friends, explore alternative religious ideas, and have access to new ideas through the media; such permeable boundaries permit new people, new ideas, and new values to enter the family. Some families retain rigid control of their children's activities to prevent them from coming into contact with what the family considers "undesirable." Or, the family may expect members to carry the

**FIGURE 2.5**
**External Boundaries**

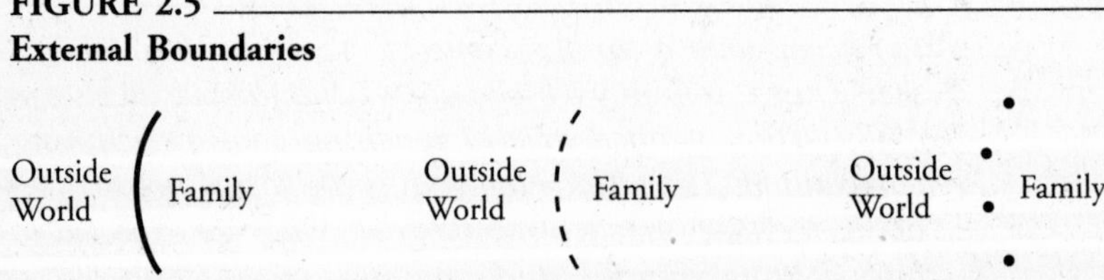

family boundaries within them as does the grandfather in the following example:

---

*The family does not end at the front step. My grandfather says, "When you are a Cammostro, you represent the entire family, (your aunts, uncles, cousins, grandparents, and your heritage) so never make a fool of yourself." This means that one must be at one's best whenever in public and never tell family stories or secrets.*

---

Extremes of such behavior result in the creation of rigid boundaries around the family system. Finally, some families provide no sense of identity for members and no control of their contact with people, places, ideas, or values. Members of this type of system experience little sense of "family," since there appears to be no collective identity.

Family boundaries will vary according to the personalities of the members, types of experiences to which members are exposed, and freedom each member has to create his or her own value system. Although the family unit system may set strong boundaries, a strong, self-assured person may challenge rigid or stereotyped positions on certain issues and reject the traditional boundaries set for him or her. An intensely emotional or sensitive child may comprehend things never imagined by other family members. This child may push far beyond the geographic limits or aspirational labels held by other family members. Beavers (1982) suggests optimal family members can switch hit, flexibly identifying with the larger world at times and yet maintain individual boundaries.

Functional families establish internal boundaries to protect members' self identities and the identity of generational groups. If the boundaries between individuals are diffuse, or nonexistent, members may experience psychological problems, such as over involvement, co-dependency, or a loss of physical boundaries, such as occurs in incest. If the internal boundaries are too rigid and strong, members will feel disengaged and out-of-touch.

Most families experience boundaries between generations, which establish subsystems of generational hierarchy. Generations establish their boundaries based on behaviors appropriate for that subsystem (Wood and Talmon 1983). For example, parents usually provide nurturance and control for their children. It is unusual for children to extensively nurture or control their parents unless the parents have become aged and ill. In two-parent families, the marital subsystem represents a critical entity in the functioning of family life. In most families, husbands and wives share unique information and give each other special emotional and physical support. Children are not allowed to share in all aspects of the marital dyad. Many types of conflict may arise if the system's interpersonal boundaries, particularly the marital boundaries, are too permeable and children or others are expected to fulfill part of the spousal role. For example, troubled families, such as those with a severely depressed spouse, may experience shifts in the marital boundary. If a depressed husband cannot provide the interpersonal support needed by his wife, she may co-opt one of the children into the marital subsystem by expecting the child to act as an adult confidant and emotional support. When boundaries are inappropriately crossed, roles become confused and pain may result for all members.

Sometimes boundary issues are played out across a series of generations. A daughter whose mother invaded her life may determine not to act in the same way toward her children, and actually distance herself from them. Her children, in turn, may resolve to develop closeness with their offspring and end up invading their children's lives.

Interpersonally testing or forcing boundaries may involve deep emotional conflicts, which could be resolved through the increased growth of all family members or by the severing of bonds with specific members who eventually leave the system. Each of you has experienced resisting boundaries or having persons challenge your systems boundaries with positive or negative results. Your family relationships may have eventually become stronger or certain relationships may have suffered. Thus, the physical and psychological boundaries set by each family strongly influence the kinds of interpersonal communication that can occur within the system.

***Biosocial Issues*** All families operate in a larger sphere that provides conventional ways of coping with biosocial issues, but each family creates its own answers within the larger framework. Hess and Handel identify the following as included with biosocial issues: male and female identity, authority and power, shaping and influencing children, and children's rights (17–18). Goldner (1989) claims gender is a fundamental, essential organizing principle of family life.

All people are faced with gender identity issues while growing up and/or while forming their own family systems and raising children. Gender identity and physical development issues affect styles of interaction and vice versa. A family that assigns responsibilities based on a member's gender operates differently than one that uses interest or preference as the basis for assigning responsibilities. If physical stature automatically determines duties and privileges, the interaction will be different than in a setting where physical development is only one factor among many by which privileges are awarded and duties are assigned to males and females.

Other value decisions in the social sphere relate to the use of power within the family structure. To what extent are leadership, decision making, and authority issues resolved according to traditional gender and role configurations? Families negotiate the use of power within the system, and members may find themselves in the renegotiation process for much of their lives. The social sphere also involves attitudinal issues related to roles and responsibilities which may be exemplified in parent-child relationships. Parent-child interaction reflects the mutually held attitudes. If a parent sees a child as a responsibility to be dispensed with at a given age, the interactions will be immensely different than if the parental attitude reflects a prolonged responsibility for his or her offspring, perhaps far beyond the years of adolescence. The extent to which a child is permitted privacy, physical or psychological, also reflects a biosocial orientation.

Hare-Mustin (1989) says that age, gender, and power interact in complex ways within family systems and argues that women may fall between the male parent and the child in some structures. Thus the parents versus child hierarchy may be too simple a concept when dealing with power.

---

*For the first eleven years of life, my stepson Travis was raised in a household that catered to his every need. He was encouraged both to be dependent and to remain a little boy in many ways. His mother Martha could not have more children, so she doted on him as her only child. Before he died Martha's first husband treated her and Travis as people who needed to be taken care of. When I married Martha, my two daughters came to live with us. They had been raised to be self-sufficient and independent. I have found myself becoming very impatient with Travis and pushing him to act like my children. As a result, Martha and I have had many fights over the children's responsibilities.*

---

The development of images, themes, boundaries, and responses to biosocial issues interacts with the functions of cohesion and adaptability. Flexible families will experience greater variety in images, themes, boundaries, and responses to biosocial issues than will rigid ones. These responses also affect the family's acceptable level of cohesion. For example, a family with fixed boundaries and themes related to total family dependence will develop extremely high cohesion in contrast to the family with themes of service or independence coupled with flexible boundaries. This entire process rests with the communication behaviors of the family members. Communication, then, is the means by which families establish their patterns of cohesion and adaptability, based at least partially on their interactions in the development of images, themes, boundaries, and responses to biosocial issues.

## A FRAMEWORK FOR EXAMINING FAMILY COMMUNICATION

There are numerous approaches to analyzing the family as a system, such as looking at a family as an economic, political, or biological system. Since concern lies with the interaction within and around the family, this text centers on the communication aspects of the family system. The following is a framework for examining family communication:

> The family is a system constituted and managed through its communication. Family members regulate cohesion and adaptability and develop a collective identity through the flow of patterned meaningful messages within a network of evolving interdependent relationships located within a defined cultural context.

> The family is a system constituted and managed through its communication.

The family may be viewed as a set of people and the relationships among them which, together, form a complex whole; changes in one part result in changes in other parts of the system. In short, family members are inextricably tied to each other, and each member and the family as a whole reflect changes in the system. Communication, the symbolic, transactional process by which meanings are exchanged, is the means by which families are constituted and regulated.

> Family members regulate cohesion and adaptability and develop a collective identity ...

Communication facilitates a family's movement on the cohesion/adaptability axis (Figure 2.3). The way in which people exchange messages influences the form and content of their relationships. Communication and families have a mutual impact on each other. The collective identity is formed through the congruence of the primary and secondary functions.

> ... through the patterned flow of meaningful messages within a network ...

Based on families-of-origin and other environmental sources, each family develops its own set of meanings that become predictable, since family members interact with one another in the same manner over and over again. Such message patterns move through boundaries, and define the relationships along specific networks, determine who interacts with whom.

... of evolving interdependent relationships ...

Family life is not static; both predictable, or developmental, changes and unpredictable changes, or crises, force alteration upon the system. Family relationships evolve over time as members join and leave the system and become closer or farther apart from each other. Family members struggle with dialectical tensions. Yet, due to the family's systemic nature, members remain interdependent, or joined, as they deal with relational issues of intimacy, conflict roles, power, and decision making.

... located within a defined cultural context.

Normality may be viewed as transactional or process-oriented. This perspective emphasizes attention to adaptation over the life cycle and adaptation to various contexts. Thus, issues of developmental stages and reaction to change combine with contextual issues such as ethnicity, gender, and socioeconomic status to create a "culture" within which families operate. Norms and expectations vary greatly across groups of families, but may remain relatively similar for families within a given cultural context. Finally the spatial context within which a family lives its everyday life affects its functioning.

Throughout the following chapters, we will examine the concepts mentioned in this framework in order to demonstrate the powerful role communication plays in family life.

---

*When you really think about it, family life is extremely complex and most of us just go through the motions everyday without any reflection. I usually take for granted that most families are similar to mine. However, the more I look carefully at other family systems, the more aware I am of the differences. Perhaps families are like snowflakes, no two are ever exactly alike.*

---

It seems appropriate to close this chapter with Handel and Whitchurch's (1994) statement which captures the crucial nature of family interaction:

> A family creates and maintains itself through its interaction, that is, through social interaction both inside and outside the family, members define their relationships to one another, and to the world beyond the family as they establish individual identities as well as a collective family identity. (1)

## CONCLUSION

This chapter described the process of communication and proposed a connection between communication patterns and family functions. Communication was developed as a symbolic transactional process. Systems theory and symbolic interactionism were established as the critical underlying theories used to understand family communication. The importance of meaning-making and managing dialectical tensions was addressed. The primary functions discussed are cohesion and adaptability, and the supporting functions include family images, themes, boundaries, and biosocial issues. The chapter concluded with a framework for analyzing family interaction.

## IN REVIEW

1. Using your own family or a fictional family, identify three areas of "meaning" which would have to be explained to an outsider who was going to be a houseguest for a month. For example, what would have to be explained for the houseguest to understand how this family views the world?
2. Describe a recurring interaction pattern in a real or fictional family in terms of the predictable verbal and nonverbal messages. Provide a statement of the effect of this interaction pattern on the persons involved or on the family as a whole.
3. Give three examples of behavior which might characterize an enmeshed family and three examples of behavior which might characterize a disengaged family.
4. Using a real or fictional family, give an example of how the family moved from one point on the adaptability-cohesion grid to another point due to changes in their lives.
5. How might one of the following themes and one of the following images be carried out in family communication patterns?

## Themes

- You can always depend on your family.
- We are survivors.
- Use your gifts.
- Take one step at a time.
- You only live once.

## Images

- Circus, army, schoolhouse, rock, corporation, octopus

# 3

# The Family as a System

"We live our lives like chips in a kaleidoscope, always part of patterns that are larger than ourselves and somehow more than the sum of their parts" (Minuchin 1984, 2). Taking a systems perspective provides valuable insights into a family's communication patterns. Because communication is a symbolic, transactional process, focus must be placed on family relationships, not on individual members. In order to understand the communication patterns of a family, the overall communication context—the family system—must be examined.

---

*Family life is incredibly subtle and complex. Everything seems tied to everything else, and it's very difficult to sort out what is going on. For example, when our oldest daughter, Marcy, contracted spinal meningitis, the whole family reflected the strain. My second daughter and I fought more, while my husband tended to withdraw into himself, which brought me closer to my son. In their own ways, the three children became closer while our marriage became more distant. As Marcy's recovery progressed, there were more changes, which affected how we relate now, two years later. That one event highlighted the difficulty of sorting out what is really going on within a family.*

---

The previous personal statement provides insight into how a family operates systemically and reflects the complexity of the task of examining families from a systems perspective. Everyday systemic patterns are often subtle, almost invisible, buried in apparent predictability, yet powerful in their effects. Individuals get caught up in their family patterns. Unless you understand people in their primary context, you may never be able to make sense of an individual's behavior. In order to understand communication within the family system, this chapter will examine what a system is, and how it works, and how it relates to everyday family interaction. We will consider the implications of applying a systems perspective of family functioning.

## CHARACTERISTICS OF HUMAN SYSTEMS

Very simply stated, a system is a set of components that interrelate with one another to form a whole. A system is characterized by its unique experience of change. If one component of the system changes, the others will change in response, which in turn affects the initial component. So, a change in one part of the system affects every part. Systems may be thought of as closed or open. A *closed system* has no interchange with the environment; this concept applies mainly to mechanical elements, such as machines, which do not have life-sustaining qualities. An *open system* engages in interchange with the environment and is oriented toward growth; living, or organic, systems such as family systems fit into this category.

A system consists of four elements: components, attributes, relationships, and an environment (Littlejohn 1983; Whitchurch and Constantine 1993). The components are the parts of a system. Obviously, in the case of a family system, these are the family members themselves. The attributes are the qualities, or properties, of the system and its members. Thus, a family or a member has generalized family system attributes, such as goals, energy, health, or ethnic heritage, but each attribute is distinctive to that family and member—attributes— such as athletic goals, high energy, ill health, or ethnic heritage.

The relationships among parts in the family system are the relationships among family members—the major focus of this book. Such relationships are characterized by communication, a point Duncan and Rock (1993) capture very succinctly.

> When two individuals come together in a relationship, something is created that is different from, larger and more complex than those two individuals apart—a system. The most important feature of such a relationship is communication. Relationships are established, maintained, and changed by communicated interaction among members. (48)

Finally, environment is viewed as a system element because systems are affected by their surroundings. Systems are embedded in larger systems, called suprasystems. Families do not exist in a vacuum; they live within a time period, culture, community, and many other influential systems, such as extended family or school district which impact them directly.

As you read about the family as a system, you will encounter some technical terminology, which may appear extremely complex at first. Unfortunately there are no simple ways to talk about these important concepts. Hopefully you will come to understand the value of a systems approach to family communication and find the terminology helpful rather than cumbersome.

From a systems perspective, persons are considered as part of an overall context, not as individuals. Decontexted individuals do not exist (Minuchin 1984, 2). When the components of a system are actually people in relationships with other people, one of the most important attributes of that system is communication behavior (Bavelas and Segal 1982, 101). From a family systems perspective, imagine a picture in which the people are in the background and their relationships are depicted in the foreground.

The patterns of interaction take precedence over the individuals. A family systems perspective should aid you in analyzing family interaction, predicting future interactions, and creating meaningful changes within a family. Remember, as we examine the systems perspective, it is important to keep in mind its relationship to the construction of meaning. As noted earlier, persons act upon the social reality they construct. Human systems behave according to the meaning something has for them (Whitchurch and Constantine 1993). Therefore, meanings impact the moves people make within their family systems.

Specifically, we will apply the following system characteristics to families: interdependence, wholeness, patterns/self-regulation, interactive complexity/punctuation, complexity structures, and equifinality (Watzlawick, Beavin, and Jackson 1967; Littlejohn 1992; Kantor and Lehr 1976; Bavelas and Segal 1982; Whitchurch and Constantine 1993; Bochner and Eisenberg 1987; Steier 1989).

## Interdependence

"How does one come to see oneself as an integral part of a larger whole?" Noone (1989) answers this question by suggesting that the process includes:

> Observing ourselves as components of an unfolding process rooted in the past and intertwined with larger living systems in the present. It is as mind boggling as gazing into the evening sky and trying to comprehend one's place in the vastness of the universe. (2)

Relationships among various parts of the family system develop their own communication patterns.

Within any system, the parts are so interrelated as to be dependent upon each other for their functioning. Thus, this relatedness, or interdependence, is critical in describing a system.

The family is a highly interdependent system with powerful and long-lasting effects on its members. Traditionally, this interdependence has been viewed as the means of maintaining a delicate balance among the system's parts, or members. In Chapter 1, you encountered Satir's image of the family as a mobile in which members respond to changes in each other. As a member moves, other members may consciously or unconsciously shift to adjust to the quivering system. As opposed to simple mobiles, families do not necessarily seek absolute balance; rather, they evolve to new states which are always slightly different from the previous state. Current thinkers support an evolutionary model of family systems which incorporates the possibility of spontaneous or kaleidoscopic change (Dell 1982; Hoffman 1980; Bochner and Eisenberg). No matter what kind of change a family is experiencing, all members are affected due to their interdependence.

You may be able to pinpoint events in your own family that have influenced all members in an identifiable way. Sometimes troublesome behaviors are encouraged, because that individual serves to keep the family relatively balanced by taking the focus off a severe problem. Examples in family therapy literature suggest that parents may use, or focus on, an acting-out child to keep the marriage together; or children may use their parents' over-protectiveness to keep them safely close to home (Hoffman 1980, 54). A behavior that seems problematic to the outside world may serve an important function within the family system. Lerner (1989, 13) describes this exact process as seven-year old Judy exhibits temper tantrums and obnoxious misbehavior:

> When specifically does Judy act up and act out? From what I can piece together, this occurs when her father's distance and her mother's anxious focus on Judy reach intolerable proportions. And what is the outcome of Judy's troublemaking and tantrums? Distant Dad is roped back into the family (and is helped to become more angry than depressed), and the parents are able to pull together, temporarily united by their shared concern for their child. Judy's behavior is, in part, an attempt to solve a problem in the family.

Thus, interdependence is a powerful element in understanding family functioning. In a family systems perspective, the behavior of each family member is related to and dependent upon the behavior of the others. When changes occur in family relationships, changes also occur in the individuals and vice versa (Kramer 1980, 45).

## Wholeness

A family systems approach assumes the whole is greater than the sum of its parts. The parts, or members, are understood in the context of that whole. A commonplace illustration is the cake that comes out of the oven, unlike the flour, oil, eggs, chocolate squares, and milk that went into the mix. A nonsystemic approach to families studies the individual members and "sums up" their personalities and attributes to describe the entire family. In this model, the whole is merely a collection with no unique qualities, "like a box of stones" (Littlejohn, 30). The systems model reflects an integration of parts while overall family images and themes reflect this holistic quality. Families exhibit a life that reflects the interplay of family members. The characteristics exhibited are assumed by others to characterize the family and each member.

The Boyer family may be characterized as humorous, religious, warm, and strong, yet these adjectives do not necessarily apply to each family member. Thus, certain group characteristics may not reflect those of each individual. You may hear whole families referred to as "brainy," "artistic," "aggressive," "industrious," or "money-hungry," yet you know at least one member who does not fit the label.

In an ongoing human system, the components, or the people, have importance; but once these parts become interrelated, these properties take on a life greater than their individual existences. According to Whitchurch and Constantine:

> There are behaviors that do not represent the parts considered in isolation; these emerge from the transactions between pairs such as the humor two siblings evoke in each other which affects the whole family. These aspects of the system are called emergent properties because they emerge only at the system level.

Communication patterns between or among family members emerge as a result of this "wholeness." Conflict or affection may become an inherent part of communication between various members. A certain cue may trigger patterns of behavior without members' awareness. A delightful example follows:

---

*Something wonderful and funny happens when my sister and I get together. We tend to play off each other and can finish each other's sentences, pick up the same references at the same time, and create a dynamic energy that leaves other people out. We don't do it on purpose. Rather, we just seem to "click" with each other and off we go!*

---

## Patterns/Self Regulation

In your family, what are the appropriate ways to greet other members? What behaviors are acceptable or unacceptable during a family argument? Human beings learn to coordinate their actions in order to create patterns together that could not be created individually. Although coordination of actions varies dramatically across family systems, each system develops communication patterns that make life predictable and manageable.

Although you may not be aware of it, you have learned to live within a family interaction system that is highly reciprocal, patterned, and repetitive. The patterns provide data to understand acts that may appear confusing or strange when in isolation. Interaction patterns provide a window for assessing communication behaviors within a system, because they provide the context for understanding specific or isolated behaviors. For example, taken as an isolated action, it may be hard to interpret an act such as Mike hitting his brother, Charles. Yet, if this act is viewed as part of a contextual pattern, it may make sense. If parental disagreements and Mike's aggressive acts are related, you may discover patterns, such as the parents stop fighting with each other when they focus on Mike's angry actions or Charles' tears. Or, Mike is scared by his parents' anger and takes his feelings out on his brother. In a personal example, therapist Harriet Lerner, describes how family members can get stuck in a pattern.

> My older sister, Susan (a typical firstborn), managed her anxiety by overfunctioning, and I (a typical youngest) managed my anxiety by underfunctioning. Over time our position became polarized and rigidly entrenched. The more my sister overfunctioned the more I underfunctioned, and vice versa (28).

Patterns provide many more clues for interpreting behavior than do isolated individual actions.

Communication rules are a very special type of relationship pattern. Rules are relationship agreements that prescribe and limit a family member's behavior over time. Rules serve as generative mechanisms capable of creating regularity out of chaos (Yerby and Buerkel-Rothfuss 1982, 2). Family rules govern all areas of life, including communication behavior. Communication creates rules and is regulated by rules. Every human system needs rules and regularity in order to function efficiently over time. Yet, rules themselves are not totally stable. These will be discussed in detail in Chapter 4.

Human systems attempt to maintain levels of constancy within an overall defined range of acceptable behavior. From a somewhat mechanistic viewpoint, a system needs to maintain some type of standard by noting deviations from the norm and correcting them if they become too significant. The function of maintaining stability in a system is called *calibration*. Calibration implies monitoring and rectifying a scale. In the case of a family system, it implies checking and, if necessary, rectifying the scale of acceptable behaviors. On occasion the changes happen too dramatically for a family to exert any control but everyday life is filled with opportunities to maintain or change family patterns. Although systems can be compared to mechanical operations, Hoffman argues against this.

> Historically human systems were talked about in mechanical terms comparing family self regulation to the regulation

> functions of the thermostat. Recently scholars question this comparison yet are struggling to find ways to conceptualize family regulative processes. (Hoffman 1990)

Systems generate negative and positive feedback processes but, in systems language, the terms are used differently than they are in everyday usage. Negative feedback processes imply constancy or maintaining the standard while minimizing change. Positive, or change-promoting, feedback processes result in recalibration of the system at a different level. No value is implied by the labels of negative and positive. You can visualize this process in the following ways. Figure 3.1a represents a system in which negative, or maintenance, feedback prevents change from occurring. For example, this may happen when a teenager swears at a parent for the first time, yet rules themselves are not totally stable. The parent may threaten, "You swear at me again and I'll ground you for six months"; or the parent appeals to the family values: "We don't treat family members like that. We show each other respect even in disagreement." If the teenager becomes frightened by the threat, or apologetic for breaking the family value system, swearing may never occur again. Therefore, swearing will not become part of their conflict pattern at that point. In another situation, if one partner indicates a desire for sexual experimentation but the other refuses, the system will be maintained at the original level of sexual intimacy at least for a while.

Figure 3.1b represents a system in which positive feedback results in change. For example, if a wife cannot stop her husband's initial use of physical abuse, hitting may become part of their long-term conflict pattern. In another example, if the partner agrees to some sexual experimentation and both partners find pleasure in it, the system may develop a wider range of sexual intimacy.

According to Olson, Sprenkle, and Russell (1979), positive feedback processes provide the family with "constructive system-enhancing behaviors that enable the system to grow, create, innovate, and

**FIGURE 3.1**
**Feedback Systems**

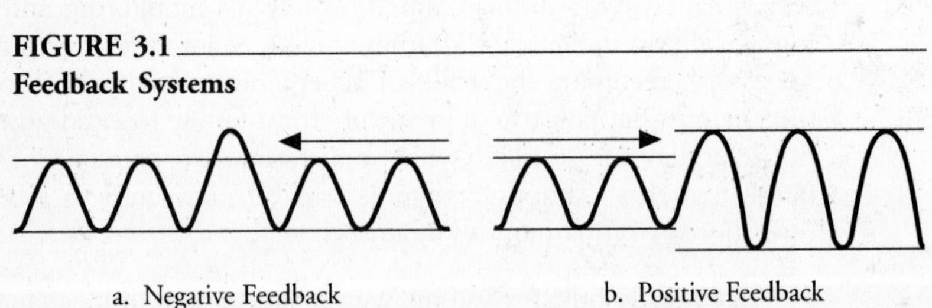

change, i.e., system morphogenesis. Conversely, negative feedback processes attempt to maintain the status quo, i.e., system morphostasis" (11). In the following situation, positive feedback processes operate as a father responds to his son's attempts to reach greater physical closeness.

---

*As an adult, I became very aware of the limited physical contact I had with my father. Although he would hug my sister, he never touched the boys, with the exception of a handshake. I determined that I wanted a greater physical closeness with him and consciously set out to change our ways of relating to each other. The first time I hugged my father was when I returned from a trip and I walked in and put my arms around him. I was nervous and tentative; he was startled and stiff, but he didn't resist. Over time I continued to greet him with hugs until we reached the point at which both of us could extend our arms to each other. I can now see my brothers developing a greater physical closeness to him also.*

---

Such attempts to regulate behavior need not occur just between two persons. All members of a family may be part of behavior regulation patterns. Constantine (1986, 61) provides an example of such a family pattern.

> When the therapist is interviewing a couple in their home, the woman says, "Dear, the boys are getting awfully noisy down there."
>
> The man goes to the doorway leading to the basement and hollers down, "Okay, you guys! Keep it down to a dull roar." The level of noise drifting up from the basement diminishes somewhat, and the interview continues. A bit later, the woman interrupts her husband.
>
> "Things are pretty quiet down there," she comments. "I wonder what the boys are up to?" Once more he goes to the basement door.
>
> "What are you two doing?" he bellows. "I don't hear the electric train anymore."
>
> "Aw, we're not doing anything, Dad," comes the reply, followed by giggles and the simulated sound of a steam locomotive.
>
> The loop involves (1) the mother, who monitors the level of noise from her sons and signals their father, (2) the

> father, who takes action intended to reverse deviation from the norm, and (3) the sons, who make the noise. Note that this system reduces deviation in either direction from the desired reference level; it exercises bidirectional control. The mother is not comfortable if the boys are either too quiet or too noisy.

When your family's communication rule has been developed over time, your family is calibrated, or "set," to regulate its behavior in conformity to the rule. If a family member or an outside force challenges the rule, the family may be recalibrated in accordance with the new rule.

The following example demonstrates this process. An unwritten family rule may be that a sick fourteen-year-old is not allowed to hear the truth regarding his illness. If anyone should suggest that he has a blood disease, negative feedback in the form of a nonverbal sign or a change of subject may keep him relatively uninformed. The family is "set" not to discuss the issue with him. Yet, the rules may be changed and the system recalibrated through a variety of positive feedback mechanisms. If the young man guesses the severity of his illness, he may confront one or more family members and insist on the truth. Once the truth has been told, he cannot return to his previous naive state, and the system will recognize his illness is known. Another source of positive feedback may be a doctor who suggests that the young man's condition be discussed with him and may require the family to do so. Again, the system would be recalibrated as family members mature and are considered able to handle certain information or experiences.

Human systems must change and restructure themselves in order to survive. Families constantly restructure themselves to cope with developmental styles and unpredictable crises. As noted in Chapter 2, regular change is a predictable part of the human experience.

Early family theorists viewed the family as a system attempting to maintain stability. Yet recent thinking about family systems views the concept of calibration as mechanistic and narrow. To view a human process in a totally mechanistic way is limiting. The constant dialectical struggles of human beings keep a system constantly at some level of movement. Hoffman maintains that human systems are capable of sudden leaps to new integrations, which reflect a new evolutionary state (54). In other words, families also experience change through leaps—as random and unpredictable forces propel members into new forms and experiences. The traditional calibration model needs to be modified and placed within an evolutionary framework, in an attempt to recogrize both types of change.

## Interactive Complexity/Punctuation

A systems perspective implies a move away from thinking about cause and effect to thinking about relationship patterns within contexts (Bochner and Eisenberg, 542). Simply put, cause and effect are interchangeable. When you function as a member of an ongoing family system, each of your actions serves as both a response to a previous action and a stimulus for a future action. The term "interactive complexity" implies that, once a cycle of behavior starts, each act triggers new behavior as well as responds to previous behaviors, rendering pointless any attempts to assign cause and effect. In most families, patterns of behavior develop and take on a life of their own. Thus, it is fruitless to assign a cause or blame to them, because the behaviors are intertwined. Family problems are seen in light of patterns of behavior in which all members have a part; one member is not to blame. One person does not carry the problems or blame. This approach has been labelled an "illness-free" lens through which to view relationships (Duncan and Rock 1993).

In order to make sense of the world, human beings tend to "punctuate," or divide up sequences of behavior. Punctuation refers to the interruption, or breaking into a sequence, of behavior at intervals in order to give it meaning. Punctuation often suggests that "things started here." Interactions, like sentences, must be punctuated, or grouped syntactically, to make sense or create meaning. Yet punctuation may serve as a trap, forcing persons into thought patterns that assign cause and blame to individuals.

Confusion may occur when people punctuate a communication sequence differently, thereby assigning different meanings to the behaviors. A son may say, "Our trouble started when my mother became depressed," whereas the mother may indicate that the family problems started when her son began staying away from home. Punctuating the cycle according to the son's suggestion would imply a placement of blame on the mother and suggest "fixing her would solve the problem." If the cycle is punctuated according to the mother, the son would be at fault for the family's troubles and should be "fixed." The "yes/no" cycle could go on indefinitely. It is fruitless to try to locate the "cause" because, even if it could be found, the current pattern is what must be addressed, not an individual's past actions. Working from the idea of circular causality within the system, it seems less important to try to punctuate the system and assign a beginning point than it does to look at the act as a sequence of patterns and try to understand this ongoing process without saying, "It started here." In Figure 3.2, you can imagine the different interpretations that could emerge depending on how the cycle is punctuated.

Some families try to explain their difficulties by going back through the past and saying, "It started when he took a job requiring travel" or "Things began to fall apart when my wife went back to work." The actions occurring since those blamed behaviors have so altered the system that a job change in either situation would not necessarily resolve the current issues, because the system has long since readjusted. In addition, specific job situations may be a response to a previous unnamed behavior. No matter how useful historical information is, only the present can be changed and the family's patterns serve as the key to change.

A classic example of this is found in the "nag-withdraw cycle," which demonstrates the pointless nature of looking for cause and effect: "He withdraws because she nags" versus "She nags because he withdraws" (Dell, 26). An example of such a cycle is found in this analysis of Eugene O'Neill's play *Long Day's Journey into Night*:

> … the family members watch the mother closely, which makes her visibly nervous, which makes them watch her closely … until the circle winds into a spiral leading to the return of her addiction, which they all fear. The above description could also have begun: the mother is visibly nervous, which makes the family watch her closely.… (Bavelas and Segal, 104)

As useful as the concepts of patterns and self regulation are, it will become clear that they cannot account for all family experiences of stability and change. These are individual issues, such as personality tendencies or genetic predispositions which also affect the system. Yet thinking in terms of patterns and self regulation can help you gain initial insight into family interaction patterns

**FIGURE 3.2**
**Circular Causality Within a System**

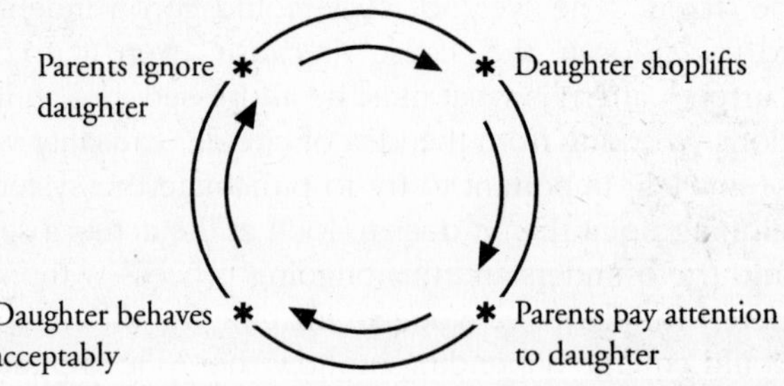

## Openness

Just as there are no decontexted individuals, so, too, there are no decontexted families. "Human systems are so organized that individuals, families, communities, and societies form nested layers of increasing inclusion and complexity" (Walsh 1985, 246). Human systems are open systems which permit interchange with surrounding environments. Describing a system as open does not mean it has no boundaries between itself and the environment. Rather, it means energy, matter, and information flow back and forth across that barrier (Broderick 1993, 37). Whereas closed mechanical systems will break down if they encounter new substances, human systems need interchange with other people, ideas, and institutions in order to remain physically and psychologically functional. Family members maintain an almost continuous interchange, not only within the system but across the family boundary to the larger suprasystem. Family systems with relatively closed boundaries develop extremely rigid family patterns.

Each family operates within the larger ecosystem, which includes legal, educational, political, health, and socioeconomic systems, as well as extended family and friendship systems. As a small child, you may have depended entirely on your family for all your immediate needs, but as you grew older, you needed to interact with nonfamily members in order to function in society. Such interchange with and adaptation to the environment is critical. Maintaining the bare necessities of life (food, clothing, and shelter) requires relating to nonfamily members. Education and work provide predictable sources of environmental contact, whereas friends and future spouses must be found outside the narrow limits of the immediate family system.

The strength of the family boundaries depends partially on how the family views the "outside world." A family's immediate environment may be experienced as harsh or threatening, such as when children can be shot walking to school, or supportive and nurturing, such as when neighbors create a kinship network of support. Individual circumstances, such as that described in the next entry, may force a family into active contact with institutions in their environment.

---

*As the parent of a hard of hearing child I am constantly managing our family's boundaries and dealing with outside systems. We deal regularly with the medical community in terms of advances which might affect Melissa's condition. The school system and I monitor which classes we should mainstream Melissa into each year. I need to keep up with legal changes to ensure that our child's rights are protected in*

(continued on page 62)

*terms of access to special programs. Finally, I am constantly aware of the effect of extended family and friends who reach out to support us.*

---

Few families can insulate children totally because school and media expose them to a range of values and beliefs, some of which may be contrary to those held by the family. Television, computers, and music open worlds to teenagers and children which parents may not even comprehend. Family systems rules include guidelines for maintaining and regulating relationships within the environment. But, in our rapidly changing world, families may not keep pace with the technological advances.

## Complex Relationships

Systems embedded in systems create a highly complex set of structures and interaction patterns and may be understood as members in relation to each other. This was referred to as nested layers in the last section. Minuchin (1974) defines family structure as "the invisible set of functional demands that organizes the ways in which family members interact" (71). Historically, the critical underlying concept of family organization was hierarchy, yet recent scholars argue there are other ways to understand system structures than just looking at hierarchy (Stier 1989; Broderick 1993).

A traditional hierarchical view establishes parents as more powerful or influential than children. In almost all cultures, authority, respect, and power go to the older generation, usually to the males of that generation. Appropriate boundaries separate generations; when these boundaries are blurred, confusion results, such as in the following case:

---

*After my father moved out I found myself playing surrogate Dad to three younger sisters who needed a lot of support. I moved into the role very easily since it seemed to take pressure off my mother who was severely depressed for almost three years. At the time I just did it. Now I wish I had not given up my adolescence so easily.*

---

In recent years, family expectations have represented this notion of family hierarchy and order through the use of a genogram, or a specialized drawing of a family tree that records information about members, events, and relationships over at least three generations

(Kramer 1985; McGoldrick and Gerson 1985). Complete genograms contain general codes which can be read by a trained eye (Figure 3.3, Figure 3.4).

Broderick, relying on his own thoughts and those of Gregory Bateson, an influential founder of the family process movement, argues families are not hierarchically structured in any stable fashion, yet how family members are positioned on vertical dimensions is a productive issue. Structural issues include subsystems and dynamics of power and privilege.

Given today's diverse family forms, the traditional hierarchical structures cannot account for the multiple family experiences. Many immigrant families in the U.S. face dramatic structural changes as young members gain power by speaking English which permits the entire family system to relate to the community. Certain responsible children find themselves as caretakers to a mother or father who is physically or psychologically unable to manage in the adult world. Extended stepfamily systems represent a range of structures, some of which are dependent on custody arrangements.

The complexity of the family system may be seen through the subsystems that contribute to the family's functioning. Multiple subsystems exist within a family, each crucial to the functioning of the whole. For example, an extended family may include many smaller family units, which in turn contain subsystems. Each family system contains interpersonal systems and individual, or psychobiological, subsystems. As noted in the discussion of wholeness, knowing the family attributes does not necessarily equal knowing the specific members or their relationships. Using the genogram in Figure 3.4, you can see that to know the Bennett family is not to know totally

**FIGURE 3.3**
**Structure of Family Relationships**

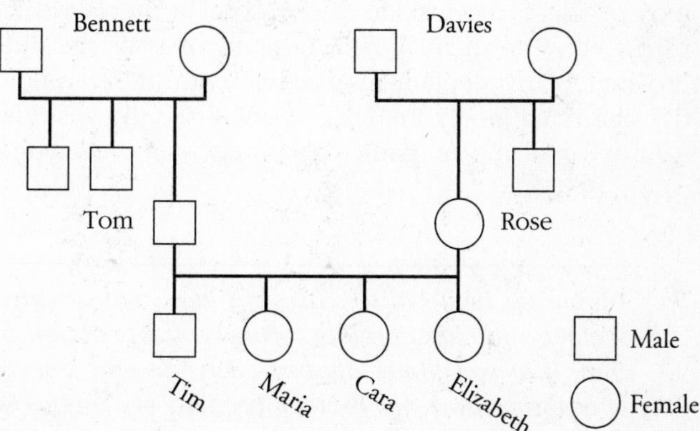

Tom Bennett or Rose Bennett, nor is it to know Tom and Rose Bennett's particular interpersonal relationship.

Every family contains interpersonal subsystems, made up of two or three persons and the relationships between or among them. Minuchin identifies subsystems as marital, parenting (involving parent and child), and siblings. Even a three-person system becomes complicated by the interpersonal subsystems within it. A mother, daughter, and grandson triad represents three such subsystems—the mother and daughter, the daughter and her son, and the grandmother and grandson.

Thus, each of the subsystems has to be considered in order to understand the functioning of the whole. Each subsystem has its own rules, boundaries, and unique characteristics. Consider the Bennett/Davis family. For example, Mom may never tease Maria but easily kids with Tim. Yet, Dad may tease both of them very comfortably and be more affectionate than Mom is able to be. Mom and Tim may spend long hours talking about his future plans, whereas Maria may choose not to discuss this with any immediate family members. Mom, Cara, and Maria may bind together to deal with problems resulting from Tom Bennett's poor health. In most cases, interpersonal subsystems change membership over time. Yet, certain subsystems may become so strong or tight that particular members feel either overwhelmed, powerless, or left out.

Coalitions develop when individuals align in joint action against others. For example, in a family with a gambling parent, the children and the non-gambling parent may form a tight group as a means of coping with the gambler's unpredictable behavior. The coalition may develop strategies for hiding money, supporting the others in arguments, or lying to those outside the system.

The triangle represents a powerful type of coalition. Under stress, two person relationships may become unstable, so they will draw in a third to stabilize their relationship (McGoldrick 1985). Family triangles are characterized by two insiders and one outsider. During periods of stress, the insiders try to rope in the outsider to reduce the stress between them. When tensions are low, the outsider may feel isolated. Many stepfamilies struggle with these issues in early years. By observing family triangles you will see the absurdity of assigning causes or blame to particular events, since everyone plays a part (Kerr 1981).

---

*I grew up in a house where my dad was an alcoholic. My mother and oldest brother formed a tight relationship against him, and sometimes against everyone else. They agreed on everything, and my brother became my mother's protector. Even when Dad started to get on the wagon, he could not break up that coalition, and I think that was one of the reasons they got a divorce. My brother discouraged my mom from ever trusting Dad again.*

---

Triangles often result in frustration and unhappiness for the "third" person. This is especially difficult when the triangle cuts across generations so the appropriate boundaries are violated, such as when a parent is aligned with a child against the other parent.

The family therapy literature identifies three powerful triangles in two parent families: the child as scapegoat, the child as mediator, and the perverse triangle (Broderick). A couple can triangulate a child into a scapegoat position by deflecting their marital tension onto the parent-child relationship, thereby labeling the child as the source of all family problems. Or a child may be cast in the role of mediator or counselor between two warring parents, a commonplace situation in divorcing families. Finally, in a perverse triangle, a coalition forms between a child and one parent whereby the child is enmeshed with one parent and cut off from the other.

As family systems grow in size, the complexity of the interpersonal subsystems develops accordingly. For example, in the Davis-Bennett family, some subsystems also represent strong coalitions (Figure 3.4).

To further complicate the issue, each family system reflects the individual, or psychobiological, system of each member as well as cultural norms which may privilege one type of subsystem over another. Each person's unique biological and psychological characteristics are influenced over the years by factors such as gender, age, birth

**FIGURE 3.4**
**Relationships Within the Family**

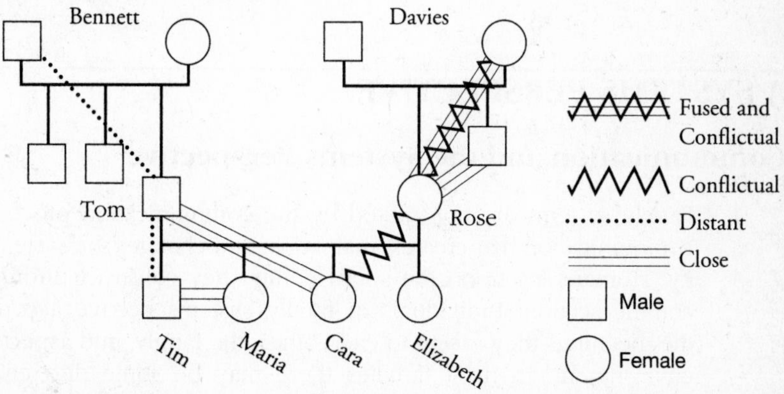

order, and the connections between family developmental stages and individual developmental stages. Therefore, no matter how much three sisters may resemble each other, each is a psychobiological entity who functions partially in an independent manner. In addition, outside factors such as their culture and socioeconomic level may strongly influence how women are treated in families.

### Equifinality

How do you know a family is resilient? Happy? Healthy? Wealthy? Adventurous? An open, adaptive family system demonstrates equifinality—the ability to accomplish a similar final goal or reach a similar state in many different ways and from many different starting points (Littlejohn, 45). In short, there are many ways to reach the same result. For example, two families may believe they achieve a "good life" based on a particular income, education, and relationship level, but appear very different to an observer. Or, two families may have a theme of: "Family members always support each other." Yet, each may work differently toward this goal of predictable mutual support. One family may interpret the theme to mean emotional support, whereas the other may view it as an economic issue. The families may differ in their definition of need for support and their demands for repayment. In short, there are as many possible ways of reaching a goal as there are families striving for that goal.

This may appear as a clean linear process of setting a goal and striving toward it, but in reality is more unpredictable. In Minuchin's words (1984), there is a "humbling conception in systems thinking having to do with change. While you can initiate, you can't entirely predict consequences" (88). Hence, a family attempting to reach security in one way may find themselves experiencing it in an entirely unpredicted yet satisfactory way after six months or six years.

## A SYSTEMS PERSPECTIVE

### Communication and the Systems Perspective

Family systems are constituted by the communication process—it is communication that creates, maintains, and changes the system's reality. Humans act upon the social reality they construct through their communication. Individuals in family systems behave according to the meanings they assign to each other, the family, and aspects of the environment. In most families there may be some differences but there is usually an awareness of congruence in how members see the world.

According to Yerby, Buerkel-Rothfuss, and Bochner (1990), communication messages way be viewed as interwoven patterns of interaction that stretch through a family's history rather than as singular events. Each message is simultaneously a response to someone else's message (real or anticipated) and a stimulus for future responses.

Finally, communication supports the self-reflexivity of human systems. "Human communication is what allows self-reflexivity to occur in a human system because it facilitates human's creation of meaning and their simultaneous activities of sending and receiving messages of symbolic contact," according to Whitchurch and Constantine (330).

## Limitations of the Systems Perspective

Just as there is no one right way to be a family, so too, there is no one right way to make sense out of family experience. The systems perspective, or family process theory, has been the primary paradigm for the past 25 years. In the early period, family scholars made a concerted effort to construct a unifying framework of family theory. The family process movement appeared to answer this need (Broderick). Although it is a well-known theory, particularly among family scholars and family therapists, decades of thinking and research revealed limitations which include gender and individual concerns and contextual issues.

***Gender Issues*** Systems theory has been criticized for ignoring the historical inequality between males and females in families, referred to as the "denial of gender" (Goldner 1989). Certain feminist theorists argue that the implicit patriarchal nature of family life goes unchallenged within the family process context, and an assumed equality of marital power is misleading and destructive. Stereotypical expectations of women as nurturing, dependent, or expressive and men as non-nurturing, independent, or instrumental are also misleading. (Boss and Thorne 1989; Hare-Mustin 1989). A commonly cited problem area which overlaps gender and individual concerns relates to abusive families in which a systems perspective removes any individual level of responsibility for problems. The concept of circular causality and mutual influence can mask the responsibility of a man and the vulnerability of a woman in a physically abusive relationship (Hoffman 1990). Greater attention to gender concerns could strengthen the systems perspective.

***Individual Concerns*** Systems theory tends to overlook individual, or psychobiological, issues. In the early years of family systems theory the growing information about genetic components of disease were largely ignored and responsibility for problems were placed equally on the members of a troubled relationship. This resulted in inappropriate responsibility being assigned to family members for actions of individuals suffering from actual illness or having biological predispositions to certain disorders such as schizophrenia, manic depression, or anxiety (Broderick). Such blame can be devastating to family members who are frustrated by the problems, as indicated below.

---

*My brother's hyperactivity was not understood in the 1970s and my parents were blamed for his inattention and the mishaps he had (ie: getting into the medicine cabinet and drinking a bottle of Dimetapp). His behavior problems were not just a product of the system and the implication that my parents were involved in causing his problem was devastating to them. The doctors, teachers, and school counselors all made my mother feel like a bad parent.*

---

Currently, theorists argue that systems approaches can be aided by individual approaches which recognize biological components of the problem.

***Contextual Issues*** Critics argue there is no culturally contextual version of family process, although, a number of efforts in this direction are underway. Until the 1980s, little thought had been given to ethnic and class variations in families and to their implications for understanding family interaction, such as in the areas of gender and power (Markowitz 1994). Throughout this text you will encounter examples of cultural impact on family functioning.

These limitations, real as they are, also represent the signs of maturity of the approach. We believe a systems approach provides a valuable perspective from which to analyze family interaction.

## Holding a Systems Perspective

What does it really mean to look at the family from a systems perspective? A systems perspective provides you with a particular set of lenses through which to view family functioning. It is a perspective with strengths and limitations, which will be addressed shortly. If you accept a systems perspective, you need to consider the following assumptions when analyzing family interaction:

- Persons do not live in a vacuum. In order to understand an individual fully you must understand how he or she functions within the primary system of the family.
- In established relationships, causes and effects become interchangeable over time. Therefore, to understand interaction, focus on the current patterns. There is little value in finding "the cause" or placing "the blame" because the current pattern is the concern.
- Any human behavior is the result of many variables rather than one cause. Since a change in one part of the system affects all parts of the system, problems must be viewed on many levels. Simplistic solutions are questionable.
- Family members operate according to many recognized and unrecognized patterns and rules. The patterns convey a level of meaning that individual behavior cannot convey.
- There is no one right way to get to a certain end or reach a certain goal. Therefore, there are many ways to be a functional family, and these may change over time.
- The whole is greater than the sum of its parts, whether those parts are individuals or subsystems. Viewing the family as a whole demonstrates its communication complexity.
- Some factors may get overlooked in the forces on relational patterns. Gender, cultural, and individual concerns may not receive appropriate attention.

Although this chapter has dealt with a systems perspective primarily in an abstract manner, this view may be applied to everyday family functioning in concrete ways. As Satir (1988) says:

> Becoming aware of their system usually opens the way for family members to become searchers and to stop berating themselves and others when things go wrong. People can ask "how" questions instead of "why" questions. Generally speaking, "how" questions lead to information and understanding, and "whys" imply blame and so produce defensiveness. (136)

Taking a systems perspective has very real consequences. It will alter the way you view families, academically, personally, and professionally. For example, an elementary school teacher who holds a family systems perspective may try routinely to discover if an acting out student's classroom behavior may be a symptom of a problem in his or her family life, or if his or her unacceptable behavior in class, such as exaggerated clowning, could serve a particular function in the family system. Therapists holding such a perspective would seek to meet and or learn about the client's family to enable them to put the individual's behavior in context. The teacher would also try to determine how changes in the family system might be reflected in a student's academic or personal school behavior.

When viewed from this perspective, the focus shifts from individual member's behavior to the family as a whole, with its interdependent relationships and patterns, which affect cohesion and adaptability. Looking at the family as a whole brings conceptions of interpersonal communication into greater congruence with the interactional complexity of family life (Bochner and Eisenberg). This perspective allows one to analyze specific behavior patterns in terms of the interpersonal context in which they occur and to understand their meaning in light of the entire family system. A systems perspective has value at an academic level and at a personal level for anyone interested in understanding how families establish and maintain their relationships through communication.

## CONCLUSION

This chapter applied a systems perspective to the family. It established that a family system consists of members, relationships among them, family attributes, member's attributes, and an environment in which the family functions. The following systems characteristics were applied to family life: interdependence, wholeness, patterns/self-regulation, interactional complexity/punctuation, openness, and complex structures and equifinality. The importance of communication to family process was established and certain limitations of systems theory were noted.

## IN REVIEW

1. Using Satir's mobile image describe how a change in one member of a real or fictional family affected the other family members.
2. Using a real or fictional family, describe its calibrated level of conflict in terms of acceptable behaviors. Describe attempts to change this calibrated level in terms of positive or negative feedback process.

3. Draw a three-generation representation (genogram) of a real or fictional family, and indicate and explain the coalitions among certain family members. See p. 63 for a model. Indicate the effect of these coalitions on other family members.
4. How would holding a family systems perspective affect your work as one of the following: a doctor, clergy person, school counselor, office manager, novelist?
5. Cite an example of a family circumstance which would demonstrate a limitation of family systems theory.

# 4

# Communication Patterns and the Creation of Family Meanings

Every family creates its own identity. Two families may share the same cultural background, uphold similar values and goals, and have members of similar ages and abilities, but they will not have identical experiences. The interaction of your family members creates an overall experience of family life that cannot be recreated by any other family. This uniqueness reflects the family meanings developed through patterned interactions. Eventually each family develops what is called a relational culture, or a jointly constructed world view. The view of reality influences all parts of a family's everyday existence and effects are felt across generations, as the following story demonstrates:

---

*My father was in his early twenties when he came to the United States from Taiwan, leaving behind his parents, three brothers, and two sisters. His first job was as a waiter in a Chinese restaurant. The job provided a small room upstairs and meals during workdays. During this time the only thing my father would spend pay on was bread and bologna to feed himself on days when he did not work.*

*He earned about $300 a month of which he sent $200 home to repay the money he borrowed for travel. He sent $50 to his family. He used the rest for chemistry books and English classes.*

*He had a hard time at the restaurant since he could not understand the American customers. One of the chefs always tried to make things hard for him. He would try to make my father work extra hard by mixing up different orders so my father had to guess which dishes went together. My father hated working there.*

*My father, who became a research chemist, has told this story many times because I think he was trying to instill in us the importance of working hard for your dreams and the importance of helping your family. This story makes me proud of his accomplishments and what our family has become. I will tell my children about their grandfather's struggles so they understand the importance of hard work and sacrifice.*

---

Such a story is a powerful example of how one creates family meanings. Wells (1986) writes:

> Constructing stories in the mind—or storying, as it has been called—is one of the most fundamental means of making meanings. When storying becomes overt and is given expression in words, the resulting stories are one of the most effective ways of making one's own interpretation of events and ideas available to others. (194)

The previous chapter examined the family from a systems perspective; this chapter centers on the meaning-making function of families. It is through communication that family members construct and manage their everyday lives, and hence, their collective identity. In order to understand the significant role meaning plays in the development of family relationships we will look at: (1) the formation of a family's relational culture through communication, and (2) the development of those meanings through four sources of communication patterns, family-of-origin influences, communication rules, family stories, and family networks. Throughout this chapter you will see how everyday ritualized experiences contribute to a family's collective sense of identity and meaning.

## MEANINGS IN RELATIONSHIPS

Communication, the symbolic, transactional process of sharing meanings, undergirds and illuminates the structure of kinship relationships. The form and content of family messages combine to create a family's view of itself and the world. Family members, through their interdependence and mutual influence, create meanings based on their interaction patterns. Meanings are formed as persons interpret what they perceive and construct a sense of reality. Yerby and Buerkel-Rothfuss (1982) maintain that "meaning in the family is achieved—behavior is interpreted and evaluated—as members coordinate their activities through communication" (2). This process of meaning-making may be voluntary or involuntary, explicit or implicit.

This meaning-centered approach grows out of symbolic interactionism, a perspective which attempts to explain the interrelationship of symbols and interaction processes. According to La Rossa and Reitzes (1993) , symbolic interactionism focuses on "the connection between symbols (i.e., shared meanings) and interactions (i.e., verbal and nonverbal actions and communications)" (135).

This approach views families as social groups and in the role of social interaction is the development of self and group identity. In summarizing key assumptions of symbolic interactionism, LaRossa and Reitzes list the following assumptions as characteristic of the importance of meaning for human behavior.

1. Human beings act toward things on the basis of the meanings that the things have for them.

Mealtime rituals are a rich source of family meanings.

2. Meaning arises out of the process of interaction between people.
3. Meanings are handled in and modified through an interpretive process used by the person in dealing with things he or she encounters. (143)

These selected tenets of social interactionism will guide our thinking about the importance of meaning-making families.

## Relational Cultures

Each of you learns to interpret and evaluate behaviors within your family system and create a set of meanings which may not be understood by an outsider. Each family system creates a world view, or "a library of framing assumptions," that organizes shared beliefs and meanings (Reiss 1981; Brighton-Cleghorn 1987). This view of reality undergirds all communication.

Communication is not only a simple interchange among people; it also shapes and alters the structure of the family system and the individuals in it. Communication serves to create a relational culture, a privately transacted system of understandings that coordinate attitudes, actions, and identities of participants in a relationship. It is based on a jointly constructed world view. According to Wood (1982):

> *Relational culture* is fundamentally a product of communication; that is, it arises out of communication, is maintained and altered in communication, and is dissolved through communication. (76)

Just as friends and romantic pairs form relational cultures, so, too, family members form powerful familial relational cultures with long lasting effects.

In order to see this more closely, consider the behaviors of a couple as they begin to form a family system. Family therapist Minuchin (1974) suggests that each young couple must undergo a process of mutual accommodation through which the partners develop a set of patterned transactions—"ways in which each spouse triggers and monitors the behavior of the other and is, in turn, influenced by the previous behavioral sequence. These transactional patterns form an invisible web of complementary demands that regulate many family situations" (17). In order to form a marital system, a couple must negotiate a set of common meanings through mutual accommodation so that, eventually, the meanings for one are linked through conjoint action with the meanings of the other. The negotiation process is both subtle and complex; some couples never accomplish this task.

A couple strives to create mutually meaningful language. General similarities in their physical and social processes assure some generalized common meanings. However, the intent of some behaviors, if not discussed, may be misinterpreted; yet, these behaviors and their interpretations will become part of the couple's meaning pattern. Usually, the more similar their backgrounds, the less negotiation is needed. With the entire realm of verbal and nonverbal behavior available, they have to negotiate a set of common meanings which reflect their physical, social, and individual processes for viewing the world. When behaviors are interpreted in the same way or interpretations are discussed and clarified, similar meanings emerge, and communication becomes clearer.

Often it is assumed that words are the key to developing a relational culture, yet in an attempt to distinguish between distressed and nondistressed couples, research concluded that nonverbal behavior was an important key. In early work, Gottman (1979) found that distressed couples were more likely to "express their feelings about a problem, to mind read, and to disagree, all with negative nonverbal behavior" (467–68). In recent work, Gottman (1994) goes so far as to suggest a husbands's facial indicators have predicted, over time, a wife's susceptibility to illness. As families add members, the relational culture becomes more complex.

As a family system evolves, the communication among members affects the continuously adapting form of the structure. Over a period of time, family members come to have certain meanings within each relationship. In their classic work, Hess and Handel (1959) suggest that interpersonal ties reflect these meanings since "The closeness between any two members, for example, or the distance between a group of three closely joined members and a fourth who is apart, derives from the interlocking meanings which obtain among them" (18–19). This can be seen in the following example:

---

*Our communication patterns tend to separate family members from each other although Mom and Amy are really joined against Dad. Here's a typical example of the family in action.*

MOM: *Sam, let's go to the zoo. The kids would love to see the animals.*

DAD: *I am tired of doing what the kids want. Let's just sit around the house.*

(continued on page 78)

SISTER: *Damn, Dad, you never want to do anything that we like.*

MOM: *Amy, watch your language. Now, apologize to your father!*

SISTER: *No, he doesn't care about us.*

DAD: *That's correct. I don't care! (Very serious facial expression)*

SCOTT: *We always have these fights. Why do we bother being a family? (Scott storms to his room)*

*By now we are so used to the "moves" that we hear the opening line and go through the predictable scene.*

---

Thus, the use of verbal and nonverbal messages—and their eventual patterns—plays a significant role in a family's existence. Yet, you will always find an exception to the norm—due to a system's equifinality, or ability to reach the same point differently, there will always be examples of the unique happily married couple or satisfied family that break all the rules.

Coordinated meanings do not emerge early or quickly within relationships. Partners may struggle for years to gain similarity in interpreting and responding to each other's behaviors. Parents and children may live with serious misunderstandings and mistaken assumptions throughout most of their shared lives as a result of communication breakdowns. For example, both may consciously avoid the subject, one may resist the other's attempt to explore the subject, or one may remain unaware of a difficulty which the other is reluctant to address directly.

A sense of self and family world views are analogous to "symbolic blueprints" which guide behavior (Brighton-Cleghorn 1987). Family disorder occurs when great differences occur among individuals' world views, such that there is no longer a family set of common meanings.

## COMMUNICATION PATTERNS THAT INFLUENCE FAMILY MEANINGS

Meanings emerge through the continuous interpretation of and response to messages. Over time, these interactions become predictable and form communication patterns or complex sets of "moves," which have been established through repetition and have become so automatic as to continue without conscious awareness. Over time these patterns serve to create meanings.

A communication pattern is distinguished by seven characteristics:

1. It is verbal and nonverbal.
2. It is specific to the relationship within the system.
3. It is recurring and predictable.
4. It is reciprocal and interactive.
5. It is relationship defining.
6. It is emergent.
7. It may be changed by forces within the ecosystem or it may influence changes in that system. (Yerby and Buerkel-Rothfuss, 7)

To fully understand how these family meanings emerge, the following areas must be explored: (1) family-of-origin influences, (2) family communication rules, (3) family stories, and (4) communication networks.

## Family-of-Origin Influences

"My son's a Kaplan, all right. He'll walk up and talk to anyone without a trace of shyness." "My family always fought by yelling at each other and then forgetting about it. My grandparents and my parents were great shouters. My wife doesn't understand this." These typical sayings indicate the potential family-of-origin influence on communication patterns in new family systems. Family-of-origin refers to the family or families in which a person is raised and is generally thought to be the earliest and most powerful source of influence in one's personality (Bochner and Eisenberg 1987). Thus, the family in which you grew up is your family-of-origin. Many of you still function primarily within your family-of-origin systems. Others of you have already formed new family systems.

The term "family-of-origin influences" refers to how current relational experiences reflect a unique combination of (1) multigenerational transmissions and (2) the ethnic/cultural heritage represented within the family-of-origin. Although the development of common meanings within a couple's relationship depends on the physical, social, and individual filters of each person, the multigenerational and ethnic background that each partner brings to a relationship is also a significant social influence. Many of you may desire a family life different from the one in which you grew up, yet you find yourself recreating that family in a new relationship. Parental socialization serves as a major factor in determining children's family-formation behavior (McLanahan and Bumpass 1988). People often work out marriages similar to their parents, not because of heredity, but because they are following a family pattern.

Certain communication patterns may be passed from one generation to another and may reflect cultural heritage.

***Multigenerational Transmissions*** Families-of-origin may provide blueprints for the communication of future generations. Initially, communication is learned in the home, and, throughout life, the family setting provides a major testing ground for new communication skills or strategies. Each young person who leaves the family-of-origin to form a new system takes with him or her a set of conscious and unconscious ways of relating to people. For example, the idiosyncrasies and culturally based communication patterns of the O'Briens may be passed on to generations of children in combination with the patterns gained from in-laws' families-of-origin. Most families develop "family words" which are only understood by a small circle, which can be traced back to a child or a grandparent, and which may be passed down from generation to generation (Dickson 1988). These may cause great confusion or humor as noted in the following:

---

*My husband gets crazy with all the odd words my family uses, especially around children. I came from a family of twelve kids and there were always words someone couldn't say or codes for things. So I talk to our kids about "I-box" (ice cream), doing a zipperino (getting dressed) or "the throne" (toilet).*

---

Just as simple language terms travel across the generations, more significant attitudes and rule-bound behaviors move from a family-of-origin to a newly emerging family system. For example, in their examination of male and female expressiveness, Balswick and Averett (1977) reported persons whose parents were expressive to them will be more expressive. The family-of-origin serves as the first communication classroom.

Wide differences in family-of-origin behaviors can lead to communication breakdowns in a couple's system. In the following example, a young wife describes the differences in nonverbal communication in her family-of-origin from that of her husband:

---

*It was not until I became closely involved with a second family that I became conscious of the fact that the amount and type of contact can differ greatly. Rarely, in Rob's home, will another person reach for someone else's hand, walk arm in arm, or kiss for no special reason. Hugs are reserved for comfort. When people filter into the den to watch television, one person will sit on the couch, the next on the floor, a third on a chair, and finally the last person is forced to sit on the couch. And always at the opposite end! Touching, in my home, was a natural, everyday occurrence. Usually, the family breakfast began with "good morning" hugs and kisses. After meals, we often would sit on our parents' laps rocking, talking, and just relaxing. While watching television, we usually congregated on and around someone else as we sat facing the set. Even as adults, no one ever hesitated to cuddle up next to someone else, run their hands through another person's hair, or start tickling whoever happens to be in reaching distance.*

---

The previous example illustrates the extent to which each partner was raised differently and how that affects communication in the new system. When you consider your parent's marriage, or your own, you can find instances of this situation in which the rules or networks affect how and what communication occurs. For instance, if you have lived in a stepfamily, you may have witnessed the stress involved in integrating your stepparent's family-of-origin influences into a system with communication patterns that already reflected two families-of-origin.

Although family-of-origin issues may be discussed as parent to child transmissions, recently greater emphasis has been placed on transmission across generations. You were introduced to this idea in Chapter 3 through the genograms. In recent years family scholars and researchers have focused more directly on the effect of multigenerational systems. The basic assumptions inherent in such an approach include:

***Multigenerational systems:***

- Influence, and are influenced by individuals who are born into them
- Are similar to, but more complex than, any multiperson ecosystem
- Are developmental in nature, witnessing changes in individuals and subsystems
- Patterns which are shared, transformed, and manifested through intergenerational transmission
- Impact nuclear families as the husband's and wife's heritages reflect cross-generational influences
- Contain issues which may appear only in certain contexts and which may be at unconscious levels
- Have boundaries that are hierarchical in nature
- Develop functional and dysfunctional patterns based on the legacy of previous generations and here-and-now happenings (Hoopes 1987, 198–204).

As a way to envision some of these influences, consider the genogram (Figure 4.1) which contains examples of powerful parent-child relationships, a theme of service as well as flexible boundaries.

**FIGURE 4.1**
**Multigenerational System**

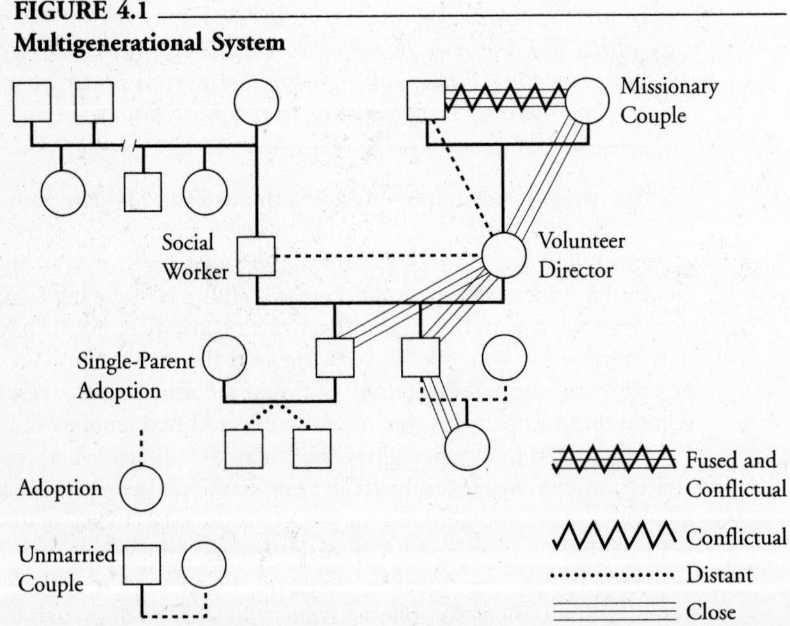

The power of multigenerational transmission is part of a puzzle which is unfolding. In the following passage a young woman reflects on her painful experiences and insights.

---

*I have come to learn that my problem of behavior was a reaction to my mother's alcoholism, and to her emotional distance during my infancy and childhood. Likewise, my mother's behaviors had a similar origin. Handicapped by her own mother's chronic depression, my mother never received the affirmation she needed and desired. Yet, having been reared by an alcoholic mother, my grandmother was in no better position to be an effective mother or role model for intimacy. With such unavailable models, the women in my family were perpetually unable to develop this essential capacity. Consequently, my own mother had to build our relationship from a faulty blue-print.*

---

Some of the issues that may be used to examine multigenerational issues include: how gender roles are played out; how families deal with losses; how ethnic patterns affect interactions; how certain people are liked, such as through names of physical similarities; how themes are played out; how rigid or loose the boundaries are; and how members deal with conflict. These and other related issues are viewed across three or four generations to see how patterns are passed down, consciously or unconsciously.

***Ethnicity*** The communication patterns of diverse ethnic heritages may bring partners into regular conflict until the source of the misperceptions can be identified and addressed. For example, the contrast between a strong Italian heritage and strong British heritage may serve as the key to unlocking marital confusion between marital partners from these backgrounds (Lerner 1989). Italian families place strongest emphasis on togetherness and absorbing new members into the family. In contrast a strong British tradition emphasizes the family as a collection of individuals who place a high premium on launching self-reliant, competent young adults. Any combination of strong ethnic heritages will cause marital issues to surface.

The role of ethnicity often is overlooked, yet its influence can be powerful, since ethnic values and identification are retained for many generations after immigration (McGoldrick 1994). Ethnic family issues may be reflected in issues such as age, gender, roles, expressiveness, birth order, separation, or individuation (McGoldrick 1993b). In their examination of Italian families, Rotunno and McGoldrick (1982) highlight the families' cultural enjoyment of celebrating, loving, and fighting and their orientation toward social skills, including cleverness, charm, and graciousness. These behaviors exist within an orientation to values that places heavy emphasis on how actions affect the family, especially its honor. In addition, Italian families function within a network of significant other relatives, gumbares (old friends), and godparents from whom mutual support is expected. This orientation stresses parental role distinction, with the father as the undisputed head of the family and mother as the heart, or the family's emotional sustenance.

This generalization about the Italian heritage comes into sharp contrast with descriptions of Scandinavian family patterns, which generally stress the importance of emotional control and the avoidance of open confrontation (Midelfort and Midelfort 1982). Within the Norwegian family, words are likely to be used sparingly; inner weaknesses are kept secret; aggression is channeled into teasing, ignoring, or silence. In terms of male/female roles, the man serves as head of the family and exacts discipline, while the woman is the communication center establishing the social network among kin. The marriage of persons reflecting these two ethnic backgrounds has the potential for misunderstanding unless differences are addressed. Strong conflicts may develop as each plays out behaviors appropriate to his or her family-of-origin. Such differences may never be resolved because of the strength of the family pattern, or compromises may be necessary as the whole family is influenced by social forces.

A family's ethnic heritage may dictate norms for communication which are maintained for generations. For example, an emphasis on keeping things "in the family," the acceptability of discussing certain subjects, or the way in which such subjects are discussed may pass from generation to generation reflecting individual and cultural influences. An examination of communication patterns through three generations of an extended Irish-American family revealed great similarities across generations in terms of culturally predictable communication patterns (Galvin 1982). Respondents from each generation reported their variations on the theme of privacy saying: "What you see and hear in this house goes no further; Don't advertise your business. Handle it on the q.t. This information doesn't leave this table." Whereas the Irish family set strong boundaries, the following description of Arabic family life portrays a different picture.

---

*Growing up in an Arab household, our immediate family and our extended family reflected the strong patriarchical influence and a theme of "family is family" which implied active support of many relatives. We lived by the Arabic proverb "A small house has enough room for one hundred people who love each other" and we shared joys, sorrows, money, and things among and across generations.*

---

The importance of a family-of-origin is summarized well by Kramer (1985) in her description of its influence on a child's view of the world.

> He observes the environment he inhabits, partakes of its ambiance. He forms values and beliefs, develops assumptions about how marriages and families are and should be, and learns about life cycles, including how to handle the changes of maturation and of aging and death. He learns about power and control and about the consequences of emotions, both his own and others. He is schooled in patterns of communication: what role to take in triangles; how to handle secrets; how to respond to pressure. (9)

Such a description captures the power of a child's family experiences to influence his or her entire life.

## Family Communication Rules

---

*When I was 15, my father had surgery on ... to this day I don't know exactly what! My parents mentioned nothing until the day of the surgery when Mom told me, that, instead of riding the bus home from school, I would take a taxi with her to visit my Dad in the hospital. It wasn't my business to know, I guess, and it certainly wasn't my business to talk about it. I got the message loud and clear—never talk about your father's health.*

---

The previous example reflects a very common family experience—the family communication rule. Every family develops rules for interaction and transmits them to new members. As noted in Chapter 3, rules are relationship agreements that prescribe and limit a family's behavior over time. A family acts as a rule-governed system: family members interact with each other in an organized, repetitive fashion, creating patterns that direct family life. Rules serve as generative mechanisms capable of creating regularity where none exists. In most cases, rules reflect patterns that have become "oughts" or "shoulds." Rules exist because social behavior depends on regularities, even though some individuals may act in unpredictable ways. Because of their regularities, rules serve a powerful function in coordinating meanings between people (Cronen, Pearce, and Harris 1979). Through rules family members gain a sense of shared reality and mutual understanding.

Although individuals may follow personal rules such as "I never discuss my religion with strangers," and society may promote standardized rules such as "tell the truth if under oath," these rules do not reflect an interpersonal generative function. Relational rules refers to the tendency of people in relationships to "develop rules unique to a specific interaction situation and to repeat them until they become reflected in patterns of behavior" (Yerby and Buerkel-Rothfuss, 3).

***Development of Rules*** Since birth you have learned to adjust to social and personal regulations, and you have expected others to do the same in a predictable way. You were raised in a world of rules, particularly communication rules, but how did you learn them? You learned some rules through conscious discussion, but you learned most through redundancy—repeated interactions.

Rules vary on a continuum of awareness, ranging from very direct, explicit, conscious relationship agreements which may have been clearly negotiated to the implicit, unspoken, unconscious rules emerging from repeated interactions. Whereas the former are rather straightforward, the latter are extremely complex and convoluted. In some families, particular rules are negotiated directly, such as "We will never go to bed without kissing goodnight" or "We will openly discuss sex with the children." But most rules develop as a result of multiple interactions. One person's behavior becomes a powerful force capable of evoking a predictable response from the other person. In most cases, these rules are both influential and invisible. They are so much a part of the family's way of life that they are not recognized or named, but they are enforced, as indicated in the following example:

---

*When I bring up a subject that is "taboo," and we are around other people, my mother gives me the cold stare as though she would deny it. When we are engaged in a one-on-one conversation, she ignores me or changes the subject. We've never talked about these topics or rules directly. I doubt we ever will.*

---

Many rules reflect the partners' family-of-origin rules which, if questioned, pass from generation to generation. Spouses from families with dissimilar rules experience greater struggles than those from similar families-of-origin. Some rules are tied to ethnic communication patterns.

Persons who form a system must be sensitive to the relational consequences of their acts. Consider the difficulties if two people bring to their marriage the following individual rules for behavior during a family argument:

> Person 1: If one person expresses strong negative emotion, the other should consider it carefully and refrain from spontaneous response.
>
> Person 2: If one person expresses strong negative emotion, the other should respond with emotional supportiveness. To avoid responding would indicate total rejection.

You can imagine the process of rule negotiation that would have to occur in order for these two people to achieve a communication pattern with which both of them feel comfortable.

Cultural or ethnic backgrounds influence family rules. In discussing problems in doing therapy with multi-generational Irish families, McGoldrick (1993b) suggests that family members may "clam up," because there are particularly strong rules about sharing personal information with those of the opposite sex or different generations. In contrast, members of Jewish families value direct verbal expressions of feelings (Herz and Rosen 1982). Each ethnic or cultural group reflects its own rules.

Analysis of any rule-bound system requires an understanding of the mutual influence pattern within which the rules function. Due to the transactional nature of communication the mutual influence process will result in new relational patterns. This process has been described as follows:

> No matter how well one knows the rules of communicator A, one cannot predict the logic of his/her communication with B without knowing B's rules and how they will mesh. The responsibility for good and bad communication is thus transactive with neither A or B alone deserving praise or blame. (Cronen, Pearce, and Harris, 36)

Once rules are established, changing them may be complicated and time-consuming unless the family has a flexible adaptation process and can recognize the rule for what it is. When a family rule has been developed over time and members are accustomed to certain "acceptable" behaviors, the family tends to regulate its behavior in accordance with the rule.

Rules are maintained or changed through negative (maintenance) or positive (growth) feedback processes. Limits can be recalibrated unconsciously or consciously. For example, rules may be renegotiated as family members pass through certain developmental stages. A child of twelve may not be allowed to disagree with his parents' decisions, but when he reaches seventeen, his parents may listen to his arguments. This recalibration may not be a totally conscious process but one that evolves as the child matures toward adulthood. On the other hand, rules may be openly negotiated or changed as the result of various factors, such as member dissatisfaction or feedback from outside sources. A teacher's suggestion to "Encourage Derrick to make more decisions" or "Encourage Patrick to state his own opinions" may affect a parent's behavior.

Breaking the rules results in the creation of a new set as the system recalibrates itself to accept a wider variety of behavior. Old patterns shift. For example, one may hear "I have broken the rule about not discussing sex by openly discussing my living arrangement with my mother. She is now completely vulnerable, because she can no longer use the familiar defensive pattern of communication." Although a period of chaos may precede the emergence of a new set of rules, the new system may be more open and flexible as a result.

Most rules exist within a hierarchy. The Parsons and the Coopers may each establish the rule "You do not swear." In the Parson family, it may be a critical concern, whereas, the Coopers may see it as desirable. Once you learn the family rules, you then have to figure out the importance placed on each of them.

For years, you have lived with certain rules without discussing them, but they are adhered to as closely as if they were printed as a list of "shoulds" on your refrigerator door. As a family insider, you make subtle adjustments to context with ease and limited awareness. The power of patterns emerges as you adjust your language in front of an older relative, refrain from raising a certain topic at the dinner table, or assess your partner's mood before discussing money.

Yet sometimes a member of a family system operates according to rules unknown to the others. A major source of conflict centers around the breaking of rules that one member of the pair may not even know exist. "You should know enough not to open my mail." "Don't listen to my phone calls." Such conflicts frequently arise as stepfamilies form. The more conscious the prescriptions, the greater the possibility of their renegotiation at appropriate times.

***Importance of Rules*** Rules are important for many reasons because they support: (1) family self definition, (2) relational development, and (3) family satisfaction (Pearson 1989). Through rule bound interaction, families establish their primary and secondary family functions. Rules set the limits of cohesion and adaptability within a family. In some families, members learn that everything is to be kept within the family, intimate physical and verbal behavior is expected, and friends are to be kept at a distance. In others, members encounter a lack of concern for the privacy of family issues, suggestions that problems be discussed with outsiders, and injunctions against changing one's position on a controversial point. Rules help form a family's images, themes, boundaries, and positions on biosocial issues such as power and gender. These in turn guide further rule development. The interaction of rules and functions supports the development of self-definition.

As individuals come together to form relationships they create an increasingly unique pattern of interaction. The higher the relational knowledge between partners, the greater their comfort and ability to predict interaction patterns. Rules provide a major means of coordinating meaning in such a developing relationship.

Finally, rules contribute to a family's sense of satisfaction. Rules provide stability in interactions and serve to socialize younger members. If every time a "hot" topic such as death or sex arose a family had to discover each member's response to the subject, there would be constant confusion. Predictable communication patterns allow a family to carry on its functional day-to-day interactions smoothly. Members know whom to approach about what under which circumstances. There is security and satisfaction in such knowledge.

***Types of Communication Rules*** Key questions provide a framework for looking at types of communication rules: What can be talked about? How can it be talked about? And to whom can it be talked about? (Satir 1988).

The first set of rules relates to what one is allowed to talk about. Can death, sex, salaries, drugs, and serious health problems be talked about in the family? Are there family skeletons or current relatives who are never mentioned? Most families have topics that are taboo either all the time or under certain circumstances. Sometimes family members may openly agree not to raise a particular topic, but usually, they realize it is inappropriate because of the verbal or nonverbal feedback they receive if they mention it. These become extremely clear, as this young person reports:

---

*At my father's house there are lots of unspoken rules which dictate unsafe topics of conversation. It's clear that I should never mention (1) my mother, (2) the way we used to celebrate holidays, (3) my need for money, (4) my mother, (5) old family vacations, (6) my mother's relatives, (7) (8) (9) (10) my mother!*

---

Although topics may not be restricted, many families restrict the feelings that can be shared—especially negative feelings. Emotions such as anger, sadness, or rage may be avoided at all costs and denied whenever necessary.

Decision making often provides a fertile field for family rules. Does the system allow children to question parental decisions, or are they "the law" which cannot be challenged? In some families, children may hear such words as, "We're moving and that's final. I don't want to hear another word about it." Other families have rules that allow joint decision making through discussions, persuasion, or voting. In such cases, all members are allowed to question the decision.

The next question is, how you can talk about it? Within your family, can you talk about things directly, really leveling about feelings on a particular issue or feelings, or must you sneak it in? For example, in a family with an alcoholic parent, the other members may say, "Mom's under the weather," but no one says, "Mom is an alcoholic." There is a tacit agreement never to deal with the real issue. In dealing with death, children learn that "Grandpa's gone to sleep" or "passed on," but the reality of death is not discussed. Many couples have never drawn up a will, because partners cannot find a way to talk directly to each other about death. Some parents prevent the treatment of their child's disability by referring to the child as "different" and ignoring the reality of the disability. Thus, the "how" may involve allusions to the topic or euphemisms for certain subjects.

Most families have rules that lead to strategies for communication—for breaking bad news, asking for money, or expressing anger. Such strategies may involve a change in both verbal and nonverbal communication behavior. A competent woman may suddenly revert to childish mannerisms to express disapproval acceptably; her husband may respond with corresponding parental behavior.

Strategy involves the timing of conversations, such as "Don't bother your father with that while he's eating," or the timing of discussion on a particular issue, such as "We won't tell Bobby that he's adopted until he's seven years old." It also involves selecting a place. Many married couples agree not to fight in the bedroom, avoiding associations of anger and conflict with that room. Some families have a place, such as a kitchen table where the "real" talking gets done. For some people, the car serves as the place for important conversations. In a family's communication system, the verbal and nonverbal strategies, including the issues of time and place, indicate how members may talk about things.

The final question is, with whom can you talk about it? Consider the following: "Don't tell Grandma; she'll have a stroke." "Don't you think Jenny is too young to hear about custody battles?" Often, the rules for "who" relate to the age of family members. For example, while children are small, they may not hear much about family finances, but as they grow older, they are brought into the discussion of how money is earned and spent.

Sometimes unforeseen circumstances, such as death or divorce, move a child into a conversation circle that would have been denied otherwise. A fourteen-year-old in a single-parent family may discuss topics that only the other parent typically would have heard. A widow may discuss previously undisclosed financial matters with close relatives. Such shifts can make a younger person uncomfortable as demonstrated in the following:

---

*Lately my father has taken to discussing his dating, and even his sex life with me. He seems to think this is a way for us to get closer, but I wish he could find a friend instead. My mother only died a year ago and it's hard for me to imagine Dad with other women.*

---

Family myths or stories dictate the directions of many conversations. The message of "Don't tell so and so—she can't take it" sets up myths which may prevail for years. Statements such as "Don't tell your grandfather. He'll have a fit" or "Don't talk to your sister. She'll just get sad." No one ever attempts to see if Grandpa will be outraged or Alice will cry—it is assumed, and communication proceeds accordingly.

In order to fully appreciate the "what," "how," and "who" of a family's communication rules, it is necessary to analyze the system to see which rules are enforced in what contexts. The following set of communication rules developed within one young woman's family indicate the interpersonal nature of rules:

- Don't talk back to Dad unless he's in a good mood.
- When Mom is tired, don't discuss school problems.
- Tell the truth at all times, unless it involves a happy surprise.
- Do not fight with Mom about your appearance.
- Don't talk about the family's finances outside the family.
- Do not discuss politics or religion.
- Don't discuss sex.
- Don't talk to Dad about Grandma growing old.
- Don't mention Mom and Dad are over 50.
- Share feelings with Mom.

- Don't talk about Granddad's two previous marriages.
- Never mention Aunt Bea's cancer.
- Tim's hearing problem is not to be discussed.
- Family deaths are discussed only in terms of religion.
- Mother's pregnancy at marriage is not admitted.

The author of these rules concluded that she had learned to distinguish among people and circumstances but had not experienced very direct open communication in her family.

The process of forming new systems through marriage or remarriage provides fertile ground for renegotiating existing rules. For example, the rules become even more complicated in blended families, where members come together having learned sets of communication rules in other systems. When widowed or divorced persons remarry, they may involve each of their immediate families in an extensive recalibration process as the new family system is formed.

***Metarules*** In addition to ordinary rules, there are metarules, or rules about rules. As Laing (1972) aptly states, "There are rules against seeing the rules, and hence against seeing all the issues that arise from complying with or breaking them" (106). When a couple does not make a will because of the difficulty of dealing with death, there may also be a rule that they not talk about their rules about ignoring death. Both pretend they are too busy or too poor to meet with a lawyer. The following thoughtful analysis of the rules in the previous young woman's family indicates this meta level of rule-bound behavior.

---

*Sex may be a topic that is never mentioned and, so, becomes one of those topics you should forget. In order to forget it, you must make the rule saying you can't mention the rule that forbids the discussion of sex. In this way, you can pretend it isn't forbidden and that deep levels of communication actually exist. We may laugh at a guest's dirty joke or my mother will set a very strict curfew for my younger sister, but no one ever directly discusses sex. Yet, we pretend we can.*

---

All family members live with powerful rule-bound patterns, giving little conscious attention to most of them. Yet, they give meaning to each relationship. According to Perlmutter (1988), as each child is born into the family, the family map changes and its rules and metarules evolve. Therefore the birth of each child increases the communication complexity.

## Family Stories

How often have you heard comments such as "Uncle Wayne, tell us how Mom drove the car into the lake" or "Ask my grandmother to tell you about the one-room school she went to when she grew up in Alabama." Stories give meaning to everyday life. "People grow up and walk around with their stories under their skin" (Stone 1988, 6).

Every family develops stories that reflect its collective experience. Some stories are too painful to remember; others are the centerpiece of any family gathering. According to Stone (1988),

> A family culture makes its norms known through daily life, but it also does so through family stories which underscore ... the essentials, like the unspoken and unadmitted family policy on marriage or illness. Or suicide, or who the family saints and sinners are, or how much anger can be expressed and by whom. (7)

Stories have a strong personal power. According to Yerby (1993), "From the narrative perspective one's sense of self is the story that a person has created about herself from the totality of her experiences" (6). A person's story brings together parts of a self into a purposeful whole (McAdams 1993). Personal stories may "fit" with family stories or may serve to separate a member from his or her family.

Stories, once voiced, take on a life of their own and collect meanings beyond the first telling. One story may be embellished to turn one member into a hero; another story may be cut short to save a member embarrassment. Each teller places a slightly different "spin" on the tale. Some stories are only told by a particular family member, whereas others tend to be told with overlapping voices. Each retelling makes this story more significant within the family's life.

Family members' stories are connected to each other's stories. You may be recruited into your brother's story of a childhood prank; your partner may delight in retelling your Thanksgiving dinner disaster. Certain family members may find their images carved in stone by the key hero or problem child roles they are given in reported stories.

Frequently a story gains one meaning which seals off alternative explanations. Sometimes families revise an interpretation to create a slightly different view of the world. For example, a mother may reframe her son's actions as "cautious" rather than "scared," or a single aunt may be reframed as "courageous" rather than "foolish" for entering the Peace Corps at age 53.

***Types of Stories*** A family develops stories that represent its collective experience. These are frequently tied to primary and secondary family functions. Family stories often respond to questions such as the following:

1. How did this family come to be?
   Most families tell some version of "creation" stories. These may be first meetings of adult partners, birth stories, the first stepsiblings meetings, or adoption stories. Such stories tell about how family members came to be in the family and therefore, how the family came to be. Often they are accompanied by strong feelings statements, such as follows:

---

*We arrived at the airport two hours before the plane from Seoul by way of San Francisco was due to arrive, because we were too excited to stay at home. We brought Grandma and Poppa and Uncle Allen and Aunt Mary. Your father kept walking up and down the concourse and we could not get him to sit down. He had your picture which he showed to the airline attendant and he started to tell all the people near the gate we were going to become parents when the plane arrived. Three other couples arrived and were waiting for their babies also. We were all beside ourselves trying to pass the time. Finally the plane arrived, fifteen minutes late, and one by one all these business passengers came out. Finally it looked like there were no more people on board when a young woman carrying a baby came struggling down the ramp. She was followed by other young people with babies. She called out "Mr. and Mrs. Ackerman" and one of the other couples ran to her. The next one called for the Fisher family. When I saw the third baby I knew it was you and started to grab you as the girl carrying you said "Dobbs." You gave me the most beautiful smile and your dad and I started to cry and laugh. We had waited two and a half years for that moment.*

---

2. Are parents really human?
   Children love to hear stories in which parents struggle with issues of growing up or making decisions—stories which take a parent figure off a pedestal. There are usually humorous ones, such as when Dad fell off a motorcycle or when Mom "lost" her baby brother. Sometimes they are serious such as the stories of a stepfather strug-

gling with drug addiction as a young man. These stories may be told for the first time as a parent self-discloses his or her mistakes at the point a child is old enough to learn from such a story. The telling represents an attempt to try to prevent a child from making a similar mistake.

3. How does a child become an adult in this family?
These are the narratives in which a child grows into adulthood by accomplishing some feat—beating a parent at a sport, earning more than a parent, solving a problem in a very mature manner. Often these are poignant because they signal a passage of time and, in some cases, a role reversal between parent and child. A middle aged adult may tell of having to watch over a parent whose recent fall left them unable to live alone.

4. Will the family stand behind its members?
There is much to be learned from stories of family support, or lack of support, at stressful times. In some families you learn that when you leave the accepted path, you will be disowned or cut off. In other families you learn that time heals many wounds and you can always return to the family. These stories link to family themes and to levels of adaptability. There are important stories behind comments such as "No one ever mentions Aunt Ginny at family gatherings because she married outside our religion and Granddad disowned her" or "My brother Terrence was in jail for dealing drugs. At first my mother wouldn't see him but over time she came around." Such stories often center on an event and begin with "When." For example, "When my uncle left the priesthood," or "When Deon got fired."

5. How does the family handle adversity?
When unpredictable crises arise, such as illness or job loss, does this family pull together and find a way through, or does the family split and force members out on their own? How does the family cope—through cunning or through hard work, or through aggression? Countless immigrant stories recount heroics of family members who battled against great odds to build a life in this country. Stories of family members facing illness, accidents, prejudice, or economic hardships may depict aggressive or passive responses. In the stories family members may fight against the stress or may be overcome by the pressure.

6. What does it mean to be a (family name)?
This is a question of collective identity. There may be a key story which serves to capture the essence or being a Pearcy or a Stone.

Family stories carry powerful messages which influence family members' lives as they organize their lives by making decisions in accordance with the dominant narratives (Sluzki 1992). These dominant narratives tell these members who they are in the world and how they should act.

## Family Communication Networks

Family members establish patterned channels for transmitting information which are called family networks. By definition, a network determines the two-way flow of messages from one family member to one or more other members or significant others outside the family. Family members regulate the direction of message flow up, down, or across the lines of the network. Horizontal communication occurs when the persons involved represent perceived equal status or power as when siblings pass messages, or when parents and children sit down and work out problems together. In such cases, all persons have an equal say, and status or role differences are minimized. The communication is vertical when real or imagined power differences are reflected in the interaction. For example, although the Turner children may share in many family decisions, they know that certain things are not negotiable. Mrs. Turner sets curfew and limits on the car, which means she hands down information on these topics in a vertical manner. An older sibling may serve as the babysitter and, therefore, disciplinarian.

Over time, families develop communication networks to deal with the general issue of cohesion and specific issues, such as carrying out instructions, organizing activities, regulating time and space, and sharing resources. Family adaptability may be seen through the degree of flexibility in forming and reforming networks. Families with high adaptability and flexible rules may use a wide variety of network arrangements. Families with low adaptability and rigid rules may consistently use the same networks for all concerns.

Although two-generation networks are complicated, most current family systems are part of multigenerational networks of greater complexity. By the year 2000, the parents of the baby boomers will be members of four- and five-generation families. Such networks are staggering in their complexity yet only key persons will relate regularly across generations.

Networks are a vital part of the decision-making process and relate to the power dynamics operating within the family. Certain networks facilitate dominance, while others promote more shared communication. Networks also play an integral part in maintaining the roles and rules operating within the family system. Thus, networks and rules operate with mutual influence—rules may dictate the use of certain networks; networks create certain rule patterns.

***Types of Networks*** To develop awareness of networks, observe the usual flow of verbal and universal exchanges between members of a family. Who talks to whom about what? Who exerts nonverbal control? This processing of communication may be horizontal or vertical and take one of several types: chain, Y, wheel, or all-channel. The choice of network types indicates much about family relationships.

---

*There are four girls in our family, and we have a very set pattern for requesting things from our mother or father. Gina tells Angela, who tells Celeste; Celeste tells me, and I talk to Mom. Usually, things stop there, because she makes most of the decisions. If it is something really important, she will discuss it with Dad and tell me their decision. Then I relay the message down the line.*

---

The example describes an operating chain network. It has a hierarchy built into it whereby messages proceed up through the links or down from an authority source. Quite often, a father or mother controls the chain network and passes out orders to children. For example, in male-dominated families, the father may control the flow of messages on vital family issues. As in all of these networks, there are times when the chain has definite advantages. All busy families tend to rely on a chain network when certain members do not experience much direct conflict.

Sometimes, chains keep certain family members separated. If Wei-Lin always avoids dealing with her stepfather, communicating all her desires or concerns through her mother, she and he will remain distant. A child may honor the communication rule forbidding direct discussion of a topic with Dad by relaying such messages through Mom. In a chain network, a two-way exchange of information may occur between all persons except those on the end. They have only one member with whom to communicate (Figure 4.2).

In the Y network, one key person channels messages from one or more persons on a chain to one or more other family members. In

**FIGURE 4.2**
**Chain Network**

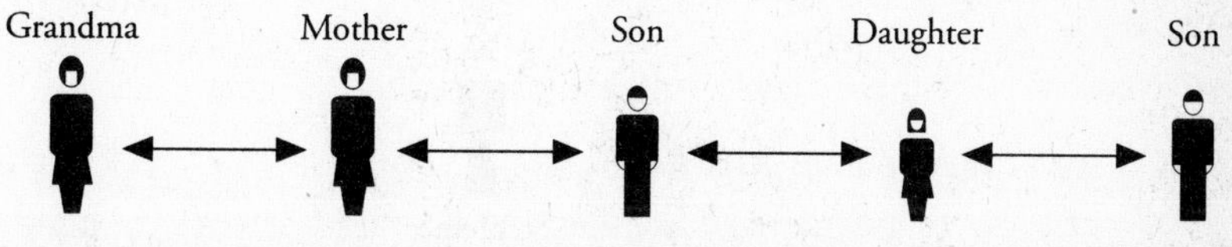

Grandma ↔ Mother ↔ Son ↔ Daughter ↔ Son

blended families with a new stepparent, the biological parent may consciously or unconsciously set up a Y network, separating the stepparent from the children (Figure 4.3). For example, a stepfamily may have a rule that only the biological parent can discipline the children. The wheel network depends upon one family member to channel all messages to other members, a position that carries with it power or control. This central figure can filter and adapt messages positively or negatively or enforce the rules about how to communicate within the family. He or she can balance tensions in the family system effectively or ineffectively. Since only one person communicates with all the others, this person becomes critical to the ongoing family functioning and may experience dominance or exhaustion as a result. When the communication load is heavy and concentrated, as it can be when all family members want to get off to work or school, the talents and patience of the family member in the wheel network can be severely taxed (Figure 4.4). In some families, the central member of the wheel network can be quite nurturing and effective in holding a family together.

---

*My mother was the hub of the wheel in our family. When we were children, we expected her to settle our problems with other family members. She always knew what everyone was doing and how they felt. When we left home, each of us always let Mom know what we were doing. Mom digested the family news and relayed the information about what each of us was doing. For several years after her death, we children had little contact. Now, seven years later, we have formed a new subsystem in which four of us stay in contact with each other. One sister, Mary Alice, is the new hub.*

---

**FIGURE 4.3**
**Y Network**

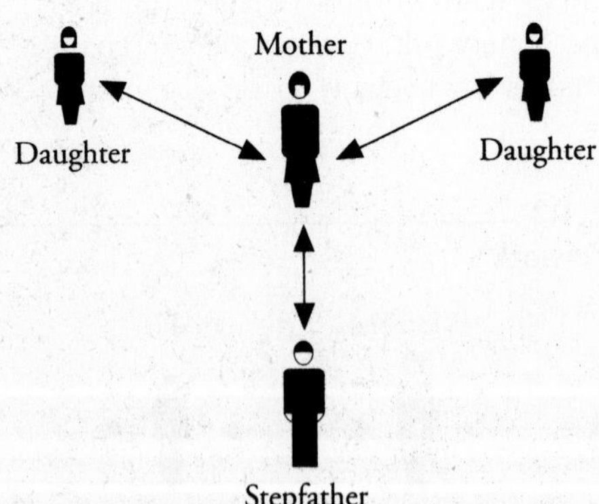

**FIGURE 4.4**
**Wheel Network**

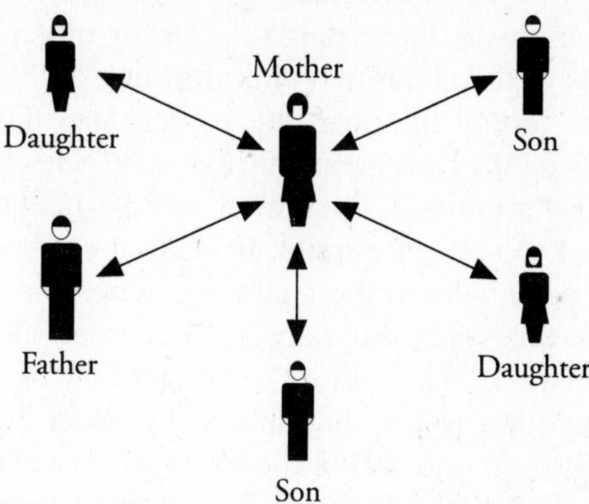


Messages in chain, Y, and wheel networks are filtered, so they may become distorted as they pass from one person to another. A family member can selectively change parts of a message. This may help to defuse some family conflicts, but misinformation could escalate others.

The all-channel network provides two-way exchange between or among all family members. Communication flows in all directions, and effective decisions can be made because all members have an equal chance to discuss family issues and respond to them. This network provides for maximum feedback. All interaction can be direct. No family member serves as a "go-between," and each participates freely in the process of sharing information or deciding issues (Figure 4.5). Yet, if the rules say that certain subjects should not be raised,

**FIGURE 4.5**
**All-Channel Network**

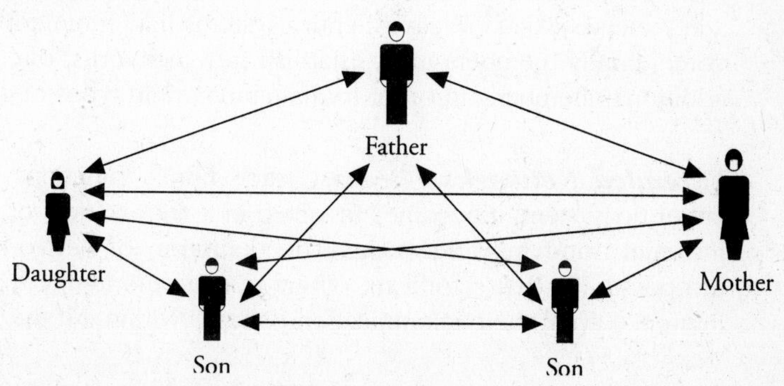

access will have little effect. Although this network allows equal participation, it can be the most disorganized and chaotic, since messages flow in all directions.

Variations of these networks occur under certain circumstances. The ends of the chain may link, forming a circle; chains may lead toward the central figure in the wheel. Most families use a variety of networks as they progress through daily life. Special issues arise that may cause a family to change the usual network patterns and adopt new ones to solve the issue. In daily life, for example, a family may operate essentially in the chain and wheel networks, but when vacations are planned, the network becomes all-channel. Multigenerational networks may add more variations when they are operational.

Subgroups and coalitions directly affect the family networks. The two people on one end of the chain may become very close and support each other in all situations. The key person in the Y formation may conspire with another member to keep certain information from the others, or control certain information. Some family members may never relate directly, as the parts of the network form small groups that support or relate only to each other. Often the family rules about "who one may talk to" determine the access. If you learn never to raise sensitive topics with your mother, the family may develop a strong Y network in which only her partner talks to her about such topics, and only when absolutely necessary.

Most functional families have the capacity to use more than one network pattern, shifting to meet the needs of a particular situation. Even families with very predictable network patterns make alterations over time. As children grow up and increasingly take over the direction of their own lives, adaptive families often move from the chain or wheel network to the all-channel. The wheel and chain networks facilitate order and discipline but may no longer be needed when children become autonomous and capable of directing their own decision making. Parents may signal their recognition of these changes by permitting more issues to be discussed via an all-channel network. As parents enter later life stages they may lose their central places in a network. The loss of a member can send the system into chaos. When a key member dies or leaves, entire systems may fragment. After a divorce, family members must establish new networks, often involving additional members, in order to maintain certain types of contact.

***Extended Networks*** Because each family functions within the larger ecosystem, it becomes involved in a wide variety of formal and informal non-family networks. The definition of networks includes the possibility that significant others outside the family may have an influence upon the communication patterns within it if the boundaries are permeable. A significant other is a person who has an intimate relationship with one or more of the family members. This may be a godparent, close family friend, lover, or a child's fiance. In long term defined relationships such a person's place in a network may become predictable and clear. For example, a parent's long term partner must be included in decisions about vacations and holidays, whereas a godmother must be consulted about the college or wedding plans of her godchild. In some cases the family member with ties to a significant other outside the family may very well make decisions within the network that were determined by this relationship.

Extended networks provide social support and serve to alleviate stress and encourage well-being during life transitions and crises (Gottlieb 1994). Families experiencing divorce or remarriage report a high need for friendship and community support (Simons et al. 1993). Yet only a few friendships manage to sustain these transitions (Wallerstein and Blakeslee 1989). In addition to friendship networks, family members become involved in formal networks created by educational, religious, and health institutions. Members must exchange information with representatives of these institutions in order to survive in our independent society.

Thus, networks serve a very important function within families. They determine who talks to whom, who is included or excluded, who gets full or partial information, and who controls certain information. Yet, the rules for what, how, and to whom to communicate exist within each style of network.

## CONCLUSION

This chapter explored how a family develops its own identity by creating a relational culture. You examined the importance of coordinated meanings between family members and how those meanings are developed through repeated interpretation and evaluation.

You also examined the patterns that family systems need to provide order and predictability for their members, focusing specifically on (1) family-of-origin influences, including multigenerational transmissions and ethnic/cultural heritages, (2) communication rules, (3) family stories and (4) communication networks. Each contributes to unique family meanings and each factor influences the others. As you will see throughout the book, patterns serve as the skeletal structure for family life, both reflecting and determining relationships.

## IN REVIEW

1. To what extent does the family-of-origin influence the communication patterns of future generations?
2. What communication patterns have been passed down from your family-of-origin which you believe reflect a multigenerational transmission?
3. Describe three incidents in a real or fictional family's development that demonstrate specific communication rules by which the members live.
4. Identify and describe the impact of a family story which you believe represents that family's collective identity.
5. Using a real or fictional family, describe how the most frequently used communication networks have changed over time due to developmental changes or family crises.

# 5

# Intimacy and Closeness Within Families

What keeps partners attracted to each other for years? How do young people move from being "the kids" to being in a caring adult relationship with a parent? Why do siblings in one family drift apart, while members of another remain connected and close throughout a lifetime? Family connections, sometimes solid and sometimes fragile, depend on the members' use of communication to sustain meaningful relationships.

Every family must engage in the kinds of communication that keep the home running, children fed, clothes washed, and bills paid. Life revolves around day by day patterns and routines, and functional communication must support such task-oriented interactions. Such communication contributes to a sense of connection. Yet, all families have the opportunity to provide their members with different kinds of communication experiences—including those that nurture the relationships involved. Nurturing communication carries messages of recognition and caring indicating: "I'm aware of you. I care about you." (Wilkinson 1989). Such communication contributes to intimacy among family members.

This chapter will focus on how communication influences the development of closeness and intimacy within a family's relational culture. In order to understand intimacy within the family realm you need to explore: (1) the development of marital and family intimacy, (2) relational currencies, (3) the communication building blocks of intimacy, and (4) barriers to intimacy.

## DEVELOPMENT OF INTIMACY

Relational culture is the hallmark of intimacy (Wood 1982). Persons, such as partners or family members, collaboratively create a unique relational culture which represents their understandings of each other and the world. Relational culture is fundamentally a product of communication—it arises out of communication, is maintained and altered in communication, and is dissolved through communication. It is within these relational cultures that intimacy and closeness develop consistent with the understandings of the members, their ethnic backgrounds, and family-of-origin experiences.

Intimate relationships may be characterized by mutual devotion and committed love involving intellectual, emotional, and physical capacities (Spooner 1982). According to Lerner (1989), intimacy means that "we can be who we are in a relationship and allow the other person to do the same" (3).

Marital and family intimacy reflect many similarities. Feldman (1979) suggests that marital intimacy involves the following characteristics: (1) a close, familiar, and usually affectionate or loving personal

Marital and family intimacy reflect many similarities.

relationship; (2) a detailed and deep knowledge and understanding from close personal connection or familiar experience; and (3) sexual relations (70). With the exception of sexual relations, these characteristics may be applied to all family relationships, understanding that intimacy is "a much different order of business among siblings than between children and parents" (Perlmutter 1988, 34). Family intimacy involves mutual devotion and intellectual, emotional, and physical dimensions demonstrated by shared knowledge and understanding and close-loving relationships, both of which are reflective of developmental stages and culture. Such a concept of intimacy translates into reality through the communication patterns of family systems and subsystems.

Acceptable levels of family intimacy reflect the interaction of members as they deal with dialectical tensions. The intimacy of a particular relationship reflects a meshing of each member's past intimate experiences, need for intimacy, perception of the other and desire for increasing predictability within a relationship. Feldman suggests that when one member of a couple feels that the intimacy is becoming too great, he or she will initiate some type of conflictual behavior to decrease the amount of interpersonal closeness. The same concept may be applied to other family relationships. Each two-person subsystem sets its limits for acceptable intimacy. A small son and his mother may cuddle, tickle, kiss, and hug. A teenager and stepmother may discuss important events, hopes or dreams, and exchange kisses on occasion. A husband and wife develop limits for acceptable and unacceptable sexual intimacy as well as sharing feelings and showing affection. These acceptable limits of intimacy reflect the family's ways of showing affection, and the depth of the particular relationship. In order to understand how intimacy may be experienced, it is valuable to look at the characteristics of developed relationships.

## Characteristics of Developed Relationships

Highly developed, or close, committed relationships display certain characteristics reflecting the coordination of meaning between, and sometimes among, family members. Stephen (1986) suggests communication between members of ongoing relationships generates a shared view of the world that bonds relationship members, a bond that reflects symbolic interdependence (29).

There are numerous ways to examine highly developed relationships. Altman and Taylor (1973) suggest characteristics that appear in committed and close relationships include richness, efficiency, uniqueness, substitutability, pacing, openness, spontaneity, and evaluation. This does not mean that all interactions are characterized by these qualities, but the relationship in general exhibits these qualities. The following description of the way in which each of these characteristics relates to communication depicts how relationships function when meanings are shared effectively.

*Richness* refers to the ability to convey the same message accurately in a variety of ways. Siblings and spouses have many ways of sharing displeasure, delight, or other feelings. Affection may be shared in words, either in a teasing or serious manner, or through looks, hugs, or kisses. Spouses report that sexual experimentation keeps a marriage vital. A relationship without richness remains in a very predictable and limited pattern of "the same old thing."

*Efficiency* refers to accuracy, speed, and sensitivity in the transmission and reception of communication. In highly developed relationships, meanings are shared rapidly, accurately, and with great sensitivity. Family shorthand abounds; the raised eyebrow conveys more than words. The comment, "I don't want another Thanksgiving scene" may conjure up similar images in everyone's head of late arrivals, charred turkey, and angry words. Only members of the relational culture can decode the meanings with efficiency.

*Uniqueness* implies the development of an idiosyncratic message system. Verbal expressions take on special meanings; words are used in unusual ways. Certain nonverbal signals may have special meanings understood only by members of the system. If a family member claims a need for "puddle time," other members may willingly withdraw, whereas an outsider would not associate a pool of rainwater with time to relax alone. In their study of the world of intimate talk and communication uniqueness, Hopper, Knapp, and Lorel (1981) identified eight types of idioms: teasing insults, confrontations, expressions of affection, sexual invitation, sexual references and euphemisms, requests and routines, partner nicknames, and names for other persons (28).

*Substitutability* refers to the ability to convey the same message in alternative fashions when necessary. For example, one need not wait for the last guest to leave the party to convey anger through yelling, because nonverbal signs such as a glare, "meaningful" silence, or a specific hand gesture will alert one member to the other's anger. Persons in a close relationship understand the meaning of the substituted behavior just as easily as they would the usual expression.

Altman and Taylor suggest that these four characteristics of richness, efficiency, uniqueness, and substitutability probably overlap.

However, together they reflect the dynamics of a close relationship which involves multiple levels of functioning, including rich, complex communication patterns and a better understanding of the meaning of transactions (132). The following example demonstrates how even a child can remain outside a highly developed marital system.

---

*My mother and father have been married for thirty-two years, and it's amazing to watch them together. They stay in tune with each other, even though many other people may be around, by relating on two levels. Words or gestures that have ordinary meanings also have special meaning for them. Even I can feel like an "outsider," recognizing that I'll never really understand what's going on between them.*

---

*Pacing,* or synchronization, refers to the coordination and meshing of interpersonal actions as people work into mutual roles and behave in complementary ways. A common metaphor for this coordination is a free and fluid dance (Rogers 1984). Members display

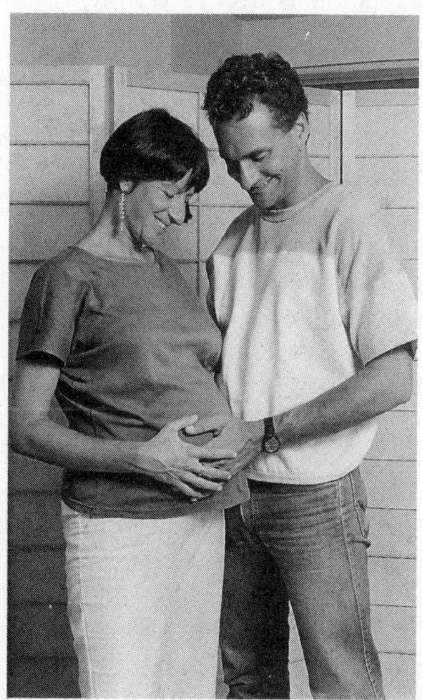

True intimacy develops over time through mutual sharing.

apparently effortless teamwork; they know when to joke, when to pull back, how to support one another, and when to stop.

*Openness* implies verbal and nonverbal accessibility. On one level, openness occurs when personal private information is expressed or received (Montgomery 1981). Yet, it is not just more intimate interactions that characterize openness, but also the individual's ability to move in and out of private areas of communication in a quick and easy way.

*Spontaneity* grows as relationships deepen. The informality and comfort of strong relationships allow members to break patterns. Unexpected lovemaking, unpredictable comments, and changed plans all have their places as a couple develops a life together. Family members may take chances with each other that they would avoid with others.

*Evaluation,* or the sharing of negative and positive judgments about one another, reflects the security that the relationship will not end if such judgments are discussed. Family members express their true feelings in hopes of finding resolution. Expressions such as praise, disappointment, or anger can contribute to strengthening relationships.

As a group, these eight characteristics provide the backdrop for communication patterns that emerge within particular family systems. Adaptability and cohesion are central to the development of such committed relationships. Adaptation is a core feature of efficiency, substitutability, pacing, and spontaneity, while cohesion underlies the development of uniqueness, richness, openness, and evaluation. The security of relationships characterized by these factors allows the widest range of interpersonal behaviors to occur and fosters the continued growth of the individuals and their relationship. These characteristics contribute to the uniqueness of a relational culture. You can recognize certain signs of unique communication characteristics as you visit an unfamiliar home as a guest and try to adapt to the message systems within that environment. The baby may walk around carrying her "doe," which serves as a blanket and psychological comforter; Grandpa may continually refer to four-year-old Neal as the "heir to the throne." You sense underlying emotions behind the parent's tone of voice that first calls "Matthew" and later "Matthew Noel Wilkinson." Although the father's manner may not appear to change, you learn to respect the whispers of the other family members to "leave him alone right now"—since they are reading nonverbal messages unavailable to the untrained eye. "In" jokes and past references abound. Family members may scream and shout. You may be hugged and touched, which could be pleasant or very disconcerting. In short, you sense many messages rather than understanding them. You recognize the connections but cannot participate directly in them.

# RELATIONSHIP DEVELOPMENT AND INTIMACY

## Developing a Relationship Culture

All developing intimate relationships reflect a history-building process. There are multiple perspectives on how this occurs, the most common of which involves stage models. Developmental models assume the persons involved are adults or older adolescents. The stage models assume all relationships exhibit points of initiation, maintenance, and possible dissolution (Wilmot 1987). Recently the issues raised by a dialectical perspective have called into question some of the assumptions of the stage model which will be addressed later.

***Stage Models*** Numerous scholars have proposed models of relationship development based on stages through which the partners move as they draw closer (Knapp and Vangelisti 1992; Altman & Taylor 1973; McWhirter and Mattison 1984). These are called linear models. Psychologists Altman and Taylor created a model called *social penetration*, which captures the stages of relational development. They hypothesize that interpersonal exchange gradually progresses from superficial, nonintimate areas to more intimate deeper layers of the self. People assess interpersonal costs and rewards gained from interaction. The future development of a relationship depends on their perception of these rewards and costs. They propose a four-stage model of relational movement relying on the eight characteristics of a developed relationship discussed in the previous section. The extent to which these dimensions exist in a relationship is reflected by the communication that occurs between the persons involved; each dimension becomes more apparent as the relationship moves through the stages toward the highest point. Movement through the stages also depends on the perceived costs or rewards of interactions as estimated by each person in the relationship.

The model is best understood by picturing a continuum (Figure 5.1) with guidelines for movement through the stages. The levels represent where the relationship is at a given time, even if one or the other persons involved wishes it were different. Although we talk about relationship within the system, each relationship reflects the connectedness or distance between two system members. For example, three sisters would not move through the stages as one relationship. These would be three separate dyadic relationships that might be very similar and overlap, but each relationship belongs to a dyad.

The *orientation stage* represents the first meetings when strangers tend to follow traditional social rules, try to make a good

**FIGURE 5.1**
**Stages of Relationship Development**

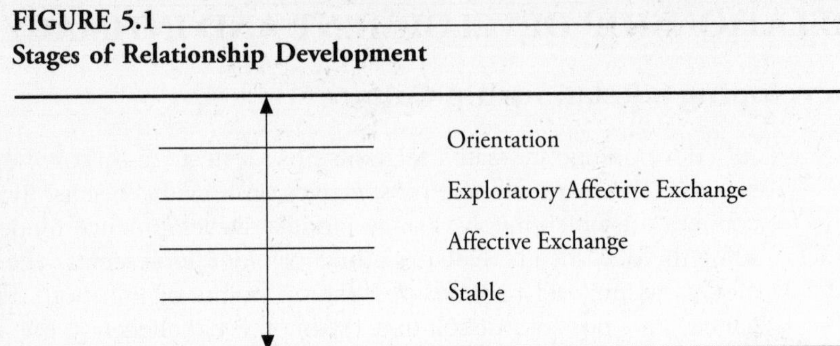


first impression, and attempt to avoid conflict. In short, they try to reduce uncertainty about the other person and increase their ability to imagine future reactions. Except for situations involving babies or small children, all family relationships start at this point, although some previous information may have been known about the "other." Future spouses may have been coworkers or classmates who met at the watercooler or in geology class. In-laws meet as strangers. Future stepfathers and stepchildren may have skirted around countless unpleasant topics as they tried to be polite "for Mom's sake."

The second stage, *exploratory affective exchange*, is characterized by the relationship between casual acquaintances or friendly neighbors. By this point, the relationship contains some honest sharing of opinions or feelings that are not too personal, but no real sense of commitment exists. Most relationships do not go beyond this second casual exploratory stage.

Countless family relationships remain indefinitely at this stage. Uncle Ned may be delightful, but you do not seek him out beyond the annual Christmas get-together. Siblings may have stronger bonds with friends than with one another. Some parent-child or husband-wife relationships function at a level of acquaintances with little sense of commitment or deep involvement.

The third stage, *affective exchange*, is characterized by close friendships or courtship relationships in which people know each other well, reflecting a fairly extensive history of association based on reciprocity. This association may be built over a long period of time or through intense short meetings. Communication includes sharing positive and negative messages, including evaluations. By this stage, members of the relationship exhibit many of the characteristics of a developed relationship.

Some family relationships may exist at this level for long periods of time, while others remain at lower areas of the continuum. As children mature and develop empathy, they can participate in the transactional process needed at this level. Often, such abilities reflect the communication modelled by older family members and the relational currencies they demonstrate. Such change is described as follows:

---

*My relationship with my daughter in college has developed into a friendship. Karen and I went through some rough times when she was in high school, but in the past two years we have developed a closeness I never thought possible. We can sit down and share some very personal thoughts. I am learning to let her be an adult and have stopped trying to impose my way of life on her. I think because of that she is willing to tell me more about her life. There are certain parts of my life I may never be able to tell my daughter about, but it is such a pleasure to have an adult female friend who is also my child.*

---

Affective exchange level relationships are likely to occur in families with themes that support close interactions and interpersonal boundaries that permit extensive sharing. Many marriages exist at the affective exchange level, and partners remain either satisfied or frustrated, depending on their spouses. Many people find this level of intimacy sufficient.

Finally, some relationships enter the fourth or *stable stage*, which is characterized most often by committed, intimate friendships or familial relationships. This stage is characterized by high symbolic interdependence and a strong "relationship world view."

Yet, even these unique relationships require extensive effort if they are to be maintained. Partners who share a stable relationship are very aware of each other's needs and changes. They are willing to work actively to maintain their relationship, as in the following example:

---

*After twenty-six years of marriage my parents seem to have an incredibly close relationship that I haven't seen in other people. They often hold hands. They share a great deal of common interest in music and will play together. They just can't get enough of each other. Life hasn't been all that easy for them, either. But they have coped with these things together. They almost sound alike and they finish each other's sentences.*

---

Relationships do not follow the four stages easily and simply. Some relationships may speed through certain stages, while others may remain at one stage for years. Other relationships may move through the levels as the partners' lives change. Relationships that proceed too quickly to core areas may have to retrace steps through beginning stages.

Altman and Taylor suggest that the stage can be reversed when considering the dissolution of a relationship. For example, a couple may reach the stable stage before the births of their children, but attending to the children may have taken so much time and energy that the couple's relationship move to the lower level of affective exchange.

Other models provide variations on the theme. For example, in an extension of Altman and Taylor's work, Knapp and Vangelisti (1992) propose a model of interaction stages in relationships that details five coming-together and coming-apart stages.

This model has a unique "bonding" stage which occurs when the partners undergo a public ritual announcing to the world a contract of commitments. In essence, bonding is a way of gaining social or institutional support for the relationship. Traditionally, this involves going steady, engagement, and/or marriage. Whereas ritual events, such as baptism, circumcision, or legal adoption, should be viewed as examples of family bonding, it is more difficult to imagine traditionally accepted bonding experiences for homosexual pairs, step-children and stepparents, or long-term foster families.

***Dialectical Approaches*** Relational culture is not static—it is constantly in process. There is a need for constant reflection and redefinition (Wood, 77). Theorists who question stage models believe they appear linear and static. That is, they seem to include predictable moves and imply relationships remain in the same place for a long time. A dialectical perspective highlights the continual tensions which relationships must manage. According to Werner and Baxter (1994), relationships are

> "maintained" by the ways partners manage competing needs, obligations, how they organize and coordinate their activities, the way they introduce novelty and pleasure into their relationship, and how they build a place in which to nurture the relationship. (324)

Montgomery (1992) argues that "sustaining" relationships is a better term since maintaining sounds like an attempt to create a steady state.

This approach does not mean that every moment or everyday a relationship experiences struggle or tension. Although at critical times, struggles may be in the forefront of a relationship's life, there are more times when the dialectical tension serves as the background to an ongoing relationship. In other words:

> Dialectics may work backstage in a relationship beyond partners' mindful awareness or ability to identify and describe them, but still contributing a sense of unsettledness or instability in the relationship. (Montgomery 1992, 206)

There are times when family members feel equal pressure to be open and *closed*. A parent and teenager may wish to be open and *close*, but also be distant to protect certain areas of privacy. Within stepfamilies there is a strong pull in competing directions. The main dialectical dilemma is to manage the voluntary marital relationship and the involuntary stepparent-stepchild relationship (Cissna, Cox, and Bochner 1990). Between steprelations there is a tension between getting close and staying distant in order to remain loyal to a biological parent or child. A dialectical approach recognizes relationships begin to develop and deteriorate, but it stresses the ongoing struggles that characterize the overall life of a relationship rather than a linear, step by step approach.

Although all humans seem to have intimacy needs—to be loved, held, touched, and nurtured—there may also be fear of intimacy: a fear of being controlled by another, loved and left by another, or possessed by another, all of which keep relationships from reaching high stages of involvement. Thus, the needs, fears, rewards, and costs become the stuff of the struggle.

Relationship development models assume voluntary involvement. There has been little careful study of nonvoluntary relationships, such as those experienced within some stepfamilies. Such relationships may begin with stages characteristic of deteriorating relationships, such as low self-disclosure, conflict, and resentment (Galvin and Cooper 1990).

Intimacy and closeness in each family system is influenced by its overall themes, images, and boundaries, which indicate some acceptable intimacy limits for family members. Family themes that stress verbal sharing, such as "There are no secrets in this family," may promote honest disclosure if a sense of community and support exists. Otherwise, such themes may promote keeping secrets. Family boundaries influence how much intimacy is shared among family subsystems and how much intimacy may be developed with those outside the immediate family. Gender related attitudes support or restrict the capacity of members in certain roles or power positions to develop certain levels of intimacy. Knowledge about another family member is not sufficient to develop intimacy. Relational growth depends on communication of and about that knowledge (Duck, Miell, and Miell 1984).

## RELATIONAL CURRENCIES: THE MEANING OF INTIMACY

*Since as early as I remember, affection has been displayed openly in my household. I remember as a young child sitting on my father's lap every Sunday to read the comic strips with him. I always hugged my father and mother, and still do. "I love you" is still the last thing said by my parents and by me when we talk on the telephone.*

Family members develop a set of behaviors, such as those just described, that have meaning within their relationships. Thus, one partner may cook beef stew to please the other, or a grandfather may rock a grandchild for an hour while telling him stories of years gone by. Both of these instances represents an attempt to share affection, but the meaning depends on a shared perception. The partner may devour the stew and interpret the message of affection, or he may wish for lasagna; the grandchild may "snuggle in" or long for escape.

Communication behaviors that carry meaning about the affection or caring dimension of human relationships can be viewed as *relational currency* (Villard and Whipple 1976). The currencies can be seen as a symbolic exchange process. As partners share currencies, they will form agreements about their meanings and either strengthen or limit their relationship world view (Stephen 1984).

### Types of Currencies

Certain currencies make a direct statement. The act is the message—a hug means "I'm glad to see you," or "I'm sorry you are leaving." Usually, the sender's intent is clear and easily interpreted. Other currencies permit a greater range of interpretation. After a family quarrel, does the arrival of flowers mean "I'm sorry," or "I still love you even if we don't agree on one issue"? There are many possible relational currencies. The list that follows shows some of the common ways family members share affection.

Each of these currencies represents one way of sharing affection. The use of each currency must be considered within the contexts of gender, ethnicity, class, and developmental stage.

**Table 5-1** Sample Relational Currencies

| | |
|---|---|
| Positive verbal statements | Gifts |
| Self-disclosure | Money |
| Listening | Food |
| Facial Expressions | Favors |
| Touch | Service |
| Sexuality | Time together |
| Aggression | Access rights |

***Positive verbal statements*** Such statements include oral and written messages indicating love, caring, praise, or support. In some households people express affection easily, saying "I love you" directly and frequently. Other families view such directness as unacceptable, preferring to save such words for unusual situations. Within families, age, gender, and roles affect this currency. For example, female relatives are more likely to receive statements of love in birthday cards (Mooney and Brabant 1988).

***Self-disclosure*** Self-revealing, or "voluntarily telling another things about yourself which the other is unlikely to discover from other sources," serves as a means of deepening understanding between people. As a currency, self-disclosure is intentionally used to show caring and commitment in a relationship. This currency is discussed later in the chapter.

***Listening*** Listening carries a message of involvement with, and attention to, another person. Empathic listening requires focused energy and practice. "It's a mental habit at which one has to work" (Ryan and Ryan 1982, 44). Listening may be taken for granted and the effort discounted unless the speaker is sensitive to the listener's careful attention.

***Facial expressions*** "Affect displays, are spontaneous displays of affection best characterized as "love in that 'eyes lighting up' sense." (Malone and Malone 1987, 14). These nonverbal displays of affect indicate joy from the other's presence.

***Touch*** This is the language of physical intimacy. Positive physical contact carries a range of messages about friendship, concern, love, or sexual interest. Touch varies greatly across genders and cultures, so it may be easily misinterpreted.

***Sexuality*** For adult partners, sexuality provides a unique opportunity for intimacy. The discourse around intercourse, as well as the act itself, combine to create a powerful currency. Sexuality is discussed in detail later in the chapter.

***Aggression*** Aggressive actions, usually thought to be incompatible with affection, may serve as the primary emotional connection between members of certain families. Persons frightened of expressing intimacy directly may use verbal or physical aggression as a sign of caring. Children find teasing or poking as a way to connect to a sibling. When adults do not know how to express intimacy in positive ways, they may use hitting, sarcasm, or belittling as the only means of contact. Some conflictual couples may maintain their contact through screaming and hitting, relational currencies within their family system.

***Gifts*** Presents are symbols of affection which may be complicated by issues of cost, appropriateness, and reciprocity. "Gifts become containers for the being of the donor." (Csikszentmihalyi and Rochberg-Halton 1981, 37). The process of identifying, selecting, and presenting the gift serves as part of the currency.

***Money*** The exchange of dollars represents an exchange of relational currencies. Money must be given or loaned as a sign of affection and not as a parental or spousal obligation for it to serve as a currency.

***Food*** A symbol of nurturing in many cultures, food has emerged as an important currency in romantic and immediate family relationships. Preparing and serving food for a loved one, serve as major signs of affection in many relationships.

***Favors*** Performing helpful acts for another may be complicated by norms of reciprocity and equality. Favors, to be considered currencies, must be performed willingly rather than in response to a spousal or parental order. The underlying message may be missed if the effort of the favor is not recognized as such.

***Service*** Service implies a caring behavior which evolved into a habitual behavior. Driving the carpool to athletic events, making the coffee in the morning, or maintaining the checkbook may have begun as favors and moved into routines. Such services are frequently taken for granted, thus negating the underlying message of affection.

***Time*** Being together, whether it's just "hanging out," or voluntarily accompanying a person on a trip or errand, carries the message "I want to be with you." This is a subtle currency with potential for being overlooked.

***Access rights*** Allowing another person to use or borrow things you value is a currency when the permission is intended as a sign of affection. This currency is not at work when you let "just anyone" use your things. It is the exclusive nature of the permission which is given only to persons you care about, that makes this a currency.

This list of currencies does not represent the "last word" on the subject. You may identify unnamed currencies which you exchange or which you have observed in family systems.

## Meanings and Currencies

The meanings attached to relational currencies have a direct impact on relationship development. Stephen (1984) proposed a framework in which interaction may be viewed as an exchange process of trading and meanings. He suggested that when meanings are shared, rewards are experienced; when meanings are missed, costs are experienced. Therefore, over time, intimate partners will create common assumptions about the importance of currencies and develop high levels of symbolic interdependence.

Although relational currencies may be exchanged with the best intentions, accurate interpretation occurs only when both parties agree upon the meaning of the act. Usually the meaning you give to another's currencies would be used in a similar situation. For example:

> Each of us tends to identify as *loving* those expressions of love that are similar to our own. I may express my love ... by touching you, being wonderfully careless with you, or simply contentedly sitting near you without speaking. You may express an equally deep love feeling by buying me a gift, cooking the veal, working longer hours to bring us more monetary freedom, or simply fixing the broken faucet. These are obviously different ways of loving. (Malone and Malone 1987, 74)

In the previous example the question remains, does the contented silent partner know that a good dinner or a fixed faucet is a way of showing love and vice versa? When you think about your relationships, you may see others as more loving if they express their love the way you do. Such similarity adds to a growing sense of symbolic interdependence and the strengthening of a relational culture. Misunderstanding may develop when two family systems attempt to blend into a new one and create a set of mutually understood currencies.

Without common meanings for relational currencies, family members may feel hurt or rejected. For example, one spouse may consider sex to be the ultimate currency in married life and place a high value on sexual relations. This partner may assume sexual relations will be exclusive and sex will be engaged in only when both people are satisfied in the relationship and desirous of sex. If the other partner holds similar views, the sexual currency will be appropriately exchanged. If not, these two people will have difficulty with the communication of affection. Such differences are very common. They also occur between parent and child as this comment indicates.

---

*After I became a parent of a teenager I realized how many ways my mother had shown love through waiting up for me at night, driving me around, sliding a five dollar bill into my wallet. I hope she understood that I was a bit too self-centered to be grateful in those years.*

---

What happens if family members wish to share affection but seem unable to exchange the currencies desired by others? Villard and Whipple concluded that spouses with more similar affection exchange behaviors were more likely to report (1) high levels of perceived equity and (2) higher levels of relationship satisfaction, thus greater relationship reward. Interestingly, accuracy in predicting (i.e., understanding) how the other spouse used currencies did not raise satisfaction levels. Just knowing that your husband sends love messages through flowers does not mean that you will be more positive toward this currency if you prefer intimate talks. Persons who were very accurate at predicting how their spouses would respond to certain currencies still reported low marital satisfaction levels if the couple was dissimilar in their affection behaviors. Unfortunately, this finding, coupled with the finding that wives are more likely to use intimate currencies, suggests that many marriages may face "unhappiness, unfulfillment, conflict, and/or divorce because of socialized differences between men and women in how they share 'who they are' and how they manifest 'affection'" (Millar et al. 1985, 15). These differences can be opportunities for growth if partners can talk about them and grow through them as this respondent did:

---

*When my wife went through a very bad time in her work, we bumped into our differences. My caring solution was to give advice, try to help more around the house, and leave some little gifts for her. These were not what was desired at the time.*

*Cybele wanted someone to listen to her—empathic listening—not a bunch of suggestions. She wanted to be held. She needed verbal reassurance. Fortunately, Cybele let her needs and wants be known, and in the midst of that self-disclosure, a crisis was turned into an opportunity for growth. Since that time I have worked to provide listening, compliments, and hugs, and the bond between us has grown stronger.*

---

A family's levels of cohesion and adaptability interact with its communication of affection. Highly cohesive families may demand large amounts of affection displayed with regularity, whereas low-cohesion families may not provide enough affection for certain members. Families near the chaotic end of the adaptability continuum may change the type of currencies valued whereas more rigid systems may require the consistent and exclusive use of a particular currency. Family themes may dictate the amount or type of currencies used. "The Hatfields will stick by each other through thick and thin" may require members to provide money for hard-pressed relatives. Boundaries may establish which members or outsiders may receive more personal types of affection.

Because the family system evolves constantly through dialectical struggles, personal meaning of currencies changes. Members may change their ways of sharing affection because of new experiences, pressures, or expectations. A lost job may result in fewer gifts but more sharing and favors within a family.

The process of exchanging relational currencies significantly affects the intimacy attained by the family members. The more similarity in the exchange process, the higher the levels of symbolic interdependence and relational satisfaction.

## COMMUNICATION AS A FOUNDATION OF INTIMACY

The basis for all relationships lies in the members' abilities to share meanings through communication. Countless studies of enduring and/or healthy marriages or families emphasize the importance of communication underpinnings of successful family relationships (Curran 1983; Stinnett and DeFrain 1985; Pearson 1992). The terminology varies but similar factors emerge. Robinson and Blanton (1993) identified key characteristics of enduring marriages as intimacy balanced with autonomy, commitment, communication, congruence, and, in some cases, religious orientation. Pearson's study of lasting happy marriages discussed the important facts such as positive distortion, commitment, understanding, and unconditional acceptance.

In this section we will examine four major factors which serve to undergird the development of intimacy within family systems and reflect the use of many of the relational currencies described earlier. These are confirmation, self-disclosure, sexual communication, and commitment. Although the importance of these factors will be stressed, their function varies with the unique marital or family system and its ethnic heritage. Also, although conflict is not dealt with until a later chapter, the management of conflict is normal and necessary in all relationships. Since closeness is co-constructed in the ongoing management of both interdependence and independence, differences and struggles are inevitable.

## Confirmation

Confirming messages communicate acceptance of another human being—a fundamental precondition to intimacy. Sieburg (1973) provides four criteria for confirming messages. A confirming message: (1) recognizes the other person's existence, (2) acknowledges the other's communication by responding relevantly to it, (3) reflects and accepts the other's self-experience, and (4) suggests a willingness to become involved with the other.

Confirming responses may be contrasted with two alternative responses, rejecting and disconfirming. Whereas confirming responses imply an acceptance of the other person, rejecting responses imply the other is wrong or unacceptable. Rejecting messages might include such statements as "That's really dumb," "You're a real pain," and "Don't act like a two-year-old." Disconfirming responses send the message "You don't exist." Disconfirming responses occur when a person is ignored, talked about as if he or she is invisible, excluded from a conversation, or excluded from physical contact.

---

*When my sister remarried, she and her new husband tried to pretend they did not have her twelve-year-old son, Wayne, living with them, because her new husband did not really want him. They would eat meals and forget to call him, plan trips and drop him with us at the last minute, and never check on his work in school. The kid was a nobody in that house. Finally, his father took him, and Wayne seems much happier now.*

---

Confirming communication is characterized by recognition, dialogue, and acceptance, which indicate a willingness to be involved (Sieburg 1973; Barbour and Goldberg 1974). Each is described in the following sections.

***Recognition*** Verbally, one may confirm another's personal existence by using his or her name, including him or her in conversation, or just acknowledging his or her presence. Comments such as "I missed you, I'm glad to see you" serve to confirm another person's existence.

Nonverbal confirmation has more subtle but equal importance in the recognition process. From earliest infancy, tactile recognition serves as the basis for relationships. Children develop their earliest sense of recognition through touch. Direct eye contact and gestures also may serve to confirm another person within norms of ethnic culture. Confirming relationships develop from a base of mutual recognition.

***Dialogue*** When family members say things in front of each other "without actually responding in an honest and spontaneous way to each other's ideas and feelings, their interaction might be described as a series of monologues rather than a dialogue" (Barbour and Goldberg, 31). Dialogue implies an interactive involvement between two people. Husbands and wives, siblings, and parents and children must be able to share attitudes, beliefs, opinions, and feelings and work at resolving their differences. Comments such as "Because I said so" and "You'll do it my way or not at all" do not reflect a dialogical attitude, whereas "What do you think?" or "I'm upset—can we talk about it?" open the door to dialogue and rewarding interactions. Nonverbal dialogue occurs in families where hugs, kisses, and affectionate displays are mutually shared and enjoyed and where hugs of consolation or sorrow are exchanged.

***Acceptance*** Acceptance gives a powerful sense of being all right. "When we feel acceptance, even though disagreed with, we do not feel tolerated; we feel loved." (Malone and Malone 73). Acceptance avoids interpreting or judging one another. Rather, it lets one another be, even if being the other is different from yourself. From a communication perspective, acceptance occurs when "we respond to the statements of another person by genuinely trying to understand the thought and feeling he or she has expressed, and by reflecting that understanding in our responses" (Barbour and Goldberg, 31). This may involve allowing yourself to hear things you really do not want to hear and acknowledging that you understand.

Confirming behavior often reflects the specific roles and cultural backgrounds of one's family-of-origin. Persons who grew up in a non-expressive family may have trouble satisfying the reassurance and recognition needs of a spouse. Cultural differences in the use of eye contact or touch may create disconfirming feelings for one partner. Family intimacy develops from each member's sense of acceptance and care. If one "learns to love by being loved," then one learns to confirm by being confirmed.

## Self-Disclosure

Self-disclosure occurs when one person voluntarily tells another personal or private things about himself or herself that the other is unable to discern in a different manner (Pearce and Sharp 1973). It involves a willingness to accept such information or feelings from another. According to Malone and Malone:

> The most powerful and profound awareness of ourselves occurs with our simultaneous opening up to another human ... It is the most meaningful and courageous of human experiences.

In addition to feeling confirmed, persons in intimate relationships need to experience openness in their communication. Such openness is experienced through sharing and receiving self-disclosure.

Trust, the essence of which is emotional safety, serves as the foundation for self-disclosure. "Trust enables you to put your deepest feelings and fears in the palm of your partner's hand, knowing they will be handled with care" (Avery 1989, 27). In her examination of family self-disclosure, Gilbert (1976) links self-disclosure and intimacy. High mutual self-disclosure is usually associated with voluntary relationships which have developed a strong relational culture and are characterized by trust, confirmation, and affection. Yet, high levels of negative self-disclosure may occur in such relationships at points characterized by conflict and anger.

Traditionally, self-disclosure has been considered a skill for fostering intimate communication within families. Jourard (1971) describes the optimal marriage relationship as one "where each partner discloses himself without reserve" (46). Many current marriage and family enrichment programs support self-disclosing behavior, as do popular texts on the subject of marital or parent-child interaction. Premarital counseling often focuses on revealing areas of feelings or information not yet shared by the couple. Yet, some cautions about unrestrained self-disclosure need to be considered, since it can be destructive.

In order to understand the importance of self-disclosure within the family system, you need to review some relevant issues and examine the practice of self-disclosure in developing family intimacy.

***Variables in Self-Disclosure*** Much of the research in self-disclosure has been conducted through questionnaires and self-reports collected from family members, usually adult partners. The actual self-disclosing behavior is not easily observed or measured. What family material exists focuses on marital couples or parent-child interactions; entire family systems have not received attention. Yet, even this limited research raises issues and implications for family relationships.

Some generalizations can be made about self-disclosure in family relationships, but much of the original research in the area is under review due to more sophisticated follow-up studies. Littlejohn (1992) has summarized the findings of research in general self-disclosure as follows:

> 1. Disclosure increases with increased relational intimacy.
> 2. Disclosure increases when rewarded.
> 3. Disclosure increases with the need to reduce uncertainty in a relationship.
> 4. Disclosure tends to be reciprocal (dyadic effect).
> 5. Women tend to be higher disclosers than men.
> 6. Women disclose more with individuals they like, men disclose more with people they trust.
> 7. Disclosure is regulated by norms of appropriateness.
> 8. Attraction is related to positive disclosure but not to negative ones.
> 9. Positive disclosure is more likely in nonintimate or moderately intimate relationships.
> 10. Negative disclosure occurs with greater frequency in highly intimate settings than in less intimate ones.
> 11. Satisfaction and disclosure have a curvilinear relationship; that is, relational satisfaction is greatest at moderate levels of disclosure. (273)

***Family Background*** Family-of-origin, cultural heritage, gender, and socioeconomic status set expectations that may influence self-disclosing behavior.

Ethnic heritage may influence the amount and type of disclosure. For example, the Mexican-American society appears to be relatively more open that the Anglo-American society when it comes to discussions of death (Falicov and Karrer 1980, 423). Whereas Jewish families exhibit verbal skill and a willingness to talk about trouble and feelings, Irish families may find themselves at a loss to describe inner feelings (McGoldrick 1993b).

Although the research on gender and disclosure is inconclusive, female pairs tend to be more disclosive than male pairs (Cline 1989). Generally, women tend to be higher disclosers than men; they disclose more negative information; they provide less honest information and they disclose more intimate information (Pearson 1989). These differences reflect socialization of females and males. Limited research on communication and social class points toward differential use of self-disclosure (Hurvitz and Komarovsky 1977; Rubin 1983).

***Partner Relationships*** Marital self-disclosure studies reveal consistent findings across groups. According to Fitzpatrick (1987, 585–586) self-report studies show a positive correlation between the self-disclosures of husbands and wives and between self-disclosure and marital satisfaction. Yet a high disclosure of negative feelings is negatively related to marital satisfaction. In addition, dual career couples appear to be more able to disclose to one another. The effect of age or length of marriage on spouse self-disclosure is unclear, since the content of discussion may vary over time (Waterman 1979, 226–227). Married men are less likely to disclose to friends than married women, although of married men and women who reported high self-disclosure within the marriage, only the women reported moderate to high disclosure to a friend (Tschann 1988, 6).

***Parent-Child Relationships*** Parent-child disclosure has received some attention, revealing that self-disclosure does not involve all family members equally. Most mothers receive more self-disclosure than fathers (Waterman 1979). Parents perceived as nurturing and supportive elicit more disclosure from children who find those encounters rewarding. College students are more likely to disclose more information more honestly to same-sex best friends than to either parent (Tardy, Hosman, and Bradac 1981).

Such a brief review only highlights certain issues but indicates the complexity of a subject that some popular writers tend to treat simplistically as they encourage unrestrained, open communication in family relationships.

***Satisfaction*** The positive effect of self-disclosure on intimate relationships has been described extensively. Clearly shared and accepted personal information or feelings enhance intimacy in a relationship. In general, marital self-disclosure is rewarding because it signals to the listener the speaker's willingness to trust and share (Fitzpatrick 1987, 585).

Yet, such sharing and acceptance is not the norm. In fact, high self-disclosure is not necessarily linked with relational satisfaction, since it is clear that satisfied couples are more likely to engage in positive disclosure or sharing pleasant feelings. Unsatisfied couples tend

Parent-adolescent self disclosure paves the way for strong adult relationships.

to disclose more unpleasant feelings or negotiate messages. These studies highlight the value of "selective disclosure" (Sillars et al. 1987; Shumm et al. 1986; Burke, Weir, and Harrison, 1976).

The valence, or balances between the positive or negative nature of the message, relates directly to how comments will be received. Most people appreciate receiving positive self-disclosure. More frequently, self-disclosure is considered "dirty laundry," the misdeeds or negative feelings that are likely to cause pain for the listener. Some of the studies cited earlier report that higher self-disclosure levels are more characteristic of happily married couples, but that unhappily married couples are higher in disclosure of a negative valence. Families characterized by pleasant self-disclosure content can experience intimacy more easily than those trying to discuss painful, negative-laden issues. For example, talking about a desire for continued sexual experimentation within a generally satisfactory relationship has much greater possibilities of leading to further intimacy than a revelation of severe sexual dissatisfaction.

***Self Esteem*** High self-esteem is the basis for much positive communication within families. According to Satir (1988), integrity, honesty, responsibility, compassion, and love easily flow from persons with high self-esteem because they feel they matter. Such people are willing to take risks whereas persons with low self-esteem constantly feel they have to defend themselves. Abelman (1975) found that the self-disclosures of adolescents to their parents seemed more closely tied to their own self-esteem than to the amount of self-disclosure received from the parents. Research literature relating self-disclosure to esteem, within the context of interaction in family systems, reveals that often people refrain from expressing their feelings because they are insecure about their marriage (Gilbert). Since self-disclosure requires risk-taking, it appears more likely that persons who feel good about themselves would be more willing to take such risks than would persons who have low self-esteem.

***A Curvilinear Perspective*** Based on a review of self-disclosure research, Gilbert suggests a curvilinear relationship between self-disclosure and satisfaction in relationship maintenance, holding that a moderate degree of disclosure appears to be most conducive to maintaining a relationship over time. The diagrams shown in Figure 5.2 will help you visualize the differences.

According to Figure 5.2a, as relationships become more disclosing, satisfaction moves from a growth pattern to a decline, whereas according to Figure 5.2b, increased self-disclosure is directly related to increased satisfaction. The research based on a curvilinear view holds that "as disclosures accumulate through the history of a relationship and as the nature of the relationship itself changes, then the connection between disclosure and relational satisfaction reverses from a positive to a negative association ... this is the way disclosure functions for most relationships" (Gilbert, 211). When you think of many of your friends or relatives, you may realize that you do not share the particularly negative aspects of yourself or discuss theirs, because this may result in the decline of the relationship. Perhaps you witnessed a family relationship in which very unpleasant disclosures seemed to diminish or end it. Members may not have been able

**FIGURE 5.2**
**Relationships Between Self-Disclosure and Satisfaction**

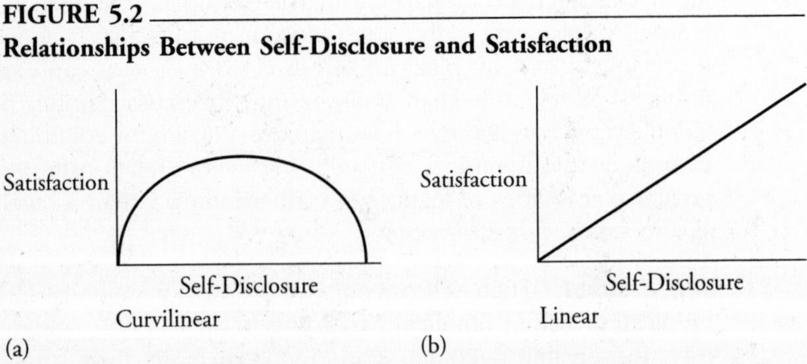

to cope with the negative information they received about themselves or other relatives, and such a situation follows:

*As a child, I never fully understood what happened, but there was a big change in the relationships in our house, and there seemed to be a dark secret that no one would talk about. Fifteen years later, I found out from my oldest brother that my father had a short affair with someone at the office, and after it was over he told my mother. She was devastated. It changed their relationship for many years.*

The linear point of view, suggesting that self-disclosure remains a positive source of relational satisfaction throughout the relationship, clearly describes "optimum state of affairs" rather than how things actually are (Gilbert, 211).

Yet, the linear relationship and its positive outcome may occur when mutual capacity to handle positive and negative self-disclosure exists. Such situations, though, are uncommon. Gilbert suggests that for a linear pattern of disclosure to work in intimate relationships, both persons need healthy selves, including high self-esteem, a willingness to risk, a commitment to the relationship and its growth, and reciprocal confirmation. The diagram showing Figure 5.3 presents the

**FIGURE 5.3**

**Disclosure Processes in Relationship Development: A Linear Versus a Curvilinear Schemata**

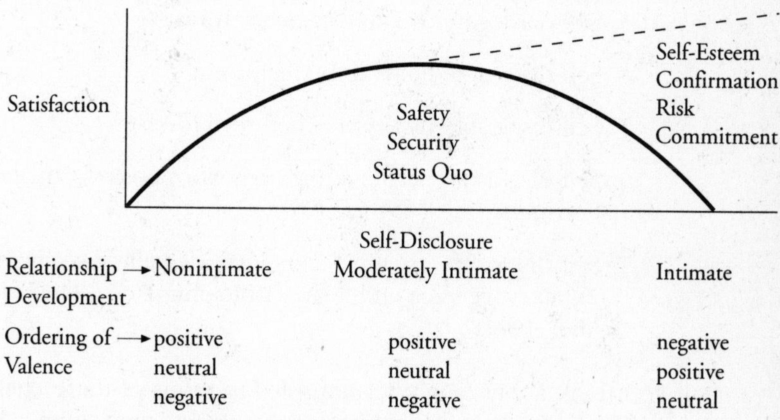


From Shirley Gilbert, "Empirical and Theoretical Extension of Self-Disclosure," pp. 210, 211–212 in Explorations in Interpersonal Communication, edited by Gerald R. Miller. 

possible combinations of approaches to self-disclosure and satisfaction found in the different types of relationships.

The diagram illustrates that, as relationships move from being nonintimate to intimate, the initial high positive self-disclosure gains in importance. In order to handle this and remain satisfied with the relationship, both the individuals involved must be characterized as high self-disclosers because of the amount of trust and risk involved. Intimate relationships are less likely to engage in high self-disclosure due to the amount of trust and risk involved (Pilkington and Richardson 1988).

Since family life involves long-term growth and change, it would be ideal if members could handle the negative and positive aspects of each other's disclosures, permitting total honesty within a supportive context. Yet, many negative self-disclosures are necessarily painful and each individual varies in a capacity to endure emotional pain. Thus, in many relationships, high levels of self-disclosure result in low levels of satisfaction. Recent research indicates partners may naturally cycle between being open and closed in their communication, meeting needs for separateness and togetherness (Montgomery 1994).

***The Practice of Self-Disclosure*** Now that you have received some of the research and thinking in the area of marital or family self-disclosure, you can think about your own family relationships according to the following general characteristics of self-disclosure:

1. Relatively few communication transactions involve high levels of disclosure.
2. Self-disclosure involves verbal and nonverbal signals.
3. Self-disclosure usually occurs in dyads.
4. Self-disclosure tends to be reciprocal.
5. Self-disclosure increases when rewarded.
6. Self-disclosure occurs in the context of positive, trusting relationships.
7. Self-disclosure usually occurs incrementally with increased intimacy. (Pearce and Sharp; Littlejohn; Duck, Miell, and Miell 1984)

If you think about family relationships in terms of these characteristics, you can see ways in which family systems tend to encourage or discourage self-disclosure. Considering the time it takes to do the functional things in families, you can understand that little time or energy may be available for nurturing communication, including self-disclosure. According to Montgomery (1994), "While self-disclosure may have significant impact in close relationships, it does not occur with great frequency even between the happiest of partners" (78). Finding everyday time to talk sets a context for the occasional self-disclosure. According to Schwartz (1994), partners can lead parallel lives and may never get in the habit of sharing their lives with each other. Vangelisti and Banski (1993) found if couples held debriefing conversations and talked about how their days went, they were more likely to experience marital satisfaction. These kinds of conversations set the groundwork for moving into riskier topics. Hence, risk-taking communication is not likely to occur frequently within family life, but certain developmental or unpredictable stresses may trigger extensive amounts of personal discussion.

The self-disclosure process has an overlooked nonverbal component. A sequence of appropriate nonverbal signals occurring in the context of verbal disclosure also contribute significantly to mutual understanding. For example, nonverbal signals may tell a husband that his wife is surprised that he is unaware of her feelings about a topic (Duck, Miell, and Miell, 305). Duck proposes the term "intimation sequences" for these signals in which both partners intimate new levels of evolving awareness within a discussion. Parents may become skilled at reading a child's face and recognizing a desire or need to talk. Thus, verbal self-disclosure and nonverbal intimation sequences are bound together in face-to face interaction.

If high levels of disclosure occur mainly in dyads, how often do two-person systems spend time together? How often does a parent of four children get time alone with each one of them? When do a step-parent and stepchild make time alone for themselves? Many family members never spend one-on-one time with each other, yet such time is important for openness to develop in their relationships.

Reciprocity is critical to self-disclosure. Many couples report a serious imbalance in openness; traditionally, the female partner discloses more and desires more disclosure, becoming frustrated with the lower male response. In parent-child situations, it is more likely that parents provide the initial impetus and model for self-disclosing behavior.

Families create unique opportunities for self-disclosure. Joint living experiences provide needed time and space for such interaction. Yet, this can take place only where positive social relationships, including trust, exist. Parents unwittingly may break a child's trust because they discussed the child's concern with another adult, not respecting the child's privacy. Unless disclosers indicate how private certain information is to them, another person may accidentally reveal that information to others and, as noted in the next quote, damage the relationship.

*I have stopped discussing anything important with my mother because she cannot keep her mouth shut. She has told my aunt and some friends at work all about my relationship with my boyfriend, my use of birth control pills, and some of my health problems. Well, she doesn't have much to tell them now since she doesn't hear about my real concerns anymore.*

In some nonvoluntary family relationships, especially those involving stepfamilies, the bases of trust and liking may be missing, thereby reducing the likelihood of openness developing within the first five years (Galvin and Cooper 1990).

In self-disclosure, as in many other areas of life, one is likely to repeat behaviors that are rewarded or met with positive response. In a family that indicates satisfaction at knowing what the members are thinking or feeling, even if the information itself is not necessarily pleasant, continued self-disclosure is likely. If self-disclosure is met with rejecting or disconfirming messages, the level of sharing will drop significantly.

Some people are dishonest or inaccurate in their disclosures (Berger and Bradac, 87). Although self-disclosure enhances intimacy development, it can be used to manipulate or control another family member. Partial or dishonest disclosures can undermine trust in a relationship. Sometimes young persons or immature adults engage in pseudo self-disclosure to see how it works or to gain something else from the relationship. In this process, they take advantage of the other by betraying a trust. Unauthentic disclosures may be difficult to detect, but once discovered, may interfere with future believability and mutual self-disclosure. In marriage, partners may be caught between desires for openness and protectiveness. A husband may be dismayed by his wife's weight gain, but he knows that bringing up his feelings would feed her low self-esteem.

Self-disclosure bears a direct relationship to family levels of cohesion and adaptation. An extremely cohesive family may resist negative self-disclosure, since it would threaten the connectedness, particularly if the family has a low capacity for adaptation. For example, a highly cohesive family with a theme of "We can only depend on each other" would resist negative disclosures that might threaten security and cause internal conflict. Such a theme might be accompanied by rigid boundaries which would resist self-disclosures to outsiders.

Families with very low cohesion may tolerate negative self-disclosure but have difficulty with positive self-disclosure, which might lead to greater cohesion. Families with moderate to high adaptation and cohesion capacities may cope relatively well with the effects of high levels of positive or negative self-disclosure. Self-disclosure is a complicated process that may result in increased intimacy. In short, self-disclosure, or "sharing what's inside—even if what's inside isn't pretty—is the supreme act of faith in another" (Avery, 31).

## Sexuality and Communication

How would you describe sexuality? As a series of isolated physical encounters? As an integral part of a growing relationship? Do you see marital sexuality as restricted to "being good in bed"? For most partners, sexuality within a marital relationship involves far more than just physical performance; it involves the partners' sexual identities, their history of sexual issues, their mutual perceptions of each others' needs, and the messages contained with sexual expression.

Feldman stresses the importance of sexual relations to marital intimacy, yet the quality of the sexual relationship affects, and is affected by, the other characteristics of intimacy—the affectionate/loving relationship and a deep, detailed mutual knowledge of the two partners. In their study of over 6,000 couples, Blumstein and Schwartz (1983) report, "Our findings lead to the overwhelming conclusion that a good sex life is central to a good relationship" (201). In recent work, Schwartz (1994) reports the importance of equitable sexuality in peer marriages.

How would you describe sexuality within the family relationship? As an important dimension of family life? As unrelated to family issues, or scary within the family context? For family members, healthy sexuality reflects the balanced expression of sexuality in family structures and functions which enhance the personal identity and sexual health of members and the system as a whole (Maddock 1989).

At both the marital and family level sexual issues directly impact communication. Sexuality, including sexual attitudes and behavior, may be viewed as a topic of communication, a form of communication, and a contributing factor to overall relationship intimacy and satisfaction. According to Sprecher and McKinney (1994) "Sex is not only an act of communication or self-disclosure. Verbal and nonverbal communication is essential for the accomplishment of rewarding sexual episodes" (206).

In this section, sexuality will be explored in terms of socialization, parent-child communication, partner communication, and communication breakdowns.

***Socialization and Sexuality*** The basis for a mutually intimate sexual relationship reflects each of the partner's orientation toward sexuality, particularly that which is learned in the family-of-origin. An individual's sexuality remains closely intertwined with his or her intrapersonal, interpersonal, and environmental systems—systems that interlock, yet which vary in importance according to an individual's age. According to Greene (1970):

> The sexual feelings (intrapersonal) and behavior of a person are a reaction to the parental attitudes (interpersonal) in which he was raised. These attitudes, in turn, were handed down by their parents and were largely molded by broad cultural viewpoints specific to their social class (environmental forces). (57)

The sexual dimensions of family life are tied strongly to developing gender identities, setting boundaries, and handling developmental change. Much of your sexual conduct was originally learned, coded, and performed on the basis of biosocial beliefs regarding gender identity, learned originally in your family-of-origin. Parents possess a set of gender-specific ideas about males and females learned from their childhood experiences and from "typical" behaviors of girls or boys of similar ages to their children. Based on these and their personal experiences, parents transmit a gender identity from earliest infancy, resulting in children establishing gender identities at a very young age. This identity is so strong that efforts to alter such socialization patterns must be presented to children before age three or they will have little impact (Gagnon 1977). Your personal identities include sexual/gender identity as a core component, which influences later sexual experiences. According to Gagnon:

> When we do begin having sex in our society, our beliefs about woman/man strongly influences whom we have sex with, what sexual things we do, where and when we will have sex, the reasons we agree, and the feelings we have. (59)

Sexual experiences contain powerful confirming or disconfirming messages which affect sexual interactions.

***Parent-Child Communication*** Many of today's adults grew up in a home atmosphere of sexual silence and now live in a world of open sexual discussion (Ryan and Ryan 1982). Much of what you learned about sexuality took place within the rule-bound context of your family. In the earlier discussion of communication rules, you may recall that many sex-related rules are negative directives—"Do not ..." The extent to which a family encourages or discourages talk about issues such as pregnancy, birth control, masturbation, menstrual cycles, the initial sexual encounters of teenage or young adult children, and the sexual intimacy of the parents is related to communication and sexuality rules (Yerby, Buerkel-Rothfuss, and Bochner 1990). Often, communication about sexual issues remains indirect, resulting in confusion, misinformation, or heightened curiosity.

Families differ greatly in their approach to sexuality. Maddock (1989) has described communication behaviors of sexually neglectful, sexually abusive, and sexually healthy families. In some "sexually neglectful" families, sex is discussed little or not at all. If it must be addressed, sexual communication occurs on an abstract level so direct connection is not made between the topic and the personal experience of family members (Maddock, 133).

---

*My mother explained the act of sex in the most cold, mechanical, scientific, factual way she could. I was embarrassed and I couldn't look at her face after she finished. I know it was very difficult for her. Her mother had not told her anything at all, and she had let her get married and go on a honeymoon without any knowledge of what was going to happen. She made a point of saying throughout, "After marriage ..."*

---

Messages like the previous example communicate an underlying attitude of anxiety or displeasure, but the direct issue remains hidden. Veiled messages often continue through adolescence and into adulthood. According to Satir (1988):

> Most families employ the rule, "Don't enjoy sex—yours or anyone else's—in any form." The common beginning for this rule is the denial of the genitals except as necessary nasty objects. "Keep them clean and out of sight and touch. Use them only when necessary and sparingly at that." (124–125)

In many families, the marital boundary remains so tight around the area of sexuality that children never see their parents as sexual beings—no playful jokes, hugging, or tickling occurs in view of the children. Children may perceive adults who are cool or distant as people who associate sexuality with shame or guilt.

Yet, in other families, the marital boundary is so diffuse that children encounter incestuous behaviors as they are co-opted into spousal roles. This "sexually abusive" family is typically a closed, rigid system with boundary confusion between individuals and generations. Communication reflects a perpetrator-victim interaction pattern, especially in cross gender relationships, resulting in marital conflict and lack of emotional intimacy (Maddock, 134). Yet, in both the sexually neglectful and sexually abusive families, sexual attitudes and sexual behavior are seldom addressed directly.

According to Maddock, sexually healthy families are characterized by (1) respect for both genders, (2) boundaries which are developmentally appropriate and support gender identities, (3) effective and flexible communication patterns which support intimacy, including appropriate erotic expression, and (4) a shared system of culturally relevant sexual values and meanings.

Maddock suggests sexually healthy families communicate effectively about sex "using language that can accurately cover sexual information, reflect feelings and attitudes of members, and facilitate decision making and problem solving regarding sexual issues" (135). Sex education is accurate and set in a context of family values transmitted across generations. Talking about sexuality has been avoided by a great majority of parents (Roxema 1986). After interviewing women in their thirties about their mother-daughter conversations about sex, Brock & Jennings (1993) reported that memories were primarily of negative, nonverbal messages and limited discussion focused on warnings and rules. The women wished for openness and discussions of feelings and choices. Interestingly most of these women excused their mother's for their silence or discomfort, but indicated a desire to do better with their own children.

Today, direct parent-child communication about sexuality is not only important for healthy family functioning but for the long term physical health of family members. Pressing issues such as AIDS, sexually transmitted diseases, and a high percentage of unwanted pregnancies necessitate such discussions. Parents need to be able to address issues of safe sex practices and ways of talking about sex with their children.

---

*In our family we did not discuss sexuality openly. When I left for college my mother (totally unprovoked) told me that if I ever decided to go on birth control, I was never to tell her, and NOT to get it through our family doctor, but through the school health service. By doing so she made sure she separated herself from ever discussing the topic—so much that she did not even ask me if I had ever thought of it. This is how much she wanted to avoid the subject.*

---

The family represents the first but not the only source of sexual information. As children mature, they gain additional information about sexuality from peers, church, school and the media. When you look back over your childhood and adolescence, what were your major sources of sexual information? What attitudes were communicated to you about your own sexuality? What could have improved the messages you received?

***Partner Communication*** As an individual embarks upon sexual experiences, his or her sexual identity influences the encounters, as does the partner's sexual identity. Couples establish their own patterns of sexual activity early in the relationship, and these patterns typically continue (Sprecher and McKinney). Open communication becomes critical for both individuals, since a good sexual relationship depends on what is satisfying to each partner. A couple that cannot communicate effectively about many areas of their life will have difficulty developing effective communication about their sexual life. In short, "Communication in the bedroom starts in other rooms" (Schwartz 1994, 74). Ryan and Ryan describe the mutuality involved in sexual experience:

> Having sex with someone is a semi-private act. It begins with an invitation, often unspoken by one, and the acceptance, often tacit but clear, by the other. It is semi-private in that the pleasure of sex is one's own, but the quality of the pleasure depends on what the other does. In sex, one is both a giver and receiver of pleasure (75).

This sense of mutuality is enhanced by direct and honest communication between partners. Some understanding comes only through a combination of self-disclosure and sensitivity as spouses reveal their needs and desires while learning to give pleasure to the other. For some spouses, this involves working on "signal clarification" to minimize miscommunication. From another perspective, we can distinguish between monological and dialogical sex—the former being sexual experiences in which one or both partners "talk to themselves" or attempt to satisfy only personal needs. Dialogical sex is characterized by mutual concern and sharing of pleasure (Wilkinson 1990).

Talking about sex appears to be easier than it used to be, especially for long term partners. After professional polls in 1984 and 1994, Clements (1994) reported that 74 percent of men today said it is easy to talk about sex with their partners, compared with 59 percent in 1984. Today, 70 percent of women find conversations about sex with a partner easy, up from 63 percent in 1984.

Yet many partners still find it difficult to talk about their sexual relationship. Adelman (1988) defines the discourse of intercourse as "sexual conversation which occurs between two people prior to, during, and after sex"(1). She maintains that the vocabulary for sex talk is impoverished and thus ineffective in many relationships. Thus impoverished language and parental socialization may combine to restrict the adult sexual experiences, preventing husbands and wives from communicating freely about or through their sexual encounters.

Sexual discussions are rife with euphemisms (Bell, Buerkel-Rothfuss, and Gore 1987; Hopper, Knapp, and Scott 1981), which may serve to romanticize or confuse the message. Euphemisms serve partners well when they promote the desired erotic reality but may serve to create disappointment or anger.

Satisfied couples report their ability to discuss directly issues of feelings about sex, desired frequency of intercourse, who initiates sex, desired foreplay, sexual techniques, or positions. They avoid "mindreading," such as "If she really loved me, she'd know I would like ..." or "If he really loved me, he would ..." This is a powerful trap. Hatfield and Rapson (1993) suggest both men and women wished that their partners would tell them exactly what they wanted sexually. However, these same people were reluctant to tell their partners what they wanted. They kept expecting the partner to mindread.

Because of their "taboos" regarding a discussion of sexual behavior, many couples rely solely on nonverbal communication to gain mutual satisfaction. For some, this may be acceptable, but for others, unclear messages result in frustration, as partners misinterpret the degree or kind of sexual expression desired by the other. Some partners report a fear of using any affectionate gesture because the other spouse always sees it as an invitation to intercourse; others say their partners never initiate any sexual activity while the partners report being ignored or rebuffed at such attempts. Mutual satisfaction at any level of sexual involvement depends upon open communication between spouses, yet intercourse, according to Lederer and Jackson is special "in that it requires a higher degree of collaborative communication than any other kind of behavior exchanged between the spouses" (117).

The current AIDS crisis has brought about a new consciousness of the need for clear discourse about intercourse (Michal-Johnson and Bowen 1989). The following vignette from an interview about safe sex talk (Adelman 1988) illustrates the depth of the problem:

> She spoke openly about her sexual practices, describing in candid terms her preferences for foreplay and certain positions. When she had finished her graphic description I asked her "So what do you *say* to your partner during sex?" She

> laughed nervously and replied, "Oh, *now* you're getting personal." (1)

Given the dangers, "partners can no longer remain silent about their sexual pasts, nor fear to voice their concerns about a mutual sexual future" (Adelman, 3). The need for safe sex talk and practice becomes more apparent daily. Thus, for couples engaged in an intimate relationship, open and direct communication about sexuality may deepen the intimacy and provide tremendous pleasure to both spouses.

***Sexuality and Communication Breakdowns*** Although sex as a form of communication has the potential for conveying messages of love and affection, many spouses use their sexual encounters to carry messages of anger, domination, disappointment, or self-rejection. Often nonsexual conflicts are played out in the bedroom because one partner believes it is the only way to wage a war. Unexpressed anger may appear as a "headache," great tiredness, roughness, or violence during a sexual encounter.

Blumstein and Schwartz found that married couples who report fighting a lot about housekeeping, income, expenditures, and whether both should work are less happy with their sexual relationship. If partners experience unsatisfying sexual encounters early in their relationship, their "mutual disappointment and embarrassment can easily lead to sensitivity and reluctance to talk about what has been happening to them" (Ryan and Ryan, 80).

As more information is gathered about sexuality through the life cycle, it becomes clear that sexual expectations are altered over time due to developmental changes and unpredictable stresses. Couples interviewed about the history of their sex lives report that they have experienced dramatic changes in sexual interest, depending on other pressures in their lives. Dual career couples report a decline in time and desire for sexual activity. There are indications that sexuality may become more pleasurable in later life when a couple's childrearing burdens cease.

Based on his work in the area of sexual communication, Scoresby developed a chart indicating areas of sexual breakdown. Table 5–2 indicates the possible areas of breakdown related to communication and possible ways to address them.

Scoresby sees the following advantages of thinking of sex as communication: (1) an awareness of complexities and limitless potential and (2) viewing the sexual relationship as a continuous process instead of as a series of isolated events (46).

**Table 5-2** Signs of Difficulty in Sexual Communication

| Common Symptoms | Possible Solutions |
|---|---|
| 1. Failure to talk openly with each other. | 1. Increase each person's ability to self-disclose feelings. |
| 2. Repeated lack of orgasm by female. | 2. Spend increased positive time alone together. |
| 3. Tension and lack of relaxation. | 3. Avoid threatening to dissolve the marriage. |
| 4. One demanding the other to perform. | 4. Check for angry conflict and reduce if possible. |
| 5. Excessive shyness or embarrassment. | |
| 6. Hurried and ungentle performance. | |
| 7. Absence of frequent touching, embracing, and exchanges of intimacy. | |

The area of sexuality and communication within the family realm has received less attention than other, less sensitive topics. Yet, since sexual standards, values, and relationships are negotiated among people through their interactions, the area of sexual communication is critical to the development of family and marital intimacy.

## Commitment

"If you have to work at a relationship, there's something wrong with it. A relationship is either good or it's not." These words capture a naive but common belief about marital and family relationships. How often have you heard people argue that relationships should not require attention or effort? Yet it is only through commitment that a loving relationship remains a vital part of one's life.

Commitment implies intense singular energy directed toward sustaining a relationship. As such, it emphasizes one relationships and may limit other possibilities.

Knapp and Taylor (1994, 155) describe kinds of relational commitments as: (1) want-to, (2) ought-to, and (3) have-to. Want-to commitment is based on personal choice and desire, usually rooted in positive feelings. Ought-to commitment stems from a sense of obligation based on a promise, a sense of guilt, a fear of hurting another. Have-to commitment is based on the perception that there is no good alternative to maintaining membership in this relationship. Frequently, partnerships and families are held together by a combination of these types of commitments. At good times, members want-to be connected; during rough times, members stick it out because they ought-to. Under sad conditions they may have-to stay together. Commitment is built on an investment of talk and effort. This talk creates its own rewards. For example, "trust is inspired when both partners communicate that the relationship is a priority; something they want to invest in for their own benefit and their partner's" (Avery 1989, 30).

***Talk*** There are direct and indirect messages that communicate commitment in a relationship. Direct relational talk occurs when partners share with each other their feelings and desire to grow in the relationship. "I love you." "It's so great to have a sister to go through life with. We are a pair, no matter, what."

Repetition, explicitness, and codification add to commitment talk. (Knapp and Vangelisti, 268–269) As described in the discussion of verbal relational currencies, certain phrases need to be repeated, certain ideas needs to be reaffirmed. Explicitness reduces misunderstanding. "I will stand behind you even if I don't agree." "We are brothers and that means I will support you." Such comments make the commitment quite clear. Codifying communication may be reflected in anything from love letters to a written agreement of rules for fighting to a marital contract. Commitment is not always easy; words may be hard to find and say.

***Effort*** Many factors compete for attention in your life. Meeting home, work, school, friendship, and community responsibilities take tremendous time and effort. The nurturing of marital or family relationships often gets the time and energy that is "left over," a minimal amount at best. In most cases, this limited attention spells relational disaster. Unless familial ties receive high priority, relationships will "go on automatic pilot" and eventually stagnate or deteriorate.

Because the family operates within larger systems including work and school, each system impacts the other. In describing the tensions between work and home obligations, Blumstein and Schwartz refer to the interaction between "where people put their emotional energy (home versus work) and their commitment to their relationship" (173). In this era of dual-career couples and families, commuter marriages, and high technology and subsequent job loss or relocation, family intimacy can be lost in the shuffle.

Only a conscious and shared commitment to focus on the relationship can keep marital and family ties high on one's list of priorities. As you will see in Chapter 14, many couples and families seek out opportunities to enrich their lives, to reaffirm their commitment to work on their relationships. According to Avery the way a couple demonstrates their commitment is tied to communication.

> It can be willingness to do things for each other, spending time together, making personal sacrifices on the other's behalf, being consistent. Self-disclosure is part of it too, because sharing what's inside—even if what's inside isn't pretty—is the supreme act of faith in another. (31)

Thus, only conscious commitment and dedication to working at relationships, particularly through talk and effort, can preserve or heighten intimacy.

## BARRIERS TO INTIMACY

Marital or familial intimacy depends on confirmation, self-disclosure, and sexual communication and commitment yet, because of the perceived risks involved in intimate communication, drawing close to another person can be frightening. For many people it is much more comfortable to maintain a number of pleasant or close relationships, none involving true intimacy, than to become intensely involved with a spouse or child. Low risk takers establish barriers to relationship development to protect themselves from possible pain or loss. Whitehead and Whitehead (1981) address this directly when they say, "The central threat of any close intimacy encounter ... is the threat of injury and loss" (223).

There are many reasons for a fear of intimacy, including the following four discussed by Feldman (1979, 71–72): merger, exposure, attack, and abandonment. People may fear a merger with the loved one resulting in the loss of personal boundaries or identity. This occurs when the "sense of self" is poorly developed or when the "other" is very powerful. Comments such as "I'll disappear altogether" or "I have to fight to keep my identity" indicate struggles with merger. Individuals with low self-esteem fear interpersonal exposure and feel threatened by being revealed as weak, inadequate, or undesirable. Persons who fear exposure avoid engaging in self-disclosure. Some individuals fear attack if their basic sense of trust is low. If you have shared private aspects of your life with another and that person has turned against you, it will take a while before trusting another person. These persons also choose to protect themselves by avoiding self-disclosure. The fear of abandonment, the feeling of being overwhelmed and helpless when the love object is gone, may affect those who have experienced excessive traumatic separations or broken relationships. Their way to prevent such helplessness is to remain distant. Once one has taken the risk to be intimate, rejection can be devastating, resulting in reluctance to be hurt again.

For most people, fear of intimacy is tied directly to issues of boundary management. Sometimes intimacy becomes confused with an unhealthy togetherness or extreme cohesion, resulting in a loss of personal boundaries and identity. In families with unclear boundaries, one person's business is everyone's business. Much communication occurs across family subsystem boundaries, and members may feel obligated to engage in high self-disclosure and even seek disclosure inappropriate to the subsystem or role. An adolescent may feel obligated to discuss dating behavior with a parent. A mother may discuss marital problems with a teenage son. Yet, the pressuring person requires the other to "be like me; be one with me." He or she suggests, "You are bad if you disagree with me. Reality and your differentness are unimportant" (Satir 1967, 13), demonstrating the difficulty of negative self-disclosure. Members may require, or sense a demand for, constant confirmation to serve as a reassurance that they are cared for. Yet, intimacy can smother, as this person relates.

---

*My father thinks we all experience life as he does. He expects us to love and hate what he does. He assumes when he's cold, tired, or hungry, we are cold, tired, or hungry. He's like a whale swallowing little fish.*

---

In some families, the adults may be so afraid of sharing both good and bad things with each other that they establish a "united front" for themselves and displace any anger onto a child. Thus, the child serves as a scapegoat while the partners convince themselves that they are experiencing intimacy. Such false togetherness becomes a barrier to true marital intimacy while seriously harming the scapegoat child.

Within disengaged, or low cohesive, families, individuals experience rigid boundaries to each other, and the members may not receive necessary affection or support. Each person is a psychological subsystem with few links to the surrounding family members. Intimacy may be undeveloped in households where each family member is concerned solely with personal affairs, remains constantly busy, and spends extensive time away from home. Yet, even if persons spend time together, unless their communication goes beyond the task-oriented type, they may remain generally disengaged. Both types of families set up barriers to true intimacy by smothering or ignoring individual family members.

One of the challenges of life is to learn how to be yourself while you are in a relationship to another person. In a truly intimate relationship the "I" and the "we" co-exist, to the joy of all persons. Lerner (1989) captures the link between the development of intimacy and communication. Her words serve as a fine conclusion to this chapter.

> "Being who we are" requires that we can talk openly about things that are important to us, that we take a clear position on where we stand on important emotional issues, and that we clarify the limits of what is acceptable and tolerable to us in a relationship. "Allowing the other person to do the same" means that we can stay emotionally connected to that other party who thinks, feels, and believes differently, without needing to change, convince, or fix the other.
>
> An intimate relationship is one in which neither party silences, sacrifices, or betrays the self and each party expresses strength and vulnerability, weakness and competence in a balanced way. (3)

## CONCLUSION

This chapter explored the close relationship between intimacy and communication. After describing the relational currencies and stages in relationship development, the chapter focused on specific communication behaviors that encourage intimacy within marital and family systems: confirmation, self-disclosure, sexual communication, and commitment effort. Confirming behaviors communicate acceptance of another person. Self-disclosure provides a means for mutual sharing of personal information and feelings. Sexuality serves as a means of communicating affection within a partner relationship. Family intimacy cannot be achieved unless members nurture their relationships through commitment. Because most people experience anxiety about intimacy this is an ongoing and sometimes frustrating process. The barriers to intimacy may prevent certain relationships from developing their full potential.

Think about the kinds of interactions you see in the families around you. Is most of their communication strictly functional? Do you see attempts at intimacy through confirmation or self-disclosure? Are these people able to demonstrate an ability to touch each other comfortably? If you think back to Gilbert's model of curvilinear versus linear development of self-disclosure, you can imagine the model applied to all relationships, knowing that only a few are likely to have the mutual acceptance, risk-taking capacity, and commitment to move towards true intimacy.

All human beings long for intimacy, but it is a rare relationship in which the partners (spouses, parents and children, siblings) consciously strive for greater sharing over long periods of time. Such mutual commitment provides rewards known only to those in intimate relationships.

## IN REVIEW

1. Create your own definition of intimacy and provide two examples of a marital and a family relationship characterized by intimate communication. Discuss some specific communication behaviors.
2. Trace the development of a real or fictional couple through some of the stages of relationship development, citing representative examples of their communication patterns at each stage.
3. Using a real or fictional family, describe the relational currencies most commonly used. Indicate any family-of-origin influences you see in the current pattern.
4. Describe some confirming behaviors that can become patterned into a family's way of life.
5. Under what circumstances, if any, would you recommend withholding complete self-disclosure in a marital and/or family relationship?
6. If you have to work at a relationship, do you think there's something wrong with it?

# 6

# Communication and Family Roles

Members of a family develop roles through an interactive dialogue with each other. All parts of a family system are affected by change, but sometimes the most obvious signs of change are reflected in roles. There are no easy answers to what it means to be in a partner, sibling, or stepparent-stepchild role relationship. Economic factors facing families in the 1990s have forced family members to reconsider aspects of their roles. Underemployment means some parents work less than forty hours a week in one or more jobs. Men are the only breadwinners in less than 15 percent of two-parent families. Single parent and minority families experience even greater role stress in trying to make ends meet (Richards and Schmiege 1993). More parents work different shifts and do trade-off parenting. Women speak of working a "second shift" when they come home from their jobs. Some parents switch or divide the provider role and we have "househusbands." All of these changes produce uncertainty and a lack of agreement on appropriate roles. Perhaps it comes as no surprise when the results in one recent study suggested that couples found it easier to function in gender-based roles than to create new role expectations (Zvonkovic, Schmiege, and Hall 1994). Needless to say there is tremendous variability across families as members interact with each other creating a sense of role relationships. In order to explore these issues, this chapter will discuss: (1) role development, (2) role functions, (3) role conflict, and (4) couple and family typologies.

# ROLE DEVELOPMENT

Within families, roles are established, grown into, grown through, discussed, negotiated, worked on, and accepted or rejected. As family members mature or outside forces impact the family, roles emerge, shift, or disappear (Lewis, J. 1993). The term "role" is so widely used that it can mean very different things to different persons. In order to understand role development you need to consider first the definitions of roles and then examine role expectations and role performance.

## Role Definitions

Early role theorists frequently disagreed on the definition of family roles (Heiss 1968; Hood 1986). However, this text supports the view that "family roles are defined as repetitive patterns of behavior by which family members fulfill family functions" (Epstein, Bishop, and Baldwin 1982, 124). This position contrasts with some theories which present a fixed, or unchanging, view of roles. For example, some theories maintain that family members hold specific expectations toward the occupant of a given social position, such as a father or grandmother. These expectations carry beliefs about how a role can and should be enacted, no matter what the circumstances.

Rather than take a fixed view of the position of a child or a parent in a family, most theorists prefer an *interactive perspective,* emphasizing the emerging aspects of roles and the behavioral regularities that develop out of social interaction. This approach takes into account the transactional nature of the encounters experienced by

Role development involves observing and imitating role models.

persons with labels such as "father" or "wife" and reflects the reciprocal nature of roles. According to this interactive philosophy, you cannot be a stepfather without a stepchild, or a wife without a husband; in fact, you cannot be a companionable father to a child who rejects you, or be a confrontive wife to a man who avoids conflict. In creating roles in close relationships, communication "involves the exchange of interrelated behaviors—action and reaction, question and answer, request and response" (B. Montgomery 1994, 69). Over time, family members negotiate their mutual expectations of one another. Family members gradually fulfill those expectations in specific situations. Over time, family members acquire role attachments and make an emotional investment in carrying out, for example, the roles of provider or nurturer. In addition, as circumstances change, members may have to give up roles, a process called role relinquishment (Hood 1986). Yet, roles do not emerge solely through interaction. Part of learning roles occurs by observing and imitating *role models*, persons whose behavior serves as a guide for others.

The interactive role reflects: (1) the personality and background of a person who occupies a social position, such as oldest son or stepmother, (2) the relationships in which a person interacts, (3) the changes as each family member moves through his or her life cycle, (4) the effects of role performance upon the family system, and (5) the extent to which a person's social/psychological identity is defined and enhanced by a particular role. For example, a woman's behavior in the social position of wife may have been very different in her first marriage than in her second, due to her own personal growth and the actions of each husband.

The distinction between interactive and fixed roles has many implications for communication. In his classic work, British sociologist Bernstein (1970) identifies two primary forms of communication that contrast and typify families, the position-oriented type and the person-oriented type. Position-oriented families usually maintain strict boundaries along the lines of age, sex, and family roles. Thus, the behaviors attached to the roles of grandparent, mother, and son become carefully defined and delineated. In a position-oriented family, an aunt does *X*, a mother does *Y*, and a husband does *Z*. Person-oriented families center more on the unique individuals occupying each label and have fewer limits or exacting rules for appropriate behavior.

Note the communication differences between position-oriented and person-oriented in this example: Dennis and his sister, Patty, grew up in a position-oriented family. They learned that either their mother or father was in charge of whatever activities went on within the family. Either parent had definite rules for the behavior expected. These remarks would be stated: "Dennis, mow the field and help your dad clean out the barn." "Patty, clear the table and don't forget to go get those clothes out of the dryer and fold them." "You can't go ride your bikes until your mother has time to check your homework." "Write that 'Thank you' note to your grandmother right now."

In a person-oriented family, Celeste and David would hear from their parents' reasons for the desired behaviors that go beyond parents' rights to command and direct. Children would experience a sense of choice or control. For example, "Which of you would like to help do some of these chores that need to be done?" "David, you might want to empty the dryer and put in those gym clothes of yours that need washing before tomorrow's game." "Find a time to write or call Grandmother, because I think she gets lonely and sometimes feels unappreciated."

A child raised in a position-oriented family learns that what can be said and done in relation to others depends on the roles one has relative to others, whereas a child raised in a person-oriented family learns that, although role relationships are important, what constitutes appropriate or inappropriate behaviors depends on reasons that transcend role relationships and depends upon the individual nature of each family member. An example of parent attention to these issues follows:

---

*I feel strongly that, in my single parent family, my children need to be flexible. I always try to encourage their direct participation in all decisions and events. I try to raise them in a non-sexist manner, giving equal responsibilities to them in the home and outside, regardless of their age and sex. My daughter cooks, gardens, and dances. So does my son. They also have to help me fix things and sometimes I feel that I am lucky to be their only role model, so they will learn to be full and open individuals with a sense of self-worth.*

---

Roles are inextricably bound to the communication process. Family roles are developed and maintained through communication. One learns how to assume his or her place within a family from the feedback provided by other family members, such as "I don't think you should argue in front of the children." Individuals talk about what they expect from another as they enter a marital relationship. In-laws are verbally or non-verbally informed about what is considered appropriate behavior; children are given direct instructions about being a son or daughter in a particular household. In general, adults tend to use their family-of-origin history as a base from which to negotiate particular mutual roles as they form a family system; children develop their communicative roles through a combination of their cognitive skills, family experiences, and societal norms and expectations. Young family members in immigrant families sometimes feel role tension when they sense that their parents' values differ from their desires to be Americanized. Recently arrived immigrants have difficulty assimilating role expectations when their parents fear their children are abandoning the family's heritage.

Family roles and communication rules are strongly interrelated, as each contributes to the maintenance or change of the other. Rules may structure certain role relationships, while particular role relationships may foster the development of certain rules. For example, such rules as "Children should not hear about family finances" or "School problems are to be settled with Mother" reinforce a position-oriented structure; in turn, such a structure contributes to the creation of this type of rule.

Current literature on family roles often centers on terms such as dual-career couples and dual-earner couples. These terms also need to be clarified. The term dual-career couple refers to a pair where each pursues full-time career advancements. Each spouse feels committed to achieve professional growth as well as marital satisfaction. By contrast, in a dual-earner couple, both spouses have taken a job in the labor force primarily for economic reasons (Hansen 1991). This couple usually cannot make ends meet on one salary, and the issue of career growth is not of major importance. Clearly there are many variations of these two spousal arrangements.

In order to better understand family roles, you need to examine the sources of role expectations and the determinants of role performance. How many of you remember making comments like "When I'm a parent, I'll listen to my kids." Most of you have spent time planning how you will perform a specific future role based on your expectations.

## Role Expectations

Society provides models and norms for how certain family roles should be assumed. Currently the media is an important societal source of family role expectations. Look at any newsstand and you will see articles on "how to" be a good parent, grandparent, stepparent, etc. Television has provided many family role models from the time of *Father Knows Best* to *The Young and the Restless* to *Roseanne.* Parents get daily advice from talk show hosts and their guests. Advertising reinforces stereotypes of how family members should act.

Daily life within a community also serves as a source of role expectations. As you were growing up, the neighbors and your friends all knew who were the "good" mothers or the "bad" kids on the block or in the community. Religious leaders presented exhortations for the "good family life." School personnel promoted "good" parenting. Each of you has grown up with expectations of how people should function in family roles, just as this example shows:

---

*My mother grew up on a ranch in the Great Uinta Basin in Utah. The women in her family were extremely strong and used to doing "men's work." Again, whatever had to be done would be done by whoever was available. It didn't matter whether one was a girl or boy, all hands were necessary and looked upon as being equal in her family.*

---

Cultural groups hold beliefs about parenting or spousal roles, which are learned by members of their community. For example, in the Jewish tradition, the role of mother is associated with the transmission of culture and, as such, carries a particular significance and implies certain expectations. In a comparative study with Anglo children, Mexican-American children described fathers significantly more as rule makers, but sensed both mothers and fathers as rule enforcers. Anglo children depicted fathers more often both as rule makers and enforcers (Jaramillo and Zapata 1987). In their study of the physical and psychological health of middle-aged and older African American women, Coleman et al. (1987) found an expectation of parenting and providing. They sensed parenting and partnering as interconnected with the providing role function primary to their well-being. Thomas (1990), in a study of dual-career African-American couples, found that family cohesion was the strongest determinant of marital happiness for the men, and quality communication ranked first for the women. She also cited evidence that indicated the division of family responsibilities into stereotypical male or female roles is significantly less apparent in African American families than in white families.

Role expectations also arise from significant others and complementary others. *Significant others* are those persons you view as important and who provide you with models from which you develop role expectations. A favorite teacher who combined a career with a family, or a close friend who succeeded as a trial attorney while she raised three children as a single parent may influence your role choices. You may have had a grandmother who taught you caring behaviors that parents should exhibit. Most people tend to seek models for particular lifestyles.

*Complementary others* are those who fulfill reciprocal role functions which directly impact on your role. Their expectations of your behavior influence your expectations. A husband has expectations for a wife, as does a parent for a child. During early stages of romantic relationships, men and women spend long periods of time discussing their expectations for what being a complementary other, a husband or wife, will be like. "I want my wife to be home with the children until they go to school" or "I need a husband who will help parent my children from my first marriage." As families blend, prospective spouses may talk with their future stepchildren about what they think the relationship should be like. If one partner's expectations are more position-oriented, they are more likely to clash than if both hold similar orientations.

Additional expectations come from each person's self-understanding. A person who expects to fulfill the role of spouse or parent has certain ideas about what such a role entails. You may find that you relied on a role model or you decided that with your skills or personality you would like to be a certain kind of spouse, parent, or lover. Sometimes one's role expectations clash with those of significant others, as this man reports:

---

*Leah and I have arguments with our parents. They expect us to "produce" grandchildren, but neither of us wants the responsibility of children. It has taken each of us over a decade to finish our education by paying for it on our own and working full time. We love our dog, but that doesn't guarantee we would be nurturing parents!*

---

Although many expectations develop prior to assuming a role, persons may develop new expectations for that role. For example, a young mother may watch her boss take his teenage daughters out to lunch every second Saturday and develop new expectations for parenting of older children.

Role expectations are influenced by an imaginative view of yourself—the way you like to think of yourself being and acting. A father may imagine himself telling his child about the "facts of life." Such imaginings are not just daydreams; they serve as a primary source of plans for action or as rehearsal for actual performance. No matter what you imagine, until you enact your role with others, you are dealing with role expectations.

## Role Performance and Accountability

*Role performance* is the actual interactive behavior which defines how the role is enacted. As with role expectations, role performance is influenced by such factors as societal or cultural norms, reactions and role performances of significant and complementary others, and the individual's capacity for enacting the role. *Role accountability* requires a family mechanism for seeing that role functions are accomplished. This may come through family members' development of a sense of responsibility for carrying out their role functions, including the creation of monitoring and corrective mechanisms (Epstein, Bishop, and Baldwin). Without accountability, the family system becomes dysfunctional.

Churches may influence whom their members can marry and how parents and children should act. School and community organizations may give feedback as to how well people are carrying out their family roles. The extent to which you respond to this feedback determines its influence upon you. You may choose to "keep up with the Joneses" or you may decide that the Joneses do not know much about how to live.

The feedback of important persons in your life affect role performance. Perhaps a friend told you he is not as disrespectful to his mother as you are to yours, and you changed your behavior toward your mother.

Persons in complementary roles have direct bearing on how you assume your role. Have you ever tried to reason with a parent who sulks, pamper an independent grandparent, or correct a willful child? You were probably frustrated in enacting your role. On the other hand, if two complementary persons see things in similar ways, it enhances role performance. A college student who believes that she should no longer have to answer for her evening whereabouts will be reinforced by a mother who no longer asks. Thus, the way others assume their roles and comment on our roles affects how we enact our roles.

Additionally, your background influences your behavior. The range of behaviors allowed by one's background limits what he or she can do. For example, if certain communication behaviors are not part of your repertoire, they cannot magically appear in a particular situation. A father may wish he could talk with his son instead of yelling at him or giving orders, but he may not know how to discuss controversial subjects with his child. Self-confidence in attempting to fulfill a role may affect behavior. A shy stepmother may not be able to express affection for her new stepchildren for many months.

Sometimes individual expectations do not match the realities. A woman who had planned to mother many children may find herself comfortable with the role of mother to only one. On occasion, people discover that they can function well in a role they did not expect or desire, as this women discovered:

---

*I was really furious when my husband quit his sales job to finish his degree. I didn't choose the role of provider and I didn't like being conscripted into it. But after a while, I got to feeling very professional and adult. Here I was supporting myself and a husband. I didn't know I had it in me.*

As you will see in later chapters, predictable and unpredictable life crises affect the roles you assume and how you function in them. Thus, although role behavior functions as a result of expectations and interpersonal interactions, unforeseen circumstances may alter life in such a way that roles change drastically from those first planned or enacted. The next section discusses the role functions that adults assume in families.

## SPECIFIC ROLE FUNCTIONS

The concept of the family as a mobile can be applied to roles using McMaster's model of family functioning. In this model, role functioning is examined by discovering how the family allocates responsibilities and handles accountability for them (Epstein, Bishop, and Bladwin 1982). In a well functioning family, allocation of tasks is perceived as fair and reasonable, and accountability is clear. According to this model, five essential family functions serve as a basis for needed family roles. They are:

1. Providing for adult sexual fulfillment and gender modelling for children

2. Providing nurturing and emotional support

3. Providing for individual development

4. Providing kinship maintenance and family management

5. Providing basic resources

These family functions can be categorized as instrumental (providing the resources for the family), affective (support and nurturing, adult sexual needs), and mixed (life-skill development and system upkeep). Within each family system, the existing themes, images, boundaries, and biosocial beliefs affect the way these functions are carried out. This chapter places a greater emphasis on those related to sexual identity, child socialization, nurturing behavior, and maintenance of the family system, since these have stronger implications for communication. As you look at Figure 6.1, imagine a mobile with the systemic parts balanced by the multiple roles operating within the family, such as providing maintenance or adult sexual fulfillment. These role functions become attached or superimposed on the family system characteristics because the ways in which the family survives financially or the children behave affect all parts of the system.

Small and Riley's research (1990) complements the earlier study of Epstein, Bishop, and Baldwin, and enriches a perspective on the interface between work and an individual's personal and family life. They examine how work spillover affects four nonwork role contexts: the parent child relationship, the couple or marital relationship, the use of leisure time for family activities and the home management role. Barnett, Marshall, and Pleck's research on men's multiple roles and stress (1992) focuses on three key roles in men's lives: the job role, the marital role, and the parental role. The same roles and stresses exist in women's lives.

## Providing for Gender Socialization and Sexual Needs

***Gender Socialization*** In a culture which provides multiple possibilities and few clear distinctions, males and females face a dilemma in trying to be both nurturing and strong, as well as both independent and interdependent in family dynamics (Leonard 1982). For example, men today can receive a double message from women who want a man who is expressive, gentle, nurturing, and vulnerable, yet he must be successful, wealthy financially, and capable of taking

**FIGURE 6.1**
**Family Role Functions**

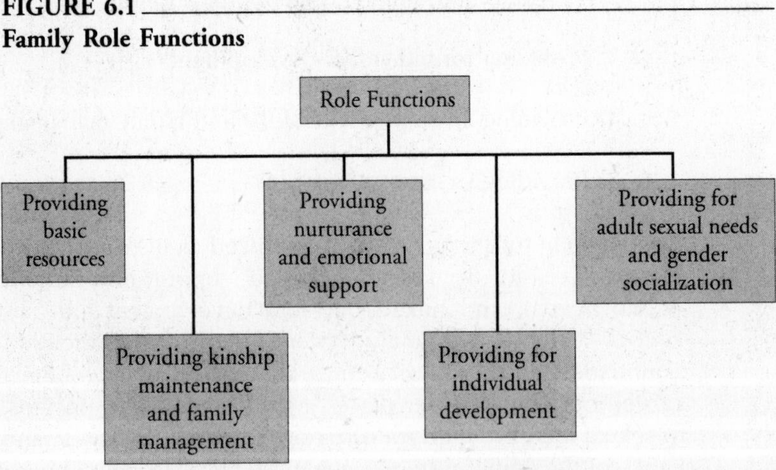

charge (Barnett, Marshall, and Pleck 1992). Women can receive similar conflicting messages (Barnett and Marshall 1991).

The process of learning what it means to be male or female begins at birth. Even as newborns, males and females are handled differently and may be provided with "sex-appropriate" toys. Males and females learn expected behaviors at an early age. Studies of kindergarten children show boys keenly aware of what masculine behaviors are expected of them and restricting their interests and activities to avoid what might be judged feminine. Girls continue to develop feminine expectations gradually over five more years. Certain religious or political groups and cultural traditions support strong male-female distinctions, seeing such practices as necessary for continued family existence and development (Kraemer 1991). For others, such sexually bound distinctions appear repressive.

In his study of male and female roles, Feldman (1982) found that both women and men expected women to care for the home and children, to be warm, affectionate, considerate of others' feelings, dependent, and submissive, and to be complaining, illogical, fragile, subjective, and easily hurt emotionally. Both sexes expected men to have more ambition, a sense of direction in the world, and remain calm, tough, independent, aggressive, and decisive. Men were tolerated when they were tough, powerful, harsh, stern, rigid, and autocratic.

These characteristics are important because of the ways they can affect family communication. Feldman concluded that the culturally defined characteristics of what was appropriate or inappropriate in sex roles indicate that "men are not supposed to act like women, and women are not supposed to act like men" (355). Further verification of differences between mothers and fathers can be found in a study of full-time employed couples who revealed their perceptions of major parental role responsibilities in raising children. Parents agreed highly on role responsibilities for a male child but significantly less for a female child. Fathers placed greater emphasis on girls' acquiring emotional skills and boys' acquiring instrumental skills and attitudes for working in the future (Gilbert, Hanson, and Davis 1982).

The gender-based communication directives you received as a child come into play when you form your own family system. Regarding self-disclosure, men are thought to disclose less about themselves than women and keep more secrets (DeVito 1994). Compared to women, men relate more impersonally to others and see themselves as the embodiment of their roles rather than as humans enacting roles. Men fear that talking about emotions reduces their competitive edge. Shimanoff (1993) reports that men do not trust other men and prefer to express their emotions to women whom they perceive to be more nurturing. If men accept a very restrictive definition of their nurturing communication, they may deprive themselves and

Gender distinctions influence family communication patterns.

their family members of desired intimacy. Vangelisti and Banski (1993) reported that husbands' expressiveness and ability to disclose affected both husbands' and wives' relational satisfaction more than wives ability to be open and expressive. Woman may suffer when female role prescriptions prohibit spontaneous, assertive, or independent communication. Wood and Inman (1993) have challenged some of the research that finds women more effective in self-disclosure via more open, expressive communication. They found that male self-disclosure didn't reduce stress as much as it did for females; men regarded practical help, mutual assistance, and companionship as better benchmarks of caring.

A variety of studies (Barnett, Marshall, and Pleck 1992) found that success in the marital-role and parental-role affected men's mental and physical health. Success in all three roles, marital, parental, and work, led to happiness and satisfaction. Another study revealed parental status moderated the relationship between job role quality and stress for women but not for men, because being a parent "is less central to men's sense of self than to women's" (Barnett and Marshall 1991, 336). Today young adults live very different lives than many of their parents did, as this person indicates:

---

*I recently received a letter from my son which reminded me of how his marriage is so different from ours. He wrote about his week as a "single parent" while his wife was in Los Angeles on business and how he survived the carpools and cooking. Their lifestyle amazes me, but I love to see Brian act as such a caring and active parent to the boys.*

---

Androgyny affects role performance. *Androgyny* refers to "the human capacity for members of both sexes to be masculine and feminine in their behaviors—both dominant and submissive, active and passive, tough and tender" (DeFrain 1979, 237). Androgyny means family members evaluate issues on their merits or demerits, without reference to the gender of the persons involved. The androgynous person is flexible, adaptive, and capable of being both instrumental (assertive, competent, forceful, and independent) and expressive (nurturing, warm, supportive, and compassionate) depending upon the demands of the situation. An androgynous communication style appears in person-oriented families. A position oriented family operates with fixed expectations and maintains strong gender distinctions. An androgynous orientation prizes flexibility and interchangeable gender expectations.

Androgynous married partners demonstrate more understanding of their spouses (Gunter and Gunter 1990). They perceive emotional messages much more accurately and listen more empathically (Indvik and Fitzpatrick 1982). This orientation has been shown to be an important psychological resource for women in high stress situations (Patterson and McCubbin 1984). Mott (1994) reports parents who are less gender-typed in their own activities were less likely to gender type activities for their children. This is especially true of single parent mothers who need more kinds of help from their children. Brown and Mann earlier found single mothers less inclined to differentiate supportive or punitive behaviors on whether their children were male or female (1990).

As noted in the last chapter, sexual behavior is a form of communication that has a powerful effect on the quality of a marital relationship. Even in today's more "open" society, many communication breakdowns stem from an inability of couples to communicate honestly about their sexual relationship. Childhood socialization and the rules of their current system may inhibit adult discussion which may result in frustration, anger, or confusion as noted in the following example:

---

*If there is anything I would wish for my daughter as she enters marriage, it would be the ability to talk to her husband about sex. It was unthinkable to me that men and women could really talk about what gave them pleasure in sexual activity. My husband and I spent years in troubled silence. It took an affair, a separation, and counseling for us to be able to begin to talk about our sexual life.*

---

Feldman (1982) observes that a woman's inhibitions against sexual assertiveness prevent her from being active in meeting her needs. This behavior reinforces the man's expectations that she is not interested but goes along with satisfying his needs. This response blocks his empathic understanding of her needs, and the circle of poor communication continues.

## Providing Nurturing and Support

In a family, members need mutual admiration, support, and reassurance. Transactionally, family happiness develops when each member meets the needs and expectations of the others. When children arrive, parents must negotiate role expectations and enactments. Stamp (1994) noted that, although advice is free and plentiful from friends, books, doctors, in-laws, etc., there remains considerable ambiguity about how to carry out the parental role. Children are socialized by their parents, peers, and the community which, in turn, affect children's capabilities to nurture and be supportive.

***Nurturing Children*** This function incorporates communication since it is the chief process used to transmit parental caring, values, and a sense of community to the children. Through advice, directives, and answers to questions, children learn what parents and society expect of them. Until recently, mothers had greater amounts of contact with their children than fathers and were more likely to contribute to the nurturing process. Children usually experienced their fathers as more distant, less empathic, and less caring, especially in verbal and nonverbal signs of love (Slevin and Balswick 1980; Shepard 1980; Mott 1994). Perhaps these differences are due to the fact that men spend less time in child care, regardless of their work schedules. In one large study, men whose wives worked full time spent 2.3 hours per day in child care compared to 4 hours for mothers (Moen and Dempster-McClain 1987). Another difference relates to single parent families. Ninety percent of the children who live with only one parent reside with their mother (U.S. Census 1992). Yet, men are becoming more active nurturers of young children, and children are finding nurturing from other significant adults ranging from childcare providers to stepparents. Pleck found that the work overload on women continues but that "men's time in the family is increasing while women's is decreasing" (1992, 4). Socialization for nurturing includes learning acceptable or unacceptable communication behaviors, such as yelling, lying, crying, hugging, directness, and silence. Each person experiences communication socialization through a family-of-origin. Cultural institutions also influence childhood and adult communication competence. Nurturing across cultures varies; silence may be affirming in one and alienating in another.

In keeping with the interactive nature of roles, children can resist socialization messages. This frustrates parents, especially those in an extremely rigid family system who cannot be flexible enough to present other options. Communications between parents can also become confused if the mother feels threatened when the father demonstrates to relatives and neighbors that he is capable of childcare. Likewise, the father can feel undermined in his providing role when the wife demonstrates her capabilities in a career and puts pressure on him to take more responsibility for the children (Feldman 1982; Harrison 1993).

***Providing Support and Empathy*** This function, sometimes called the therapeutic function, implies a willingness to listen to problems of another and provide emotional support. The listening must be empathic in order to give the other the understanding needed or the chance to ventilate pent-up feelings of rage, frustration, or exhaustion. Not only should adults do it for one another, but their children require the same kind of listening. This is a gift which may not be appreciated until a child becomes a parent as indicated by the following example:

---

*My father's way is to be very calm and patient with his children. When he helped me with my homework, he would never leave until he knew I understood it completely. He would recall how hard it was to deal with math and science assignments. Now when I explain something I try to see that my children understand because I remember the good feelings that I had when I finally understood my homework.*

---

Empathy implies nonjudgmental understanding of what another family member is sharing with us. In addition to having someone available in times of crisis or to hear about a problem, family members need someone to give them a sense of belonging—a sense of occasional refuge from the realities of the world they want to ignore or gain time to cope with. If the communication channels between family members encourage and permit the expression of open feelings, various individuals in the family can function therapeutically, which includes offering advice and questioning motives.

## Providing for Individual Development

This role function includes those tasks that each individual must fulfill in order to become self-sufficient. While each family member is part of a system, each must develop his or her own personality in order to take pride in his or her self-concept. Baxter speaks of how individuals must simultaneously seek to sustain a "sense of uniqueness from other relationships yet the sense of commonality with other relationships" (1990, 16). Family members who do not develop this role function can easily become dependent or enmeshed in the system. A "take care of me" attitude on the part of any member diminishes the wholeness and interdependence aspects of the family system.

Family members must facilitate for one another opportunities for self-discovery and development of talents. Parents do the majority of this task in their children's formative years, but, from an early age, children influence one another's talents. Competition for grades, positions on sports teams or musical groups, and membership in organizations all create opportunities for self-growth. In many cases, children's activities require the family to communicate regularly with outside persons and institutions, such as coaches or music teachers. An important study indicated that fathers who actively involved themselves in child care compared to those who did not reported higher self-esteem and satisfaction in their parental role. These same fathers complained that they had too little time for their careers, and family responsibilities interfered with their jobs (Barnett, Marshall, and Pleck 1992).

## Providing for Maintenance and Management

***Kinship Maintenance*** One important maintenance function involves kinship ties with the extended family network, as well as ties with neighbors and friends. The kinship maintenance function has direct implications for family communication. Kinship involves sharing, participating in, and promoting the family's welfare as contacts are maintained with relatives outside the family home. In short, it involves boundary management. Parents, children, sisters, brothers, uncles, aunts, and steprelatives are all involved in maintaining a family network. Whether or not one is included or excluded from family events or hears the latest family gossip signifies one's place within the family system. While fulfilling the kinship function, family members may operate within their own rules or rituals, and outsiders may not feel welcome or included in the unique family communication patterns.

Holidays are a special time for family communication. In some families, particularly highly cohesive ones, attendance at get-togethers is mandatory, and only illness or great distances may be acceptable excuses. In some households, the events are painful, since "cut-off" members may be excluded, or members of low cohesive families may feel they are missing something. Blended families must work to create their own rituals to provide members with a sense of identity (Whiteside 1989).

Women do most of the communicating with relatives. One study found that husbands maintained fewer kinship contacts with their relatives and actually had more contact with their wife's relatives. Ninety percent of interaction with the kin was concentrated in three areas: visiting, recreation, and communication by letter and telephone (Bahr et al. 1976).

The single-parent and blended family systems encounter special kinship concerns. For example, in divorced families, there may be special problems in communication with the ex-spouse and his or her new family. One of the ex-partners may refuse to communicate with the other; children may become pawns and resent forced separations from legitimate kinship ties. One study indicated that remarried families' kinship issues differed for spouses. Men were less affected by problems their wives had with their children. Wives were affected more by problems with their stepchildren and former husbands. This resulted in the father curtailing his kinship ties with prior-marriage children (Hobart 1988).

Family networking in order to maintain kinship also varies according to family-of-origin and ethnicity. For example, in a large study of New York City Puerto Rican families, both men and women had equally strong relationships with their relatives. However, Puerto Rican men networked more with other persons outside their families, whereas the women formed their strongest relationship ties within families (Rogler and Procidano 1986).

Since a family consists of persons who consider themselves to be a family, kinship ties often include extended family members bound together by caring, as noted in the following example:

---

*Since my immediate family is dead and any other distant relatives on my husband's side or my side live thousands of miles away, we have worked at creating a "local family." Over the years we have developed close friends who serve as honorary*

(continued on page 162)

*aunts and uncles for the children. The highlight of our Christmas is our annual dinner when we all get together to decorate the tree and the children get to see Uncle Bernard or Aunt Lois within a family context. I feel closer to these people than I do to many of my blood relatives.*

---

Such activities represent a special way to communicate the message that kinship is important. In this age, where families often live great distances from their kin or have few relatives, this idea has merit. When family members feel safe in sharing their problems, joys, and family celebrations, they reap the benefits of the kinship function.

***Management of Daily Needs*** Other role maintenance and management functions include decision making to facilitate housekeeping, childcare, recreation, and taking care of family budgets, bills, income taxes, savings, and investments. Discussions of decision making occur in a later chapter. Housekeeping, childcare, and recreational aspects of family roles will be noted briefly.

The housekeeping function has traditionally meant that the wife performs the cooking, cleaning, and maintenance of the home, but this is changing slowly. Although surveys show men believe housekeeping should be shared, they held that it was more the responsibility of the women. In spite of the facts that most women are working full-time or part-time and involved in careers, cooking, cleaning, laundry, and childcare duties are seldom shared equally (Perry-Jenkins and Folk 1994). Coltrane and Ishii-Kuntz (1992) examined five areas of household labor (meals, dishes, shopping, laundry, and cleaning). Husbands spent an average of 8.6 hours per week on these tasks compared to 20 hours for women. They concluded that wives that had traditional attitudes toward gender roles had husbands who performed less work. They also found that, in couples who married later and delayed children until their late 20s, the men did more housework, and that men whose wives contributed more than they did to the family income performed more housework. Another study of the division of household labor among older couples indicated that, when both worked, the wives did most of the domestic work. The same result was true of a comparative group of older couples where both had retired (Lee 1988b). Yet, wives whose spouses help with household work report far less depression than those with men who do not (Shamir and Boas 1986). Gottman (1994) found that men in successful marriages who do housework were happier and more involved in their marriages. They were less distressed, less lonely, and in better physical and psychological health.

The changes in this area reflect active negotiation between partners since most are creating a housekeeping system different from that in their families-of-origin. In many single parent or dual-career homes, children are taking on increasing responsibility for housekeeping functions, especially daughters. In a large national sample of adolescent chores in dual and single earner families, Benin and Edwards (1990) reported that sons in full-time, dual-earner families spend only one third as much time on chores as sons in traditional families, but daughters in dual-earner families spend 25 percent more time on household duties. The researchers suggested that mothers saw their daughters as more competent to replace them in the house or else were repeating the stereotype that males cannot do housework as well.

Childcare management, or the keeping of the child physically and psychologically safe, is also changing. For the child, management means being bathed, dressed, fed, housed adequately, and protected from terrifying experiences. In a society of smaller families and couples who are child-free by choice, childcare has diminished in importance for some families. Yet, even in small families, the arrival of children requires parents to assume childcare responsibilities for a long period of time.

Even when the children leave home, certain aspects of childcare continue. You can have an ex-wife or ex-husband, but never an ex-child. Also, more young, single mothers are opting to raise their children, and more single parents are taking full responsibility for childcare—making it an enormous task in some cases.

Recreation management implies coordinating those things you do for relaxation, entertainment, or personal development. Families vary as to who is responsible for carrying out the recreational function. More husbands than wives value family recreation activities. Yet, with the rise of dual-career families and increased opportunities in sports for women, this may change. Family recreation can be complicated, because individual members have their own interests as well as the desire or obligation to participate in family activities. Extremely cohesive families encourage much group activity, whereas families with low cohesion may not.

Although the recreational function provides opportunities for nurturing communication, in some families, people perform the role in isolation or non-familial settings. Stereotypically, men have found a recreational niche in strong, masculine, athletic behaviors. Parental behavior telegraphs to children what is expected recreational behavior, and conflicts may result if a child does not measure up. Most of you have seen parents yelling at a Little League umpire or at their eight-year-old batter who has struck out. In some families, recreation, such as bowling or bridge, provides a means to escape from the family. If all recreation is separate, important communication opportunities may be missed.

## Providing Basic Resources

The current economic climate impacts families. Inflation continues, many positions are being eliminated as business and government agencies restructure and downsize, and computers are replacing people, creating a need for both partners to work to pay the bills (Larson, Wilson, and Beley 1994). This may force families into stressful lifestyles.

Traditionally, men were expected to be major providers in families (by a ratio of three to one in most studies) and laws and customs help to carry out these expectations. Women have been limited in terms of the providing function, which historically has affected their decision-making power within the family system. Pleck, who has studied men's roles over a long period of time, declares it is a myth that men are obsessed with their work and ignore their families. His data has shown over many years that men value their family roles "as far more psychologically significant than their paid-work role" (Barnett, Marshall, and Pleck 1992, 359). As more couples share responsibility for providing resources, greater potential for shared power and decision-making results. Stepfamilies often face conflicts as the stepparent may feel he or she has lost control of resources that go toward the stepchildren. Single parents often feel that providing economic stability has become their primary role, when they would wish for a greater balance with nurturing or recreation.

Each family combines these five role functions in unique ways. For example, in the Kondelis family, childrearing and child socialization may no longer be important functions, although recreation may be highly valued and organized by the husband/father. If finances permit, most housekeeping functions may be provided by a cleaning service, whereas providing may be done by both husband and wife. In the Rosenthal family, the single mother may engage primarily in the providing and therapeutic functions, partially delegating childcare and socialization functions to the two older children. Recreation may be more individually oriented, while kinship functions may receive limited attention. Again, ethnicity influences role function, For example, research on two-parent African American families indicate that there is more role flexibility between the partners. As children mature, they participate more actively in many functions. Yet, in some single-parent, dual-career or dual-earner families, children may be inappropriately required to engage in a type or amount of activity usually reserved for a spouse. For example, an older child may assume total childcare or housekeeping responsibilities in a busy dual-career household. In a single-parent system, children may be expected to provide therapeutic listening that might be expected of a spouse in a two-parent household.

# ROLE CONFLICT

*I have had a great deal of experience with conflict in my marriage. I spend most of the time with my in-laws wearing the mask of the "wonderful little woman-wife" who does all the traditional things while they act like guests in my home. I feel such a sense of relief when our visits are over because we each know this is a big fake, but no one will remove the mask.*

This painful statement well describes a serious role conflict. Family roles emerge from the repetitive pattern of behaviors that members use to carry out family functions. If not analyzed or planned, these patterns can cause interpersonal and individual conflicts. Repetition can be boring and confining to individuals who find themselves expected to behave in certain role functions in certain ways. Much negotiation occurs as system members attempt to work out their own definitions of the role interchange. The discussion of role conflicts is divided into interpersonal conflicts over roles and intrapersonal conflicts over roles.

## Interpersonal Conflicts

While individuals may know what is expected of them in a family, not all members perform the expected behaviors. For example, a husband may relinquish the provider function by deciding to write "the great American novel," or suffer a fall that prevents him from returning to work, or being laid off. Consequently, his wife may be thrust into providing for the family which results in potential conflict. When this happens, the organizational structure in the system changes; a new kind of interdependence must evolve. Role changes, especially by parents, upset the balance in the system.

If complementary or significant others have different expectations of the way a person should be performing a role, conflict may occur. A child or adolescent may expect far more nurturing from a parent and complain about the lack of emphasis on it. A wife may expect her husband to assume half the provider responsibility and resent his limited attention to what she considers his duty. The reverse can be true if the wife refuses to work outside the home and the husband feels all the responsibility is unfairly his. Swanson (1992) writes of men being treated as "success objects" who must provide well for their families or else lose respect. Today, most parents face the dilemma of being a good provider and measuring up to new societal expectations of being a sensitive nurturer.

If the priorities or goals of system members are not congruent with each other, role conflict occurs. If money is critical to one spouse and recreation has a high priority for the other, there may be major fights over providing resources versus playing. For many couples, the addition of the first baby signals a whole set of role changes, which are often accompanied by conflict. One spouse may suddenly devote extensive time to the childcare function, thereby neglecting the therapeutic or kinship functions that the other spouse expects and values. The new child changes the allocation of family dollars and brings added pressure on the provider role (Ambry and Margaret 1993).

Feelings for the other person may affect the extent to which conflict occurs. A parent may react differently to each child by basing his or her actions on the child's behavior. For example, a mother with extensive childcare responsibilities may abuse one child and not another. A child of a single parent may be co-opted to serve as a surrogate spouse to provide emotional support. Usually, such actions lead to later conflict as individuals struggle to maintain roles that are not appropriate to their ages or relationships, such as noted below:

---

*As the oldest daughter, I ended up with a great deal of responsibility and feel as if I lost part of my own childhood. My mother was an alcoholic and my father and I almost became the "adult partners" in the house. He expected me to take care of the younger kids and to fix meals when Mom was "drying out." I hated all the work I had to do and all the responsibility. He didn't even want me to get married because he didn't know how he would cope.*

---

These behaviors affect all parts of any family system. Although these and other issues lead to interpersonal role conflict, some people experience role conflict within themselves.

## Intrapersonal Conflicts

Occasionally, people find themselves performing role functions that do not fit their self-concepts, which leads to internal conflict. Some new parents experience difficulty adjusting to childcare responsibilities expected of them. Others find that they did not expect to be breadwinners or do not see themselves as integral members of an extensive kinship network. Such differences between how you see yourself and how you act may lead to intense intrapersonal struggles.

People sometimes find themselves in roles that they expected to assume comfortably but which they cannot perform adequately. Although the new "supermom" is pictured as balancing a career, household duties, and childrearing duties with equanimity, many young women have discovered that there are not enough hours in a day to maintain such a schedule, and they cannot fulfill their ideal wife/mother role. This often leads to disappointment and anger at themselves for not fulfilling expectations.

In a study of the stages in a marital relationship, Cahn (1987) found that acceptance and appreciation functioned as a self-concept support. Communication behaviors such as the desire to participate in a number of social activities with the partner, to share many interests with each other, and to respect one another enhanced their relationship. Couples who took time to debrief and share work experiences greatly increased their relational satisfaction (Vangelisti and Banski 1993). Certainly increasing each partner's sense of worth would affect their role performance and lessen conflicts.

Such interpersonal and individual role conflicts necessitate sensitive and extensive communication among members of a family system if it is to be recalibrated to fit the needs of individual members. Role performance constitutes an important way of regulating family life. Yet, if roles are viewed as "set in stone," they will limit personal and system growth.

## COUPLE AND FAMILY TYPOLOGIES

Couple or family typologies represent another way to explore how roles develop through family interaction. Many family researchers and therapists believe family behavior and organization can be classified into various typologies, or family types, depending upon the patterns of its interactions. When these types emerge, some predictability is possible, and it enables researchers and therapists the opportunity for analysis. A few typologies will be discussed.

### Couple Oriented Typologies

***Fitzpatrick's Couple Types*** The most extensive work done in classifying couple types is found in Fitzpatrick's research (Fitzpatrick, Fallis, and Vance 1982; Noller and Fitzpatrick 1993). In her early work, influenced by Kantor and Lehr, Fitzpatrick (1976; 1977; 1988) tested a large number of characteristics to find out which made a difference in maintaining couple relationships. She isolated eight significant factors:

1. Conflict avoidance
2. Assertiveness
3. Sharing
4. The ideology of traditionalism
5. The ideology of uncertainty and change
6. Temporal (time) regularity
7. Undifferentiated space
8. Autonomy

All eight affect role enactment. An individual or couple fits a type when their answers indicate they possess a number of characteristics. Fitzpatrick designated relational definitions of traditionals, separates, and independents, plus six mixed couple types wherein the husband and wife described their relationship differently. She found 20 percent are traditionals, 17 percent are separates, and 22 percent are independents (1988, 79). Thus, 60 percent can be classified as pure types and 40 percent as mixed.

Independent types accept uncertainty and change. They pay limited attention to schedules and traditional values. Independents represent the most autonomous of the types but do considerable sharing and negotiate autonomy. They do not avoid conflict. Independents are more likely to support an androgynous and flexible sex role (Fitzpatrick 1988, 76).

Separates differ from independents in greater conflict avoidance, more differentiated space needs, fairly regular schedules, and less sharing. In relationships, separates maintain a distance from people even their spouses. They experience little sense of togetherness or autonomy. Separates usually oppose an androgynous sexual orientation and tend to avoid conflict.

Traditionals uphold a fairly conventional belief system and resist change or uncertainty because it threatens their routines. Physical and psychological sharing characterize the traditional type. This leads to a high degree of interdependence and low autonomy. Few boundaries exist in the couple's use of physical and emotional space. They will engage in conflict but would rather avoid it. Uncertainty and change in values upset them. Traditionals, like separates, demonstrate strong sex-typed roles and oppose an androgynous orientation.

The other six mixed types (approximately 40 percent) included traditional/separate, separate/traditional, independent/separate, separate/independent, traditional/independent, and independent/ traditional (Fitzpatrick 1988). In mixed types, the husband is designated by the first term.

Which relational type experiences the greater satisfaction? Which couples are the most cohesive? The answers follow and have implications for role enactment. In their summary of the research, Fitzpatrick and Best (1979) reported traditional couples significantly higher than the other three types on consensus, cohesion, relational satisfaction, and expressing affection. Independents were lower on consensus, open affection to one another, and dyadic satisfaction. However, their lack of agreement on issues regarding dyadic interactions did not impair their cohesiveness. Separates were the least cohesive, but on relational issues appeared high on consensus. Separates demonstrated few expressions of affection toward their spouses and rated lower on dyadic satisfaction. In the separate (husband)/traditional (wife) category, couples had low consensus on a number of relational issues, but they were moderately cohesive. These couples claimed high satisfaction for their relationship and outwardly expressed much affection (Noller and Fitzpatrick 1993).

Table 6–1 summarizes the ways in which couple types responded to a variety of relationship measures, including sex roles and gender perceptions. In predicting communication, you might expect that traditional families would demonstrate affection and sharing of the role functions discussed earlier in this chapter, with males and females remaining in defined positions. You could expect male dominance in attitudes and values regarding the providing, recreational, housekeeping, sex, and kinship functions, since the traditional type resists change. Since independents are more open to change, they might be

**Table 6-1 Couple Type Differences on Relational Measures**

| Couple Types | Marital Satisfaction | Cohesion | Consensus | Affectional Expression | Sex Roles | Psychological Gender States (Wives Only) |
|---|---|---|---|---|---|---|
| Traditionals | High | High | High | Moderately high | Conventional | Feminine |
| Independents | Low | Moderately high | Low | Low | Nonconventional | Sex-typed androgynous |
| Separates | Low | Low | Moderately high | Low | Conventional | Feminine sex-typed |
| Separates/ traditionals | Moderately high | Moderately high | Moderately high | High | Conventional | Feminine sex-typed |
| Other mixed types | Moderately high | Low | Low | Moderately high | Depends on mixed type | Depends on mixed type |

more open to dual-career marriages and sharing the providing and housekeeping functions. Because independents value autonomy and avoid interdependence, individual couple members may be freer in their role functions. This self-reliance might better equip independents to handle the unknown and accept the inevitable changes that occur in roles and life.

The potential for problems when communicating about role functions relates especially to the separates who have not resolved the interdependence/autonomy issue in their marriage. Fitzpatrick uses the label "emotionally divorced" for this type, because separates are least likely to express their feelings to their partners. Thus, if a partner is dissatisfied with the role expectations of the other spouse, yet cannot freely express these feelings, the relationship suffers. Baxter (1991), in her explorations of dialectical theory, suggests Fitzpatrick's traditionals "privilege continuity over discontinuity, with independents privileging change over continuity, with separates somewhere in the middle" (17). She states that traditionals in their families reproduce or continue the conventional ideology of marriage while independents produce a special relationship that departs from societal norms.

***Other Couple Typologies*** Two more recent typologies that have applications to roles in couples are presented in Hochschild's *The Second Shift* (1990) and Gottman's *Why Marriages Succeed or Fail* (1994).

Hochschild's research revealed three types of marital roles for working couples: traditional, egalitarian, and transitional. Although women in traditional couples work, they view themselves primarily as mothers, community members, and gain acceptance through their commitments such as school board member or Scout leader. Husbands in traditional couples focus on their work and expect their wives to manage the home. As a couple they prefer the man base his identity on his work and hold more power in the relationship. Both accept this role definition.

In an egalitarian marriage both partners wish to jointly share home responsibilities as well as take advantage of career opportunities. Power is to be shared and each partner strives to maintain a life balance between career and family, while supporting the other in this effort. The transitional couple holds some of the values, and exhibits some of the behaviors of both the traditional and egalitarian couples. This couple sees the husband's identity as the provider who accepts some responsibility for household management. They see the wife as primarily responsible for home management although involved in a career. Therefore, both experience their identity as involving home and work, but the male focuses more energies on work while the female focuses more on home. Hochschild found most of the couples she interviewed described themselves as transitional in ideology but occasionally they held contradictory views, choosing at times to act in a traditional or egalitarian way.

Gottman classifies his couple types depending upon the style of the conflict interactions between the couple as validating, volatile, and conflict avoiders. He found that lasting marriages existed in all three types if a ratio of five positive interactions to one negative developed over time in the relationship (1994A). In the validating type, partners respect one another's point of view on a variety of topics and, when they disagree, they work out a compromise. This type agrees on most basic issues of sex, money, religion, and children. When they disagree about roles, they listen to one another and refrain from shouting or "hitting below the belt." The volatile type of couple represents the other extreme. It's as if they were born to fight. Any questions over roles and who does what and when, leads to open conflict. They don't fight fairly, and they do it often. Both at work and back in the home, they monitor one another's activities to see who has more power or does more work. The third type, conflict avoiders, abhors negative messages and goes to any length to lessen potential conflicts. They placate and please one another rather than meet their own needs. They walk away from arguments, often giving family members the silent treatment. The attitude on roles is that, "if you can't say anything good about my job in the factory, please say nothing!" This type recognizes that they disagree, but that's okay. They are comfortable with "standoffs," and uncomfortable with rage or protest.

## Family Typologies

Kantor and Lehr's work, *Inside the Family* (1976), serves as the touchstone study of family types. As a means of dealing with the basic family issue of separateness and connectedness, or what Kantor and Lehr called "distance regulation," they developed a six-dimensional social space grid on which family communication takes place. All communication represents efforts by family members to gain access to targets, i.e., things or ideas members want or need. Specifically, family members use two sets of dimensions. One set reaches targets of (1) affect, (2) power, and (3) meaning through the way they regulate the other—the access dimensions of (4) space, (5) time, and (6) energy. In carrying out the functions in any role, all family members have a target or goal of gaining some degree of affect, power, or meaning. Affect means achieving some kind of intimacy or connectedness with the members of the family and receiving some reward in the form of nurturing behavior in their verbal and nonverbal communication. Power implies a member has the independence to select what he or she wants and the ability to get the money, skills, or goods desired. This freedom to choose what an individual wants gives a family member power and the separateness needed to develop autonomy. The third target is meaning. Each family member in the system seeks some philosophical rationale that offers reasons for what happens to them in the family and outside world. The acquisition of meaning by each member develops a stronger self-concept and provides an explanation of why members live as they do. When family members collectively find meaning in their interactions, cohesion develops.

Kantor and Lehr provide descriptions of the access dimensions (space, time, and energy) from an analogical as well as physical point of view. The spatial dimensions include the way a family handles its physical surroundings (exterior and interior) and the ways in which the members' communication regulates their psychological distance from each other. The time dimension includes a consideration of clock time and calendar time in order to understand a family's basic rhythmic patterns. Increasingly, the time couples have to communicate when one or both are working has diminished. The energy dimension deals with the storing and expending of physical and psychological energy. Each of these dimensions would affect role enactment because they regulate behavior. Family communication usually involves at least one access dimension and one target dimension. For example, a wife moves physically closer (space) to her husband in order to gain more affection (target) from him.

Using these six dimensions, the authors have created a typology for viewing families, consisting of open, closed, and random types, acknowledging that actual families may consist of mixtures of types. The ways in which these three family types maintain their boundaries, or regulate distance through access and target dimensions, account for their differences in role enactments.

Closed families tend to regulate functions predictably with fixed boundaries. Such families interact less with the outside world. They require members to fulfill their needs and spend their time and energies within the family. Usually, there are emphases on authority and the continuation of family values. Events in closed families tend to be tightly scheduled and predictable. Family members often focus on the preservation of the past or plan for the future. Energy is controlled, used to maintain the system, and dispersed at a steady rate. Moderation, rather than excess, prevails.

In the open family, boundaries tend to remain flexible as members are encouraged to seek experiences in the outside space and return to the family with ideas the family may use if group consensus develops. Open families seldom use censorship, force, or coercion because they believe family goals will vary, change, and be subject to negotiation. They carry these characteristics into intimacy and conflict situations. Members are more likely to concern themselves with the present, while energy in this type is quite flexible. Family members in their roles do not have total freedom because they cannot use methods of refueling their energy that cause excess harm or discomfort to other family members. For example, a teenager cannot play tapes at the loudest level after eleven o'clock at night when other family members wish to sleep.

Unpredictability and "do-your-own-thing" aptly describe the random family. The boundaries of space surrounding this family are dispersed. Family members and outsiders join in the living space based on interest or desire, or they voluntarily separate from one another without censure. Social appropriateness holds little importance for such members. Time is spent on an irregular basis. Each individual functions according to his or her own rhythm, resulting in high levels of spontaneity. People may change their minds and plans at any time. Energy in the random family fluctuates. No one source for refueling has been predetermined by the family. Members may rapidly spend high levels of energy and then need long refueling periods. The following example illustrates a random family:

---

*I am next to last of eleven children and by the time I came along, the family was in chaos. The younger kids lived with different relatives off and on until we were almost adolescents. When we did live at home, things were always unpredictable. Every morning my mother would put a big pot of cereal on the stove and people would eat when they wanted. You never knew exactly who was going to be sleeping where each night. When I was about ten, my parents got their own life straightened out and enough older kids were gone so that we could live a more "normal" life, although I found it hard to suddenly have rules that were enforced and times when I had to be places.*

---

Table 6–2 summarizes the characteristics that Kantor and Lehr delineated for each of these family types. You may identify more closely

**Table 6-2** Characteristics of Family Types

| Type of Family | Use of Space | Use of Time | Use of Energy |
|---|---|---|---|
| Closed | Fixed | Regular | Steady |
| Open | Movable | Variable | Flexible |
| Random | Dispersed | Irregular | Fluctuating |

with one of the types, or you may find that your family incorporates two of the types. You may also realize your family has shifted in typology over the years.

The following example indicates how a family can change from a closed type to an open over time as circumstances develop:

---

*As I grew up, my parents kept a watchful eye over my three sisters' activities by scrutinizing friends, watching phone calls, keeping strict curfews, chaperoning dates, and generally isolating our family from "them," that is, the rest of the South Bronx community. Dad and Mom knew where you were going and whom you were with and told you what time to return. The communication pattern, mostly nonverbal, was also simple: the better you behaved, the more privileges you were allowed.*

*Then things changed. When my father died, I found myself closer to my mother and vice versa. My sisters also found themselves closer, not only to my mother but to each other. My family has gradually become more open. Today, any requests for either joining or separating are viewed as reasonable and legitimate.*

---

A speculative comparison can be made between Fitzpatrick's and Kantor and Lehr's research. Olson's model of cohesion and adaptability (Chapter 2) can also be integrated into their thinking. Fitzpatrick's and Olson's early work was greatly influenced by Kantor and Lehr. The terminology each theorist uses can be clarified by remembering that Fitzpatrick's autonomy/interdependence is similar to Olson's cohesion dimension and Kantor and Lehr's affect dimension. Adaptability as used by Olson is similar to power (measured behaviorally) in Fitzpatrick and Kantor and Lehr. Fitzpatrick's "ideology" refers to "meaning" in Kantor and Lehr's thinking but does not appear in Olson's work. Communication is included in the behavioral data collected by Fitzpatrick. In Olson's model, communication appears as an enabling dimension, and as distance regulation in Kantor and Lehr's study. Whatever the family or couple type, adults use communication strategies in their various roles which maintain their type and which are important socializing information for children.

## CONCLUSION

This chapter took an interactive approach to roles, stressing the effect of family interaction on role performance. The distinction between position oriented and person oriented roles was developed and applied to communication. The development of roles takes part in a two-step process, role expectations and role performance, both of which have communication components. The five role functions were presented in a mobile model and explained in detail. They are:

1. Providing gender models and adult sexual fulfillment
2. Providing nurturing
3. Providing for individual development
4. Providing kinship maintenance and family management
5. Providing basic resources

Finally, the couple and family typologies, with their predictability, are viewed as sources for understanding the communication that helps to carry out role functions. The recent research cited throughout the chapter indicates the directions in which roles are changing.

A major consideration in examining roles or couple/family types is their dynamic nature, which is viewed in accordance with the personal developments and unpredictable circumstances faced by the people involved. Barnett, Brennan, and Marshall (1994) found role patterns in men and women becoming increasingly similar, especially in dual-earner families. This may well indicate a future trend in roles.

## IN REVIEW

1. Discuss what you think will happen to roles in families by the year 2000. What directions do you see families taking in the future?
2. Compare and contrast the communication tasks required in carrying out the role functions involved in providing resources and nurturance for the family. Describe these functions in a family with which you are familiar.
3. Identify a real or fictional family that has changed over time. Note the role changes and give your reasons for these changes. What has been the effect on the system?

4. Give examples of partners you know that fit Fitzpatrick's couple types. Describe sample communication strategies they use.

5. Using one of the family typologies for roles (for example, Fitzpatrick's, Hochschild's, or Gottman's), analyze your family or another real or fictional family and explain how it fits or doesn't fit the type. Cite examples of communication patterns.

6. Take a position and discuss: A family needs to be more position-oriented than person-oriented in order to function through crises over time.

7. To what extent are role models actually teachers of communication?

# 7

# Power

Power, a central factor in all human life, has a unique impact on family dynamics. In family systems, the issue of power surfaces in the interactions between members. Family members engage in power maneuvers in an attempt to control their lives (Dell 1989). Haley believes that "the struggle for status and the question of who is going to be in charge is basic to human relationships" (Simon 1982, 33).

Where does the power lie? What constitutes power? Do customs, laws, and religion give men in marriage more power than women? Who controls the rules about who can come and go out your front door and at what hours? By the end of this chapter you should have some insights that will enable you to answer these questions. You will sense that power does not operate in a simple, linear way. It is not a physical thing, belonging to one or two and sought by many. It is easy to talk about power as a tangible, or easily observed "thing," but relational power cannot be classified simply. Power resides in the interactions in a relationship; it does not reside with one person in a relationship. The following comment captures this idea:

---

*I see my family as a three ring circus. There are always three or four things going on at once. My mother is the ringmaster! She stands center stage and calls the shots. My father is the promoter and the producer. He keeps everything ready for the arena. My sisters and I are the performers. We compete for the spotlight and each of us thinks our act is the star attraction. Since I'm the oldest, my name always comes first. However, it's hard to say one person has more power than another since we are so very interconnected. Yet, Ringling Brothers had a much easier time getting the show on the road than my parents had.*

---

No family member can remain unaffected by how power operates in the family, because power serves as a subtle and persuasive aspect of family life (Gerber 1991). It's like air, invisible but always present. McAdams (1985) suggests that each family member constructs stories that become organized around two general life themes, power and intimacy. Haley sees interpersonal power struggles as the central issue in human life (Simon 1982).

In order to begin to understand the complexity of power and its communication dynamics within family systems, you need to examine: (1) the concept of power, (2) various aspects of power which impact family systems, (3) the development of power in family systems and (4) communication strategies which affect power.

## THE CONCEPT OF POWER

Power has been defined frequently as the ability or potential to influence others (Mantz and Gioia 1983), but this definition is too limited for application to the family. Power does not belong to an individual; rather, it is a property of a relationship between two or more persons. Thus, the following definition evolves: "Power, a system property, is the ability, potential or actual, of an individual(s) to change the behavior of other members in a social system" (Cromwell and Olson 1975, 5). From a dialectical perspective, power is defined by the way it is used to reduce or increase tensions as individual family members interact with each other over goals or attempts to change behaviors. What irritates one person and causes tension may not bother another. Each responds differently to power moves by other family members. This perspective emphasizes change and flux (Baxter 1991, 1993). The exercise of power becomes an important factor in regulating relational tensions between closeness and distance. The closeness or distance affects cohesion, and power shifts relate to adaptability in a family system.

Family power is dynamic; it is not static, or fixed. The power dimension in a family system may vary greatly over time, depending upon a host of factors, such as the family structure, the developmental stages of the children or parents, the predictable and unpredictable stress encountered by the family, and the economic, cultural, or intellectual resources and opportunities of the family. The power dimension also varies greatly in culturally diverse families. Because the values, histories, and current socio-economic factors of ethnic groups are different from the dominant white culture, power processes may operate differently (Walker 1993). Yet, one cannot assume that most African American, Hispanic, or Asian families exercise power in similar ways.

Power operates transactionally in a family, and any power maneuvers within it have a system-wide effect. One member cannot assert independence or dependence on an issue without affecting other members. As one or more members exert power or respond to others' power moves, the whole system recalibrates itself. The transactional nature of power within a family reflects a member's interdependence. Each member affects the relationships within the family and is affected in return. The system, through its adaptability mechanisms, reacts to all pressures and maintains balance between the power plays and players.

Power affects perception and behavior. The way in which one family member perceives the power dynamics helps determine and explain the reasons for that member's actions. However, the same power issue may be perceived differently by every other family member. Montgomery (1992) noted how a couple imitates other couples, and thus coordinates their relationship with a larger social order. Couples use their knowledge of how power operates in various families within their culture to inform them about how to use power in their own relationship. At the same time the couple sends unique messages to one another that demonstrate their desire for autonomy from society and their desire to interpret their specialness and differences as a couple, as parents and as lovers. Baxter (1987) reported that couples use special interaction routines, games, nicknames, references to events, places, or objects to symbolize relational significance. Power is part of all these messages and routines.

Think of family power as a way of examining the process by which group activity is accomplished. The family collectively interacts about an end or goal that one or more family member desires. This specific goal sometimes conflicts with group or family goals. Power is the ability of one or more family members to prevail in a family setting of conflict so that goals are achieved. To understand power, one must identify the pattern of verbal and nonverbal interaction the family goes through to accomplish a goal. In the following example a student explains how one family member attempts to seize power:

---

*When my parents separated and Dad left the house, my grandmother became the ruling force. She was very domineering and wanted everything done her way. My mother would go along, out of respect for her age, even though she would disagree many times and secretly do what she wanted.*

(continued on page 180)

*Grandma would yell and scream if something wasn't done the way she wanted. She could not accept our opinions. We had no voice in her rulings. Each of us left home sooner than we might have in order to escape her domination.*

## ASPECTS OF POWER IN FAMILY SYSTEMS

McDonald's model of the interrelatedness of units of analysis and dimensions of power (Figure 7.1) helps to depict visually the complexity of power issues (1980a, 844).

**FIGURE 7.1**
**Units of Analysis and Dimensions of Power**

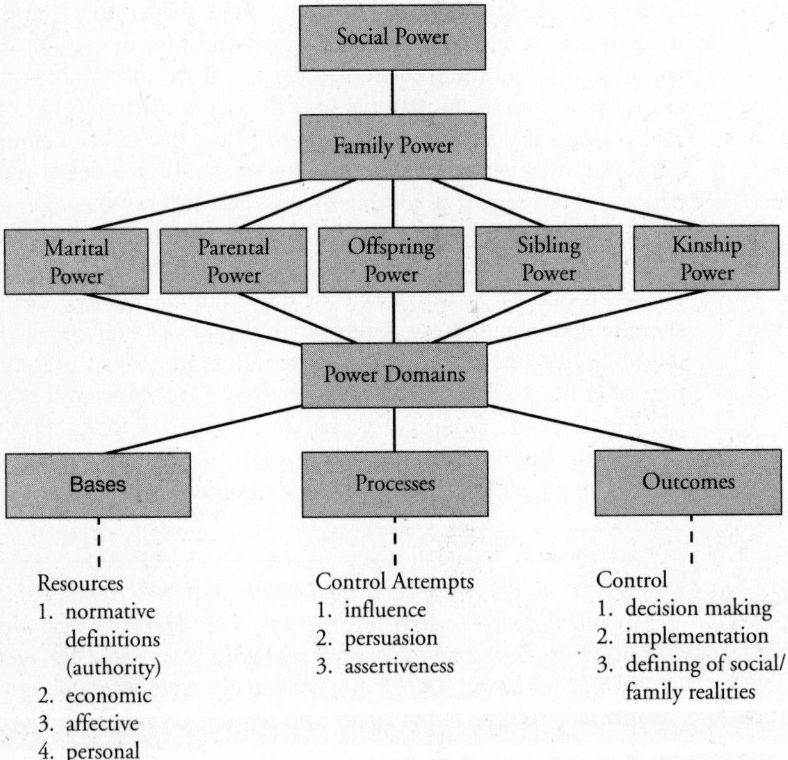

The model begins with social power found in the environment, including the laws, customs, and traditions surrounding any family in the culture or community in which it operates. This model demonstrates how the family is influenced by other systems in the social sphere, such as government, education, business, or religious organizations. Family power is tied directly to the family system's interactions with this ecosystem or a larger social system. Family power is a system property, which McDonald divides into marital (husband/wife power dynamics), parental power (mother/father power), offspring (children/parent interactions), sibling (brother/sister, or combinations of sister/sister and brother/brother), and kinship (grandparent/ aunts/uncles/stepfamily members). When you consider the large percentage of stepfamilies in today's society, you can imagine some of the complex power issues which are included under the term kinship power. The power domains include the areas along which power develops, ranging from the bases of power, through the strategies or process of control to the outcomes. Yet, in real life this is a dynamic rather than linear experience. The following discussion attempts to clarify the concept of power, by discussing three family power domains: (1) power bases, (2) power processes, and (3) power outcomes.

## Power Bases

The bases of family power are the sources of power or resources family members can use to increase their chances of exerting control in a specific situation. Resources consist of whatever is rewarding to an individual or a relationship. Thus, a resource is anything that one partner makes available to the other to satisfy needs or attain goals. No two family members within a system utilize exactly the same resources to achieve their ends. You may exert power because of your education or assertiveness. Your sister's power may come from her strong personality, while your mother may have the authority to veto decisions. Yet, unless others respond to these power positions, no power can be exerted. If your brother does not respond to your assertiveness, you are powerless in relation to him. Montgomery (1994) noted how families over time find ways of relating that work for their family but wouldn't for another. Families develop a relational culture through the ways they engage in, interpret, and evaluate the communication behaviors in their use of power resources with other family members. The power outcomes represent and reinforce the special identity they have in comparison with other families.

There are many models which explain bases or resources of power (McDonald 1981; French and Raven 1975, 1959). McDonalds' five resources serve as bases from which persons may derive power.

They include normative, economic, affective, personal, and cognitive resources.

1. *Normative resources* refer to the family's values and to the cultural or societal definitions of where the authority lies. The expectations of how power is generated and later used depends upon cultural factors, often going back to the families-of-origin. Some families have norms that expect the father to do the providing while other families expect power to emerge based on individual strengths or talents. Normative definitions represent the culturally internalized expectations of the nature of the marriage relationship and perceived role expectations and obligations of the parents and/or children of the family (McDonald, 1981).

2. *Economic resources* refer to the monetary control exerted by the breadwinner and/or persons designated to make financial decisions. Economic power comes from wages earned and money saved or inherited. The ability of each partner or family member to earn a living affects power.

3. *Affective resources* refer to the level of involvement with and degree of dependence on others. Affective resources reflect who in the family nurtures others and how each member in the family meets his or her needs for feeling loved or belonging to the system. These resources may be seen in the use of relational currencies.

4. *Personal resources* refer to each family member's personality, physical appearance, and role competence. They also include interpersonal factors which may cause the individual to be perceived as attractive or competent, and, therefore, accorded power. One's self perception of attractiveness or personality strengths relates to self concept and in turn to perceptions of powerfulness or powerlessness.

5. *Cognitive resources* refer to the insight family members have, or how their power influences their own actions and affects others. It deals with using intelligence to logically sense what power options are available. Not all family members cognitively achieve the same level of awareness, especially when under stress or conflict.

McDonald's bases of power go beyond the earlier work of French and Raven (1975, 218–19). French and Raven listed six resource bases of power: (1) punishment or coercive power, (2) positive reinforcement or reward power, (3) expertise or knowledge power, (4) legitimacy or power gained through a position, (5) identification or referent power gained through affiliation, and (6) persuasion or information power. McDonald (1980a) suggests French and Raven's bases of social power could be viewed as resources according to his model.

Although not a perfect match, French and Raven's work can be integrated with McDonald's model if you think of punishment and positive reinforcement as related both to what's normative in a family and who has the authority or who is expected to enforce the rules. Reinforcement or reward power often has an economic tie or may be affective in the forms of hugs or messages of praise. Expertise relates to McDonald's personal and cognitive bases of power. When you believe another family member knows more about a subject than you do, you defer to them and grant them the power to use their skill or knowledge. Identification may relate to both McDonald's personal and cognitive resources as affiliation may add to one's self concept and knowledge. These speculative linkages demonstrate how such approaches complement each other.

Note that these power terms are defined by the way in which the situation is perceived by others. In a family relationship, no member possesses all five of these power sources equally or uses all of them in a given situation. Some may never be used, while others may be used in combination. It is possible for a husband to use normative and economic power resources extensively in his interactions and simultaneously for his wife to use cognitive and affective resources in her interactions. Children in the same family might use affective and personal power resources, especially when they are younger. This process is described by a young respondent:

*I can influence Ryan. I simply have to go about it the right way! There are times he sets rules and expects the rest of us to follow them. Then I join with my sisters and together we find ways to go around the rules. We tease him and keep bugging him until we wear him down.*

Power becomes a resource base wherein family members perceive ways in which they can use communication in order to establish their status in various family situations. Family members accumulate power options in attempts to define their relationships (Barge 1984).

Power bases are related to many factors such as income and culture. In a large cross-cultural study of spousal organization, spousal resources, and marital power, it was found that wives in biological rather than extended family structures and in societies with matriarchal rather than patriarchal customs of residence and descent had far more power (Warner, Lee, and Lee 1986). Thus, the more complex the family structure is in a culture, the less power wives possessed and the more supervision they experienced in extended families. According to Blumstein and Schwartz (1983), discovering how money bestows power reveals crucial things about a relationship (53). In their study of American couples, money established the balance of power in all couple types except lesbians. According to Blumstein and Schwartz, money represents identity and power to men, security and autonomy to women. Within various cultures power may reflect age and family position. Whereas parents in Jewish families tend to have democratic relationships with their children, in Italian families the father tends to be an authoritarian and undisputed head of the household (McGoldrick 1982a).

## Power Processes

The ways in which power operates in a family are revealed by its power processes, or by studying ongoing interactions among family members. These processes affect interactions in family discussions, arguments, problem solving, decision making, and especially in times of crisis. In his model (Figure 7.1 on page 180), McDonald refers to these processes as control attempts through influence, persuasion, and assertiveness. Power processes include the interactional techniques individual family members use in their attempts to control the negotiation on decision making. Since each family member exercises different degrees of influence, persuasion, or assertiveness, the power process is unique for each family system. No two are alike.

These power processes reflect the internal resources that each family member accumulates by living interpersonally together. The internal resources are the amount and types of information family members process from one another within the family. When Dad wants a positive response from Mom or a daughter, he must use an appropriate message stimulus. The effectiveness of the message depends upon Dad's abilities to perceive how Mom or the daughter will react to different message strategies. Family members learn how to discriminate in the selection of the right stimulus message to achieve their goals. In other words, Randy could have ample economic or affective resource power and still fail to gain his son's compliance to accept a curfew if he doesn't select the right message. Power is transmitted through the use of messages that discriminate in specific situations how best to implement an idea to meet a need or goal. Over time, each family member accumulates a knowledge of what internal resources will communicate better in different situations, both positive and negative (deTurck and Miller 1986).

Researchers have examined the number of times people talk, how long they talk, to whom they address their comments, and how long a talk session lasts (Johnson and Vinson 1990). They have also analyzed questioning, interrupting, and silence patterns and concluded that family members who talk most frequently and for the longest periods of time are dominant, and those who receive the most communication are the most powerful (Berger 1980).

Yet, as you know from your own experience, the longest or loudest talker may not hold the power in each situation. One must distinguish between the power attempts a person makes and the final outcomes. Assertiveness and control maneuvers affect family power. Assertiveness means the number of attempts, for example, that Debra makes to change the behavior of her sister. Control represents the influence or number of effective attempts that Debra made that changed the behavior of her husband or sister.

As you remember, all messages in a family are co-created by the senders and receivers. Family members may send mixed messages, which are difficult to analyze accurately. When an individual says one thing but means and wants something else, confusion results. Contradiction often appears in the nonverbal aspects of a message. In analyzing power messages, both the content and relationship dimensions must be analyzed carefully to understand family communication. A family member who acts helpless attempts to control the behavior in a relationship just as effectively as another who dominates and insists on specific behavior, as this respondent reports:

---

*My sister, I think, has a great deal of power in my family because she positions herself as dependent and helpless. Everyone is supposed to help Charmaine because "she can't cope." I think she is highly capable, deliberately or not, of manipulating everyone to meet her needs. She has always possessed this quality. She preferred to remain unemployed while she was single! And, now that she has a kid, she has a very good reason to not work and to need help in every way—money, child care, home, car. My mother falls for it all the time.*

---

Some studies indicate wives display "powerless" language in that they use two and one-half times more tag questions, (e.g., "This is what I'm saying, isn't it?") and five times more hedges (e.g., We agreed to do this, didn't we?") than their spouses. However, closer analysis reveals that although men use less of them, they do indeed use them also to get complete attention and more detailed answers. In addition, women use tag questions and hedges creatively and assertively to accomplish their communication goals and improve interpersonal relationships (Giles and Wisemann 1987; Johnson and Vinson 1990).

Messages created by ill or dysfunctional members can influence family power. Families with alcoholic members have learned just how powerful that member can be. Everyone may learn to tiptoe around the drinker and develop a proactive way of living—planning personal moves in order to minimize the alcoholic's verbal abuse. This places the alcoholic into a central and powerful position in the family although he or she may be talked about as weak or helpless. Such a situation is described in the following example:

---

*My sister and I would meet at the front door to our house after school to report to each other on our father's mood. He was either in a "good" mood (sober) or a "bad" mood (drinking) and Robin and I tailored our actions and plans to his mood. We learned to adapt to whatever mood and situation came our way.*

---

## Power Outcomes

The final area, family power outcomes, focuses upon those issues involving who makes decisions and who wins. In this aspect, one or more family members get their way or receive rights or privileges of leadership. McDonald's model also equates power outcomes with control through decision-making, implementation activities, and further defining the social-family context in which the power is carried out. In this last item, which is number three under "outcomes" in his model, McDonald cautions readers to remember that what becomes a power outcome depends on who controls the family situations, which determines the range of possible decisions. Also, who in the family, or what alliance of members, decides which decisions to make or which to ignore? If the decision is also to delegate authority, who in the family can decide who will or who will not do something?

Conflict can function as a necessary condition for power. Through conflict, family members attempt to settle their differences. However, power resources can influence outcomes by suppressing potentially conflictual situations. Power hierarchies in the family system also establish guidelines for power processes that avoid conflicts yet affect power outcomes. Family members have orchestration power and implementation power. Orchestration power means that a family member usually makes decisions that do not infringe upon his or her time but determine the family lifestyle and major aspects of the system. The one with orchestration power can delegate unimportant and time-consuming decisions to the spouse or older child who derives implementation power by carrying out these decisions. In the

Family power outcomes focus on the issues involving who makes the decisions and who wins.

model of power (Figure 7.1 on page 180), orchestration (related to decision making) and implementation appear under outcomes as controls.

Power bases influence power outcomes. Family members who hold normative positions of authority may have the greatest power. Often, the balance of power rests with the partner who contributes the greatest economic resources to the marriage. Sources of power may be tied to rewards, which affect outcomes. It may be rewarding to receive praise, to gain information, to learn from an expert, to identify with another person, to be persuaded, or, most importantly, to be confirmed by others. In a study of control in marriages, Ross (1991) equated control to various power dimensions. She concludes that marriage represents a trade-off for women. Marriage increased married women's income resources, which increased their sense of control, but decreased their autonomy, especially their sense of independence. Marriage had less effect upon men's sense of control. She attributes this difference to the fact that 88 percent of the husbands earned more and held the dominant position largely because of the economic resources they contributed to the family (835–837).

Some family members who give much to others, both emotionally and economically, expect much in return. The family member who suffers a real or perceived abuse of power or an injustice caused by one or more members may become upset, and this upsets the family system's balance. A family member who cannot achieve harmony within the system because he or she feels powerless may, in extreme circumstances, resort to separation, divorce, desertion, suicide, murder, or beating. The exit act may be an important power play to a family member, but it can create new problems. Children may feel trapped and have to wait until legal age to exercise their power to reject a defective family system. Family members consciously and unconsciously obtain certain outcomes from the actions they use in a power struggle. In many well-functioning families, members attempt to provide resources for each other in order to maintain a certain level of harmony.

In his review of power in families, Berger suggests that, although the classic Blood and Wolfe study found a positive relationship between the income, educational level, and occupational prestige of the husband and the extent of his power, "the absolute number of resources a person brings to the marriage does not determine his or her power, but rather the relative contribution of resources to the relationship" (210). He maintains that most of the studies he reviewed provide support for the resource theory but found notable exceptions, particularly in studies of other cultures. Berger concludes that resources have been defined narrowly—mainly as economic contributions and social prestige—and suggest that family research should include an analysis of resources, such as interpersonal skills, and personality orientations such as dominance, physical attractiveness, and sense of humor.

Marital power involves the extent to which one spouse loves and needs the other. Safilios-Rothschild's (1970) extension of Waller's important research on the "principle of least interest" suggests that the spouse with the strongest feelings puts himself or herself in a less powerful position, because the person with less interest can more easily control the one more involved. She also suggests that the existence of an alternative relationship provides power to one or another family member. This concept is described in the following example:

---

*One of the ways I was finally able to live at home with some degree of peace was to make it clear to my father that I could and would go and live with his sister if he kept hitting me. My mother agreed with my position although she didn't like it, and he finally realized I was serious. Once he understood that I had somewhere else to go, he began to treat me better.*

---

In discussing options for couples, Berger states, "The mere existence of alternatives does not ensure increased power for the spouse who has them; in addition, the other spouse must have some degree of commitment to the relationship so that the alternatives of the other spouse represent a real threat" (215). If Mark does not care deeply about Kristie anymore, he may not become terribly upset by Kristie's affair with another man, and Kristie may not be able to use this new interest in a power play to win Mark back. According to systems theory, this change of feelings will affect the mutual influence and punctuation of messages. Remaining in the relationship requires system recalibration if the affair continues.

Couples may enter a relationship with unequal power, but the relationship can achieve balance over time. One family member may have most of the power in one area, and both may perceive their power as balanced. Also, the sharing of decisions and tasks causes the systemic balancing principle to operate. Many couples may attempt to develop family themes that stress equality of power, and those with children may encourage sharing of power with them. Finally themes such as "Each person is an individual" or "We respect all opinions" may lead to shared power. The following example illustrates how power changes over time in a relationship:

---

*In the beginning of our relationship, Jack, who is older, tended to dominate. He had a lover for several years and when that commitment ended, he made up his mind to be more autonomous in any future relationship. I resented his treating me as if I were his former partner and assuming that we would conflict in similar situations in the same way. His behavior limited my trust in our relationship. Now that we have been together over five years, he realizes that the past is not the present. We can make joint decisions, and both of us are much happier.*

---

Each family uses a variety of power sources relevant to its needs and the personalities involved. In some families, traditional roles, including the biosocial issue of male dominance, are clearly defined, and since no one challenges them, the family operates as if that were the only way to function. In other families, negotiation has resulted in mutually acceptable compromises on power issues. The following section considers the development of power within marital and family systems.

## DEVELOPMENT OF POWER IN FAMILY SYSTEMS

Due to the systemic nature of a family relationship, power occurs in a transactional manner. An alcoholic cannot control a spouse unless the nonalcoholic spouse permits it. A mother relinquishes her own personal control when she gives an "acting-out" child power over her. Only the small child who has limited means of resisting power moves must accept certain power outcomes; for example, an abused toddler has few means of resisting punishment. Women have argued that they also have limited means of resisting power because in our culture, power outcomes have been largely, and sometimes unfairly, managed by men. Society has affected the development of power within families.

These thoughts about power relationships relate to family boundaries, themes, and biosocial issues. If a family decides that each member, regardless of sex, should develop his or her potential in order to be self-sufficient, the power process and outcomes will differ from a family that believes men should take care of women. This belief limits the boundaries and possible future power options of female members. If, however, the family cultivates a theme of achievement for every member, such as "The Nicholsens rank at the top of their classes" or "The Garcias will be active in politics and public service," the power dimensions will reflect these goals. Over time, the family system creates patterns of power that reveal to outsiders how these themes operate.

### Types of Power Patterns

Spousal authority may be examined by the number and type of areas over which each spouse exercises authority. The spouse with the greater range of authority has the higher relative authority. Spouses may have shared authority, where there are areas of life jointly managed. There are four authority types: wife-dominant, husband-dominant, syncratic, and autonomic. In husband- or wife-dominated families, such as described in the following example, major areas of activity are influenced and controlled by the dominant spouse:

*Mother decides things and gets her way by using her temper, yelling, screaming, and crying if Dad or any of us strongly object. Dad determines when to cut the grass, time for sons to get haircuts, how long my sisters can wear their hair, where to eat or go for entertainment or groceries, and when any of us kids can leave the house after supper. I wait and wait—until he finally decides when he wants to eat dinner, which determines when I can get ready to go out, and so on. I never get anywhere on time.*

---

Dominance by one spouse permeates all areas of family power: the use of resources or bases, power processes, and power outcomes. One spouse demonstrates control of power in the system, while the other accepts such control. Thus, one spouse often orchestrates and the other implements the power. However, the type of power that families use depends upon the mutual activity or inactivity of all members of the family. Support groups for families with addicted members recognize how power transactionally affects all members. In these groups family members learn how to cope with some of the power maneuvers they encounter. This includes learning how to ignore power moves that hook family members into nonproductive behaviors. Highly skewed relationships, such as extreme husband- or wife-dominance, have greater violence (Allen and Strauss, 1979). A further finding indicates that the lower a husband's economic and prestige resources were relative to his wife's, the more likely he would use physical violence (coercive power) to maintain a dominant male power position (85).

The amount of violence or abuse each parent experienced in his or her family-of-origin relates directly to the use of coercive power in families. The frequent observation of abuse in the family-of-origin consistently indicated a risk for wife abuse (Marshall and Rose 1988, 414). Vangelisti (1993) states that negative emotions in family relationships can become more intense and irrational than those in other close relationships because families are together longer in an environment with closer and more frequent contact. Thus, there is more opportunity for power maneuvers on a daily, even hourly, basis. Because family members assume their relationships have a long future, individual members may see this as a "license" to violate conversational and relational norms that they would not otherwise violate (49). This may explain why some family members make coercive power moves that they wouldn't make with close friends.

In couples with more equally divided power, the structure can be described as either syncratic or autonomic. A syncratic relationship, characterized by much shared authority and joint decision making, implies that each spouse has a strong say in all important areas. The next example reveals a couple that realized the value of their syncratic relationships:

---

*When Jim and I married, we agreed never to make big decisions alone, and we've been able to live with that. This way we*

(continued on page 192)

*share the risks and the joys of whatever happens. It just works out best between us if we wait on deciding all important matters until we sound out the other's opinions. Neither of us wants to force the other to accept something disliked. It's when we decide over the little things that I know that each of us respects the rights of the other and wants equal consideration.*

---

In the autonomic power structure, the couple divides authority, i.e., the husband and wife have relatively equal authority but in different areas. Each spouse is completely responsible for specific matters. The division of areas usually coincides closely with role expectations.

Shared power situations reflect specific agreements or role definitions about who controls what situations. The wife might have more power over the budget, vacation plans, and choice of new home and the husband more power over the selection of schools, buying anything with a motor in it, and whether the family moves to another state.

## Power and Marital Satisfaction

As you might imagine, certain power arrangements can increase marital satisfaction (Giblin 1994). High levels of marital satisfaction occur most frequently among egalitarian (syncratic or autonomic) couples, followed by husband-dominated couples, and least among wife-dominated couples (Corrales 1975, 198). In a study of 776 couples in the Los Angeles area, over two thirds of husband-dominant, syncratic, and autonomic couples reported themselves "very satisfied"; however, only 20 percent of wife-dominant couples were "very satisfied" (Raven, Centers, and Rodriges 1975).

Research by Corrales also suggests that women do not seem satisfied when dominating a marriage. In a study in which the wives indicated they dominated, they gave themselves low satisfaction scores. This outcome suggests that wives exercise power by default to compensate for a weak or ignoring husband. In this same investigation, one quarter of the systems were wife-dominant; these same wives had only 10 percent of the authority regarding final decision making. Corrales explained this discrepancy as follows: "The spouse with little authority may seek less visible ways to make her or his power felt. Interactive control appears to be one such way" (208). One sidelight is that husbands in wife-dominant marriages indicated they were not as dissatisfied as their wives. Kolb and Strauss (1974) explained this outcome with their "role incapacity" theory, which posits that, when a man relinquishes his traditional leadership role or fails to carry out his part in an egalitarian relationship, the wife becomes dissatisfied, because she feels she married a less competent man.

Women often feel that power options benefit men in our society. They are expected to carry the primary burden of child care and nurturing, yet increasingly expected to succeed in jobs as either dual-earner or dual-career participants. Boss and Thorn (1989) maintain, "Women have long been asked to 'stand by their man' when he has a demanding job to do in the work world; while needing her to do this, he is not labeled pejoratively as 'overfunctioning' but positively as doing his job well. He is labeled as a 'success' while she is labeled as 'hovering,' 'smothering,' and 'overfunctioning.' She can't win" (1989, 85). Indeed in some families men are granted powers that women are not. A number of women have to challenge men to establish some semblance of equality.

Wives and husbands react differently to dissatisfaction in marriage (Roberts and Krokoff 1990). Men tend to take a coercive stance toward their partners whereas women take an affiliative position which uses communication strategies such as reconciling, resolving, and appealing to fairness. Men express coerciveness in strategies that indicate rejecting, blaming, or using guilt (White 1989). In a study of dissatisfied marriages, when the husband withdrew from interactions, the wife's hostility increased. In satisfied marriages, the husband's displeasure predicted the wife's displeasure, and the wife's withdrawal predicted the husband's withdrawal (Roberts and Korkoff). In a study of gender and power in violent marriages, Gerber (1991) found few differences between how men and women were perceived when the roles were reversed. Violent women who abused their husbands were rated much the same as violent men when they asserted themselves negatively and exerted their wills over men.

If the question arises, "Do men or women have more power?," remember that, historically, research indicates that men overestimate and women underestimate their respective power in the family. Self reports reveal individuals may underestimate their power and overestimate their partner's.

deTurck and Miller (1986) found that husbands and wives who carefully discriminated and then adapted messages to their partner's individualistic beliefs, attitudes, needs, and desires experienced greater marital satisfaction and better conjugal power outcomes than those couples who communicated using more stereotyped cultural, social, and role expectations. Both husbands and wives were happier when they had the ability to exert social control over their partner. This kind of marital power, however, influenced greatly wives' self-esteem, but not their husbands'. An interesting sidelight of their research using the Conjugal Understanding Measure is that adaptability frequently determines the quality of marital relationships.

A study of marital happiness in dual-career African-American families reveals that family cohesion was the strongest determinant of happiness for the husbands, but quality communication was the most important for wives (Thomas 1990). In this and other studies cited, these interesting results have to be connected to the way power is processed in different families.

Wives' successful use of coercive control enhanced their self-esteem and confidence that other family members appreciated their company. This research and other studies indicted that, as women adopt more male oriented persuasion tactics, they equalize the power between the spouses and suffer less from the challenge (deTurck 1985; Burgoon, Dillard, and Doran 1984). Males use more coercive power in resolving conflict if either they or their wives were dissatisfied. Although women had higher rates of coercive behavior overall than their spouses, the use of this kind of power was not related to their marital satisfaction with partners or self-esteem (White 1989).

The type of power processes used by couples can often be traced to their experience in their respective families-of-origin. Growing up in a family in which people were physically controlled may lead a person to adopt the same method, particularly when other alternatives are not immediately available. A son who had a dominant father may find it very difficult to visualize himself in an equal-dominance relationship with his wife. The next example illustrates how children can be influenced by their parents' use of power:

---

*My German father and my Irish mother both exercised power over us in different ways. My father used to beat us whenever we got out of line, and that power move was very obvious. On the other hand, my mother never touched us, but she probably exercised greater power through her use of silence. Whenever we did something she did not approve of, she just stopped talking to us—it was as if we did not exist. Most of the time the silent treatment lasted for a few hours, but sometimes it would last for a few days. My brother used to say it was so quiet "you could hear a mouse pee on a cotton ball." I hated the silence more than the beatings.*

---

A family-of-origin serves as the first power base in which a child learns to function. The strategies used there are often repeated later in a child's adult life. Certain types of power strategies, such as silence, seem to move from generation to generation, because such control was learned at an early age and often not questioned.

## Children and Power

Children have great influence on family power situations. Early studies often ignored them, possibly on the assumption that parents controlled decisions and that children had to follow their directions. Traditionally, parents are expected to control and be responsible for their children's behavior. The law also supports the idea of power in the parents' hands. In no other relationship within a family system does a person have such complete power over another as parents do over young children. Children need to be included in any study of power because of their impact on making the family system more than the sum of its parts. Parents replying to questionnaires indicated that they possessed power, but when trained observers used behavioral methods to measure power, they found that children definitely exercised power in a family (Turk and Bell, 220). With the large percentage increase in the number of working mothers, both children and adolescents assume more personal and domestic responsibilities. This affects not only children's power but enhances their maturity and sense of self-reliance (Demo 1992).

A whole new power scheme emerges when two family members become three, four, or more. Alliances can form between and among family members, upsetting the original balance of power. The door is open for two-against-one power plays and all other possible combinations. In an era of smaller families, an only child or two siblings may have four living grandparents who divert many resources to the grandchildren or the parental generation to support them in child rearing, and, thus, the children gain resources for themselves and the system.

The number of children definitely affects power because couples who have been married fewer years and had less children were more satisfied with their marriage than those couples married longer and with more children (White). Children also gain power by forming alliances with one parent, as in the following example:

---

*When I was growing up, I was very close to my father and we usually agreed on things, so my mother began to see it as "the two of you against me." I thought it was silly because we enjoyed being together, and we did not mean to be against her, but, as I've grown older, I can understand that she felt left out. Now, I often feel outmatched when my son and my husband agree on things and I do not.*

---

***Power Interactions and Alliances*** Often children influence the interaction and outcomes of power struggles in families by using power plays such as interruptions or illness. Adolescents identify with the parent who has the most power over their behaviors; they see the father as holding more outcome-control power (McDonald 1980b). They seem to identify more closely with their same-sex parent, making for power alliances (Acock and Yang 1984). However, daughters identify with the father when they perceive that he has more legitimate power than the mother. Sons identify with the mother only to the degree that she controls outcomes and has referent power. In a cross-cultural study of Japanese and American fathers, results revealed American fathers on weekends spent two hours per day with their adolescent sons and one hour per weekday. This contrasted to Japanese fathers spending one half that time. However, Japanese fathers spent slightly more time with daughters than sons. American fathers spent much more time with sons (Ishii-Kuntz, 1994).

In many families one spouse consciously or unconsciously coopts a child into an ally position in order to increase the strength of his or her position. Similarly, children become adept at playing one parent against the other. "Daddy said I could do it" or "If Mom was here, she'd let me" has echoed through most homes as new alliances form. Blended families are especially vulnerable as children quote exspouses' ideas and unsolicited opinions.

Alliances take varied forms. Many alliances often follow a same-sex bias, as boys and girls are expected to be like their respective parents. "My mother and I stick up for each other against the men" represents such a power move. Children pick up patterns of behavior at an early age from observing their parents. Note this in the following example:

---

*I couldn't believe it when I heard my four-year-old grandson announce to his mother and two-year-old sister, "The men will go the store; the women will stay home." He then turned and followed me out to the car. When I asked him about it, he replied, "Men do things together."*

---

Parents may form an alliance against the children, establishing an inflexible boundary that prevents negotiation or discussion. The extended family can become a part of the power block to be used in both everyday and crisis situations. Single-parent families display unique power alliances, due to the presence of one adult. A potential advantage for a child in a single-parent family is that the child may negotiate directly with the parent for immediate answers and have direct personal power (Wieting and McLaren). Most single mothers cannot say, "I'll let you know after I talk it over with your father." However, the same child cannot form a parent-child alliance to try to change a decision the way a child can in a two-parent family. Yet, either the parent or the child may create an alliance with a grandparent. Blended families often contend with children's playing one side of the family against the other. "She can't tell me what to do, she's not my real mother" is the kind of communication that may cause years of pain as new roles are negotiated.

Some alliances continue in families over a period of time; others exist only for reaching a specific decision. The results of past alliances can obligate family members to feel they must support another on an issue to repay a debt. For example, "Roy helped me convince Dad to let me buy a new ten-speed bike. Now I ought to help him argue with Dad to get his own car." Wives and husbands can also form alliances with one another or their children and behave in this way. Alliances in some families demand loyalty and "payoffs," which affect a fair use of power in the family system. It is also a way members of families adapt to the needs and frustrations of living together in the same system. Alliance members are able to pool their individual assets so as to increase their chances of dominance. Parents should not ignore their adult power responsibilities, and no child should feel persuaded to assume premature responsibilities (Beavers 1982).

***Power Development*** Although young children exercise power, they develop more independent power as they grow older when they demand and can handle more power within the family structure. Whereas a six-year-old may fight for a later bedtime, a sixteen-year-old fights for independence. A school age child may begin to have expertise in some areas unknown to his or her parents, thereby gaining power. Each of you has seen a small child explain computers, metrics, or a board game to a confused adult. Parents often provide their children with educational opportunities and material advantages they never had. The resulting knowledge and prestige can give children an additional advantage over their parents in power struggles.

Adolescence is a difficult time in certain families as sons and daughters rebel against normative parental power, yet, for adaptable systems, the adolescents' talents and skills may be welcome. In a study of the differences in the perception of power by adolescents in four different ethnic family groups, the researchers found that, during late adolescence, girls increasingly perceived their mothers in a variety of power roles, in addition to nurturing roles. Boys in late adolescence continued to see their fathers in more power roles and not their mothers (McDermott et al. 1987). The next remarks describe how the family of origin and cultural background influence power outcomes:

*Within our Thai culture, children are taught early to defer and show respect to their elders. Given names are rarely used in conversation, except for older family members talking to younger ones. Respect for relationships are formalized verbally by the use of the term "phi" for elder sibling and "nong" for younger sibling. The boy child is very important to Thai families and outranks any girl children.*

As families change, the original power relationship of a couple undergoes enormous modification as the family network increases, fragments, or solidifies. In addition to developmental issues, many other forces affect changes in family power: separation from the family-of-origin or outside influences that affect the family—varying from inflation and environmental factors to changing cultural norms. Parents' competency in relating their needs and desires, first to one another and then to their children, affects power. Spouses' or children's acceptance or rejection of these requests influences power outcomes. The increasing or decreasing independence or interdependence of the couple alters power in the entire family system. Ishii-Kuntz (1994) noted in his research that children with highly involved fathers had higher cognitive competence, increased empathy, less gender stereotyped beliefs, and more self control. If a spouse falls ill, dies, or leaves, the remaining parent may return to the family-of-origin seeking everything from shelter to advice. The single parent left with children must modify family power processes. The family power structure changes constantly as members achieve or change goals.

## COMMUNICATION STRATEGIES AND POWER

Many families develop predictable communication strategies for addressing power issues. Yet any given strategy is effective only if it is met with a response which engages it. Such is the transactional nature of communication.

### Sample Strategies

Confirming, disconfirming, and rejecting behaviors are strategies that affect power. These three strategies can become a part of power messages as family members attempt to separate and connect in one-up, one-down subsystems. In a one-up position, one family member attempts to exercise more power control over one or more other members. The one-down member accepts from the one-up member the control implied in the messages.

Confirming implies acknowledgement and may be used to gain power as one tries to get another to identify with him or her, or as one tries to give rewards in order to gain power. The careful, nonjudgmental listener may wittingly or unwittingly gain power through the identification or information learned by such behavior. A highly complimentary father may be given power by a child who needs positive support. Such approaches to marital power are found in certain self-help books which exhort wives to use positive, confirming approaches as a way to gain power in the marital relationship.

The "silent treatment" probably represents the most powerful and most often used disconfirming behavior—a behavior which does not acknowledge the other person's existence. One family member can put another in a one-down power position through the punishment strategy of disconfirmation. "I ignore him; he'll come around" represents such an effort. On the other hand, disconfirming a power message may serve as an effective method of rejecting power. The child who pretends not to hear "clean up your room" messages effectively deflects the parental power, at least for a while.

Rejecting messages tie directly to punishment messages and are often used as control in family power plays. "I hate you" or "I don't care what you say" may effectively halt control attempts, just as "If you don't behave, you can't go" may serve to pull a reluctant family member into line. The negative conflict behaviors of displacement, denial, disqualification, distancing, and sexual withholding can also be used as rejecting power moves.

Self-disclosure serves a major means of gaining intimacy within a relationship, but it can also be used as a power strategy as one attempts to control the other through the "information power" gained by self-disclosure. For example, when a self-disclosure is thrown back at a spouse during a fight, that person loses power. "Well, you had an affair, so how can you talk?"

Self-disclosure may be used as a means of offering power to a loved one in an intimate relationship. The disclosure gives power to the listener in an effort to gain connectedness. Such sharing involves risk and gives the listener "information power," which he or she could use to cause pain or separation in the relationship. In such cases, the more knowledgeable person has the capacity to control the relationship. Self-disclosure is often difficult for parents, but the mother cited in the following example gained greater closeness with her daughter:

---

*One of the most meaningful times in my life occurred when my teenage daughter and I had an all-night session about love, sex, and growing-up problems. It was the first time I honestly told her about what I went through growing up and how we faced some of the same things. I had always kept those things to myself, but I suddenly realized that she shouldn't feel like she was different or bad because of her feelings. It's scary to tell your daughter your faults or fears, but it certainly resulted in a closer relationship between us.*

---

## Power Transactions

According to a transactional view of relationships, power must be given as well as taken. In short, it is negotiated between and among family members. This transactional quality may be seen in the research of Rogers-Millar and Millar (1979), in which they examine the distinction between dominance and domineering behavior. They defined domineering as the sending of "one-up messages," or verbal statements claiming the right to dominate. For example, "Be sure and have my supper ready at 6:00 p.m." Domineeringness comes from an individual's behavior, while dominance relates to dyadic relational behavior (Courtright, Millar, and Rogers-Millar 1979, 181). Courtright and associates' research focused on the area of power processes; they studied the messages exchanged between spouses as they accepted or rejected one another's statements. Pure dominance meant all one-up remarks made by an individual were followed by a one-down response from the other.

Correlating domineering behavior to self-report data, Rogers-Millar and Millar found that "higher rates of wife domineeringness related to lower marital and communication satisfaction for both partners and higher role strain" (244). They found some further important results when they analyzed the interaction data, or messages between the spouses. The dominance of one spouse correlated positively to the number of support statements (i.e., agreement, acceptance, approval remarks) and negatively to the number of nonsupport statements made by the other spouses. Nonsupport statements were in the form of rejections, disagreements, or demands. Talk-overs, defined as verbal interruptions or intrusions that succeed in taking over the communication while another is speaking, occurred more frequently in couples who used the domineering style.

KEN: *"I've got to tell you about this wonderful movie I saw last ..."*

KIM: *"You won't believe who I saw in the bar last night."*

KEN: *"This movie has such beautiful ..."*

KIM: *"He came over to me, acting as if nothing happened and tried to buy me a beer."*

In both wife-domineering and wife-dominant interactions, the discussions were longer. The reverse was true of husbands. A second study provided additional conclusions: the more domineering one spouse was, the more domineering the partner became. This indicated a more defensive or combative style of conversation developed from a domineering style (Courtright, Millar, and Rogers-Millar). Frequent question-asking characterized the wife's style of interaction when the husband dominated (Rogers-Millar and Millar). The more domineering the husband, the less accurate were both spouses' predictions about the other's satisfaction with the marriage. The same held true for domineering wives in predicting their mates' satisfaction. The researchers suggested that if you did not want to be dominated, you should increase your domineeringness. However, they added that if you do so, be prepared to accept the possibility that both your satisfaction and your partner's will decrease.

Other aspects of one-up, one-down communication have been described by Haley as dysfunctional communication strategies. He suggests that helplessness will influence another person's behavior as much as, if not more than, direct authoritarian demands. One who acts helplessly defines the relationship as one in which he or she wants the other to take care of them. This kind of behavior in a relationship can be avoided by using qualifications in part of the message that indicate that an individual takes responsibility for his or her decisions. For example, Carlos might say to his brother, "I want your opinion, but I know it's my problem to solve." This approach to communication lessens the likelihood of control by another, thus giving persons possession of their own powers. Thus, the communication strategies used to enhance relationships or to increase intimacy also may be used to gain power.

In order to achieve cohesion, each family has to work out a communication pattern that allows intimacy without overpowering certain members. According to Corrales, "in this culture, behavior that is more conducive to building self and other esteem seems to be more effectively communicated in an egalitarian interaction structure than in either type of dominant structure" (216). The equalitarian structure includes the syncratic and autonomic types of power sharing. In either of these family types, individuals can deal honestly with their feelings and aspirations. Their more open nature encourages freer communication exchanges than either the husband or wife dominant types.

Steinor (1978) distinguished between "gentle power" and "control power." Gentle power sends the message: "I can give you what I feel and think. You can understand it and you can compare and decide. This makes people powerful." Ideally, to use communication effectively to counteract the negative aspects of power, there can be no power plays between the persons involved. Steinor suggests that power should not be used to rescue others from solving their own problems. When parents take over their children's problems, they also assume power that is not rightfully theirs. Husbands, wives, or lovers who, through power plays, make decisions for the other, reduce that partner's power potential. An egalitarian family relationship requires that each member have the power to solve the problems they encounter.

All human beings find themselves in power struggles in all areas of their lives. Just as power struggles in the larger social system affect the family, so, too, family struggles influence how one functions at work or school. Individuals and families can operate more effectively when they can identify power issues and develop a repertoire of communication strategies to address these issues.

## CONCLUSION

This chapter presented an application of power issues to the family. We discussed power bases, power processes, and power outcomes as described by McDonald's model and indicated how they affect cohesion and adaptability in family systems. The research has indicated that a rigid power structure, characterized by dominance and little sharing, restricts family flexibility, reduces cohesion, and adversely affects satisfaction in families. Power in the system changes as the family system grows and develops. Spouses create power patterns such as wife dominant, husband dominant, syncratic, and autonomic. Children wield power, often through power plays which gain attention. Families often involve member alliances which make certain issues predictable. Each family serves as a context for certain predictable communication strategies which fail or succeed only as they function within the transactional context. All power maneuvers take place within the boundaries the family has established; thus, all communication and activities that take place affect the images, themes, and degree of unity, or cohesion, the family desires. Power operates within a dynamic, growing, interdependent, transactional family system. The sum total of family power is greater than the individual power of each member.

## IN REVIEW

1. How may power affect a family's cohesion and adaptability?
2. Describe how cultural and gender patterns influence the basis of power used in family systems.
3. List ways in which power might be effectively shared in an egalitarian family.
4. Analyze the power resources used regularly by members of a real or fictional family. Indicate how members use communication to convey their use of these resources.
5. Describe the type of power exhibited by a real or fictional couple. If power has changed over time, what accounts for the change?

# 8

# Decision Making

Decision making is the process whereby differences between individual family members can be addressed. It is one of the most important activities in families and ranges from the trivial (Where do we buy groceries?) to the serious (Do we want children?).

Decision making helps regulate the closeness or distance each family member desires or needs from other members. The kinds of decisions and the quality of them determines how family roles, rules, or themes are satisfactorily or unsatisfactorily enacted. Potentially all power dimensions can come into play when difficult decisions must be made within a family system. It is through decision making that family members can negotiate dialectical concerns of autonomy and connection. Couples have available to them a set of strategies that they use in the negotiation process to deal with the shifting needs they have between wanting to be connected and autonomous within the family systems (Montgomery 1992). Some kinds of decision making must take place to adjust these dialectical tensions between individual and family needs and societal norms to achieve satisfaction in any family. Today's families have to struggle to find time to make decisions. The pressures on single parents, dual earner, or dual career couples to set aside time to do intelligent decision making requires prioritizing among competing demands within the family system. For example, to take the time to debrief and shift focus from outside jobs requires the couple making a decision to do so, a decision that results in high relational satisfaction for these couples (Vangelisti and Banski 1993). Families need patterned decision processes so members know what to do in certain circumstances. The more complex the family system, the more important the decision patterns, as indicated in the following example:

---

*Both Mom and Dad work overtime. The oldest one home is in charge of decisions that involve those in the house. For*

(continued on page 206)

*example, when my older brother is home, he makes decisions on who can go somewhere or what friend can come over. If he's at work, I take over. My next younger sister does the same when I have something after school.*

---

Decision making, like power, is a process that belongs to the family system, not to an individual. Therefore, decision making varies greatly among families because each family processes its interactions and resources into roles and power domains differently. Keeping McDonald's model (Figure 7.1 from page 180) in mind will help you to understand how complicated decision making can be in families. Remember, decision making appears under power outcomes. According to Scanzoni and Polanko (1980), decision making means getting things done in a family when one or more family members need to agree with others to accomplish something.

Many decisions have a moral component involving a sense of what is right or wrong that affects family behavior. Kohlberg (1969) and Gilligan (1982) stated that moral development progresses through a series of stages from meeting individual desires, to societal norms, to universal ethical principles. Kohlberg believed morality centered around concepts of justice, but Gilligan found care and responsibility more important in decision making, especially for women (Evans 1987). These differences highlight the inherent complexity of the decision making process.

Your family differs from a small group that comes together merely for the purpose of doing a particular task. Your family has a history of continuous interaction and consists of a combination of interdependent individuals. Even if the decision making process results in turmoil, your family remains a unit, although sometimes a factional and unhappy one. This is not true of outside groups. If the members cannot reach a decision, they usually disband rather easily. Short of death, divorce, or moving out, families tend to remain together even if members disagree. This causes what to outsiders may appear as irrational decisions or negative communication. Because family relationships are both involuntary and lengthy, members may use negative messages that ironically function to maintain the family system and the separate identities of a husband or daughter (Vangelsti 1993).

Family decisions can be either instrumental or affective. *Instrumental* decisions require solving rather mechanical issues, such as getting a job to pay the family bills or providing transportation. *Affective decisions* relate to emotions or feelings. Epstein, Bishop, and Baldwin (1982) concluded that "families whose functioning is disrupted by instrumental problems rarely, if ever, deal effectively with affective problems. However, families whose functioning is disrupted by affective problems may deal adequately with instrumental prob-

Satisfactory family decisions require good listening and negotiation skills.

lems" (119). Feldman (1982) indicates women in traditional roles experience difficulty with instrumental problem-solving skills.

The location of a family along the cohesion and adaptability continuum affects their decision making behavior. Highly enmeshed, rigid families may pressure members to reach predictable and low-risk decisions, since change or separation would be threatening. Disengaged systems may have trouble sharing enough information to make reasonable decisions, while families characterized by chaos probably experience few real decisions that stand. The length of the relationship also influences decision making. Early in the marriage or cohabitation, the couple may conduct themselves in arguments like others they have known or observed. Later they operate on their own pattern. Montgomery noted how couples can cycle between periods of high autonomy and periods of high connection over time (1992).

In order to understand the family as a decision making system, you need to examine: (1) a model of decision making, (2) types of family decision making, (3) modes of family governance, (4) steps in decision making, and (5) factors that influence decision making. This chapter extends the study of power to look in greater detail at decision making as a negotiation process that influences power outcomes. Who influences the decision and how is the influence felt? Who decides what, when, and how certain necessary aspects of family life are resolved? The answers will vary according to how communication is used to maintain the way rules, roles, and power operate within a given family. Decision making patterns often set the tone for a lifetime of sibling difficulties as seen in the following example:

---

*My brother, Tim, a very dominant personality, has always needed to be heard! This was particularly difficult for his youngest brother, Denny. If he disagreed with Tim, he would put him down and call him an idiot—especially if he would make a different decision, not necessarily a "wrong" decision. Tim was older and assumed he made the rules and knew more information on all subjects.*

---

## DECISION MAKING MODEL

The ways in which decisions are made differ greatly within families. Wood and Talmon (1983) present the idea that decisions represent a type of territory that a family develops. In this "decision space," the family allows some decisions to be made by individuals, while other decisions require approval from certain sub-systems or the whole family. For example, Marissa may ask the whole family's opinion of her Girl Scout project, while her parents' decision to go on a trip without the children may not be submitted to the whole family for approval. Sometimes family members take over another's decision space. For example, a divorced father may offer suggestions and persuasions that are not needed or welcomed yet pressure the person or subsystem making the decision. The following model should help clarify the decision making process.

This model supports the idea that marital negotiations that lead to decisions can be analyzed in terms of social contexts, processes, and outcomes. In drawing upon earlier work by Straus (1978), Scanzoni and Polonoko (1980) devised this model to demonstrate the ongoing nature of process and outcome in decision making. They divided family social context dimensions into four areas:

1. *Composition,* meaning ages of spouses, cohabitors or lovers, length of marriage, ages and number of children, and time available before deadline.
2. *Resources,* including amount of education, salary, job status, amount of work each year, and experience negotiating decisions.

3. *Orientations,* including self-esteem, sex-role attitudes, amount of concern about the outcome, and importance of the issue.
4. *Actor's orientations* refers to each partner's past bargaining experience and how the Actor (spouse) perceives that his or her partner will negotiate. This includes perceptions the couple has about how hard each will bargain, how fairly, and how cooperatively. It also includes how much each can be trusted to follow through on decisions.

**FIGURE 8.1**
**A Model of Explicit Marital Negotiation**

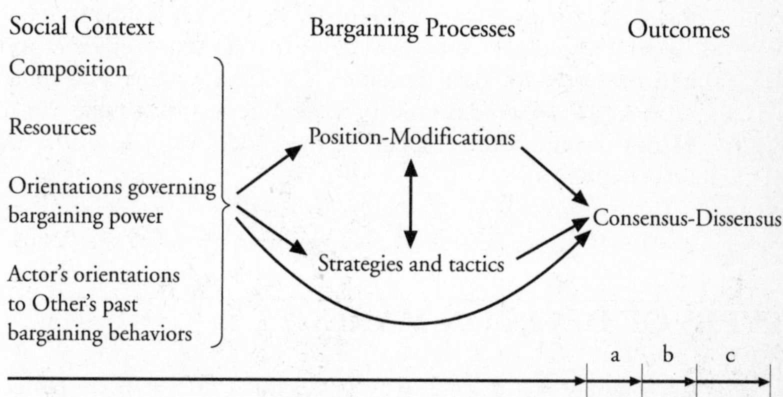


The main part of the diagram indicates how the "one-shot" negotiation works. For example, Emily and Carmen negotiate a problem, making use of various strategies and tactics and modifying their respective positions as necessary. The horizontal arrow at the bottom of the model represents the interaction that takes place in the course of the bargaining process. The outcome that results is labeled "a" on the time line at the bottom of the model. Once this outcome has been reached, it becomes a part of the social context within which additional decision making negotiations occur, affecting the future outcome "b." Outcome "b," in turn, provides context for outcome "c," and so on.

This model emphasizes the importance of bargaining as a mediator of power. Scanzoni and Polonko state that this idea "sensitizes us to the notion that power is intrinsically associated with ongoing movement, or process, rather than outcome" (33). This model makes us aware that outcomes often do not end issues. Family members are not always equally satisfied with decisions. The model provides for repeated series of negotiations occurring over varied periods of time before true consensus happens. Power resides in each partner's or child's shifts or changes in bargaining position. The degree of flexibility, or willingness to compromise, enhances the probability of reaching consensus.

Social context variables such as disparity in tangible resources (schooling or salary), differences in intangible variables (self-concept or sex roles), and insights into a family's decision making history usually have significant impact on process and outcomes variables (Hill and Scanzoni 1982). Research indicates that the greater the educational disparity, the larger the amount of disparity will be on three other dimensions: income, self-esteem, and perceptions of past bargaining. Income and self-esteem positively correlate, as do self-esteem and perceptions of past decisions. Other findings show that style of communication has a powerful, pervasive effect in determining spouses' responses. A defensive style increases the number of disagreements, as do verbal strategies that are ego centered and evoke bad memories of past decisions. Decision making is a multifaceted process. Understanding the process helps us determine the meaning of an outcome. Other aspects of this model will be discussed later in this chapter.

## TYPES OF DECISION MAKING

Each family has its own way of reaching decisions on issues. In his early study of family decision making patterns, Turner (1970) differentiates decision making outcomes according to the degree of acceptance and commitment of family members. He identifies three kinds of decision making which remain valid categories: (1) consensus, (2) accommodation, and (3) *de facto* decisions (98–100).

### Consensus

In consensus decision making, discussion continues until agreement is reached. This may require compromise and flexibility, but the desired goal is a solution acceptable to all involved. Because each family member has a part in the decision and a chance to influence it, they share the responsibility for carrying it out. In some families, all major purchases are decided on the basis of group consensus. This type of decision making does not occur as frequently as the other two. The complexity of such decision making is described in the following example:

*Every Tuesday night is family night, and everyone must be present from 7:00 until 8:30. This is the time when we make certain family decisions that affect all of us. We may make a joint decision about vacations and try to find a plan that will please everyone. Sometimes Dad will let us decide on a big item to buy with his bonus. Each of the six of us has to finally agree for us to go ahead with the decision.*

## Accommodation

Accommodation occurs when some family members consent to a decision not because they totally agree but because they believe that further discussion will be unproductive. They may give their consent with a smile or with bitterness. The accommodation decision may represent a great deal of give and take, but no one really achieves what he or she desires. For example, you may want to go to church family camp while someone else wants to play in three ballgames that weekend. Eventually, the family may agree to go on a picnic while the baseball player gets to play one game in the schedule. The wants of no one has really been satisfied with the decision; individual wants have been merely placated or postponed to some future time. This kind of decision making tends to leave some or all family members disappointed. When decisions are made this way, factions may emerge, and you may feel obligated to repay people who argued for your goals. This type of decision making may occur in families that pressure for high cohesiveness by maintaining their themes and boundaries as indicated in this somewhat manipulative example:

*It's just easier to agree with Dad and let him think his ideas are what we all want than to argue with him. He's bound to win anyway, since he controls the money. Sometimes when we humor his wishes, Mom, my sister, and I can then get our way on what we want to do—sort of a trade-off!*

Sometimes accommodation results from voting as family members line up on one side of an issue and the majority wins. The minority views held by losing family members might have genuine merit, but the losers accept majority rule rather than cause trouble.

Anyone who loses consistently finds this to be an unacceptable way to make decisions.

One danger of accommodation is that it encourages dominant behavior. Too often, decisions favor those who dominate, and less aggressive family members develop a pattern of submitting to their wishes. Accommodation may appear to be a decision making approach that furthers family cohesion and adaptability, but this is not the case. The results are temporary at best, because the communication that goes into accommodative decisions represents compromises made by members out of fear or lack of equal power. Such decisions over time accent separateness and lessen connectedness among family members. Accommodative decision making can also enforce negative family themes and images while implementing stereotyped thinking on biosocial issues, especially in case of male dominance.

## *De Facto* Decisions

What happens when the family makes no decision or when the discussion reaches an impasse? Usually, one member will go ahead and act in the absence of a clear-cut decision. This is a *de facto* decision—one made without direct family approval but nevertheless made to keep the family functioning. A fight over which model of television to buy while on sale may be continued until the sale nears an end and Dad finally buys one by himself.

*De facto* decisions encourage family members to complain about the results, since they played either no part or a passive part in the decision. The family member who acts in a vacuum created by the lack of a clear-cut decision has to endure the harassment or lack of enthusiasm of those who have to accept the decision. Again, dominant family members can easily emerge victorious in too many decisions—their wishes are carried out while those of others are unfairly suppressed.

Although many families, particularly rigid ones, seem to use only one type of decision making, more flexible families vary their styles according to the issues. Critical issues may require consensus, while less important concerns can be resolved by a vote or a *de facto* decision. As we will see later, the style of decision making experienced in his or her family-of-origin by each member of a couple has a great effect on the decision making styles they adopt when they form their own system.

Another way to type decisions is to distinguish between social decisions, economic decisions, and technical decisions. Social decisions help reduce disagreements over values, roles, and goals of parents of their children. Economic decisions require family members to compare and communicate about alternatives within the family's resources. This often requires compromise in order to reach one decision that the family members agree to follow. With economic decisions, the outcome cannot always be known. It takes time to know whether the decision enhanced or diminished the family's resources. Technical decisions deal with how the decisions will be carried out (Noller and Fitzpatrick 1993).

## STYLES OF GOVERNANCE

In an interesting approach that combines ideas about family power and decision making, Broderick (1975) set up three styles of governance based upon Kohlberg's (1964) study of children in different cultures and the universal steps in reasoning that they go through to reach moral maturity. The lowest level of reasoning for decisions was hedonistic self-interest, or zero-sum; the next was based on conventionality and obedience to rules; the third was based on social contract and principles of conscience (118).

### Zero-Sum Decisions

Applied to decision making in conflict situations, the first and most primitive way to reach a decision is simply to insist upon your own way. Broderick labeled this approach a hedonistic, "zero-sum" power confrontation. This means that in an argument, one person wins and one loses. The sum of the wins (+) and losses (-) is always zero. You have seen this operate between small children who refuse to share. Instead, they shout, "That's mine, you can't have it." Unfortunately, such behavior does not always stop as family members move beyond the toddler stage. In this kind of decision making, each family member insists upon his or her own way without compromise. This approach can lead to threats, yelling, browbeating, and slanting of the truth. The following example represents zero-sum decision making:

*With regard to my wife, I have to put her in her place. She thinks I am unfair and everything is for me and nothing is for her: I go to bed on time each night. I don't take "no" for an answer. When I go to bed, she goes to bed! No ifs, ands, or*

(continued on page 214)

*buts. She thinks she is too busy, but if I don't insist, she'd go to bed very late.*

---

Broderick suggests only two circumstances in which families could survive using zero-sum confrontations. For example, if the wife and husband are closely matched, with each getting an equal number of wins and losses, the relationship could continue. Also, if the consistently losing partner feels there are no alternatives and lacks the emotional or financial resources to leave, he or she may remain in the relationship in spite of the heavy psychological cost of lower self-esteem. Children can be victims in this kind of household, because they have no way to escape. Young people caught in this kind of family make such statements as "I can't wait until I graduate and can get out of here" or "I don't like it, but it's not worth fighting over." In time, the losers either leave the family or define their role as second class. In zero-sum governance, decisions are static and predictable.

The maintenance of a zero-sum relationship requires coercive power, or punishment, especially the use of fear and threat. Information is of little use, because too much evidence might weaken the position of the hedonist family member who insists upon his or her views. Of even less use is reward power, because the "winner" does not usually sense the need to give anything in return for acceptance of the decision.

---

*In our house you went along with parental decisions or you were punished—it was as simple as that. I had one brother who was a rebel, and my father would beat him. My mother usually went along with whatever my father said, because I think she was scared of him, too.*

---

Some family members use force in decision making. Violence is a problem-solving method learned in a family setting, which reflects society's attitude toward permitting the use of physical force in intimate relationships (Steinmetz 1977; Ford 1983). The method parents used to solve their problems became the method usually employed to solve parent-and-child and child-and-child problems. Thus, the parental approach to decision making became the model for other family interactions. When verbal aggression and physical force characterized the parents' attempts to make decisions, the same behavior appeared in that of a parent with his or her children or between the children when they disagreed. As unfortunate as it seems, many people use fists rather than words to settle family problems.

According to the process model of decision making, to be a constant winner requires defensive behaviors and putting up with the loser's submissive behaviors. To lose constantly requires a person to live with low self-esteem and continually try to subvert the more powerful person. The images maintained in zero-sum family relationships foster separateness and reduce the chance for much cohesion. The pattern of adaptability required to maintain zero-sum relationships does too little to develop positive self-esteem for individual members within the family system. In many families, victories are hollow because they curb or destroy ideas and limit decision making skills in others that might lead to better and more meaningful solutions.

## Decisions Based on Rules

A second mode of governance involves the creation and enforcement of rules. Family members may live most of their lives according to the rules and avoid certain power clashes, as well as certain opportunities for growth. Rules affect decision making because, over a period of time, they become accepted ways to operate when problems arise. Rules evolve from the social contexts of the family members plus repeated family interactions. Rules in decision making certainly become a part of what relational maintenance strategies affect equity in marriages (Canary and Stafford 1992). These strategies maintain a relational definition and safeguard the status quo, reduce or heighten the dialectical tensions, and increase or decrease affection between family members. The goal is for family members to more evenly share responsibilities. These strategies are incorporated into the decision making processes, especially decision making via rules. Broderick distinguished among three types of rules used in family decision making: (1) rules of direct distribution, (2) rules of designated authority, and (3) rules for negotiation.

***Rules of Direct Distribution*** Rules of direct distribution imply the dividing of family resources directly among members. This includes the distribution of family income into the amounts available for food, housing, tuition, vacation, and entertainment. Similar distribution can be made with living space—which child gets which room, or has to share a bedroom, which shelves belong to which child or parent, and where personal items are to be kept. These rules function to avoid confrontations and reduce power plays in the family through resolving conflicts before they become problems. Rules of this kind require that family members carry around in their heads a whole series of predetermined decisions about matters of family living. They also carry a knowledge of what relational maintenance strategies worked in the past and can recall what rules went into the decision making that solved the problem.

***Rules of Designated Authority*** Designated authority rules indicate who has the authority over certain areas. For example, Mother pays the bills and, thus, collects the checks and does the budgeting. Dad does the painting and refinishing and, thus, decides on the materials to use. Lois plays in the band, and thus, does not need to explain her absence from home after school or help with housework on weekends when the band travels. Sometimes, rules allocating authority contain a series of steps. For example, either Dad or Mom can go out for an evening with friends if the other knows who is going and where. Either can veto such a decision if his or her job requires overtime work and the children will be home alone. This type of rule, dispersing authority, often relates closely to roles in the family. Whoever controls the kitchen and all of the activities that take place there has the authority to make the decisions in that area. Culture may play a significant role in desiginating authority as the following example notes:

---

*As an immigrant Assyrian family living in the United States, my family is quite different. I would describe our family as "closed" because we have learned that this works better if we are to keep our culture, language, religion, and traditions. My father makes all important decisions, so we don't make decisions like other families in our neighborhood.*

---

Rules of designated authority tend to set clear boundaries for who may get involved with what. Certain people may have far more decision making power than others. Yet, children can also have areas of decision making assigned to them. For example, if they do their expected tasks, they can make decisions about their free time. If a son likes to bake and does all of the buying and preparation of baked goods, he may be given the authority over the oven and that part of the kitchen. The autonomic family described in the previous chapter quite often operates its decision making in accordance with this rule.

***Rules for Negotiation*** The third type of rule is based on negotiation. Over time, families can establish rules that govern the process that decision making will follow when conflict occurs. Rules of this type imply greater family input in settling differences. It may mean placing a limit on the amount of force or threats one member can use against another. Certain tactics, such as yelling or hitting, can be outlawed and negotiation done only when all involved agree not to interrupt. This approach implies that the decision reached may require compromise or sacrifice on one or more family members' part. Many current marital or family enrichment programs stress how to negotiate differences according to rules that allow all members of the system some input (Renick, Blumberg, and Markman 1992).

In some families each person has a right to decide what is negotiable and what is non-negotiable for himself or herself. Others intimately involved have a right to know what is non-negotiable and can question or evaluate it, but the final decision is up to the individual and is respected. For example, in some interfaith marriages couples agree that each has the right to continue his or her religion. Thus, a choice to attend religious services is non-negotiable.

---

*Ever since the children have grown older, I have declared Saturday as my day to do whatever I desire. It is sacred to me and I only do what I want on that day, even if somebody else will be disappointed. I am wife or mother to four people during six days of the week, and I really need some scheduled time to myself and Saturday's it!*

---

Thus, the third type of rule involves potential negotiation about what is usually not negotiable. This approach has the potential to increase family cohesion and provide a method for adaptability. To be successful, family members have to communicate their wishes directly to all other members and take responsibility for their comments. Negotiation implies change and flexibility. If this expectancy of later possible change is recognized by the family, its members realize that negotiation can be another communication skill to use to gain adaptability within their system. It can help keep a system open and flexible. Not only are there rules for negotiation, couples who decide to parent must renegotiate their roles. This leads to numerous decisions to recalibrate the family system as it goes from two to three members. Parents can argue over how to care for the child. Stamp states, "Couples must decide which differences in technique are unimportant enough to be left alone and which issues are sufficiently critical to discuss" (1994, 103).

## Decisions Based on Principle

Broderick's third mode involves government by contract or principle. As you might imagine, few families actively operate at this high of a level, and those that do usually include older children and adults. It is based on a belief in the basic human goodness of each family member and their desire to put the family's welfare above their own. Individual family members operate on principles of fairness and concern. For example, if either Dad or Mom works late, he or she calls the other and explains. The operating principle is that neither partner unnecessarily inconveniences the other. Both respect the other's right to make overtime decisions, but fair play motivates each of them to inform the other. This prevents one from preparing food that is not eaten or planning activities that are later canceled. Through this, there is no rule about hours to come and go but a principle operating that neither will waste the time of the other.

This type of governance works in families with children if the parents have taught them how to use good judgment and value the rights, strengths, and limitations of one another. It requires harmony and cooperation. Disharmony can be handled as a temporary condition that will be resolved by fair decisions that restore balance to a family system. Children realize that they play an integral part in the successful operation of the system. A family might have a contract in which areas of work and play are shared—each member has duties assigned so that time remains for individual and joint family activities. Compromise is a part of this form of governance so that all members' legitimate needs are met.

You have examined both Turner's and Brodericks's ways of viewing family decision making. The former relates to the actual behavior, while the latter takes more complex issues into consideration, since it involves a level of moral reasoning reached by the members. This last approach also carries out Kohlberg and Gilligan's emphasis upon the importance of justice, care, and responsibility in all decision making. Another way to combine approaches would be to divide them into either policy-guided or non-policy-guided choices. If family policy has been established on a given matter, decision making would then be guided by that policy. This would involve the rules established to deal with similar situations. Nonpolicy choices could require either accommodation, consensus, or some form of negotiation to reach decisions.

Littlejohn stated that in conflict situations people make decisions by coalitions, judications, and negotiations (1992). Coalition decisions base outcomes on numbers with the majority of family members winning and the others losing. This kind of decision making is similar to the zero-sum type. In judication, a family member with authority, probably a mother or a father, makes the decision. Other family members may be heard but the outcome is determined by the family member with the power to judge. Negotiation in family decision making would involve two or more family members making proposals and counter proposals in order to find a solution to a problem. The important feature of negotiation is that its outcome aims to achieve a joint solution that pleases the involved family members, rather than one based on an authoritative (judicial) or numerical (coalition) decision.

## STEPS IN DECISION MAKING

No steps in problem-solving work in families until members sense that their input in decision making has any chance of support. In dysfunctional families, change through effective decision making is blocked by rigid rules and images that protect the status quo. In order for any decision making to take place, it has to be a priority. If it isn't important or the risks involved are perceived to be too great, the process never gets underway. In some families, procrastination avoids decision making until crises occur or deadlines prevent the parents or children from having enough time to negotiate decisions.

Decisions are never as simple as they appear. In examining the five problem-solving steps in decision making, it is important to realize that the process may be short-circuited at any point by a family member or subsystem alliance that does not agree with certain choices. Or, the family group may reach a decision by skipping some steps.

The first step requires definition of the problem, including isolating the parts of it that family members agree need attention. At this stage it is helpful to make sure everyone understands the problem's key terms in the same way or to establish that the definitions differ. Sometimes, differences in meaning cause part of the problem and delay in decision making.

The second step includes an exploration of the problem and analysis of the differences. At this stage, all pros and cons should be discussed, with every involved family member having a chance to be heard.

The third step involves setting up criteria that any solution or decision should meet. Sample criteria might be: the family can afford the money to do it; there will be enough time available to do it; the decision will be equitable and not take advantage of any member; and the advantages will outweigh possible disadvantages. This important step tends to be overlooked, yet it can help clarify the family's goals and lead to better decisions. It is a listing of what is needed to be fair and just in making a decision that will solve a problem.

The fourth step focuses on listing possible solutions that might solve the problem. In this phase of decision making, alternative ways to solve a problem are brought out. If democracy prevails in the discussion, this step gives submissive family members a chance to express their ideas. All participants should be encouraged to contribute suggestions. This way, if they have a part in the process and are later outvoted, they can feel their ideas were at least considered.

The last step requires selecting the best solution. The decision made should represent the members' best combined thinking and meet the criteria agreed upon in the third step.

Finally, a plan of action for implementing the decision needs to be agreed upon—a plan that will strengthen and enhance the operation of the family system, because a problem that had reduced the efficiency of the system has been solved. Note the steps followed by the family in this example:

---

*My two brothers and I and our wives actually went through a formal decision making process as we decided how to take care of our elderly mother after she was unable to live alone. We went through all kinds of hassles on terms such as nursing homes, residential facilities, and social security benefits. We had to set a monetary criteria for any solution based on a percentage of our salaries and based on a location that everyone could reach. Mother had to agree to the solution also. We agreed we could not force our solution on her. Each couple investigated different options, specific senior citizen housing options, live-in nurses, nursing homes, and specialized group homes. Then we all sat around and hashed ideas over. We finally reached two options that we could live with—a particular senior citizen facility or a nursing home that accepted people who were not severely ill. We discussed these with my mother who rejected the nursing home instantly but who agreed to the senior citizen housing facility.*

---

This planned approach to decision making does not just happen in families. In fact, left to their own ways, most families do not solve their problems in an organized way. Many families become bogged down and never get beyond the first or second step.

No matter how decision making occurs, whatever style or type of governance is used, the actual process involves many factors. Unfortunately, it is not a very predictable or streamlined process. In order to understand the complexity of the process, we need to examine what affects family decision making.

# FACTORS THAT AFFECT FAMILY DECISION MAKING

Over the years, each family evolves some patterned ways of solving problems. The decision making process is more than trial and error, although that may be a part of it. Family decisions are related to a variety of factors that explain the actions taken. According to Kurdek (1991), ineffective decision making is based on poorly developed interpersonal cognitions and skills. In this section, we will discuss: (1) how children affect decisions, (2) how gender influences modify outcomes, (3) how the individual's involvement and resources influence decisions, and (4) how time availability and quality communication skills affect family decision making.

## The Role of Children in Decision Making

By now, you are aware that your family-of-origin experiences affect all areas of your life. Thus, your decision making experiences as a child partially determine your approach to adult decision making situations. On the other hand, your children may have some interesting effects on family decision making processes. The arrival of the first child opens the door for the formation of triangles or alliances in the family and provides the first opportunity for a chain network by which decisions may be relayed. The new baby forces decisions that test Dad or Mom's role expectations; the facilitation/inhibition of others on the parent's role expectations and the openness/closedness in making decisions about how to carry out the parental role with the spouse (Stamp 1994, 89).

Children often influence decisions by forming alliances with one or the other parent or by presenting a united front to a certain proposed decision. In some families, permanent alliances seem to exist as indicated in the following example:

---

*A trite axiom the two of us share is "together we stand, divided we fall." My brother and I took tremendous advantage of the concept of joint pressure throughout our college years. My brother and I dreamed up strategies to combat our parents in order to achieve our ends. At times, we add complexity to the tension-filled situations by pairing one parent off against the other. Sometimes it works, but sometimes we end up losing.*

---

In certain circumstances, children share the leadership in decision making. Russell (1979) found that this happened in a family atmosphere in which a child or spouse felt support from other members. This atmosphere also made it easier for a less assertive member to take charge of a problem and try to solve it (42). Results from a study of high school students from diverse socioeconomic and ethnic backgrounds in California revealed that granting adolescents autonomy in decision making too early led to lower levels of effort and lower grades for youth of both sexes (Dornbusch et al. 1990). In another study conducted over three years, boys as late adolescents continued to think their fathers had the strongest influence on decision making, but girls changed and saw the process as more equal or shared between parents (McDermott et al. 1987). Decision making may be different in single parent families with adolescents headed by a mother. A comparison of households revealed that youth in the single mother homes were more likely to make decisions without direct parental input and more likely to get into trouble in the community. If there was an additional adult in the single mother's household, the mother exerted more control over decisions and there were fewer reports of adolescence deviance (Dornbush et al. 1985).

In family problem-solving, children responded best to positive emotional patterns of communication and performed less effectively when parents expressed negative emotions. Although negative feelings need to come out in decision making, the way in which they were treated affected the outcomes. The sometimes "let it all hang out" philosophy hindered family problem-solving (Forgatch 1989). When too many negative feelings surface during decision making, the focus shifts from problem-solving to personalities. This triggers more emotional responses which fuel each other. Children can withdraw or manipulate these situations, both of which are undesirable responses. Farrell and Barnes (1993) found that, for daughters, the more adaptability the more positive the outcomes on behavioral, psychological, and relationship measures. Such was not true for other family members. The results for boys showed that more adaptability affected communication with parents and caused depression, but not cohesion or other behavioral and psychological outcomes.

## Gender Influences

The ways husbands and wives define their roles and responsibilities directly affect family decision making. In a study of couple allocation of responsibility for eighteen family decisions and thirteen tasks, Douglas and Wind (1978) asked husbands and wives to group decisions and tasks into areas of responsibility in their families. The findings revealed basic spousal agreement with a group of wife-dominated activities, including washing and drying the dishes, laundry chores, and food budgeting and buying. Other decisions were joint decisions, such as places to go on vacations, who is invited to dinner, which movie to see, the amount to spend on appliances, what furniture to buy or replace, and if the wife should work.

Couples differed on other decision areas. Wives made more distinctions than husbands. Certain tasks were perceived as male-dominated: getting the car repaired, choosing the liquor, or maintaining the yard. The same held true on family financial decisions, such as investments and insurance. On financial decisions, some wives indicated more competence and joint participation and involvement. On clothing decisions, wives indicated they often acted as influencer or consultant.

It is interesting to note that in this study and several earlier ones, the couples had a harder time identifying who made a decision than who performed a task. For example, a husband could not recall who influenced what in their decision to buy a new sofa or whether he or his wife asked friends over for a barbecue, but he knew who did the dishes or balanced the checkbook regularly. In talking about how they make decisions, Krueger (1983) concluded that "both spouses tend to avoid singular responsibility" (99). White (1989) found men use coercion to distance themselves in order to analyze a situation and take charge of a problem before it escalates. Women by contrast sought affiliation to maintain connections long enough to find a solution, thus maintaining their relatedness. Adverse maternal work experiences related more to negative parenting styles, including less acceptance and warmth toward their children (Menaghan and Parcel 1991). Thus the interface between the job/career and the family impacts upon decision making.

A family's role ideology determines who carries out certain decisions and tasks. Thus, in male-dominant households, the husband will take over the financial decisions and the wife the household operation. Egalitarian couples will make more joint decisions. However, Douglas and Wind found little systemic relationship between couples' role attitudes and responsibility patterns. These findings indicate that responsibility in families for various decision areas and tasks seldom demonstrates a dominant authority pattern. In later research, Schaninger and Buss studied differences between happily married and divorced couples. They found happy partners practiced, "More role specialization, with greater influence of the wife and less husband dominance in family finance handling, and greater joint and wife influence in decision making" (1986, 129).

Floyd (1988) conducted a study of couples in problem-solving discussions and found, in decision making, men more often than women misinterpret their partner's communication behaviors, especially nonverbal expressions. This insensitivity results in what Weiss (1984) defined as a "sentiment-override." If the men felt positively toward their partners, they interpreted their communication behaviors positively in spite of the fact the women were indicating reservations in the decision making. Fitzpatrick (1988) also found wives more accurate in predicting their spouse's feelings. Her 'Separates' type were the least accurate. In casual conversations she discovered both 'Independents' and 'Mixed Couples' types employed challenges and justifications to assert control over spouses whereas 'Traditionals' used orders in decision making (133). If men worked in a participative work setting where the management encouraged job autonomy, self-direction, and group problem-solving skills, they in turn as fathers were more democratic in child-parent relations, including more use of family decision making and consensus (Grimm-Thomas and Perry-Jenkins 1993).

Spitze concluded from a number of studies that employed women had more power than their husbands in decisions about money matters (1988). In decision making, a wife's income was found to be highly correlated with direct bargaining and reward strategies (Zvonkovic, Schmiege, and Hall 1994). However, rural women who didn't work outside the home, but indeed did field work on family farms had no more and possibly less influence on decision making (Lyson 1985; Rosenfeld 1986). Doherty (1981) discovered that newly wed wives attributed events to causes differently than their husbands. Wives who attributed other couples' marital problems to negative personality traits and attitudes were more likely to use verbal criticism of their husbands in problem solving discussions. The same was not true of husbands, suggesting that an attributional style, which requires assigning causes to events, affects men less in marital problem solving. This finding relates to an earlier review of 100 bargaining and negotiation studies that concluded that women negotiate in a reactive, nontask-oriented manner that decreases their skills in problem solving. Women had greater difficulty ignoring provocations and frequently overreacted to situations (Rubin and Brown 1975). Decisions may appear final at one moment and then be reconsidered at a later time. What seemed to be the best decision may, upon experience, be proven otherwise and necessitate a search for a better one. In a viable, open family system, this would be a healthy state—all decisions subject to re-evaluation and study whenever new information or changes seem important to any family member.

The role functions carried out in a family affect the decision-making process. If one partner has more power, decision making can become unilateral. This may make one partner satisfied with the relationship but create intense tension for the other. For both to be satisfied in decision making, the less powerful partner would have to use more direct influence strategies, such as gaining resources to use as rewards or bargain for making an autonomous decision, rather than a shared or compromised decision (Zvonkovic, Schmiege, and Hall 1993). These roles vary greatly from family to family, so each family's decision making must be studied to see whether it fits the generalizations from the research presented.

## Individual Involvement and Resources

How many times have you dropped out of or avoided a family decision making session because you did not care about the result? If you do not see how things affect you, you are not likely to get involved, even though, as a system member, you will probably be affected. Not all family members care equally about the outcome of decisions. Antonio's desire to go to college away from home may be a major concern for his little brothers. Mom's desire and need for a new refrigerator may not be perceived as important to a teenager. If money or any other shared resource is scarce, decision making can become a competitive process for the limited resources. Decisions may be unimportant to some individuals in families; even if relevant, the decisions may not be points of disagreement.

Communication in making decisions changes greatly as children grow and develop their own sense of self-sufficiency. The same holds true for parents who also go through great changes and growth. Network formations reflect these changes, as do rule adjustments. As parents grow accustomed to problem solving and encounter different situations demanding solutions, they cannot replicate previous decisions, even if they so desire. The real world does not remain constant. Their personal investment in decisions varies over time with the degree of separateness or connectedness within the family system. The dependence-independence of the members fluctuates as children become adults and leave home. Parents learn from their decision successes and failures with older children and, as a result, the communication going into decision making with younger children may be quite different than it was with older children. A study of decision making with retired adults over 65 found that dominance by the wife related to the wife's positive self-concept (Lederhaus and Paulson 1986). These results agree with Ross' (1991) study in which people with a high sense of control actively solved problems and often took action before problems occurred.

Empathy, an important element in effective communication, relates to power and decision making. Empathy may be operationalized as the individual's ability to predict the decision of another family member about a problem. The greater the empathy regarding a particular decision, the greater the agreement between the measures of predicted and actual power.

Since the family is never static, individual members can also be involved in several decision making matters simultaneously, both within and outside the family. Matters requiring decisions, depending upon their importance, affect the members involved and determine their degree of active or passive commitment to new decisions. Investment in an issue impacts directly upon decision making, as shown in the following example:

---

*My brother has more decision making skills as a result of not only living but working with my dad in a contracting business. My dad is dependent on him to assist him directly. My brother has the technical computer ability to pull the rug out from under my dad which would "disable" my dad from maintaining his livelihood, home, car, and girlfriend. My brother and father have a love-hate relationship and their continual contact, both night and day, frequently tests their relationship.*

---

If one member of a family exerts too much power in the form of coercion, control, or suppression over another, decision making falters. Problem-solving requires an equalization of power. You can achieve a favorable power balance by employing problem-solving methods consciously as noted in the following example:

---

*I have learned over the years that the best way to reach my partner is through persuasion. I suggest Carl consider the situation and see if he can think of some plan that will accomplish his goals with as little impact on me as possible. With a little charm thrown in, I might even venture an idea. I reveal my feelings, explain the situation as I see it, and listen to what he has to say. Then I ask for time to think about what we've said. Later I can bring up the subject again and we'll both be better able to discuss it. Other decisions about our relationship, where there is not so much friction, are either made by whoever really cares about the issue or by the person the situ-*

*ation will most inconvenience. Issues are usually negotiated until we reach a fair outcome.*

## Outside Influences

Since each family is one permeable subsystem among many, all sorts of outside factors affect how a family makes decisions. Mom's salary, BJ's friends, and Mary Frances' teacher may all affect how a decision is resolved.

Decisions within a family system often represent compromises or adaptations to other societal systems. School, corporate, and government systems impinge upon families and influence decisions. The interface between the family and any other system can make problem-solving easier or more difficult. Other systems also have rules, images, and boundaries that require maintenance and a change process that helps them continue as viable systems. For example, think of how a business where one parent works affects decision making. If the mother must travel, work overtime, or take customers out in the evening, the family makes decisions differently than if this were not necessary. The school/home interface requires other adjustments in decision making, particularly if both parents work or a single parent has chief responsibility for providing income, childcare, and nurturance. "Latchkey kids," filling time between the end of the school day and the time a parent arrives home, make different decisions than children greeted by a parent at the door.

Government, business, and education are deeply and permanently involved in policies that impact upon families. Decisions forced upon a family by outside agencies restrict individual member's choices and require flexibility and adjustments, sometimes for poor reasons, often resulting in added tension in families. Divorce, desertion, or death can greatly alter the decision making processes in a family. If separating partners cannot reach decisions about equity issues, then attorneys and judges intervene. If there are children, decisions must be made regarding custody, visitation rights, financial arrangements, and property or inheritance rights (Buehler 1989). This is painful, as the following respondent indicates:

*In this age of "experts" our family was almost ripped apart as my parents tried to make decisions about how to raise my younger brother who has a serious attention deficit disorder.*

(continued on page 228)

*My mother was always wanting to follow the advice of a doctor or teacher; my father wanted the family to make the decisions about Robert's care. My parents were constantly disagreeing with each other and the medical and educational experts.*

---

According to Sporakowski (1988), "Decision making processes used in previous generations may not work under the conditions in which families find themselves functioning" (367).

## COMMUNICATION IN DECISION MAKING

Remember the discussion of these family decision making factors as you read the following results of a comparison of communication and decision making between married couples and unrelated single couples. Note how communication differs in decision making because a couple operates within their own system, while unrelated single individuals do not have those systemic ties to consider before deciding. Winter et al. (1973) measured seven aspects of communication:

- Spontaneous agreement (the shared values and like preferences that exist prior to the decision making process)
- Decision time
- Choice fulfillment (the number of times a positive or negative choice by one agrees with that of the partner)
- Silence (the length of time no one communicates)
- Interruptions
- Explicit information (a definite statement of a liked or disliked choice)
- Politeness (overall impression of how couples treat one another—tone of voice, asking questions, listening quietly, and being supportive).

The results indicated that married couples had more spontaneous agreement, were less polite, made more interruptions, and exchanged less explicit information. A higher degree of spontaneous agreement would be expected, because a married couple has learned the values and wishes of one another, and each has a history of sharing these values. Married and unmarried couples took about the same amount of time to reach a decision and were almost equally effective in reaching mutually satisfying decisions. Unrelated stranger pairs listened more respectfully to one another than married couples—a sad commentary on marital communication.

In another study, Krueger found that disagreements serve as a functional part of the decision making process, particularly when each partner uses positive communication strategies to express their differences. She found this was true except when a sequence began with a disagreement followed too rapidly by another disagreement, which signaled the beginning of conflict escalation. She also noted that partners change subjects sometimes as a transition and at other times to avoid conflict. These changes indicate that couples do not focus for long periods of time on a single issue, thus demonstrating a cyclical model of decision making, with the couple taking up a topic and leaving it, returning later to reach a decision.

Throughout this chapter, you have seen that communication plays a key role in determining the outcomes of family decision making. The way in which family members use verbal and nonverbal communication determines decision making outcomes. The sending of mixed messages by one or more members affects decisions and may alter the cohesion and balance of the family system. Recent studies indicated that relationship satisfaction is highly related to skill in problem solving in married couples (Renick, Blumberg, and Markham 1992) and cohabiting gay and lesbian couples (Kurdek 1991). In the Kurdek study the use of problem solving strategies of negotiation and compromise led to constructive decision making; negative strategies such as coercion, withdrawal, and avoidance produced poor decisions and relational satisfaction. In comparing race and gender differences in using a problem solving model in a sample of dating African American couples compared to white couples, Sanderson and Kurdek (1993) did not find significant differences in problem solving and happiness in relationships between the two samples or between the men and women in the samples. What they did find was that couples, regardless of race, reported higher relationship satisfaction when there was frequent positive problem solving. Thomas listed the following communication difficulties that hinder decision making:

> … overtalk, overresponsiveness, quibbling, over-generalization, presumptive attribution, misrepresentation of fact or evaluation, content avoidance, content shifting, content persistence, poor referent specification, temporal remoteness, excessive opinions, opinion deficit, excessive agreement, excessive disagreement, too little information, too much information, illogical talk, and excessive negative talk (123).

Researchers have argued over whether the dominant authority structure in a family can be determined from the manner in which decision making responsibilities have been allocated or from studying the decision outcomes. The conclusion is that family authority and decision making operate together as a dynamic, interactive system, requiring give and take among family members.

The following principles, based on Kohlberg's and Gilligan's concerns for justice, care, and responsibility could help guide family members in their decision making: (1) create a sense of justice by treating family members equally, regardless of sex or their power resources, (2) create a sense of autonomy by respecting each family member's rights to free choices in order to carry out actions that enhance their lives, (3) create a sense of caring by helping other family members achieve their goals, (4) create an awareness of which decisions lead to actions and behaviors that harm family members or place them at risk, (5) create a sense of loyalty via keeping promises and carrying out decisions mutually agreed upon. These principles should enhance the self concepts of each family member. More importantly, the use of these ethical guidelines in decision making should enable family members to self disclose more easily and achieve greater intimacy. This complex process of decision making can be streamlined by experiences of a life of shared communication as described in the following example:

---

*For fifty years, Lambert and I have always tried to make decisions together. We try to spend our money as we both see fit and discuss what is important to us. We usually shop together: groceries, machinery, cars, and so on. Even on buying our tombstone, we looked them over and decided on one we both liked. We've had our differences, but we always tried to see things from the other point of view and eventually we'd resolve the problem.*

---

## CONCLUSION

This chapter, with the help of the model, discussed a process-oriented approach to understanding decision making. Through communication interactions, power is used and decisions made often using consensus, accommodation, or *de facto* decisions. These decisions may occur in families that govern their systems by styles such as zero-sum confrontations, by the creation and maintenance of various types of rules, or by guiding principles of fairness based on conscience.

There are five decision-making steps that families often use to communicate differences yet solve their problems: establishing definitions, exploring and analyzing the problem, establishing solution criteria, listing possible solutions and selecting a solution. Although compromise may be required, this problem-solving approach has the potential to strengthen cohesion in the family. The chapter concluded with a variety of factors that affect communication in decision making.

## IN REVIEW

1. Give an example of a decision that was made in a real or fictional family that illustrates one of the types of decision making.
2. Give specific examples of how factors such as gender, age, individual interests or resources affected a family's decision making process.
3. To what extent should children be part of the family's decision making process? How can they be guided to develop the communication skills necessary to participate effectively in such discussions?
4. Decide and explain what kinds of decisions the family members in a television sitcom usually make under a variety of situations.
5. If you wanted to improve your decision-making skills and make decisions easily with a significant other person in your life, what communication behaviors would you try to demonstrate? Make a list of suggestions based upon your understanding of ideas in this and other chapters.

# 9

# Communication and Family Conflict

Normal families fight! Controversies in families enable the systems to grow and change. The mere absence of conflict does not make a family function well. Both functional and dysfunctional families conflict, but the functional family processes conflict more positively (Gottman 1994). In other words, family members use conflict as they struggle to make their differences more tolerable. In spite of the best decision-making strategies, individual family members can feel cheated or misunderstood in attempting to meet their needs within the family system. The ways in which a family agrees are important, and the more agreement between members, the less likelihood of disastrous conflict. The way in which a family disagrees is equally important. You probably have already observed great variations in how families handle conflicts. Some battle openly while others covertly do one another harm. What is accepted as rational in one family may be perceived as irrational in another (Vangelisti 1993). All family members help in either negative or positive ways to regulate the dialectical tensions that conflicts create within family systems. It's hard as an individual family member to remain neutral when conflict develops between or among other members.

One strong parent or sibling can suppress or avoid conflicts and provide necessary stability for other members to take coordinated actions that make the family system appear to be balanced. Over time, however, such suppression can have negative effects. Dysfunctional families may get stuck in a powerful conflict cycle and devastate one or more members.

Conflict affects and is affected by all areas of family life. Family members use rules and their roles to help solve the problems through communication strategies. They escalate or avoid conflict. Conflict may create boundaries, yet boundaries may serve to reduce potential conflicts. A family's themes or images will influence the amount and the type of conflict that develops. Conflicts can cause negative outcomes: divorce, marital distress, confused children, depressed family members, or loss of property and money (Renick, Blumberg, and Markman 1992, 141). A family theme of "no conflict" can lead to future problems, as the daughters experienced in the following example:

---

*In our family we were not allowed to fight. My mother wouldn't tolerate it! She would say, "God only gave me two little girls and they are not going to kill one another." Arguments were cut off or we were sent to our rooms. After she died we fought most of the next ten years! We each had so many old resentments—scores to settle. For over two years we didn't speak! Fortunately, we relearned how to relate to one another and now conflict only when necessary.*

---

This chapter will examine the conflict process, a model of conflict styles, factors related to the conflict process, and communication strategies for managing inevitable family conflicts.

## THE CONFLICTUAL PROCESS

Family members who confront their differences can improve their relationships and accomplish more joint benefits that increase love and caring. Conflict can provide opportunities for more effective feedback that leads to innovations that enhance adaptability and cohesiveness. Think of conflict and communication as interdependent. Each affects the other. Communication either helps or hinders conflict and serves as a way to resolve conflicts or continue them (Hocker and Wilmot 1991). The intensity of the conflict determines the kinds of messages produced, the patterns the confrontations follow and the interpretations placed on the communication cues (Roloff 1987).

### Conflict Defined

Conflict is a process in which two or more members of a family believe that their desires are incompatible with those of the others. It may be a matter of perception, as when Jose believes that the degree of intimacy expected of him is too threatening or requires more of him than he is willing to deliver. Conflict may also develop over a difference in attitudes or values. Robin, a full-time working mother, does not enjoy cooking and would rather the family went out to eat pizza than expect her to fix dinner. Conflict may also arise when one person's self-esteem is threatened. If each person can reach his or her own goals, there is no conflict. Conflict occurs when one person's behavior or desire blocks the goals of another, resulting in "a struggle over values, behaviors, powers, and resources in which each opponent seeks to achieve his goals usually at some expense to the other" (Scanzoni and Polonko 1980). From a communication perspective, conflict may be viewed as "an expressed struggle between at least two interdependent parties, who perceive incompatible goals, scarce resources, and interference from the other party in achieving their goals" (Hocker and Wilmot 1991, 12).

The conflictual process is very complex. Conflict has an individual dimension. The conflicts going on within an individual family member often can cause trouble with others in the family such as when a father or daughter senses an incompatibility or inconsistency within their own cognitive elements (Roloff 486). A frustrated family member who doesn't like his or her job and feels inadequate about coping may have individual issues that affect behavior within the family's conflict situations. In addition, family members may use conflicts in a dialectical sense to gain autonomy when they feel trapped and need to reduce connectedness. It is important to understand that not all dialectical contradictions involve conflict. Those that do are referred to as antagonistic contradictions. Other contradictions that regulate tension are non-antagonistic when they don't lead to conflict. Werner and Baxter (1994) state "non-antagonistic contradictions are intrapersonal in nature; the individual experiences internally the dialectical pull between contradictory oppositions" (353). Antagonistic contradictions become external and result from a mismatching of interests and goals of individual family members, causing a different kind of dialectical tension.

Change may trigger uneasiness and conflict. A new family member, the acquiring of a new job, the trauma of a divorce, or loss of income all have an impact within the family system. Disturbances in equilibrium lead to conditions in which groups or individuals no longer do willingly what they are expected to do. Family systems experience a constant level of friction, since they continually change to survive and cope with conflict, either realistically or unrealistically. In his classic work, Coser (1967) defined *realistic conflicts* as those that result from frustration of one family member wanting something from another member who does not see the necessity of granting the request or meeting the need. *Nonrealistic conflicts* are those characterized by at least one antagonist's need for tension release. Within family systems, conflict directed toward members for the improvement of conditions and rights are realistic. Nonrealistic conflicts may result from frustrations caused by persons other than those against whom the original conflict was directed. Such behavior may result in misdirected anger or scapegoating. For conflict to be realistic, the communication must be between the family members directly involved in the matter.

If a couple or family plans to share experiences and realizes the advantages of family solidarity, conflict will be an inevitable and valuable part of the process. Gottman and Krokoff (1990) found in their research that "some forms of confrontation during marital conflict precede increases in marital satisfaction" (504). These researchers concluded that conflict avoidance had negative long term consequences. Sometimes, family conflict evolves into either a stalemate or a bitter fight, and no members emerge happily. By exploring the process of conflict and how it can develop realistically or nonrealistically, plus becoming aware of better communication practices to use during conflict, one can better understand the development and management of family conflict situations.

Several studies have concluded that conflicts are present in successfully functioning marriages as well as in dysfunctional marriages (Schaeffer 1989; Gottman 1993). While all relationships have problems, successful ones have partners who learn how to negotiate conflicts. In addition, conflict outside the home in jobs, social groups, or friendships can cause unrealistic conflicts within the family. Individuals who live together in a close and intimate relationship cannot expect a conflict-free existence. In certain stages of courtship for some couples, there is little conflict, but conflicts develop as the relationship progresses.

In his early important work on measuring family conflict, Straus (1979) states that conflict is an inevitable part of all human association and keeps social units, such as nations or families, from collapse. "If conflict is suppressed, it can result in stagnation and failure to adapt to changed circumstances and/or erode the bond of group solidarity because of an accumulation of hostility" (75). Attitudes toward conflict emerge partially from cultural background; in some cultures open struggle is commonplace and comfortable, in other cultures differences are avoided at all costs.

## Model of Conflict Styles

Every family member has a distinct conflict style. Each conflict is different for every member. Your personality in conflict changes with regard to one family member or another. For example, your mother and brother have a conflict style that is not exactly the same as the way each of them conflicts with you. You also conflict differently with your mother than you do with your brother. In addition, your experiences within your extended family, plus your perceptions of conflict in other social systems, affect your conflict style. As you grew up, you learned how to survive conflicts; this learning influenced the conflict strategies you tend to use.

Kilmann and Thomas (1975) developed a model (Figure 9.1) to demonstrate that conflict style consists of two partially competing goals: concern for others and concern for self. Conflicts contain elements of both cooperation and assertiveness, as well as the need for interdependence.

Each of these styles warrant discussion. Avoidance implies you are nonassertive, and not particularly interested in cooperation. You will not participate. The storm brews but you seek cover. However, remember that while you might behave this way in a dispute with your older sister, you might be more assertive, and hence competitive, with a younger brother on the same issue. This conflict style particularly hampers communication about intimate matters in cases where one partner simply ignores such topics.

At the lower right of the model is accommodation. This style of conflict happens when you are nonassertive but cooperative. It is the opposite of competition, because you meet the demands or needs of the other person but deny your own. Where do you think the following example would fall on the model?

---

*My father left my mother last year to live with someone else. I have become my mother's main support. She calls me at college almost every day and demands I come home for all kinds*

(continued on page 238)

**FIGURE 9.1**
**Conflict Styles**

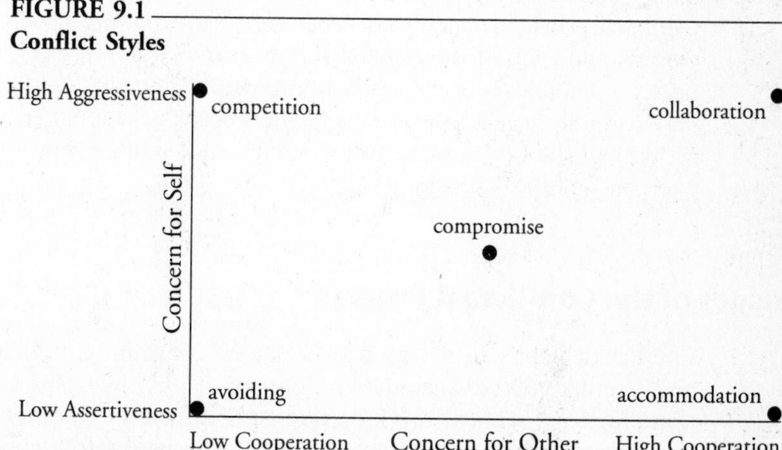

*of silly reasons. Right now I can't seem to tell her to back off so I do whatever she wants and hope this stage will pass.*

---

Competition and collaboration are at the top of the model. Competitiveness requires aggressiveness and going after what you want. Your concern for self is high and, thus, you see conflict as a way to get what you need, regardless of the concerns of others. Competition can be quite selfish if it is your only style of conflict. It can mean "I win, you lose" too often and destroy cohesion within a family. The challenge is to compete to achieve personal goals without taking unfair advantage of other family members. Wilmot and Wilmot changed the term in Kilmann and Thomas' model from high assertiveness to a highly competitive condition. Assertiveness, a more positive term, recognizes the rights of others to disagree.

Collaboration occurs when you show concern for those other family members. Collaboration requires that conflicting members seek a solution that enables all parties to feel they have won without compromising issues vital to their needs. Again, remember that your collaboration style varies from member to member. You use your personality differently in conflict, depending upon the family members involved and your closeness to them.

Compromise occupies the middle ground of this model. A compromise represents a solution that partially meets the needs of each member in the conflict. It is an adjustment to the differences that all can accept. In some families, the motto is "Be wise and compromise." Such a family theme recognizes that too much independence detracts from family cohesion and that adaptability via compromise enables more intimacy and tasks to be accomplished in a family.

This model of conflict style provides a way of sensing how one family member's fights affect another's counter arguments through feedback. This feedback varies between parents and also between parents and each of their children. For example, you are not permanently competitive; it depends upon whom you are fighting. You may carefully watch your conflict style with your stepfather because of his high blood pressure but not with your mother who enjoys—even encourages—speaking out.

## Stages of the Conflictual Process

Conflict develops in stages with a source, beginning, middle, end, and aftermath (Vuchinich 1987; Gottman 1979; Filley 1975). Understanding how conflict develops permits you to unravel some of the complexity and places a point of anger or blowup into a larger context. The following six stages provide a model for analyzing the conflict process:

1. Prior Conditions Stage
2. Frustration and Awareness Stage
3. Active Conflict Stage
4. Solution or Nonsolution Stage
5. Follow-Up Stage
6. Resolved Stage

As these stages are explained, think about a recent conflict in your family. Did each of these stages emerge as a distinct entity or was it difficult to know when one ended and the next began?

***Prior Conditions Stage*** Conflict does not occur without a prior reason or without a connection of the present event to the past experiences in the family. It does not emerge out of a vacuum but has a beginning in the background of the relationship of the conflicting people. The family system or its context establishes a framework out of which conflicts arise. The participants are aware of the family's rules, themes, boundaries, biosocial beliefs, and accepted patterns of communication.

In conflict, at least one member perceives that the rules, themes, boundaries, or beliefs have been violated or that they have been threatened by something inside or outside the family. Prior conditions are present in the absence of conflict but, under pressure, come into play. Prior conditions that may affect a new conflict situation include: ambiguous limits on each family member's responsibilities and role expectations; competition over scarce resources such as money or affection; unhealthy dependency of one person upon another; negative decision-making experiences shared by those involved in the conflict; necessity for consensus and agreement by all on one decision; and the memory of previously unresolved family conflicts (Filley 1975, 8–12). Thus, past experiences set the groundwork for new tension.

***Frustration Awareness Stage*** The second conflict stage involves one or more family members becoming frustrated because a person or group is blocking them from satisfying a need or concern. This leads to an awareness of being attacked or threatened by something they have seen or heard, which may be a nonverbal message in the form of a stern look or avoidance of eye contact. If you closely monitor any developing conflict, usually nonverbal cues of conflict appear before verbal ones. As you nonverbally become aware of the conflict, you may ask yourself, "What's wrong?" "What's his problem?" "Why am I not being understood?" This frustration depends upon the mutual perceptions of the individuals involved. It is in this frustration awareness stage that one family member becomes increasingly aware that he or she is not communicating effectively with other family members. If two persons align their respective interests and goals to set up a struggle, "the dialectical struggle is antagonistic, that is, likely to involve interpersonal conflict," according to Werner and Baxter (1994, 353). This mismatching may be due to misperceptions.

Inaccurate perceptions can create conflict where none exists. Frustration is affected by whether members are having an isolated disagreement or if they are functioning in a general state of disagreement at this point in time (Schaeffer 1989). Perceptions also affect the degree to which the participants feel they will be threatened or lose if the conflict continues. Conflict may end at this stage if one party perceives that the negative consequences outweigh the possible advantages. In families, this happens when one of the members shows signs of power and expects compliance. "Backing off" from the issue ends the conflict but does not remove the causes or satisfy the needs that provoked it. This kind of unrealistic conflict may be avoided through self-disclosure. "I'm really just upset about the test tomorrow and I'm taking it out on you," or "You're right—I was selfish and I'm sorry."

It is during this stage, labeled "agenda building" by Gottman, that cross complaining occurs via a series of negative messages that the involved family members are unwilling to stop. They also refuse to recognize nonverbal signals asking for affection or cooperation. Each family member defends his or her view in this stage.

***Active Conflict Stage*** In this stage, the conflict manifests itself in a series of verbal and nonverbal messages. This symbolic interchange can either be like a battleground or be relatively calm, depending upon the family's rules and style of fighting. In some families, yelling and screaming signals the fight of the decade, whereas others exercise their lungs weekly over minor issues:

*Unfortunately, my husband is the type who would rather yell. He is not always a fair fighter. When I want to talk and explain my feelings, and then give him a chance to explain his, he either goes into moody silence or explodes. I find both approaches useless.*

Typically, conflict escalates from initial statements and queries to bargaining or an ultimatum. In the active conflict stage, there is a discernible strategy, or game plan, as one or more family members try to

**FIGURE 9.2**
**Stages of Family Conflict**

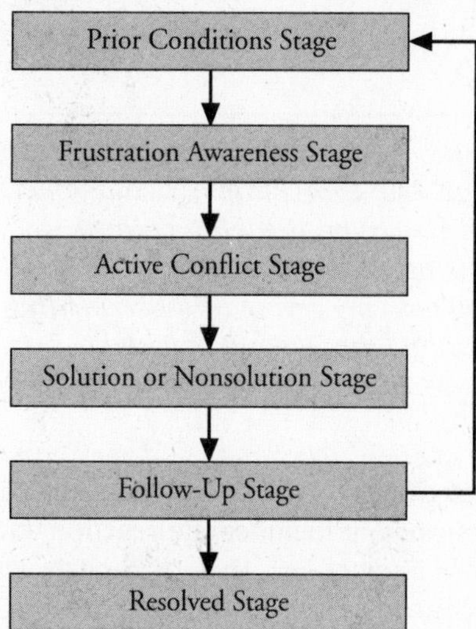


maneuver and convince others of the merits of an issue. The longer the conflict continues, the more the participants' behavior may create new frustrations, reasons for disliking, and continued resistance. Dysfunctional couples usually return negative remarks, matching their partner's complaints. This is called cross-complaining. When partners complaints are acknowledged, it is called cross-validating (Warner 1991a). Functional couples tended to match positive remarks or coordinate negative with positive remarks. Family subsystems may take sides or form alliances.

***Solution or Nonsolution Stage*** The active conflict stage evolves into either a solution or nonsolution stage. The solution may be creative, constructive, and satisfactory to all involved, or it may be destructive, nonproductive, and disappointing. The solution may represent a compromise or adjustment of previously held positions. In this stage, how the conflict is managed or solved determines the outcome and whether positive or negative results follow.

Some conflicts progress into a nonsolution. Family members may not have the resources or talents to solve the problem, or, after going this far into the conflict process, they may recognize that they do not want the responsibility of carrying out what they demanded. Perhaps they decide they do not want to pay the trade-off costs of accepting a change they earlier demanded. This nonsolution brings the conflict to an agreed-upon impasse. Obviously, communication problems can develop if too many conflicts end with nonsolutions. However, every family lives with some unresolved conflicts, because the costs of an acceptable solution outweighed the disadvantage to one or more family members. Sometimes, when children mature, they look back on conflicts quite differently, as in the following example:

---

*My sister and I are thirteen months apart. We fought like cats through our teens. Jamie would always keep at me until I would reach the breaking point. I would say that my anger was rising. Naturally, that was the red flag, and we would end up with my crying and her goading me on. It's ridiculous now when I think about how she manipulated me into crying.*

---

***Follow-Up Stage*** The follow-up stage could also be called the aftermath, because it includes the reactions that follow the conflict and affect future interactions, such as repeats of the same conflict, avoidance, or conciliation without acceptance. Grudges, hurt feelings, or physical scars may fester until they lead to the beginning stage of another conflict. The outcomes may be positive, such as increased intimacy and self-esteem or honest explorations of family values or concerns. This aftermath stage is linked by a feedback chain to the initial stage, because each conflict in a family is stored in the prior conditions "bank" of the family and comes into operation in determining the pattern of future conflicts.

***Resolved Stage*** This stage occurs when conflicts move out of the family system—they simply no longer affect its balance. For example, a husband and wife may conflict over priorities on bills to be paid. They negotiate and compromise on demands, then stick to their agreement. Time and developmental stages of each family member affect solutions to conflicts. For example, parental conflicts over who will take Steve to school decrease or disappear after he becomes old enough to walk there by himself; the same will be true of parental conflicts over dating rules and curfews when he becomes a young adult. Conflicts over space and territory among six children competing for three bedrooms no longer require solutions when all have left home and the "empty nest" remains.

It is important to remember that in the model (Figure 9.2) participants may "exit" at any stage. A drop-in visitor may interrupt during the frustration awareness stage and actually defuse the tension. One or the other party may disengage from the issue, give in, or shift the focus. Gottman (1982) found in analyzing the sequential nature of conflicts that an essential difference between distressed and adjusted couples was the ability of happy couples to de-escalate verbally potential negative effects. Vuchinich (1987) discovered in his study of conflicts at the family dinner table that 61 percent ended in standoffs that were used as the easiest way to get out of conflicts. The different family members involved most frequently used submission and compromise to close off conflicts. Renick, Blumberg, and Markman (1992) noted that nondistressed couples exited out of the beginning stages of negative interaction cycles while distressed couples engaged in negative escalations.

## The Conflict Model in Action

To demonstrate the operation of this model of conflict, follow the example of the Hanrahan family: Dad (45), Mom (45), Frank (21), Louie (19), and Nellie (17). The boys attend the local junior college because the family's funds are limited. At an evening meal in January, Nellie asks her mother if she can apply to a distant four-year college to major in her specialty, marine biology. Mom responds positively, because Nellie has high grades and has been promised financial help on her degree. Frank frowns, because he assumes that Nellie's request means that he cannot go away to college and silently begins to react. He thinks about the other family hassles and recalls other encounters between his sister and himself when Mom took Nellie's side. Frank wonders if Dad or Louie would agree with him that his education was more important than Nellie's. In the past, the men in the family have banded together. All of these prior conditions are important to the outcome of this conflict.

Communication shifts into the second stage. Louie clears his throat and nonverbally gains his mother's attention by waving his fork. He enters the frustration stage, because he too wants to go away to school and fears that planning between Nellie and Mom will move fast. He thinks there is no way Frank or he can go away to finish their degrees if Nellie insists. Louie announces, "I was going away myself next year." Both his mother and Nellie cease talking and nonverbally check out Louie, their eyes asking the question, "Are you serious?" They discover he is and also that he looks angry enough to fight. They check out Frank, and he looks equally agitated. The sons eye one another for support. The women look at one another as if to say, "Where do we go from here?" This leads to the third stage—active conflict.

"I asked Dad on Wednesday if I could go to the university," Frank declares. The women exchange glances again and then each looks at Dad, who nods in agreement. "Also, I checked with Louie and he didn't disagree." Louie nods to confirm this.

"I never get to do what I want in this family," Nellie says in a defeated voice. "When all of you get through planning, there is nothing left for what I want." Nellie looks at each of the men. Her voice begins to rise as she pushes back her chair and begins to noisily pile up her dishes. "The junior college doesn't even have one course in my field, and I'll lose credits when I transfer."

Mom anxiously glances at all the children and then at her husband, who catches her eye and then looks toward Nellie and Frank. His silent message seems to be, "How are we going to solve this?" This scene of conflict could continue in countless ways. The parents could remain silent, and Frank and Nellie could escalate the conflict into a series of harsh remarks, including charges of favoritism or wasting family money, thus repeating unsolved family brawls. The development of the controversy will depend upon what the prior conditions "bank" includes and the family's problem-solving style. What rules does it follow in conflict situations? What rules do the father and mother assume in such disputes? If Mom is the peacemaker, she will smooth things over. If Dad is dominant, he will negotiate a settlement—fair or otherwise.

The solution stage of the conflict starts as Dad speaks up: "Wait a minute! Perhaps Mom and I can help this argument." Mom smiles at Dad to let him know she likes this approach. In this family's conflicts, the parents present a unified position, and the father usually asserts that "he and Mom" will be the arbitrators. Dad asks, "Can Nellie go another time?" Nellie shakes her head "No." Dad then looks at Frank with an unstated question, inquiring if he has any flexibility and could change his plans. Frank sends back a "no compromise" message. So does Louie. "Well, what can we do?" Dad asks. "Are there any other options?"

This leads to a series of possible solutions. "Couldn't Nellie go to the junior college like we did?" Frank volunteers. "It might take her longer, but by that time Frank and I would be through school and there would be more money for her," Louie suggests.

"Would that work?" Mom asks Nellie. She shrugs, for she does not really prefer that solution. This leads to a discussion of how much money each of the children thinks they will need in the next few years for college expenses. Since education has been a high priority theme in this family, all participants have a vested interest. Both parents want all of their children to have the degrees that they were unable to obtain. Another theme has been to "pay as you go," and, thus, loans have not been considered.

In this family, a compromise solution works. Mom agrees to accept a full-time position she had been offered and use the income to help pay the increased expenses when Frank and Nellie go away to school. Since this discussion occurs in January, she has nine months before tuition is due.

Dad agrees to increase his credit union savings by 15 percent. Frank and Nellie agree to secure loans and to work part time. Louie stays at the community college, because it has an excellent pre-engineering program, but he receives assurances that he could have additional future support. The family reaches the decision that each child receives the same amount of money from the parents and that each would have to earn or secure loans for the rest.

The follow-up stage continues the conflict process. The family will store in their prior conditions bank the positive aspects of this experience. Louie may feel Nellie owes him a favor, and Nellie may be more willing to agree in a future encounter because Louie accommodated her. They will also store the amount of self-worth and self-confidence each family member has received in this conflict. That is why the feedback link from this follow-up stage back to the first conflict stage is so important. Future conflicts are affected by the positive or negative aspects of current conflict: this family may one day have to renegotiate the allocation of resources for college educations.

If the compromise works effectively, eventually the conflict moves into the resolved stage, a kind of "They lived happily ever after" stage. The family comes to closure with this conflict over resources. However, disagreements or favoritism can lead to the cycle of conflict all over again. The reaching of this resolution stage is a major goal of effective family communication.

## FACTORS IN FAMILY CONFLICT

You fight with each member of your family in different ways. Over time, most families develop their rules for conflictual situations, and each member stays within the calibrated levels, except for unique situations when he or she may go beyond acceptable fighting levels or reconciling behaviors. A tearful embrace may jolt the family pattern far more than a flying frying pan. A family's systemic nature affects its conflictual patterns, which emerge and maintain themselves. Dialectical tension generated in conflicts is not a negative force but rather a part of the ongoing dynamic interaction between opposite views and needs of family members. It can be a positive force because the "interplay of opposing tendencies serves as the driving force or catalyst of ongoing change in relationships" (Werner and Baxter 1994, 351).

Scanzoni (1972) classified couple conflicts into two major types: those that concern the basis of the relationship and those that concern less central issues (73). In the first type, basic values and goals held by one family member are ignored or challenged by another.

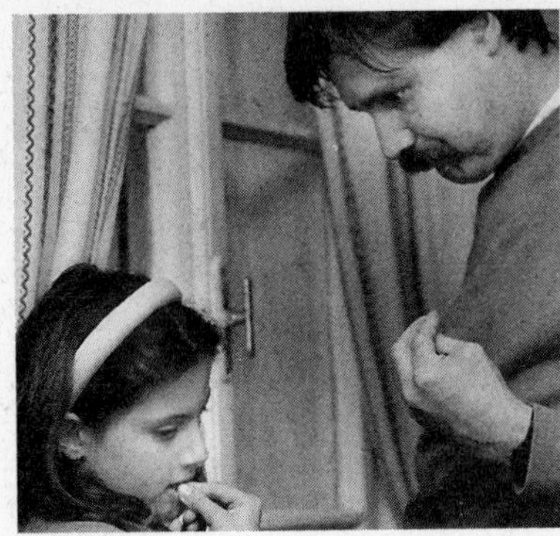

Family pairs develop their own conflict styles.

Conflict over such values as religion, having children, or the need for education can become quite painful or have a dysfunctional effect upon the family system. Unresolved, these conflicts could result in separation or termination of the relationship. The second type occurs when family members seek ways "to change or maintain some part of the distribution of rights and privileges in the relationship" (76). Such conflicts might deal with problems over which bills to pay first or where the family should go for vacation.

## Patterns of Family Conflict

In their major study of conflict in early marriage, Raush et al (1974) found that "whatever the contributions of the specific partners, the marital relationship forms a unit, and the couple can be thought of as a system." Their analysis revealed that the marital unit was the "most powerful source in determining interactive events" (201). Couples developed their own styles of conflict, which were unique to them. Soon after marriage, the system had its own fight style.

How does a fight style form so quickly? Do yellers marry yellers, apologizers pair with apologizers? Common sense says this is not always the case, yet, within a short time, a couple appears to acquire a set of characteristic conflictual behaviors. Raush and his colleagues found similar responses to be one of the major determinants of interaction, i.e., certain conflictual behaviors of one partner were more likely to elicit similar responses from the other. The same reciprocal pattern held for negative behaviors, such as coercive tactics or personal attacks. The only exception occurred when one partner rejected the other. Rejection is usually met with either coercion or emotional appeals. If both partners rejected each other, communication ended. Family members' use of appeals, whether to fair fighting, justice, promises, or future favors kept the communication process going. Thus, partners were more likely to send similar reciprocal messages than they were to shift to a new message style. Interestingly, Warner's (1991b) more recent research on cross-complaining and cross-validating supports these ideas.

Such reciprocity is a tendency, not an absolute; conflict does not function as a totally predictable ritual with foregone conclusions. Certain partners may have such different approaches to fighting that reciprocity does not emerge. As you saw in the Fitzpatrick typologies, separates, traditionals, and independents each display particular conflict styles, and it may be more difficult to create reciprocity when different types marry than when similar types marry. Rosenblatt, Titus, and Cunningham (1979) have found that when one or both partners use disrespect, coercion, and other abrasive factors in their communication, conflicts escalate and couples spend less time together. Before togetherness, or cohesiveness, can be increased and conflicts settled amicably, couples "must first deal with abrasive aspects of the relationship" (54).

Who starts conflicts? Do family members in their roles as father, mother, son, or daughter initiate more fights? No consistent pattern developed. According to Vuchinich (1987), parents started 47.6 percent of the conflicts and children began 52.4 percent of them. More importantly, the father had less conflict initiated against him. Mothers, sons, and daughters shared about the same number of conflict attacks. Children started conflicts twice as often with the mother. Sons initiated conflicts three times more frequently with the mother. Fathers started disagreements with their daughters three times more frequently than with their sons. Mothers countered this with starting conflicts twice as often with their sons.

Another pattern appears in the closing of conflicts with mothers most frequently involved in working out compromises, or "stand-offs," in which the family members agree to disagree and no one really wins. Daughters more readily than sons or fathers participated in the above ways of closing conflicts. In solving conflicts via submission, children acquiesced three times more frequently than parents. After stand-offs occurred, females initiated nonconflict activities twice as often.

Feldman (1979) views a couple's conflictual behavior as part of an intimacy-conflict cycle. Couples move from a state of intimacy as one member became anxious or fearful, which leads to conflict and separation. Eventually, one partner makes an attempt to patch up the differences. The desire for intimacy draws them back together. The need to be touched, reaffirmed, comforted, and nourished is a powerful conciliatory force in conflicts. At first, one partner might reject attempts to resume more positive communication, but the need for intimacy provides the motivation for repeated efforts to achieve it.

This research relates to our emphasis upon the element of cohesion in all families.

The couple's coming back together does not mean the problem between them has been resolved. Quite often, the issue has not been satisfactorily discussed or even fairly treated in the best interests of one or the other. This means that future communications on the same issue will take up where the old conflict leaves off. Intimacy will again evolve into conflict when one partner feels threatened by the issue or aggressive enough to challenge. Have you heard people fighting and had the feeling you were hearing a rerun or rehearsed battle? Communication reaches the conflict stage because some rules in the relationship have been violated; the system tries to recalibrate itself. The degree and limits of acceptable intimacy and acceptable conflict are important dimensions of a marital system's calibration. When these limits are violated, the intimacy-conflict cycle starts again.

Parts of Feldman's intimacy conflict theory can be related to Baxter's views that individuals respond to contradictory demands by seeking to fulfill each demand separately. They do this through either cyclic alternation or segmentation responses. In cyclic alternation, first one partner complains or yells and the other responds. In segmentation the family members try to verbally group their complaints around a conflicting point. In conflict, husband and wife can "cycle or spiral between the two poles of contradiction, separating them temporally with each contradictory demand gaining fulfillment during its temporal cycle" (Werner and Baxter 1994, 363). These authors report that cyclic alternation and segmentation are the most frequently used responses couples enact to manage the dialectical exigencies of their relationship.

## Rules for Family Conflict

Members of family systems develop implicit and explicit rules governing the communication of conflictual messages. In their study of rules used in conflicts, Jones and Gallois (1989) found couples generated or implied four kinds of rules in resolving their differences. They identified (1) rules governing consideration (e.g., don't belittle me; don't blame the other unfairly; don't make me feel guilty), (2) rules governing rationality (e.g., don't raise your voice; don't get me angry; don't be so aggressive), (3) rules governing specific self expression (e.g. let's keep to the point; let's be honest, don't exaggerate), and (4) rules governing conflict resolution (e.g., explore alternatives; make joint decisions; give reasons for your views) (961–962). These researchers found that rules governing conflicts differed when couples were in public or in private. The rationality rules were used more in public settings than in private. They were also more important to husbands than wives. However, both agreed rationality rules were the least important. These results agreed with Schaap et al (1987) who discovered that in conflicts husbands tended to use rational arguments and distance themselves while their wives used more emotional strategies.

Rules relating to conflict resolution were more important to both husbands and wives in private conflict. Rules governing consideration helped prohibit behaviors that would hurt others and helped maintain intimacy. Self expression rules operated in conflicts to regulate the process of communication and helped maintain intimacy by encouraging the exchange of opinions and enhancing a problem-solving style of discussion. Couples rated respect for self-expression rules second in importance in conflict resolution rules. Couple roles frequently influence the conflict behaviors of their children:

---

*As a child I remember my parents referring to their rules for fighting such as "Never go to bed mad" or "Never call the other person names." It seemed a bit silly at the time but after the kinds of fighting I experienced in my first marriage I made sure that my fiance and I discussed fighting and set some rules for disagreeing before I would consider a second marriage.*

---

## Costs and Rewards

Part of a family's systemic function relates to how costs and rewards are negotiated. Conflict may result if a teenager believes the costs of living in a family (rules, obligations, and pressures) outweigh the rewards (emotional and/or economic). Partners stay together as long as the rewards for remaining in a system outweigh the pain or costs of leaving it. Caring for children may be part of a reward and responsibility component in a marriage and hold a family together for a time, but eventually, if serious conflicts continue, one of the partners will leave. To avoid constant conflicts, there must be sufficient rewards in the family system to justify remaining together.

Conflicts may follow when these expectations are not met. When one family member does something special for another, a debt is owed. If the other fails to reciprocate, especially after several requests, conflict will start. Reciprocity becomes, or is a part of, the exchange of costs and rewards in the family. For the family to operate emotionally as a system, this reciprocity does not need to be equal either in amount or kind. Most family members do not keep an inventory up to date, but they know generally who owes them favors.

"This reciprocity," according to Scanzoni, "helps to account for marital stability because it sets up a chain of enduring obligations and repayments within a system of roles in which each role contains both rights and duties" (64). Gottman (1994) would agree with Scanzoni, pointing out that the positive forms of reciprocity must outweigh the negative ones. To ignore these obligations and repayments creates conflict in families.

The amount of equity in different relationships impacts conflict. DeVito defined equity in relationships as one in which each family member receives rewards proportional to his or her costs. He stated, "If you each work equally hard, then equity demands that you each get aproximately equal rewards" (1993, 285). A partner or sibling who feels unequal in a variety of ways will respond differently from one who feels equal. Although members may not have the same status or title, they can share in a sense of give and take or help each other feel confirmed and recognized. Canary and Stafford (1992) found that, in equitable relationships, more maintenance strategies were used, such as positivity, openness, assurances, sharing tasks, and doing networking with family and friends. The implementation of these maintenance strategies within a family system would certainly modify conflict behaviors.

## Roles in Family Conflict

Role expectations affect conflict. Position-oriented parents may require their children to ask them for what they want, while person-oriented parents look for consensus among the members and share leadership roles, especially with their children. Conflict may begin when role demands do not coincide with a family member's desires or abilities. He or she may not be prepared to fulfill certain functions. The expectancy that the individual can fulfill the present role causes anxiety and unhappiness. Young husbands raised in households where men never entered the kitchen to help with household chores will find difficulty in doing so, even if they are willing to change. In conflict, family rules determine who can do what, where, when, and how, and for what length of time (Jones and Gallois 1989; Miller, Corrales, and Wackman 1975).

Stereotyped sex-role conditioning hampers effective decision-making and heightens marital conflict. Many men in our society receive training that inhibits emotional feelings and the expression of empathy, but permits physical violence as a way to defend oneself. Many women receive counter-training that encourages over-expressiveness of feelings and inhibits constructive assertiveness and negotiation. This lack of expressiveness in husbands during conflicts causes "an emotional overreaction in wives which interferes with their rational problem-solving skills and leads to pressuring and coercion" (Feldman 1982, 356). Other researchers have found that women repress or suppress conscious reactions to threatening, unpleasant messages (Watson and Remer 1984). Another study reported that better educated women use more direct influence strategies in disagreements than less educated women (Zvonkovic, Schmiege, and Hall 1994). In a comparative study, men could identify with confrontation only to a moderate degree, and they had difficulty with empathy and seeing themselves accurately in conflict situations (Remer 1984). Fitzpatrick's independent type couples have little commitment to traditional sex roles and thus more readily negotiate and bargain with their spouse. This can lead to more conflict because independents won't tolerate stereotyping.

Men react differently in conflict, especially in unhappy marriages. In one study, wives reacted to small affective changes in their partners but their husbands seldom responded to large emotional changes in their wives (Giles and Wiemann 1987). In discussing conflict topics, satisfied wives used higher proportions of supportive and informational behaviors while dissatisfied wives used more competitive behaviors and individualistic utterances. Husbands responded similarly. However, in general, both satisfied and dissatisfied husbands used many more neutral communication cues while satisfied and dissatisfied wives need a higher ratio of positive cues (Maxwell and Weider-Hatfield 1987). Later research revealed that women are more concerned with conversational detail and monitor their conversations more seriously than do men (Duck et al. 1991). In a study of sex-role socialization, Arnston and Turner found that kindergarten children have different role expectations for fathers than mothers. Children in role playing would allow fathers to talk more and exert more power. They also would argue or conflict more with the mother (1989).

Family members' ties to kinship networks also influences conflicts. For example, in a study of urban families moving to the suburbs, Anderson (1982) found that working-class women who moved felt more isolation and experienced more marital conflict than middle-class women who had more resources in solving transition problems, including staying in contact with kin and friends. Couples who disagree about a wife's desire to work conflict more. They also argue more about how the children should be raised (Blumstein and Schwartz 1983). For working couples, both wives and husbands found the time spent in debriefing one another increased their marital satisfaction (Vangelisti and Banski 1993). Taking time to talk about their work outside the home should enable couples to shift role functions more easily and reenter the family environment in a less conflictual manner.

## Family and Couple Types and Conflict

Family types and structures can affect their conflict patterns. As a family evolves, the system develops conflictual behaviors, which characterize the group if not the individuals. Using Kantor and Lehr's (1976) types, one can predict how open, closed, or random families will behave in crises or conflict situations. These researchers hypothesized that closed families in conflicts frequently suppress the individual. This type of family operates successfully in conflict if members agree on solutions or accept those handed down to them. However, rebellion results when a member differs, and a permanent schism develops if one or more members refuse to comply with a major decision. Conflict in open families is usually resolved via group consensus in a meeting in which decisions are reviewed and modified. Conflicts are expected and welcomed if they make family living more meaningful. In decision making, every family member can reveal his or her feelings about an issue. This openness means that promises made in family conferences are kept. The random family demonstrates no set way to solve conflicts. No one person's views dominate, and ambiguity characterizes the negotiations. Emotional impasses occur when no solutions can be agreed upon. Solutions come spontaneously. Crises are not taken as seriously as in the other two family types and are viewed more as an interruption of day-to-day events.

The Fitzpatrick (1988) couple types demonstrate distinctive conflict behaviors. Traditional couples seek stability and resist change by confronting rather than avoiding conflict. However, they may avoid conflicts more than they realize. Traditionals more often collude with one another to avoid conflicts. Independents more readily accept uncertainty and change by confronting societal views on marriage in a much more direct communication style than traditionals. Independents do not run from conflicts. They resent a spouse who withdraws. Separates stress autonomy, especially by keeping their own space and distance as a strategy to avoid conflict. They hope to keep conflicts neutral and to a minimum. Separates appear angry toward a spouse who pushes conflict but withdraws when confronted. In conflict situations, independents receive satisfaction from self-disclosure, description, and questioning to receive further disclosure (Sillars et al. 1983).

## Family Developmental Stages

Conflict patterns change over the years because the issues to be resolved in families vary greatly over the years. During the early years of marriage, a couple develops a fight style that may be modified as the family grows. In their analysis of couples who had a child within the first two years of marriage, Raush and colleagues identified three stages of development (newlywed, pregnancy, parenthood) that were characterized by varying conflict behaviors, including rejection. They compared these couples who became pregnant to couples who did not have a child during these same years. During the newlywed stage, the developmental couples behaved more coercively than the matched couples, which may indicate greater stress due to impending parenting responsibilities.

Finally, during the parenthood stage, four months after the child's birth, both members of the couple appeared to handle conflict less emotionally and more cognitively than their matched counterparts. Yet the reconciling behavior of the husbands returned to prepregnancy levels. The early stage of being a threesome may lead to difficulties, since roles need to be reworked when a new person begins to compete for affection, often causing one of the other adults to feel left out. Although a joyful time in most families, early parenthood provides great stress that can lead to significant conflicts.

In the early childhood stage, parents often make decisions and solve conflicts by offering few options. As the child's ability to reason increases with age, the resolution of conflict relates closely to the type of family structure previously outlined. The adolescence period usually presents a greater number of family conflicts as young people search for independence and test rules and role expectancies. Intense peer pressure heightens conflict as family beliefs and practices are questioned. Teenagers make space and privacy demands, which may also cause conflict. Conflicts occur when adolescents question the patterns, images, and rules in their families. When dating starts, mothers have more conflicts with children, especially daughters (Silverberg and Steinberg 1987). Both adolescents and parents struggle as they face differences, as this student reports in the following situation:

---

*When I decided to go to New York for a "cattle call" for a possible movie part, it was the first time I actually argued with both my parents. During most of the argument, my father would not agree that we were in the midst of an argument. "We're just raising our voices," he insisted. This was his way of handling the conflict. He didn't want his little boy to grow up and leave. Finally, I stopped arguing about New York and argued about how he always denied we were fighting. Finally he admitted we were fighting. Two weeks later I went to New York City.*

---

If families undergo separation and divorce, children witness a recalibration of the system which usually involves a wider range of conflict behavior. One study of family conflict and children's self-concepts found no significant differences in self-concept scores of children from intact, single-parent, reconstituted, and other types of families. However, "self-concept scores were significantly lower for children who reported higher levels of family conflict" (Raschke and Raschke 1979). A later study clearly revealed the same, that, if high parental conflict before and after the divorce continued, adolescents performed poorer on both social and cognitive functions (Forehand et al. 1988). The stress and depression reported by single mothers (Webster-Stratton 1989) can create a conflictual climate for children at home. Broken homes did not yield broken lives, but excessive family conflict was definitely detrimental. In Cissna, Cox, and Bochner's study of stepfamilies (1990), they reported that the main dialectical dilemma was to adjust to the voluntary marital relationship and the involuntary step-child/parent relationship. Often there is great conflict between children and a step-mother or step-father over accepting the new person with her or his different rules and expectations.

The "empty nest" stage, defined as the period when the youngest child leaves home, presents fewer problems in flexible families than in rigid types. Parents' loneliness, uncertainty, or worry over capabilities of young adult "children" to care for themselves largely disappear after two years. In fact, this stage has positive effects upon the psychological well-being of some parents, because their child has been successful in making it on his or her own merits. Conflicts develop when the youngest lingers and takes extra years to leave (West, Zarski, and Harvil 1988; Suitor and Pillemer 1987).

Older married couples report significantly less conflict and greater happiness and life satisfaction than do younger couples. Morale increases over time, and older couples evaluate their marriages in a positive manner and describe the quality of their marriages as improving (Steinberg and Silverberg 1987).

## DESTRUCTIVE CONFLICT

You have probably been involved in a variety of conflict situations, some of which were difficult but resolved themselves well, and others that caused great pain or increased anger. On other occasions, you may have discovered that you were upset but could not put your finger on the exact cause of the problem. Conflict styles may range from the very overt (pots, words, or fists flying) to the very covert (the burned dinner, late appearance, or cutting joke). Destructive conflict is illustrated in the following example:

---

*One member of our family, a stepson, twenty-years-old, enters the house with a barrel full of hostilities and problems. He overwhelms my wife with yelling and screaming and a string of obscenities. My reaction is to tell him to shut up and not to have anything to do with him; certainly not to do anything for him. My wife seethes until she can no longer cope; then she explodes. After a litany of verbal attacks, she retreats behind a closed bedroom door—sealing herself off from the problem.*

---

Although all overt conflict cannot be labeled constructive, it does let you know where you stand. Sabourin, Infante, and Rudd (1990) discovered that abusive couples exhibited significantly more reciprocity in verbally aggressive exchanges than did distressed, non-abusive control groups. Covert conflict, on the other hand, places you in a guerilla warfare situation. "Is she really angry?" "Am I reading things into his behavior?" "Are those mixed messages?" In almost all cases, covert conflict falls into the destructive category.

In a study of the aggressive potential on the expressing of complaints in intimate relationships of college students, Cloven and Roloff (1993) found what they called a "chilling effect" when one partner had more punitive power and the other sensed less power in the relationship. The less powerful partner hesitated to complain or express grievances. This chilling effect increased when they felt their more aggressive partner was less committed to the relationship, had more alternatives, or had less dependent needs upon the love continuing. This research may have implications for later marriages, and undoubtedly the chilling effect exists in many marriages and leads to destructive conflict.

## Covert Destructive Conflict

Covert, or hidden, conflict usually relies on one of the following five communication strategies: *denial, disqualification, displacement, disengagement,* and *pseudomutuality*. You experience the *denial* strategy most directly when you hear such words as "No problem; I'm not upset" or "That's OK, I'm fine" accompanied by contradictory nonverbal signals. *Disqualification* occurs when a person expresses anger and then discounts, or disqualifies, the angry reaction: "I'm sorry, I was upset about the money and got carried away," or "I wouldn't have gotten so upset except that the baby kept me awake all night." Admittedly, some of these messages are valid in certain settings, but they become a disqualification when the person intends to cover the emotion rather than admit to it.

*Displacement* occurs when anger is directed to an inappropriate person. Everyone has heard a story about the man whose boss yelled at him, but he could not express his anger at the boss. When he arrived home, he yelled at his wife, who grounded the teenager, who hit the fourth-grader, who tripped the baby, who kicked the dog. In some families, this type of incident is not just a story. When you believe you cannot express anger directly, you may find another route through which to vent the strong emotions. Thus, displacement occurs. One type of displacement happens when a couple who cannot deal emotionally with their own differences turn a child into a scapegoat for their pent-up anger. Many families tend to single out one person who appears to be the "acting-out" child but who, in many cases, receives covert negative messages with such regularity that he or she finds it necessary to act-out to release the feelings (Minuchin 1974; Gurman and Kniskern 1981). Dogs, children, in-laws, friends, and spouses all may bear the brunt of displaced anger.

The *disengaged* couple or family lives within the hollow shell of relationships that used to be. Disengaged members avoid each other and express their hostility through their lack of interaction. Instead of dealing with conflict, they keep it from surfacing, but below-the-surface anger seethes and adds immeasurably to the already tense situation. Some families go to extremes to avoid conflicts, as in the following example:

---

*My wife and I should have separated ten years before we did because we hardly had any relationship. I was able to arrange my work schedule so that I came home after eleven o'clock and slept until Norma and the kids had left in the morning. That was the only way I could remain in the relationship. We agreed to stay together until Nick graduated from high school. Now I feel as if we both lost ten years of life, and I'm not sure the kids were any better off just because we all ate and slept in the same house.*

---

*Pseudomutuality* represents the other side of the coin. This style of anger characterizes family members who appear to be perfect and delighted with each other because no hint of discord is ever allowed to dispel the image of perfection. Only when one member of the perfect group develops ulcers, nervous disorders, or acts in a bizarre manner does the crack in the armor begin to show. Anger in this situation remains below the surface to the point that family members lose all ability to deal with it directly. Pretense remains the only possibility.

Very frequently sexual behavior is tied to these covert strategies. For many couples, sex is a weapon in the guerilla warfare. Demands for, or avoidance of, sexual activity may be the most effective way of covertly expressing hostility. Sexual abuse, put-downs, excuses, and direct rejection wound others without the risk of exposing one's own strong anger. Such expressions of covert anger destroy rather than strengthen relationships.

Often covert behavior is a rejection of family themes that discourage conflict or independence. Themes such as "We can only depend on each other" or "United we stand; divided we fall" encourage conflict to occur.

## Overt Destructive Conflict

In the first of the following pair of quotations, a daughter states her views on the way conflicts are handled in her family. She reveals how her expectations of her mother in the parent role function differ from the mother's actions. In the second quotation, her mother perceives the siblings' conflicts from a different vantage point:

---

*In my family, conflict is settled by the laissez-faire method. My single-parent mother refuses to negotiate conflicts among her four daughters. We fight but with mixed results. I believe this is bad because it brings out the worst in each of us at times. We never learn from one another; more like survival of the fittest.*

*I used to get involved in my daughters' conflicts, especially arguments over borrowing clothes without asking one another's permission. I now try to divorce myself totally from these conflicts when they try to get me to intervene on their side. I let them handle it themselves.*

---

Perhaps you could list overt forms of destructive conflict that you have participated in or lived through. The following are some commonly used negative behaviors.

***Verbal Attack*** In all conflicts, the language used by family members has a great impact on the outcome. Word choice reflects the degree of emotion and reveals the amount of respect the conflicting individuals have for one another. Emotional hate terms ("You idiot!", "Geek," or "Liar") quickly escalate conflicts. In some families, swearing is an integral part of venting rage. In others, the rules do not permit swearing, but name calling replaces it. Each generation has its own slang terms used to put down opponents. Put-downs heighten conflicts and slow the solution process by selecting words that describe and intensify bad feelings. These attacks are usually accompanied by screaming or other negative nonverbal cues. Families handle verbal attacks in special ways, such as gunnysacking and game playing.

***Gunnysacking*** A gunnysack is a burlap bag, but according to some family members, a gunnysack is a deadly weapon that implies storing up grievances against someone and then dumping the whole sack of anger on that person when he or she piles on the "last straw." In some conflicting families, members store resentments instead of dealing with them as they occur. Eventually, those members dump out the gunnysack when a spouse, sibling, or parent does that "one more thing." The offender usually responds by attacking back, and the war escalates. A variation of gunnysacking has been labeled "kitchen sinking" in which a partner introduces a number of topics at the same time, expecting attention will be paid to each of them (Montgomery 1994). The following example represents a form of gunnysacking:

---

*My husband is a workaholic. I resent that my husband does not share in the child raising. In fact, it really bothered me when he referred to his staff as his "family." It bothered me even more when his paralegal became more involved with him than we were. They went to play golf and to ballgames. I held my anger in for over a year and finally dumped all my resentments. We are at a standstill. Now he never talks about work; I resent him even more, and so the cycle goes.*

---

***Physical Attack*** Hitting, screaming, kicking, teasing, grabbing, and throwing objects characterize some family conflicts (Straus and Gelles 1990). In one study of persons between the ages of 18 and 30 and in families with more than one child, physical aggression was used in 70 percent of the families to settle conflicts between parents and their children and by the children to settle disputes among themselves. Thirty percent of the husbands and wives used physical means to resolve their conflicts (Steinmetz 1977). Instead of solving conflicts, violence led to more violence. A related study also confirmed previous findings that physical punishment increased rather than decreased aggressive behavior in children (Burnett and Daniels

1985). Further evidence has indicated that child abusers are likely to have been abused children (Straus 1974; McClelland and Caroll 1984). Aggressive nonverbal abuse as a way to manage conflicts causes more harm than good.

A large national study of marital aggression has revealed that teenagers who observe their parents hitting one another are likely to hit their own spouses in later years. This has a greater influence on future behavior than the children being hit by their parents. Further, seeing the father hit the mother increases the chances that their children will be both victims of such abuse and instigators of it. This means that aggression can be transmitted across generations and is not sex specific (Kalmuss 1984).

In a study of abusive couples compared to nonabusive couples, the abusive couples showed more imbalanced patterns of cohesion and adaptability (Sabourin 1992). This research found abusive couples focused on relational issues but had no sense of intimacy between them. In their digressions in conflicts, abusive couples complained about each other or their children, argued over relational problems, and expressed their own feelings. Nonabusive couples were more focused on accomplishing tasks and expressed their beliefs that life is good and in the value of cooperation. By contrast, abusive couples had these themes: "It's the same old thing; we're in a rut," "If only we had more money," "If only he/she would change." Sabourin concludes that "balanced cohesion enabled autonomy and connection. Balanced adaptability enables both change and stability ... Hence a truly balanced family must be willing to be imbalanced at times—another contradiction that reinforces the family's dialectical properties."

The research on family violence indicates that parent-parent and parent-child abuse becomes a part of role relationships. In physically combative families, such behaviors occur frequently enough for children, husbands, wives, or lovers to become accustomed to it. Kalmuss maintains that "exposure to aggression between specific family members teaches children the appropriateness of such behaviors between inhabitants of those family roles" (17). Children grow up accepting beatings as part of parents' rights in governing them but not accepting their parents' hitting one another. Children know about other neighborhood children receiving physical punishment, but they also know Mom's hitting Dad or vice versa violates a societal norm. Burnett and Daniels found that young men from violent families-of-origin differed significantly in their conflict resolution skills, especially when under stress, when compared to young men from nonviolent families-of-origin. The effects of physical conflict in families takes a severe toll on members' relationships as indicated in the following examples:

---

*There is a great distance between my father and me. This began when I was very young. My father was physically and verbally abusive toward my mother. On occasions their fights would be so bad that my mother would leave the situation and lock herself in her bedroom. These instances frightened me, but I also felt great anger that my father would so deeply hurt my mother.*

---

---

*As I got older and more mischievous, I became more and more familiar with the sting of my father's belt and the resultant welts and bruises that were not only across my legs and backside, but around my wrists where my father held me so I couldn't get away. Finally, when I was about eleven and tired of being embarrassed to wear shorts in gym class, and of making up highly plausible stories to explain my welts, I turned on my father as he brought down the belt to spank me one night, caught it and tried to yank it from his hand. I was never spanked again.*

---

Because abuse in conflicts occurs intermittently, children learn to live with it, because they also see periods of affection and love between conflicts (Burgess and Conger 1979). The mixed message of love followed by hate and violence causes children to mentally seek ways to avoid getting hurt themselves. They adopt a "wait and see" attitude and hope the conflicts will not lead to additional violence. There obviously are influences from the outside world that affect the handling of conflicts within the inside world of the family. For example, one study indicated that fathers were less likely to use extreme measures of psychological control and guilt with their children when they had positive co-worker relations and clarity from their bosses about their work role (Grimm-Thomas and Perry-Jenkins 1993). Reduced work stress meant reduced home conflict.

Incest is the most extreme form of family violence. The increasing evidence of this problem has led some researchers to warn that incest occurs in families that are not classified as pathological or perceived as dysfunctional. Incest is related to family stress, and poor management of conflict certainly heightens stress. It is important to note that extreme male dominance of the family, plus weakness in the mother caused by illness, disability, or sometimes death, correlates highly with rates of incest. Further, women who have been abused both in their families-of-origin and by their husbands are more likely to be forced to accept abuse, resulting in submissiveness. This fear toward male assailants increases the likelihood of incest also happening to their children (Breines and Gordon 1983).

There may also be differences in how these negative conflict strategies, gunnysacking, and physical attacks are played out in the communications between men and women. If the power dimensions are not equal between the sexes in the family, especially in the marital dyad, the conflicts that use negative strategies could be attempts to more equitably balance the power domains. Goldner (1989) warned that viewing men and women differently in arguments led to a "conflict of interests" perspective rather than a "consensus of interests." In a conflict of interests viewpoint, each sex belonged to a "distinct social group, but one having more power than the other" (55). Sometimes power moves are expressed during talk about the most mundane activities, as in the next example, where the mother asserts her expertise in shopping:

---

*My mother always seemed to think that my father had some type of "problem." Every once in a while she would give him the shopping list to pick up a few things. Every time when he would return home, my mother would find something that he did "wrong." For example, my dad did not get the exact meat that was on sale; he got four bags of grapefruit instead of three, or bought the wrong brand of napkins. Comments such as "Can't you follow simple directions?" served as a spark to really set him off.*

---

This conflict is probably about more than shopping. It is probably about their overall inability to communicate positively with one another. Often what couples fight about is a coverup for larger issues.

How a couple feels about their relationship influences their complaint behavior (Langhinrichsen-Rohling, Smutzler, and Vivian 1994, 69). Functional couples made behavioral complaints, used more positive verbal and nonverbal cues, and replied more frequently with agreement responses. Dysfunctional couples made more personal character complaints, used more negative communication cues, and responded more often with counter-complaints (Alberts 1988).

## CONSTRUCTIVE CONFLICT

Constructive conflict provides a learning experience for future conflicts. As noted earlier, a couple's manner of dealing with conflict is probably established during the first two years of marriage and remains quite consistent. Therefore, partners may create a fight style in the first 24 months of marriage that will characterize the next 50 years. Raush and colleagues have discovered that harmonious couples consist of two types: "those who manage to exhibit constructive conflict and those who deal with conflict constructively" (204). Those who exhibit constructive conflict show "even within the space of a single scene, sequential communication exchange, growth, development, and sometimes even creativity" (203–4). Both types of harmonious couples can avoid conflict escalation.

In successful conflict management, happy couples or children go through validation sequences (Gottman 1979). They know they can either agree or disagree in arguments and bring out their ideas and feelings. If family members can listen to one another, they can better understand motives, opinions, and feelings. In a study of couples and how they argue, it was found that, when disagreements were negatively responded to by both partners, they had an unhappy relationship. In this research, agreements and acknowledgements correlated positively with control mutuality and relational length (Canary, Weger, and Stafford 1991). Parents can effectively model conflict management, as illustrated by the following example:

---

*One of the things that characterize both my parents is their willingness and ability to listen. They may not always agree with us or let us do the things we want, but no one feels like they don't care. At least we feel like they heard us, and usually they explain their responses pretty carefully if they don't agree with us. As a teenager, I was always testing my limits. I can remember arguing for hours to go on a coed camping trip. Mother really understood what I wanted and why I wanted to go, but she made it clear that she could not permit such a move at that time. Yet I really felt that she shared my disappointment, although she stuck to her guns.*

---

In a comparative study of the communication patterns of couples who had problems and sought counseling and couples who did not, Gottman, Markham, and Notarius (1977) found that in conflict situations, the happier couples began with remarks that told the partner that, although they disagreed on an issue, the other party was a decent human being. They also avoided negative exchanges and ended discussions with some sort of verbal contract to solve the conflict.

Gottman has studied marital conflict over 20 years and recently concluded from his research with 2,000 couples that satisfied couples maintain a five to one ratio of positive to negative moments (1994). He found that it wasn't the way couples handled their compatibilities that prevented divorces, but how they communicated about their incompatibilities. The single factor, five to one positive over negative encounters, determined longevity, despite fighting styles that ranged from openly combative to passive-aggressive.

Other studies reveal that satisfied family members often overlook conflicts or choose communication behaviors that decrease the chance of escalation (Roloff 1987), and families that control negative emotional behaviors have an easier time of solving problems (Forgatch 1989). In conflict the use of direct strategies related positively to marital satisfaction. The use of indirect coercive strategies, such as complaining, criticizing, put downs, and ignoring, led to unproductive negative conflict outcomes (Aida and Falbo).

Families seem to be able to manage conflict creatively by recognizing that they have a twofold responsibility: to meet their individual needs and wants and to further the family system. This requires give-and-take, resulting in compromise. The attitude behind this view enhances flexibility and helps avoid conflicts that result from being too rigid and assuming that one family member's views must be followed. A conflict that presents something new to the family system, requiring accommodation or assimilation, tests the strengths and capacities of the system. If the system is flexible and differentiated, family members can more readily accommodate one another, learn new ideas from other members and themselves, and change. In a comparison of gay and lesbian couples and heterosexual couples, Kurdek found similar results for both. Relationship satisfaction depended upon the degree of investment in the partnership and the use of positive strategies to problem solve and resolve conflicts. Undifferentiated family members become enmeshed in their system and lack the assertiveness or autonomy to handle conflict constructively. In a flexible family, new ideas do not threaten the stability of the relationships, and members can learn from both outside and within the system.

## Strategies for Constructive Conflict

Conflicts usually end in one of four ways: submission, compromise, standoff, and withdrawal. Submission involves one or more family members' going along with others. This submission may be culturally biased with male family members assuming their ideas and feelings deserve more consideration. In compromise, family members find not always an ideal decision, but one that the majority of individuals can accept. When family members can't agree, they reach a standoff. They recognize that in their particular conflict no one wins or loses. Withdrawal ends conflicts when one or more family members walks out or refuses to communicate. Vuchinich (1987) found 36 percent of all conflicts ended early by family members' accepting corrections or ignoring the threat. However, if conflict starts, there is a 68 percent chance it will continue for up to five communication turns, when most conflicts subside. Most conflicts (61 percent) end in a standoff. Submissions ended 21 percent. Compromises ended 14.2 percent, while 3.8 percent ended in withdrawals (599). Although Chapter 14 describes specific methods of improving family communication, three constructive conflict behaviors will be briefly discussed here: listening, fair fighting, and managing the physical environment.

***Listening*** A cornerstone to constructive conflict may be found in good listening behavior. Listening is an important communication skill to use to defuse conflict and help clarify and focus on the issues being debated. Empathic listening requires that you listen without judging and try to hear the feelings behind the remarks. This means accurately hearing what the other is saying and responding to those feelings. Remarks like "You're really angry; I hear that" or "I hear you say that you've been misunderstood" indicate to a family member that you have listened yet not become trapped within your own emotions or thinking about "How can I best turn off this complaint?" Restating what you have heard a person say can be most helpful in slowing or stopping the escalation of conflict. "Bill, are you saying … ?" Asking Bill to repeat his contention is another helpful approach.

Some partners will go so far as to switch roles in a conflict and repeat the scene to check out the accusations. It gives the one partner a chance to try out the other's feelings. Parents may also have their children role-play their conflicts.

Gordon (1975), in his Parent Effectiveness Training program, has developed a "no lose" method for solving conflicts that depends on careful listening and involves compromise elements. This approach asks for partners to hear each other out, find the areas of agreement, and then zero in on the specific differences. Both sides seek some reward in the solution of the conflict. "If you let me do X, I'll do Y." The philosophy of caring and pleasing one another is basic to its success. Even on difficult family problems, the method can work because all parties recognize that no one can totally win or lose.

***Fair Fighting*** Many bitter conflicts in families result from the use of unfair tactics by various members; such behavior can be changed with commitment to fair fighting. In a fair fight, equal time must be provided for all participants, and name calling or "below-the-belt" remarks are prohibited. In this system, family members agree upon how they will disagree. The procedures are agreed upon with time and topic limitations. They can be used only with the mutual consent of the parties involved and the assurance that each will listen to the other's messages. An unfair example of conflict and the use of name calling to "hit below the belt" is demonstrated in the following example:

---

*My mother always used a lot of verbal attacks to "handle" conflict. Put-downs definitely intensify bad feelings. My mother knew the exact names to call me that really hurt. She used to call me chubby, fatso, and other similar words. These words only made me angrier and never settled any argument. My mother rarely used swear words when she was yelling, but if she called me those names, I would usually start swearing at her. When she went into treatment for drug abuse, the whole family got involved and through counseling we learned to avoid the "red flag" words which would set each other off.*

---

In fair fighting, family members try to stay in the here and now. They specify what it is that they feel caused the conflict. Each family member takes responsibility for their part in the fight and doesn't blame the others. The following example illustrates these ideas.

Jim tells his wife, "I need to share a concern with you." "OK," Michelle replies, giving permission for Jim to release his feelings without interruption. "I really felt angry this evening when you told Marissa she didn't have to go to the program with us. You let her run wild."

In this approach, Jim continues to release his anger during the time granted to him by his wife. According to the rules of fair fighting, he can express his anger only verbally—no hitting or throwing things. Also, Michelle could have asked to postpone hearing the gripe until she had time to really listen. The idea of asking permission to be heard is essential, because it implies the obligation of the other party to listen.

Michelle can deny the charges Jim makes, which can lead to a careful recounting of what was said and with what intended meanings. This often helps clear the air. She can also ask for a break until later if she becomes angry and cannot listen. She can also admit her error in judgment, if one was made.

Sometimes flexibility and compromise will not solve conflicts. The consequences outweigh the advantages. An individual's self-worth may be more important than family expectations. Some families permit members to decide what is negotiable and nonnegotiable for them. Stating "This is not negotiable for me at this time" enables one to own his or her position and part of the problem. Being tentative and including the phrase "at this time" leaves the door open for future discussion. Other items may legitimately be nonnegotiable for you on a permanent basis.

---

*If I feel like Italian food and Roger, my husband, has his heart set on Chinese food, Chinese it is. I have never thrived on conflict, and will avoid it by settling for less than I would have liked, especially on "little things."*

*In the case of a more serious conflict, I try to problem-solve. I believe that two people in conflict should never go to bed mad at each other. If the problem is big enough to cause conflict, it is worth the time and effort to solve it, for the sake of the relationship.*

---

It goes without saying that cross-complaining defeats the purposes of fair fighting. In cross-complaining you ignore the complaint of your partner and counter with your complaint about them. Both parents and children can get caught up in an endless cycle of "You did this!" followed by "But you did the same yesterday!"

Whatever rules or methods couples use in their fighting, the nonverbal aspects of conflict need special attention. Careful monitoring of nonverbal cues often reveals the true nature of conflict (Gottman 1994). Gestures of threat, harsh glares, and refusals to be touched or to look at others indicate the intensity of the conflict. In a study of marital communication, Beier and Sternberg (1977) found that the subtle nonverbal cues in a couple's messages determine the climate in which either conflict or peace reigns. By observing nonverbal cues, they discovered that couples who reported the least disagreement "sat closer together, looked at each other more frequently and for a longer period of time, touched each other more often, touched themselves less often, and held their legs in a more open position than couples who reported the most disagreement" (96). This finding correlates directly with Gottman and colleagues' conclusion that "nonverbal behavior thus discriminates distressed from nondistressed couples better than verbal behavior" (469).

Sometimes nonverbal cues contradict verbal statements. A receiver of such mixed messages must decide "Do I believe what I hear or what I see?" On the other hand, supportive nonverbal cues can drastically reduce conflict. For example, a soothing touch or reassuring glance has great healing powers.

***Managing the Physical Environment*** Choice of space may dampen certain conflicts. Reducing the distance between adversaries may help reduce the noise level. Sitting directly across from someone makes for easy eye contact and less chance for missing important verbal or nonverbal messages. Conflicting family members need to be aware of all the factors that can escalate a fight. Choosing a quiet and appropriate space lessens distractions or related problems, as the following example illustrates:

---

*One thing I have learned about fighting with my teenage son is never to raise an argumentative issue when he is in his bedroom. Whenever we used to fight, I would go up to talk to him about school or about his jobs in the house, and five minutes after we started arguing, I would suddenly get so upset about the state of his messy room that we would fight about that also. By now I've learned to ask him to come out or to wait until he is in another part of the house to voice a complaint.*

---

The rewards of better-managed family conflicts are numerous. Better use of positive communication practices stops the cumulative aspect of conflict. A series of minor conflicts left unsolved can escalate into separation, divorce, or emotionless relationships. Successful resolution of conflict that goes through the stages of our conflict model (Figure 9.2) leads to emotional reconciliation and affirmation of the participants. It also decreases fear and anxiety within the family. Future joint enterprises become possible for family members. Knowing how to manage conflicts leads to a greater appreciation for the talents of family members and enjoyment of each of them in the here and now of living together. Gottman and Krokoff (1989) stated that for long term marital satisfaction wives need for husbands to confront areas of disagreement and to openly vent disagreement and anger. They also noted these differences: men in satisfied marriages de-escalate negative affect in low-conflict interactions; women in satisfied marriages de-escalate negative affects in high conflict interactions. Both partners, however, in unsatisfactory marriages abandoned the de-escalation role.

Yelsma's research further indicated that couples that had high scores for managing conflict reported the highest degree of marital satisfaction. Also, too high a concern for one's own uniqueness appeared to lessen one's chances for happiness. However, reasonably high self-esteem and high task energy enhanced marital adjustments.

The following summary of strategies for constructive conflict reflect integration of many pieces of prescriptive advice. As you will note certain strategies are valued, but across different cultures other strategies may be seen as more critical.

## Elements of Constructive Conflict

The following characterize successful conflict management:

1. A sequential communication exchange takes place in which each participant has equal time to express his or her point of view.

2. Feelings are brought out and not suppressed.

3. People listen to one another with empathy and without constant interruption.

4. The conflict remains focused on the issue and does not get sidetracked into other previously unsolved conflict.

5. Family members respect differences in one another's opinions, values, and wishes.

6. Members believe that solutions are possible and that growth and development will take place.

7. Some semblance of rules has evolved from past conflicts.

8. Members have experience with problem solving as a process to settle differences.

9. Little power or control is exercised by one or more family members over the action of others.

These goals are not achieved in families in which young people fail to learn these communication and problem solving skills, because their parents either shield them from conflict or typically make the decisions. Remember, guidelines must be culture-sensitive to be effective. A student presents a humorous summary of how problems are solved in another "culture" in the following example:

> Even in "Star Trek: The Next Generation" the characters periodically checked with the psychologist, Deanna Troi, who helped individuals understand family problems, both current and in their families-of-origin. Deanna adroitly guided characters on the Starship Enterprise to solve and understand their conflicts. Perhaps her experiences with her own indomitable, new age mother, Lwaxana Troi, prepared her for such competent counseling in outer space.

## UNRESOLVED CONFLICT

What happens in the family if conflict cannot be solved? Usually, a loss occurs, which affects all members as psychological and/or physical estrangement creates and fosters separation among members. Young family members may remain in the home but withdraw from family activities until they go to school or establish a way to support themselves. If circumstances force a continued joint living arrangement, a wall of silence may become part of the family's lifestyle. Some members may be cutoff from all contact with the family and may be treated as nonexistent, as in the following example:

---

*When I married my husband, I was essentially making a choice between my parents and Joe. Joe is black, and my parents said they would never speak to me again if we married. Although I knew they were angry, I thought that they would come around when we had a baby. Melissa is two years old now and my parents have never seen her. My brother and sister have been to see me, but I am "dead" as far as my parents are concerned.*

---

Many unresolved marital conflicts result in divorce, clearly a rejection strategy. One or both members withdraw, seeing the ending of their formal relationship as the only logical solution. Yet, when children are involved, spouses are divorced from each other, not from the children, and the children not from one another. The system alters itself rather than ends. The original family system evolves into new forms, which may include new spouses and children. Legal action does not stop interaction of family members.

Some couples stop their conflicts short of divorce, because the cost of the final step may be too great; yet the rewards of living together are too few. For these people, destructive conflict characterizes much of their continued shared existence. Such unresolved conflict may add great tension to the entire family system, but not always. When an issue is unresolvable, it may be more functional for the family to avoid the issue and direct its communication to areas that bring cohesion (Fitzpatrick, Fallis, and Vance 1982). Gottman would modify this advice if the anger could be directed at a particular issue, and be expressed without contempt and general criticism. Gottman found in his research that "Blunt, straightforward anger seems to immunize marriages against deterioration." (1994, 46). Yet, over time, family members may learn to live with topics which are avoided because the pain of addressing them is too great.

## CONCLUSION

Given the many stresses families face in today's world, conflict management becomes an important critical skill. Giblin (1994) summarized several studies and stated "whatever the stress, the more partners are able to support each other, to understand and respond empathically, the greater their marital satisfaction. Marital satisfaction exists in a reciprocal relation to communication and conflict resolution skills, belief systems, and time spent together" (49). Each of these ideas have been discussed in this chapter.

Some families develop effective conflict styles through discussion and negotiation. One family realistically faced their problem when they sought outside help—a step that can reward a troubled family system:

> *When I asked my wife what she wanted for our twenty-fifth anniversary, she said, "Marriage counseling. The next twenty-five years have to be better than the first." I knew we had many fights, but I never knew she was that unhappy. I agreed to the counseling, and we really worked on our differences and ways of resolving them. After a few months, we were able to talk rationally about things we always fought over—money, my schedule, our youngest son. Next month we will celebrate our twenty-eighth anniversary, and I can say that the last three years were a lot better than the first twenty-five.*

## IN REVIEW

1. Take a position and discuss whether conflict is inevitable and necessary for the development of family relationships.
2. Describe how an individual's conflict style may vary with specific members of the family. Relate to the model of conflict style in Figure 9.1.
3. Using the stages of family conflict, describe a recurring conflict in a real or fictional family.

4. Create a position statement detailing your perception of how constructive conflict might function in families, and provide four or five reasons why this style of conflict may be difficult to achieve.
5. Interview three persons about the attitudes toward conflict they learned in their family-of-origin and how they perceive they have learned to manage conflict today.
6. Relate examples from your own experiences with families that might agree with Gottman's conclusion that couples can conflict, but the ratio needs to be five positive experiences to one negative over time if a relationship is to last.

# 10

# Family Communication and Developmental Stress

Families evolve over time as each system and its members encounter developmental and unpredictable changes, each generating some elements of stress (Feist 1993). Any time there is either a natural change in the life of a family member or a catastrophic change, communication plays an important part in negotiating the transition from one stage to the next. No two family members move through these stages identically. One family life cycle evolves into another, like a great chain with connections from previous generations to the present. Family patterns affect three or more generations (McGoldrick and Gerson 1985). Like a mobile that can't stop gyrating or a teeter-totter that dumps the one partner when the other jumps off, families experience extremes when a variety of stresses pile up. It is unrealistic to take a simplistic system's view and assume that strain can be reduced or completely eliminated by realigning priorities and renegotiating responsibilities. We can't assume that a family or individual members have the resources to go through the years easily carrying out all the aspects of their roles they occupy as parents, dual earners, siblings, or stepchildren.

The pressures that adolescents can place upon a family system is illustrated in the following example:

---

*"Jesus, Mary, and Joseph, save my soul!" can be heard from the lips of my mother at least once a day. Mom thought three in diapers was bad but since has decided three teens are worse. Presently, we have three teens in driver's ed, three teens tying up the phone, three teens falling in and out of love. Mom threatens to run away once a day. Dad says we drive*

(continued on page 274)

*him crazy and should be locked up until we go away to college. We must be driving our parents nuts.*

---

Think about your own family. What has marked family changes? Some families emphasize *marker events*, or the transition stages in human development, more than others do. A child's first steps, a confirmation or bar mitzvah, a teenager's drivers license, or a wedding may serve to mark major changes. Other families emphasize unpredictable crises as significant symbols of change. A parent's cancer surgery or the death of a sibling may symbolize the greatest sense of change.

The ways individual members "organize their experience in their personal stimulus world ... influence the shared perceptions of the social world in which they live" (Reiss and Oliveri 1980, 290). In other words, families view the world differently, thereby affecting their perceptions of stresses that enter their systems. If one family perceives the world as chaotic, disorganized, and frequently dangerous, any change may be upsetting. If another sees the world's operations as predictable, ordered, and greatly controllable, change may be perceived as manageable. How the family responds to stress depends upon its organizational structure prior to the stress (Lewis 1986). The family's first response to stress may be to maintain the balance in the family system, but this may fail if individual family members don't have the interest, time or energy required.

This chapter and the next chapter address family communication patterns in relationship to developmental and unpredictable stresses. This chapter provides an overview of life change processes that affect communication followed by an extensive overview of stages of family development as they relate to family interactions. Moving through these stages creates stress as family members separate from their families-of-origin, form their own systems, and live in those systems over a period of time. The next chapter focuses on those relatively unpredictable stresses that occur when families suffer losses such as illness, divorce, or death. Any time there is a change in the life of a family, either natural or catastrophic, communication plays an important part in negotiating the transitions and coping processes. We also recognize that stress can be related to gender issues and that men differ from women in how they handle stress.

## OVERVIEW OF FAMILY CHANGE

### Sources of Family Stress: A Model

In their work on change in the family life cycle, Carter and McGoldrick (1988) present a model depicting stressors that reflect family anxiety and affect the family system (Figure 10.1). Within the same family, individual members experience and react to these stresses differently. Stress varies with the age of each family member and their position in their life cycle.

The vertical stressors include patterns of relating and functioning that are transmitted down generations. These patterns involve family attitudes, expectations, secrets, and rules. In other words, "these aspects of our lives are like the hand we are dealt: they are given" (8). Many of these communication-related stressors were discussed as the images, themes, myths, rules, boundaries, and expectations that come from your family-of-origin.

The horizontal flow in the system includes the anxiety produced by the stresses on the family as it moves across time—both the predictable, or developmental stresses, and the unpredictable events that disrupt the life cycle. Pressures from these current life events interact with one another and with the vertical areas of stress to cause disruption in the family system. The greater the anxiety generated in the family at any transition point, the more difficult or dysfunctional the transition will be.

The past and present family stresses are affected further by all levels of the larger systems in which the family operates. The social, cultural, economic, and political context influences the level of stress. One's community, extended and biological family, and personal resources also contribute to the process of moving through life. As you

**FIGURE 10.1**
**Sources of Family Stress**

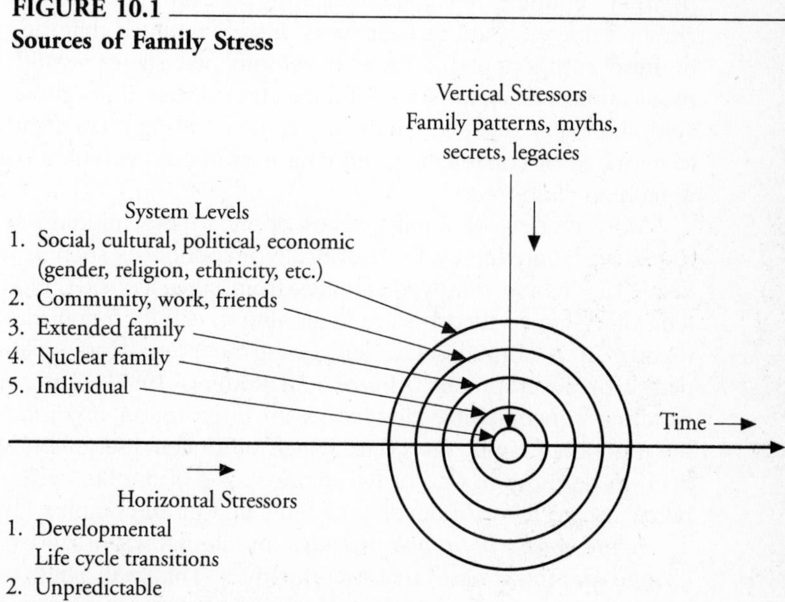

move through phases of your individual and family existence, these forces will positively or negatively influence the process. Thus, these three major factors—vertical stressors, horizontal stressors, and system levels—taken together put the family life cycle into perspective.

## General Developmental Issues

Most researchers accept the position that individuals experience critical periods of change, or life stages, until death (Erikson 1968; Levinson 1978; Gilligan 1982). All of the stages lead toward a sense of integrity, having lived authentically and meaningfully, so that one can accept old age and death with dignity. Kohlberg (1969) recognized that the communication between people not only reflected their environment but depended upon their experiences and which stage they were at in the life cycle. Hayes (1994) applied Kohlberg's ideas to what he calls a developmental constructivist perspective in which an individual moves through stages. Each stage enables the person to make more sense of a greater variety of experiences in more adequate ways. Stress occurs when the individual's levels of functioning and problems in his or her social environment don't agree. The constructivist approach to this dialectical tension is to attempt through communication to integrate the differences so the individual family member or couple can move on or be happier.

Early thinking about family life cycles reflected the position that "normal" couples remained intact from youthful marriage through child rearing to death in later years. It was assumed that the communication components of these developmental stages would also be predictable. For example, communication differs throughout the developmental changes in family life as the courting relationship moves to marriage or cohabitation and decisions about becoming parents or remaining child-free.

Most models of family stages apply to the middle-class intact American family life cycle. Historically, experiences such as untimely death or divorce removed families from stage considerations. Contemporary family theorists are beginning to call for a consideration of divorce as a normal stage, suggesting a "Y" or "fork in the road" model of development (Ahrons and Rodgers 1987). Carter and McGoldrick conceptualize divorce as an interruption or dislocation of the traditional family life cycle, which produces disequilibrium and a need to go through one or two more stages of the life cycle to restabilize and go forward developmentally at a more complex level.

A *life course approach* provides an alternative for understanding change and the stresses that accompany it. The focus shifts to understanding the individual family member and "how varying events and

Like individuals, whole family systems also pass through various "seasons" of their lives.

their timing in the lives of individuals affected families in a particular historical context" (Aldous 1990). Life course analysis looks at an individual's lifetimes, his or her existence in a social and an historical time. This perspective, for example, recognizes that individuals and families living in the mid–1990s, approaching the year 2000, are dealing with stressses unique to this historical period such as: environmental concerns, downsizing of industries causing layoffs, abortion debates, homelessness, concerns about adequate medical care, computerization replacing workers, a global economy increasing percentages of employed couples, increasing single parent and cohabiting families, plus the emergence of openly gay and lesbian family lifestyles.

The life course approach is broader and operates at a different level of analysis because it is not focused primarily on change in families but "with how individual family members in connection with their participation in other groups orchestrate family event sequences" (574). Events in the life course perspective often get labeled as "on time" or "off time." Individuals now marry later; have babies later, even into their early 40s; start or are forced into entirely new careers, often at midlife; return to complete degrees—all "off time" with a strict time sequencing family process. One way to recognize this is by adding a greater number and variety of family stages. For example, add a stage for 18–29 year olds who haven't left home because of poorly paying jobs or need for job retraining or have returned because of failed marriages. Taking a life course perspective suggests that when crises occur, an individual family member's education, income, occupation, values, and satisfaction or dissatisfaction with life may cause more changes than timing in family stages. Although we take a stage approach, we recognize the significance of the current world in which family members function.

No single model can reflect all developmental complexities. The stages presented in this chapter reflect one perspective, variations of which will be addressed in the next chapter. What follows contains some perspectives on family development and change and draws some implications for family communication patterns.

## FAMILY STAGES

Family researchers have attempted to apply the stage concept to whole families so that the entire system may be thought of as moving through particular stages. Experts describe six (Carter and McGoldrick), seven (Glick 1989), eight (Duvall 1988), nine (Hill 1986), or twelve (Hohn 1987) stages. Such analysis has difficulties, because families consist of several individuals in different life stages, but it becomes more manageable than trying to account for each person. Such schemes provide simplicity but do not account effectively for families with numerous children or widely spaced ages of children as they go through the middle stages of development. Nor do they focus on adult developmental stages or tasks unrelated to child rearing. More detailed perspectives exist, but their complexity limits their use. No matter which framework is adopted, communication emerges as a critical issue at each stage. The following stages are most appropriately applied to the two parent middle-class American family life cycle. Other family styles will be addessed in Chapter 12. The following stages, detailed by Carter and McGoldrick, will be used for discussion. Table 10–1 describes the stages of the family life cycle.

Although this first stage is not found in other life-cycle lists, McGoldrick and Carter include it as an essential stage that recognizes the young adult coming to terms with his or her family-of-origin and separating or leaving home to enter a new cycle. In short, this stage of

**Table 10-1 The Stages of the Family Life Cycle**

| Family Life Cycle Stage | Emotional Process of Transition: Key Principles | Second-Order Changes in Family Status Required to Proceed Developmentally |
|---|---|---|
| 1. Leaving home: Single young adults | Accepting emotional and financial responsibility for self | a. Differentiation of self in relation to family-of-origin<br>b. Development of intimate peer relationships<br>c. Establishment of self (re: work and financial independence) |
| 2. The joining of families through marriage: The "New" couple | Commitment to new system | a. Formation of marital system<br>b. Realignment of relationships with extended families and friends to include spouse |
| 3. Families with young children | Accepting new members into the system | a. Adjusting marital system to make space for child(ren)<br>b. Joining in child rearing, financial, and household tasks<br>c. Realignment of relationships with extended family to include parenting and grandparenting roles |
| 4. Families with adolescents | Increasing flexibility of family boundaries to include children's independence and grandparents' frailties | a. Shifting of parent-child relationships to permit adolescent to move in and out of system<br>b. Refocus on midlife marital and career issues<br>c. Beginning shift toward joint caring for older generation |
| 5. Launching children and moving on | Accepting a multitude of exits from and entries into the family system | a. Renegotiation of marital system as a dyad<br>b. Refocus on midlife marital and career issues<br>c. Realignment of relationships to include in-laws and grandchildren<br>d. Dealing with disabilities and deaths of parents (grandparents) |
| 6. Families in later life | Accepting the shifting of generational roles | a. Maintaining own and/or couple functioning and interests in face of physiological decline; exploration of new familial and social role options<br>b. Support for a more central role of middle generation<br>c. Making room in the system for the wisdom and experience of the elderly, supporting the older generation without overfunctioning for them<br>d. Dealing with loss of spouse, siblings, and other peers and preparation for own death. Life review and integration |

the unattached young adult comprises that period of time when the individual has " ... physically, if not emotionally, left his or her family-of-origin, but has not yet established a family of procreation" (Aylmer 1988; 191). Until recently, this developmental task was not considered necessary for females, because it was assumed they would move from one attachment to another, defining themselves more as a supporter than as a self, thus reflecting attachment rather than autonomy.

Unless this task is successfully handled, communication problems can develop in the stages that follow. Young people need sufficient autonomy to separate and achieve their goals independently. If they remain enmeshed and overly dependent, this will affect their choices or options throughout their lives. The goal is healthy interdependence, with the parents letting go and the young adults establishing careers, completing school, finding close friends, and establishing peer networks, defining the "self" as separate yet a part of the family-of-origin. An abrupt cutoff is not the answer. Bowen (1978) insists that an angry cutoff leaves the young adult emotionally bound to the old system. Cain (1990) indicates that young adults faced with their parents' divorce may experience severe life disruption. The ideal would be for the young adult to feel free to achieve his or her own goals and command the respect and encouragement of the parents, even if they might have hoped for other outcomes. Successful resolution of the single young adult stage requires "(1) an ability to tolerate separation and independence while remaining connected; (2) a tolerance for differentness and ambiguity in career identity of adult children; and (3) the acceptance of a range of intense emotional attachments and life styles outside the immediate family" (Aylmer 1988, 195). Young people and their parents need to find less hierarchical, or vertical, ways of communicating and to adopt more horizontal, or adult to adult, communication patterns. This is not always as easy, as seen in following example:

---

*Ending college has been a period of great stress for me. My family always refers to me as the "gazelle"—frightened by conflict. Yet I'm now battling with my parents to support my desire to go on a year long mission for my church. They see this as inconceivable. I am struggling with my need for independence and the chance to move on my own.*

---

There is a definite connection between what happens to single young adults in their leaving home and their transition into the next stages of family development. Fiese et al. (1993) go so far as to state that "the marital dissatisfaction reported during the early stages of parenting is best predicted by premarital relationship satisfaction" (634).

Part of this process involves investing in intimate peer relationships, some of which may be romantic, and beginning the process of exploring deep interpersonal connections. Thus, young single adults must experience an individual orientation, or autonomy, in order to move toward future interdependence and attachment. Orbuch, Veroff, and Holmberg (1993) found individuals do this in the stories they recall about how their relationship developed in the courtship period. In forming a couple relationship, each partner uses stories "to weave disparate events of their courtship into a coherent whole" (815).

## The Couple

You have heard the two classic explanations as to why people are attracted to each other—"opposites attract" or "birds of a feather flock together." Some people support the theory of complementary needs—that persons tend to select mates whose needs are complementary rather than similar to their own. Others hold out for similarity. However, research indicates that most people select a mate of similar socioeconomic background who shares similar values, interests, and ways of behaving. This suggests most persons find partners within a limited social network, or mate the persons with whom they regularly interact.

Proximity plays a large role in whom one encounters and eventually with whom one develops close relationships. People are more likely to date those who live nearby, attend the same school, or share their work and social backgrounds, which makes it likely that a large proportion of their attitudes and values will be in basic agreement from the start. Once a relationship becomes established, the couples' gradual discovery of just how much agreement exists becomes crucial in determining whether or not they decide to marry. Courtship may be viewed as a decision-making time because "the decision to marry is a prediction about how one person's life with another person will evolve in the future based on how it has evolved in the past" (Yerby, Buerkel-Rothfuss, and Bochner 1990, 98).

Lewis believes all couples entering a relationship must resolve three developmental challenges in order to achieve satisfaction in later stages: commitment, power, and closeness. Commitment requires each to make the other his or her primary partner and lessen their ties to parents, siblings, and friends. Power refers to the ability to influence one family member to do what another wants. According to Lewis, power works most effectively when a couple shares it. Closeness relates to establishing a balance between separateness and attachment that is mutually satisfying for the couple. It is in this early stage that a couple develops distance regulation that enables them to find a mutually satisfactory degree of separateness and connectedness. The resulting cohesion comes from much trial and error. In this developmental stage, couples use verbal and nonverbal cues to negotiate what is an acceptable and nonacceptable distance, as the following example illustrates:

---

*Sometimes I feel like a piece of Swiss cheese—full of holes. I grew up in a nontouching, often violent family. I realize I hunger for touch and affection. I can cuddle and hold my partner for long periods of time, but he gets uneasy after a while. We have to reach a point where both of us are comfortable.*

---

The system formation period, usually involving courtship and engagement, involves a couple's attempt to move to deeper levels of communication. Partners find out through permissions, granted verbally or nonverbally, that indicate the limits to their communication. Certain topics, feelings, or actions may frighten or offend the other. They create unwritten rules that will govern their communication when they encounter these issues.

The engagement communicates to outsiders the seriousness of courtship. Quite often, prior to the announcement, verbal and nonverbal signals from the couple indicate a deepening relationship. Significant jewelry may be exchanged; invitations to attend special family events such as weddings, bar mitzvahs, or reunions are extended. As you read the following example, think of the way it would happen in your family:

---

*In my family, we always knew when relationships were serious when the annual family reunion time arrived. If you were serious about someone, you were expected to introduce this person to each member of the clan. However, you didn't go through this and take all the teasing that followed unless an engagement followed. Bringing a partner to the reunion signalled an impending marriage.*

---

An engagement serves as a type of bonding, a statement to the world that the relationship is formalized and that a new familial unit will be established. The act of bonding, or institutionalizing the relationship, may change the nature of the relationship. Some parents may not be prepared for the separation issues involved. Mothers es-

Engagement involves a couple's attempt to create a strong intimate relational culture.

pecially may feel abandoned. Each family faces the questions of realignment: How willing and able are we to accept a new member as an in-law?

The premarital period provides the time for self-disclosure and negotiation. The following issues may need discussion: time with friends, desires for children, sexual needs, career and educational planning, religious participation, money management, housing, in-laws, and acceptable conflict behaviors. The trend today is for shorter engagements, with many couples living together during this period.

Each person has to deal with the move from autonomy to attachment. This shift from self to mutuality with another requires time and examination. Yet, for many couples, the final part of the engagement period becomes hectic with rituals—wedding plans, bridal showers, and other events that may keep the focus off the separation issues until the ceremony is over. The vows may be repeated before a judge or clergy, and before three or three hundred beaming friends and relatives, as two individuals formally create a new family system. The actual ceremony is a communication event—a sign to the outside world that the ultimate formal bonding has occurred.

Marriages between young adults involve certain predictable tasks for most couples (Aldous 1990). It is a time of: (1) separating further from the families-of-origin; (2) negotiating roles, rules, and relationships; and (3) investing in a new relationship. Some young people find it difficult to separate from their parents, establish an adult identity, and assume the role of spouse. Marriage at this time may continue unresolved conflicts with the parents. The new mate becomes the victim of angry projected feelings he or she did little to deserve. This is a period of unconscious negotiation between the couple and their families-of-origin regarding how the old and new systems will relate to each other (Fiese et al.). Sometimes marriage holds surprises even for old friends, as noted in the following example:

---

*I had known my husband since childhood, and we dated since our junior year. Our parents knew each other and we attended the same church, yet we had some real difficulties in the first years of our marriage. I had difficulty in the following areas: First, learning to live with my husband's habits. Second, trying to be a full-time employee and a housewife. Third, deciding at which family's house to celebrate holidays. Fourth, telling my husband when I was angry, and fifth, dealing with the biggest problem—my husband's mother.*

---

The initial stage of marriage is characterized by close monitoring of the relationship and more frequent and intense communication about the relationship that at any other stage (Sillars and Wilmot 1989). As spouses move through this period many report that romance moves into reality. Most couples experience a shift in their social networks. Early marriage is accompanied usually by a decline in contact with friends. Much negotiation relates to the role of the "old friends" and autonomy. How much time will the spouses spend apart? How much togetherness will be demanded?

Equally important, but far more subtle, is the verbal and nonverbal negotiation related to cohesion and adaptability. Each person jockeys for the amount of togetherness he or she wishes as well as for the amount of flexibility that can be tolerated. Such moves are rarely dealt with openly, but the results have long-lasting effects on communication within the system. In recalling stories about how they met and became a couple, there definitely were cultural differences between African-American and white couples. African-Americans reported more conflict in the early stages of their relationship than whites (Orbuch, Veroff, and Holmberg 1993). Further results from this study indicated that men initiated more relationship manuevers than women, women had more vivid memories of relational events than men, and that couples that remembered a positive relational development were happier in the third year of their marriages than those who told negative stories.

As you may well imagine, the images, themes, boundaries, and biosocial beliefs experienced by each partner in his or her family-of-origin affect the new system's development. A woman whose image of a husband is one that is strong, unemotional, and powerful puts great pressure on her new husband to deal with such expectations. If one partner has experienced themes of open sharing and flexible boundaries and the other partner has experienced the opposite, much negotiation will be required.

Couple conflict patterns tend to establish themselves within the first two years of marriage and demonstrate great stability (Raush et al. 1974). In addition, a greater proportion of communication is devoted to marital conflicts which gradually surface (Sillars and Wilmot). Usually, the balance of power between a couple is established early in the marriage and is based upon decision-making behaviors and role performance. Many couples set long-term patterns at this point. In their study of couples over the first year of marriage, Huston, McHale, and Crouter (1986) found couples engaged in increasing conflict and decreasing intimacy. By the beginning of the second year, couples spent less time talking with each other about general topics and about their relationship.

A couple's ability to invest in their new relationship relates directly to the quality of their communication. This is a time of investing in the system, risking self-disclosure, and building a pattern of sexual communication. Time, energy, and risk-taking nourish the relationship and establish a range of acceptable intimacy for the system.

For some couples, this two-person system will be their permanent form. Partners may choose not to add children to their lives or may find it difficult to bear or adopt children. Yet, for most young couples, the two-person system eventually becomes a three-person one, with pregnancy heralding the transition to a new stage, as in the following example:

---

*The period before the children began to arrive was a critical point. If we had not established a really strong, trusting relationship in those first two years, we would have drifted totally apart in the next twenty-three years of childrearing. We lost most of our time together. If I had it to do over, I would have waited five years before having children, to share who we really were before we tried to deal with who the four new people in our lives were.*

---

## Families with Young Children

As parents, adults move up a generation and become caretakers to the younger generation. One of the most important choices a couple makes concerns childbearing. Such a decision should, but does not always, involve intense communication—self-disclosure regarding the needs of each partner—and how a child could fit into their lives. Input from all sources affects such a decision. The media, parents, friends, and other relatives often pressure the couple to fulfill parental roles and subtly suggest that they are being selfish if they do not. Men may perceive children as a way to prove themselves as mature and responsible. Children with divorced parents may be ambivalent toward parenting. For both spouses who want children, producing a child is partially ego fulfilling, and they may desire to be the kind of parents that they never had.

In examining the periods of child growth and outward movement, three phases will be discussed. Remember that each family will experience each phase differently, depending on its size and the ages of its members. The three phases are:

1. Family with first child
2. Family with preschool children (three to six years, possibly with younger siblings)
3. Family with school-age children (oldest child six to twelve years, possibly with younger siblings)

***Family with First Child*** Parenthood is now coming later in life for most couples because the age at marriage has steadily increased to twenty-four for women and twenty-six for men. (On the other hand, twenty-five percent of children are born to unwed mothers, frequently teenagers.) For young couples, pregnancy occurs relatively close to the marriage. Because about one-fifth of all children born to married couples in the United States were conceived before marriage and many others are conceived during the first two years, many couples do not experience a lengthy period of intimacy before the child arrives.

In contrast, some couples postpone having children for several years, so the first pregnancy forces choices and may cause far more interruptions in the woman's life than marriage did (Issod 1987). Many dual-career couples are having their first child in their early to mid-thirties. No matter when it occurs, the first pregnancy signals significant change in the couple's relationship. The intensity of the desire for a child by one spouse or both greatly influences the communication about the parenthood stage from the very beginning. When a couple desires a child and the pregnancy is uncomplicated, this can be a time with much intimate communication. There is still time to talk and to share without interruptions. Yet subtle communication changes occur as well as changes in conflict patterns. Contrary to popular myth, Rauch and colleagues found no indication that wives become more emotional in dealing with conflict during pregnancy. However, in the last stages of their wives' pregnancy, husbands do make greater efforts at nurturing and conflict avoidance.

Three factors influence couples during the transition to parenthood: their views on parental responsibilities and restrictions, the gratification child rearing holds for them as a couple, and their own marital intimacy and stability (Steffensmeier 1982). Middle-class mothers differed from lower-class mothers in their response to the stress of motherhood both during pregnancy and in the years following. Middle-class women took more time to adjust and feel fewer pressures than lower-class women, who must worry more about support and work roles (Reilly, Entwisle, and Doering 1987). Stamp (1994) stressed the importance of the transition into parenthood when he stated that new parents "need to renegotiate the reality of their marriage due to both the presence of the child and to their transformed presence with one another with the addition of a new role" (109).

As the wife's body dramatizes the life changes, some couples begin to feel pregnancy has trapped them into a loss of independence. This is a time when the spouses need mutual confirmation as individuals and as a couple evolving into parenthood. Women may need extra reassurance as to their continued physical desirability.

Naming the child becomes a communication event. Names may serve to link family generations. Often they reflect attitudes or dreams of a parent. Additional important communication may center around the role of the father in the birth process. Decisions concerning this issue require careful examination, because years later, one may feel left out or abandoned by the other at this crucial moment. Being present when the child is born has a great impact upon a couple. Read the following example:

---

*I have never felt closer to my wife than at the moment of Brian's birth. I helped her breathe, wiped her forehead, and rubbed her back between contractions. I actually felt a part of the birth process. When Brian was finally delivered, Wilma Ruth and I cried and laughed and cried again because of the power of the drama we had created. It's indescribable—to share in the birth of your own child.*

---

If you have ever lived with a newborn baby, you are well aware how one extremely small person can change an entire household. Sillars and Wilmot compare the adjustment following childbirth to the adjustment following marriage, saying, "There is a gradual decline from the emotional high experienced initially to a state more tempered by negative as well as positive feelings" (233). The initial question is, To what extent is there space in the environment for a child? According to Bradt (1988), children can be born into an environment that has space for them, has no space for them, or has a vacuum the child is expected to fill. "Whether they are living with one parent or two, and whether living with biological parents or stepparents, family processes are critical to children's development and well being" (Demo 1992, 110). It is different with adopted children because the child has been wanted usually for a longer period of time and fills a void.

At the point when the dyad becomes a triad, alliances or subsystems emerge. All family members cannot receive undivided attention at the same time. Simply put, all three people cannot experience eye contact or direct speech from each other simultaneously. One person is temporarily "out." Such triangling has the potential to evolve into powerful alliances.

Within this stage, the couple must deal with the following communication-related issues: (1) renegotiating roles, (2) transmitting culture and establishing a community of experiences, and (3) developing the child's communication competence. Moderately flexible families are likely to weather this period more easily than are relatively rigid systems.

Parental roles may become so powerful that the spouses may lose sight of each other for a period of time. New parents may feel inept at caring for their child. Because mothers traditionally have taken the major responsibility for childcare, until recently few fathers have been exposed to much modeling regarding how to share the caregiving role. Currently, family life education is increasingly supporting equal roles for male and female, and young men are presented with a wider range of models of male family life (Hey and Neubeck 1990).

When fathers do become involved in childcare, some evidence demonstrates that they are just as sensitive and responsive to infant needs as are mothers. In fact, fathers of newborns are as competent as mothers in providing attention, stimulation, and necessary care (Sawin and Parke 1979). Due to societal and economic changes, many more families are experiencing shared parenting responsibilities as they share the provider role. Although men's roles are changing slowly, there are indications that men, especially those with working wives, are accepting more family responsibility, particularly if the system is adaptable (Patterson and McCubbin 1984). A study of 180 dual-earner couples (Barnett, Brennan, and Marshall 1994) revealed that "parent role quality is significantly negatively associated with psychological distress for men as well as for women" (229). This may not apply to less advantaged couples or single-earner or career couples.

It does lend credence to Pleck's views (1993) that work and family roles have similar psychological significance for men and women.

Women may have to deal with the demands of motherhood and with the loss of a job or profession that held high interest or economic value. If they return to work, they must deal with separation from their child. Husband, wife, and infant must communicate to work out their relationships within the context of their roles. Intimacy between the couple certainly changes with the birth of a child. Privacy is almost impossible when the baby needs attention (Kelly 1988). Although research points to increasingly positive involvement of the father in parenthood, the birth of a first child tends to have a "traditionalizing influence in marriage, prompting greater role specialization, male-dominated decision making and a shift toward traditional ideology" (Sillars and Wilmot).

The first child represents a link to posterity and continuation of the family name and heritage—a potentially heavy burden. Couples that become involved in talking to one another, talking to friends and kin who have children, or take parenting classes reported less stress in the first year transition to parenthood (Gage and Christensen 1991). Thus, parents become involved in transmission of culture and the creation of a community of experiences for their new family. When you think about your own children or of your future children, what parts of your background do you wish to pass on to them? Do you wish they could experience the same type of Passover Seders you did as a child? Do you want them to have a strong African, Italian, or Norwegian identity? Are there family traditions, picnics, or celebrations you want to continue? What type of sexual identity or religious belief should your child develop? Such are the issues of transmission of culture, as indicated in the following example:

---

*The birth of our first child revived many issues that we had fought about in our courtship period and that we finally agreed to disagree about. Sean and I were from very different backgrounds, religiously, culturally, and even economically. As a couple, we were able to ignore many of the differences, but once Wendy was born, we each seemed to want certain things for her that we had experienced growing up. And our families got into the act also. We've dealt with almost everything except religion, and we are due for a showdown, because Wendy is now five and should begin some religious training soon.*

---

For many people, a child represents a link to the past and the future, a sense of life's flow, and a sense of immortality. Hence, children often serve as receptacles for what we consider our best parts, strengths, and expectations for the family. Once a couple becomes a triad, certain dormant issues may arise—particularly unresolved ones. A father's unfulfilled dreams may be transferred to his son. The couple's difference in values, religious beliefs, traditions, or ethnic background may be highlighted by the small member of the next generation. Thus, spousal conflicts may arise over what is to be "passed down." The transmission of both the cultural heritage and the family's own heritage is a demanding, frightening, and exciting task that depends on marital intimacy. Simultaneously, three people are forming a community of experiences, a process begun by the couple but deepened and intensified by the arrival of their offspring. As additional children arrive, the process will be repeated and extended, as this observer reports in the following example:

---

*It was amazing for me to watch my sister and her husband with their first child. After almost 25 years, my sister could remember so many of the songs that our mother sang to us as little ones. She and Lee took great pleasure in creating new words and expressions from things that Jonathan did. They set certain patterns for birthday parties, established Friday nights as "family night," and began to take Jonathan to museums, children's theater, and library storybook programs together. They created their own world, which now incorporated a little boy.*

---

Through communication, new patterns of life are formed and maintained that reflect the uniqueness of the three-person system. Young married couples who have not had extensive contact with their parents may suddenly feel a need to connect their child to grandparents and other relatives. In most families, contact with the extended family increases after the birth of a child. However, the amount of support and quality of help from a couple's parents depends more on their relationships prior to the birth of the child. Other couples may find themselves resisting overly eager relatives who wish to envelop the child. Appropriate boundaries usually require careful consideration and negotiation.

Finally, parents are deeply involved in providing their children with a means to deal with interpersonal relationships. Their relationship serves as the first model for the child's development of communication skills. From the earliest weeks of existence, a child learns how much connectedness or separateness is acceptable within the family system and how to attain that level through verbal and nonverbal means.

The moment of birth exposes the child to the world of interpersonal contacts, as a powerful parent-child bonding process begins through physical contact, facial/eye contact, and reciprocal vocal stimulation. The child makes its first contact with the world through touch, and this becomes an essential source of comfort, security, and warmth. According to Worobey (1989), maternal holding as a soothing strategy is employed over 80 percent of the time. Newborns recognize and prefer their mothers voice over other sounds. He concludes that "watching and smiling behaviors that characterize adult forms of sound communication, contribute greatly to the success of early mother-infant interactions" (16). He suggests that such encounters facilitate later interactions.

The first few months mark the critical beginning of a child's interpersonal learning. A child's personality is being formed in the earliest interchanges with nurturing parents. Children begin to respond to words at six to seven months; by nine or ten months, they can understand a few words and will begin to use language soon thereafter. Parents set the stage for positive interpersonal development by verbally and nonverbally giving a child the feeling of being recognized and loved.

As couples experience parenthood, their lives undergo massive changes. Most couples experience a decline in marital satisfaction with the birth of the first child (MacDernid, Huston, and McHale 1990). Because infants cause the couple to feel fatigued, frustrated, and tied down with little time for self or spouse, there is a corresponding decrease in marital satisfaction (Belsky et al. 1991). The baby's fussy behavior is stressful to both parents, but less to the father. Men avoided spouses whom they perceived to be unfriendly and distanced themselves until the wife adapts to the mother role. Sometimes this period has been described as the "baby honeymoon is over!"

In a comparative study of couples who became parents in either the first or second year after they married with couples who remained childfree, the parents' group became more instrumental and child oriented and the division of tasks more traditional. Those new parents with more traditional sex role attitudes and less traditional divisions of labor complained of less love and more conflicts (MacDermid, Huston, and McHale). Women's expectations and adjustments to parenthood after one year were significantly less than they indicated they hoped for when interviewed during pregnancy. Adjustments were more difficult when expectations of more help from the husband and extended family diminished, or when mothers felt less competent and satisfied with mothering (Kalmuss, Davidson, and Cushman 1992). In summarizing 20 years of research, Cowan et al. (1991) concluded that first-time parents are at risk for personal and marital distress that often continues until after a child is two years old.

As more children arrive, variations of this process occur. Nevertheless, later births do not cause as many major changes as the first one (Terkelsen 1980). Increasingly, with the declining birth rate, many parents raise only one or two children. Today the average child has only one sibling, creating greater rivalry and intensity in sibling communication (Gudykunst, Yoon, and Nishida 1986). Children at an early age pick up cues on stress between their parents. In marriages that were deteriorating, fathers, more often than mothers, were more negative and intrusive in child care and the children at three years were exhibiting more negative and disobedient behaviors (Belsky et al.).

***Family with Preschool Children*** The preschool family (child three to six years) experiences less pressure than in the previous period. Parents have learned to cope with a growing child. Barring physical or psychological complications, the former baby now walks, talks, goes to the bathroom alone, and can feed and entertain himself or herself for longer periods of time.

Watching three- or four-year-olds, you may be amazed at language skills. A four-year-old may produce well over 2000 different words and probably understands many more (Wood 1981). Children at this age begin to develop more sophisticated strategies for gaining such ends as later bedtimes or favorite foods. They are likely to express their gender roles nonverbally. As children become more independent, parents may directly influence their language acquisition skills through enrichment activities such as reading, role playing, and story telling. The parents' own communication behavior in this stage serves as an important model for the child. In a large national study of maternal competence and the effects upon children four years and younger, representing varied ethnic and socio-economic backgrounds, it was found that "the characteristics of the mother, household, and child collectively influence the quality of the home environment and success of the child's developmental processes which mediates the influence of demographic and socioeconomic variables" (Garrett et al. 1994, 147).

As noted in the discussion of roles, communication with children will differ depending on whether the family is position-oriented or person-oriented. Whereas a child in a position-oriented family is required to rely on prescribed communication behaviors, the child in a person-oriented family is more likely to use a range of communicative behaviors. The difference is essentially the degree to which the child is provided with verbalized reasons for performing or not performing certain communicative functions at certain times with certain individuals. Persons growing up in a household where things are done "because I am the father and you are the child" do not gain training in adapting to the unique individuals involved.

Children must not only learn to relate to parents and other adults, but they may have to incorporate new siblings into their world. During this period, many couples have more children, increasing the complexity of the family's relationship network. The arrival of second and third children moves the triad to a four- or five-person system and places greater demands on the parents. Each additional child limits the amount of time and contact each child has with the parents and the parents with each other. In a comparison of parenting and children's social, psychological, and academic success across varied family structures, it was reported that biological or adoptive parents in never divorced families used more positive parenting and co-parenting practices than did other single parent or cohabiting couples. Children in intact families showed higher levels of adjustment (Bronstein et al. 1993).

Additional children trigger a birth-order effect, which combines with sex roles to affect parent-child interaction. You may have heard characteristics attributed to various people because "She is the middle child" or "He is the baby of the family." There appear to be differences in parent-child communication based on sex and position. Boys may be allowed to ask for more comforting and receive more comforting and praise, particularly if they are firstborn. Mothers tend to become intensely involved with their firstborn children and appear more anxious about their performance in other settings. Whereas mothers are more likely to praise firstborn boys and secondborn girls more often, they will generally correct firstborn girls and secondborn boys. Finally, mothers are more likely to control their daughters than their sons (Toman 1976). Hoopes and Harper (1987) in a study of birth order, characterized firstborns as self-assured and responsible high achievers. Secondborn children question their place and have some difficulty with expectations, feelings, and expressing wishes in their communication. Thirdborn offspring develop trust slowly, but, once committed to a relationship, remain connected and find it difficult to end relationships. Fourthborn siblings are quite personable, adventurous, and less ambitious. They are often caregivers, and family members may want more from them than they can give. Fifthborn children tend to repeat the patterns of firstborn; sixth of those secondborn, and so forth (1989). In short, triangles and subsystems multiply. "Each time a new person is added, the limited time and other resources of the family have to be divided into smaller portions but the mother and father still have only two arms and two ears" (Satir 1972, 153). The pressures of parenting are captured in the following example:

---

*Angie was three when Gwen was born, and it was a very hard period for her and, therefore, for us. Angie changed from being a self-sufficient, happy child to a whining clinger who sucked her thumb and started to wet her pants again. Jimmy and I had to work very hard to spend 'special' time with her, to praise her, and to let her 'help' with the baby when she wanted to. Luckily, Gwen was an easy baby, so we could make the time to interact with Angie the way she needed us to.*

---

The previous example illustrates why parents need direct communication with an older child or children before the next baby's birth or adoption and during the months that follow. This may include hospital phone calls or visits and time alone after everyone is home. Siblings three or more years older are more likely to treat the baby with affection and interest, because they are more oriented to children their own age and less threatened by the new arrival. A sibling closer in age may engage in aggressive and selfish acts toward the baby.

How parents relate to children affects sibling cooperation. In keeping with the system of mutual causality, Bradt suggests that parents should hold all children in a particular conflict situation accountable for working things out, rather than judging one child as "the cause." He also suggests that children may help each other understand relationship issues.

In the three- to six-year stage, children begin to communicate on their own with the outside world. Some attend preschool. At five years old, most enter kindergarten. At this early stage, some parents experience difficulty in letting their children go, and the parents develop patterns of possessiveness. From their young peers, children learn about friendship and establish relationships outside the family. Children's interactions with one another vary in response to each other's gender and social characteristics such as dominance or shyness (Haslett and Perlmutter-Bowen 1989). These researchers suggest life-long implications of improving children's social skills, saying "New social skills and experiences may occur as a result of improving a child's communication abilities, and some negative consequences, e.g., relative isolation, social rejection from peers, and benevolent neglect by adults might be avoided" (50).

As children grow and become more independent, parents gain more control over their own lives, but time alone for the couple remains a problem. Even after they have adjusted to any possible income losses from the new members, husbands and wives are likely to fight over the absence of joint recreation.

***Family with School-Age Children*** The school-age family experiences new strains on its communication as the children begin to link further with outside influences. The family system now overlaps on a regular and continuous basis with other systems—educational, religious, and community. Families with very strong boundaries are forced to deal with new influences. Schools provide an introduction to a wider world of ideas and values. New beliefs may be encountered, and old beliefs may be challenged.

School age children may spend many hours away from the home environment and influence. In addition to the school experience, religious organizations provide educational and recreational events. Community organizations such as the Scouts, sports leagues, or 4-H clubs compete for family members' time. Parents establish rules that set boundaries in space, time, and energy that their children can expend in these new activities. During this period of growth, the child comes under the influence of peer pressures, which may conflict with parents' views. Often, conflict develops, because the child feels compelled to please friends rather than parents. Mothers who took time to communicate with their children and listen empathically to them when disciplining or comforting had children who were less rejected by their peers and more frequently chosen as companions (Burleson, Delia, and Applegate 1992).

As children continue their emotional and physical growth, their communication skills change. Negotiation and priority setting become important aspects of child-parent communication as extra familial demands conflict with family time. Family role orientation continues to influence behavior. For example, Bearison and Cassel (1975) found that first-grade children from person-oriented families are more able to accommodate their communication to the perspectives of listeners than are children of the same age who come from position-oriented families. The authors attribute the differences to the more differentiated role systems of the children from person-oriented families. Children at this age prefer peer communication with the same sex, often declaring dislike for the opposite sex. Knowing that this normally characterizes interactions of children between ages of eight and twelve helps parents understand the messages they receive from their children.

During the school years, the identity of the family as a unit reaches its peak. The family can enjoy all kinds of joint activities, which bring a richness to the intimacy of the family relationship. Due to the intense activity level, some partners neglect their own relationship or use the children as an excuse to avoid dealing with marital problems. Involvement with children may lower parent self esteem, a reflection of the stress of active parenting (Hawkins and Belsky 1989).

This period may be very comfortable for highly cohesive families, because joint activities can be enjoyed, and children still remain an active part of everyday family life. The more parents know about child development in this stage, the more skill they have in creating a supportive environment. In fact, the more parents are aware of the importance of providing play material and interacting with their children in fun and learning activities, the better the language development of their children will be in these important early stages (Stevens 1984).

## Families with Adolescents

A family system may be transformed as members attempt to manage the adolescent stage. Although a number of investigations suggest that the extent of adolescent and parental turmoil during this period has frequently been exaggerated, there is general agreement that adolescence, and particularly early adolescence, has traditionally been a challenging and sometimes trying time for both the young and their parents (Amato 1986; Richardson et al. 1986; Giblin 1994). Research has consistently shown that marital satisfaction is at its lowest when children are school age and later when the oldest child becomes an adolescent (Silverberg and Steinberg 1987). Wives reported that their marriages were most difficult in the 16–20 year period which coincides with adolescents being in the home (Giblin 1994).

According to Offer and Sabshin (1984), a wide range of adolescent experience can be identified. A minority experience a tumultuous adolescence. A larger percentage moves through the period in spurts, emotionally and mentally demonstrating less introspection than other groups. A third group appears to exhibit high levels of confidence. Very few of this final group reported anxiety or depression, but they did report receiving affection and encouragement for independence from their parents. The switching of moods in adolescents, varying from helplessness and dependence to defiance and independence within the span of two hours, can be explained in terms of the struggle for individuation, the development of a sense of self. The life-cycle task is the mutual weaning of parents and children (Herz 1980). The more time parents spent with adolescents, the more frequent but shorter the conflicts (Vuchinich, Teachman, and Crosby 1991). Conflicts with adolescents occur most frequently over simple items, such as chores and dress, rather than over bigger issues, such as drugs and sex (Barber 1994).

Teenagers experience internal struggles in coping with changes and individuation particularly in areas of sexuality, identity, autonomy, and friendships (Garcia-Preto 1988; Blieszner 1994). These struggles affect the entire family system at a time when parents may be facing predictable midlife issues. Prior interest in same-sex relationships switches to a growing interest in the opposite sex. "All he does is chase after girls now instead of fly balls." "Keep Out" signs appear on doors; phone calls become private. The upsurge in sexual thoughts and feelings serve as an undercurrent to many interactions that may make parents uneasy because they are forced to consider their child as a sexual being. Young people begin to set their own physical and psychological boundaries, which may limit communication with some or all persons approaching adulthood.

Adolescent self-esteem is related to family relationships. Through communication interactions, adolescents gain a sense of their own identity. Parental support, involvement with their children, and willingness to grant autonomy and freedom for decisions lead to high self esteem (Gecas and Schwalbe 1986). Self esteem for boys is more closely related to good family relations than it is for girls. Perhaps boys express their self esteem needs in ways that encourage Mom and Dad to respond with support, control, and communication behaviors, whereas girls use fewer overt nonverbal and verbal cues that initiate the same responses from parents (Demo, Small, and Savin-Williams 1987). The need for privacy often accompanies the search for identity, as illustrated in the following example:

---

*I grew up in a home where doors were always open, and people knew each other's business. I remember going through a terrible period starting at the end of junior high when I hated sharing a room with my sister. I would spend hours alone sitting on my bed listening to music with the door shut, and if anyone came in, I would have a fit. I even locked my sister out a number of times.*

---

A major task of adolescence is to loosen family bonds while establishing friendship bonds with peers. According to Erikson, the identity work that a child goes through within the family needs to be similarly repeated within society. Blos (1979) concurs that all youths reach puberty with intrapsychic tensions that require reworking in adolescence if full adulthood is to follow.

Adolescents are engaged in a process of forging a "workable, acceptable identity" (Douvan 1983, 63), a process dependent on communication experiences with peers. Such companions serve as relatively noncritical confidants, supporters, and listeners (Bleiszner

1994). Concurrent with this move, a young person becomes more other-centered and begins to develop a true sense of empathy and the ability to take another's perspective (Ritter 1979). Research on adolescence reveals the importance of self esteem and how it indicates the success adolescents are having in proceeding through this stage of development. Parents can raise self esteem in adolescents by being supportive, demonstrating physical affection, maintaining contact over these years, and offering companionship (Barber, Chadwich, and Oerter 1992). These parental behaviors would certainly improve communication by reducing tensions within the family environment.

Personal decision making provides a sense of autonomy for teenagers. The changes between the ages of 13 and 19 coincide with the individuation that occurs when a young person becomes self-reliant and insists upon making up his or her own mind. This leads to independence and confidence in decision making. By asserting his or her developing talents to speak out, work, or perform tasks without constant help and supervision, the adolescent signals to parents that past communication directives no longer fit the situation. In a study addressing gender issues in adolescent development, the authors highlight females' relational concerns as they differ from males and their communication components (Gilligan, Lyons, and Hammer 1989). Boys sometimes feel they are caught in a trap between their mothers and fathers. While still wanting their mother's care and protection, they sensed their father's expectations that they not become "feminized" and "not man enough to win father's approval" (Goldner et al. 1990, 353).

In a revealing study of middle class families, parents related quite differently to their adolescents. Girls reported better relationships with their mothers than did boys. Daughters not only spent more time with mothers but felt mothers were less strict. The closeness in age between children also influenced their communication with parents. The wider the spacing in years, the more likely the adolescents perceived the discipline from their fathers as fair. Spacing did not affect mothers in this way (Richardson et al. 1986).

The adolescent's struggles to work through developmental tasks of sexuality, identity, and autonomy send reverberations throughout the family system. The sexual awakening of their children has a powerful effect on many parents. Opposite-sex parents and children may find a gulf between them as a response to the power of the incest taboo in society. Unfortunately, in many families this results in the end of nonverbal affection, as illustrated in the following example:

---

*I will never forget being hurt as a teenager when my father totally changed the way he acted toward me. We used to have a real "buddy" relationship. We would spend lots of time together; we would wrestle, fool around, and I adored him. Suddenly, he became really distant, and I could not understand whether I had done something. But I did not feel I could talk about it either. Now that I am older, I can see the same pattern happening with my two sisters. Obviously, within his head there is a rule that when your daughter starts to develop breasts, you have to back off; and for him, that means having almost no relationship at all. Now I can understand that it hurts him as much as it hurts us.*

---

In spite of differences, data indicates that between two thirds and three fourths of adolescents feel close to their parents, accept them, and say they get along (Demo 1992; Jackson and Hornbeck 1989).

Same-sex parents and children may face internal conflicts if they perceive a major contrast between their children's budding sexuality and their own sexual identity. Such conflicts are tied to the parents' stages of development and negative self-evaluations. Because facing this issue would be uncomfortable, such perceptions may result in conflict over more "acceptable" issues such as friends, money, independence, or responsibility. Adolescents are more likely to accept parental guidelines when they have clear, open lines of communication and feel that their parents respect their values. A cross-generational coalition was found to exist when young people described themselves as emotionally closer to one parent than the other. This affected their later development of satisfying intimate relationships in early adulthood. If the parents had problems with intimacy, it was more likely their offspring would experience the same (West, Zarski, and Harvil 1988).

In his study of adolescent communication, Rawlins (1989) reports that adolescents viewed parents as more likely than their friends to criticize them, yet they felt their parents cared for them more than their friends did. The criticisms reflected genuine concern. Parents were seen as viewing adolescent concerns through the historical lens of "having been through it." Parent-adolescent conversations reflected a choice of topic, anticipated response, and perceived degree of caring. Yet maintaining a caring and supportive relationship with parents aids the development of an adolescent autonomy (Youniss and Smollar 1985). Both sons and daughters rated equally their perceptions of the importance of behavioral and emotional involvement with both the mother and father. Closeness to parents during childhood and through the years of growing up was "more telling for the well being of adolescents than is father presence during childhood" (Wenk et al. 1994, 229)

The exploring adolescent often challenges family themes, boundaries, and biosocial beliefs (Barber 1994). He or she is forever introducing the family system to people or modes of behavior that may threaten the family's identity. The adolescent's new input forecasts the eventual departure of the exploring child and forces the family to reevaluate itself (Ackerman 1980). A relatively flexible family may encounter less difficulty with an acting-out adolescent than a family with rigid rules. For example, Kantor and Lehr (1976) noticed that stress during the adolescent stage causes the system, particularly a closed one, to change form by developing open strategies. This change produces "a curious hybrid such as a family with closed-system goals and open-system means of attaining these goals" (157).

Parents, preadolescent, and adolescent children do not agree when describing parental behaviors. Selecting one member of a family to report on family dynamics led to inaccuracies (Tein, Roosa, and Michaels 1994). By testing both parents and the children, a clearer picture of the family system appeared and the differences between individual family members could be recognized. This study examined the differences in perceptions between children and their parents on five parenting behaviors: acceptance, rejection, inconsistent discipline, firm control and hostile control. The preadolescents and adolescents in this study gave mothers higher scores on four of these parenting behaviors compared to fathers but reported no difference on firm control. Higher agreement was found on adolescents' perceptions of mothers being more accepting and less consistent than fathers.

Some adolescents get caught in perverse triangles, finding themselves an emotional support for one parent, thus establishing a cross-generational coalition. This affected their later development of satisfying intimate relationships in early adulthood. If the parents had problems with intimacy, it is more likely their offspring would experience the same (West, Zarski, and Harvil).

Adolescents are more likely to accept parental guidelines when they have clear, open lines of communication and feel that their parents respect their values. Communication that supports gradual separation, rather than pushes persons away from one another or holds them rigidly close, eases the transition. Failure to negotiate the adolescent stage successfully, as reflected by an increase in suicides, has caused concern among family experts.

## Launching Children and Moving on

The departure from home of the oldest children signals one more major stage and necessitates major family reorganization. At this stage, it is very difficult to generalize about specific predictable events, because so many different things may be occurring. Most theories propose some variation of one of the following scenarios: (a) the "empty nest" model, which suggests that at least one of the parents is having difficulty letting the children go, and (b) the curvilinear model, which concentrates on the increased freedom and independence of the parents (McCullough 1980). The transitions and tasks related to this stage include (1) the development of parent-child, adult-to-adult relationships, (2) changes in function of marriage, (3) family expansion to include in-laws and grandchildren, and (4) opportunities to resolve relationships with aging parents (McCullough and Rutenberg 1988).

This is the period when parents move from being responsible for children to a sense of mutual responsibility between caring adults. When young people start living on their own, especially if they totally support themselves, they more readily take on the responsibilities of adulthood and caring for themselves and begin the process of becoming emotionally comfortable living apart from their families-or-origin. It is a time of vacating the bedrooms, sending along the extra coffee pot, and letting go of the predictable daily interactions at breakfast or bedtime that tied parents and siblings into a close, interactive system.

If the separation takes place without conflict or parental strings attached, communication usually remains open and flexible. Frequent contact with parents and siblings via phone calls, letters, or visits maintains family links and strengthens the bonds. At this time, communication issues may involve handling money, negotiating living space, making career decisions, keeping regular hours, or staying in contact, as illustrated by the following example:

---

*Since I've been in college, I call home about once a week and sometimes I sense that my mother is upset about something. If I ask about it, she will say something like "Oh, don't you worry about it. It's not your problem; you don't live here anymore." That upsets me, because I still feel I am part of the family.*

---

The high cost of living today makes leaving home difficult. In fact, some leave home and later return because they miss the comforts of their parents' homes and don't make enough to live on their own. In fact, most young adults are now living with their parents. In

1988, 55 percent of 20–24-year-olds did just that (Glick 1990). Another trend is married children divorcing and returning home as single parents because of financial difficulties. A countertrend has been young people leaving home to live independently prior to marriage, with some of them entering cohabiting relationships (Santi 1987). More women than men who moved away from home married later than those who stayed with a parent (Waite 1987).

Conflicts may occur when young people remain home during their early twenties, since established family rules and regulations tend to be challenged. "You don't need to wait up for me—I'm not seventeen!" "Pay room and board? I can't afford it and make car payments," may typify certain interactions. If young adults remain longer than expected, some families develop adverse effects (Aquilino 1991). If parent-child conflicts created problems in earlier years, this pattern was likely to continue (Suitor and Pillemer 1987). Some aging parents want time alone as a couple, and if the children delay leaving, this may create frustrations and negative communication patterns. Rather than separate from the family, a young person may remain connected, enjoying the advantages of home and family comforts without working to function as an independent adult.

Leave-taking varies greatly. Stress seems less for males, but females often used leaving home as a way to cope with problematic family issues. Other factors that cause increased parent child conflict were adult children remaining financially dependent and being unemployed. The returning home of divorced or separated children, especially with their children, increases parents' dissatisfaction with joint living arrangements (Aquilino and Supple 1991).

Some parents force a leave-taking before their children may feel ready for the break. This often results in hard feelings, conflict, and resentment. Many children resist being "on their own" while others can't wait "to get out of the nest." In some communities or cultures, it is expected; in others, children may remain home indefinitely. For example, many Hispanic, Italian, and Polish families prefer, and sometimes insist, that daughters remain at home until marriage. In many cultures, getting an apartment would be quickly vetoed for a twenty-one-year-old working woman. Parenting varies from culture to culture, but a large study of African-American, Hispanic, Asian-American, and Caucasian two-parent families revealed that there were more similarities than differences in parenting attitudes, parenting involvement, and parenting behaviors including leave-taking (Julian, McKenry, and McKelvey 1994).

Major changes occur in the husband-wife relationship after children leave as opportunities for increased intimacy present themselves. Mothers in the launching stage, whose children are getting ready to leave home, are seldom enthusiastic. It is only after the children are gone that the second honeymoon occurs—if it is going to. It is impossible to state which parent is more affected by the shift. Some men have psychologically invested more in the parenting relationship than in their spousal relationship. Fathers with fewer children report greater unhappiness over their leaving than do fathers with more children. Also, older fathers react more strongly than younger fathers. This finding further relates to family communication: the most unhappy fathers reported they felt most neglected by their wives, received the least amount of understanding, sensed loneliness most, were least enthusiastic about wives' companionship, and believed their wives least empathic. Ironically, Bart's research with women revealed many of the same complaints about men and the same communication barriers. Silverberg and Steinberg (1987) found husbands' marital satisfaction closely related to the quality of their relationship with firstborn sons and wives' happiness related to firstborn daughters.

Stages which involve active parenting contain specific role stresses. Such stress affects men differently than women. In a study of the interface between the work role and the parent role in dual career couples, stress led to role strain when work schedules lacked flexibility, when children were young, and when there were several children (Guelzow, Bird, and Koball 1991). Compared to women, men reported greater role conflict and parental stress when the children were older, but greater marital stress when the children were younger. In this study, women were committed to their careers and combined full time work with marital and parental roles without experiencing high levels of stress. The researchers concluded that the higher marital stress for men in dual career marriages may be evidence of "more intense marital negotiations when children are young and when there are more children. The resulting increase in sharing by men may well be worth the conflict for women ... marital strain may be a short term cost of social redefinition of family roles" (160).

Throughout the life cycle there are differences in the strategies couples use to cope with stress in their careers and roles as parents. Dual career couples differed from dual earner couples in both gender and strategies chosen. Prior to the birth of the first child and again after children have been raised, couples establish a more equal allocation of household work and less mention is made of feelings of overload. Women in all but the last cycle stage use more cognitive restructuring (telling themselves their family is better off if both are employed, etc.), delegating, limiting hobby activities, and using social support (relying on extended family, making friends who can help out, etc.). Men used the same strategies to a lesser degree and this research showed men more significantly involved than in the 1970s studies (Schnittger and Bird 1990).

In many families, the postparental period presents few crises and becomes a part of the sequence and rhythms of the life cycle. The effects of the empty nest largely disappear two years after the departure of the last child. In a study of roles throughout the life cycle, Schaefer and Keith (1981) found that equity in the tasks of cooking, homemaking, and providing increase across the stages, with the highest increases in the launching stage and middle years after the children leave home. Another study confirmed again that older couples with no children in the home are happier than those with children (Pittman and Lloyd 1988).

In the middle years of adulthood, communication in the family mainly involves the original dyad. As opposed to earlier days when families were larger and life expectancy was shorter, the empty nest transition now occurs in middle age rather than old age. A century ago a typical couple lived together for 31 years before losing a spouse; today the figure is 44 years (Glick 1989). Many contradictory reports about this period appear in family literature. "Second honeymoons" are counterbalanced by a high divorce rate. Images of decreasing sexuality are matched by reports of this as a period of sexual revitalization. Such factors as health, economics, and social class tend to interact with the couple's development and satisfaction at this stage. Fear of job loss in these days of increasing layoffs or the loss of insurance or pension benefits haunts many midlife Americans. Wives' adjustments to midlife concerns more than husbands' affect marital satisfaction. Women undergo a reappraisal and achieve more autonomy and power as they let go of child-raising responsibilities, but they may be faced with caring for adult parents as a tradeoff.

Spouses who have allowed their children to become their main focus for so many years may find themselves somewhat unconnected. Partners may sense a distance between them and feel unable, or unwilling, to try to reconnect. For many couples, the readjustment to a viable, two-person system requires hard work. Divorces occur frequently in this midlife transmission period. How difficult the transition can be for some women is reflected in the following example:

---

*When the children left, I discovered myself living with essentially a mute man. We hadn't realized that for years we had talked little to one another—that most of our communication was with the children or about them. Since we both worked, always took vacations with the kids, and kept busy chasing after kids' activities, we never had time for ourselves. Now I've got time to talk and I have to compete with TV—that's the "other woman" in my house.*

---

Much adult parent-child interaction appears to be carried out through the female networks rather than through male ones, resulting in a potential distancing of the adult child's father (Troll, Miller, and Atchley 1979). Mothers tend to remain in even more constant contact with adult daughters, especially those who have children. The presence of grandchildren contributes significantly to changes in family communication.

The experience of being a grandparent or grandchild is becoming increasingly common given increased longevity. Currently a child has a 50 percent chance of having two living grandparents (Cryer-Downs 1989). Children in blended families may experience up to eight grandparent figures. Given the reality of a mobile society, some grandparents and grandchildren experience limited and formal or distant contacts. In a comparative study of African-American and white grandmothers, African-American grandmothers had a greater number of exchanges, plus contacts with grandchildren, than white grandmothers. In later years, however, aging African-American grandmothers received more help from grandchildren than did white grandmothers (Kivett 1993). Parents tend to give priority to adult children with greater needs, especially to divorced daughters with children and to unmarried daughters (Aldous and Klein 1991). Indeed, in some families the aging parents welcome and even long for the empty nest and resent the stress of the cluttered nest returning. Yet grandparents are being called on to take a more participative role in modern families, particularly in situations of divorce and dual-career marriages.

In a society where "grandparents range in age from 30 to 90 plus and grandchildren range from newborns to retirees" (Hagestad 1985), styles of grandparenting vary. Neugarten and Wernstern classified five grandparent styles: (1) formal, (2) fun seeker, (3) second parent, (4) family sage, and (5) distant figure. Such roles may vary across ages. For example, one study found that children ages 4–5 liked indulgent grandparents, at ages 8–9 preferred fun loving ones, and at ages 11–12 began to distance themselves (Barranti-Ramirez 1985).

Assuming the role of grandparents opens the door for unique communication experiences. Grandparents and grandchildren who interact frequently express feelings of closeness; some grandparents experience continuity, and grandchildren develop added self-identity through the narration of oral history.

Grandparenthood provides an opportunity for new roles and meaningful interaction, since it usually does not entail the responsibilities, obligations, or conflicts of parenthood. Also, grandparents and grandchildren may have a "common enemy" in the parents (Walsh 1982). Conflicts can result if grandparents are drawn into parental conflicts. On occasion, grandparents act as a refuge for children in a strife-torn family.

In certain cultural groups, grandparents are expected to assume a major role in childrearing. However, in other cultures, if grandparents are coerced into childcare, they are likely to resent it. Such cross-generational contact provides opportunities for extended transmission of culture and for development of a sense of family history. Grandparents serve as one source of a child's sense of identity. Children gain access to their roots and have the opportunity to see the functioning of the two families-of-origin that influenced their parents, and hence, themselves. In contrast to embarking on grandparenting, the middle-aged generation has to deal with changing relationships with their parents and their retirement, disability, dependency, or death.

In spite of the decisions about major changes in midlife, this period can be a happy one for families. Financial worries lessen if money has been managed well over the years. The period between the time the children leave home and the retirement of the parents is when family income is at its highest level. Husbands earn most between 55 and 64 years of age (Glick 1989). Children become less of an everyday concern and a couple or single parent may have the opportunity to focus on old or new relationships and experiences.

Many families have to negotiate the relationship between parents and grown children, who may now be entering parenthood. Highly cohesive families may attempt to keep inappropriate ties. For example, if a child or grandchild is constantly more important than a spouse, the partners are not dealing with their own development.

## Families in Later Life

Family relationships continue to be significant throughout later life. According to Walsh (1989) seventy percent of older adults live with spouses or other relatives, including children, siblings or aged parents. Eighty percent of those who do live alone tend to be elderly widows. Yet most of those with children report that a child could be there within minutes if needed and tend to maintain at least weekly contact. The myth of the isolated elderly is not reality for the majority of older Americans. Total isolation is very rare. As families grow older, the more frequently they interacted with relatives, and the higher they ranked their happiness (Ishii-Kuntz 1994).

Older family members face issues of self-identity related to retirement, health concerns, interpersonal needs (especially if they lose a spouse), and facing their own death. Some couples experience "re-entry" problems when one or both return to the home and remain there 24 hours of most days. The increased contact may lead to a deepening of the relationship or result in friction from the forced closeness. The retired persons may undergo severe role adjustments and the loss of certain functions (e.g., providing) that served as self-definition. The loss of a large social communication network places increased pressure for intimacy on the couple. Yet this may be a time of rejuvenation. The couple now has time to enjoy one another. A study of couples married for over 50 years shows the aging stage as one of the happiest, with more time together for travel and activities which they previously could not manage (Sporakowski and Hughston, 1978). When postretirement activates previously developed needs and hobbies, couples remain happy (McCubbin and Dahl 1985).

A second issue that affects all communication involves the health and declining strength of the couple. Ill health creates a need for nurturing communication and taps the couple's physical, mental, and financial resources. Aging predictably involves some sensory loss such as changes in visual or auditory acuity as well as taste, smell, and tactility which affects interpersonal communication (Benjamin 1988). Such health concerns compound the problem of maintaining relationships. Frustration and low self-esteem may make individuals reluctant to initiate contact, while listeners may decline, because of their impatience with the older person's infirmities.

Interpersonal communication becomes increasingly important at this stage. "Satisfaction with an intimate relationship is related to life satisfaction and psychological well-being, especially for elderly women" (Thompson and Nussbaum 1988, 95). Many older family members engage in the "elder function," or the sharing of the accumulated wisdom of their lives with younger people, usually family

Many grandparents relate to grandchildren as nurturers and caretakers.

members. There is a need to feel useful to the coming generation, and, for many older persons, such feelings come from revealing information or spinning stories designed to guide the younger listener. The focus of reminiscence is usually the family. It can be used as a coping mechanism, to defend self esteem, feel loved, gain self-awareness, or see oneself in a larger historical context. This oral history can enrich a family, especially its members' sense of their family-of-origin (Wolff 1993). It gives the elderly a chance to communicate to those they love, helped raise, or even harmed. Some need to "set the record straight" or to correct, and express sorrow for, mistakes. The importance of this storytelling is demonstrated in the following example:

---

*I'm glad my Dad, Bill, lived past seventy-five. Only then did we come to terms with one another. Long after he retired, he mellowed, had a stroke, and became approachable. He talked about the depression, the war years, and the struggle to pay for the farm. Then I sensed what had made him so tough and noncommunicative.*

---

Elderly individuals who remain interested and have opportunities for keeping abreast of world and national events enjoy life more and disengage themselves less from the family (Nussbaum 1983, 317).

Two basic functions seem to be served by the elderly parent-adult child relationship: affect and mutual aid. Positive affect provided to the elderly by their children significantly increased their feelings of well being (Barnett et al. 1991). Although older Americans see their children with some regularity, many older persons are prevented from maintaining the interpersonal contacts they desire due to concerns of economics, safety, and health (Aldous and Klein 1991). Rising costs of living restrict the travel and entertainment aspects of older persons' budgets, and many urban senior citizens do not feel safe attending evening meetings or social activities. Inflation has increased stress upon older Americans as more fall below the poverty level. Poverty rates are higher for elderly women, African-Americans, Hispanics, and single persons. In 1992, 16.2 percent of those 75 or older were below the poverty level (Lewis 1993).

Older couples who reach their retirement together may turn inward toward each other and share their remaining years intensely. Loss becomes a part of aging, and this increases when close friends and relatives die. In order to prevent their becoming "the last one out," older couples often move beyond their age range and establish friendships through communicating with younger adults. This may be difficult if infirmities prevent mobility.

The developmental stages of both middle and older years are important periods for introspection. Intrapersonal communication about the meaning of one's life allows an individual to see his or her life in perspective. Turning to oneself for insights can be painful and lead to despair, because some aging adults sense their faults and shortcomings and recognize that too little has been accomplished, and too little time and energy is left to change. This affects their self-concept and interpersonal communication with other family members. The intrapersonal communication has systemic affects, because how the aging individual comes to terms with his or her own sense of wholeness affects other members' sense of identity.

After the death of a spouse, cohabiting partner, or lover, the other must face the adjustment inherent in becoming a widow, widower, or single person without a lover. Working through the grief period, an older person may make great demands on friends or family members who may be resentful of, or unprepared for, such pressures. This is coupled with the friends' or family members' personal grief at the loss of a significant other or a parent. The surviving member of a couple has to renegotiate roles and boundaries as he or she attempts to create or maintain interpersonal contacts. It is important that older family members have a say in their care and be a part of all communication that concerns them as long as possible. Friedan declares, "I began to wonder why people would voluntarily put themselves into an age ghetto, paying hundreds of thousands of dollars to wall themselves off from the rest of society. Is it because they accept that senior citizen stigma and voluntarily retreat from its pain?" Her advice throughout her book, *The Fountain of Age*, is for older family members to assert themselves and continue active lives.

Much to the surprise of their adult children, many widows or widowers begin to date. The importance of dating among older persons is growing, not necessarily as a prelude to marriage. Interpersonal motives for dating include meeting possible mates, meeting other possible dates, exchanging intimacies, remaining socially active, interacting with the opposite sex, engaging in sex, and maintaining a stable identity (Thompson and Nussbaum).

Eventually an elderly person must confront his or her own death (Thompson 1989). Many families resist addressing the issue directly with the elderly member, yet relationships that allow discussion of death and that provide direct emotional support are more helpful. Family members—particularly adult children—may face their own crises as they try to (1) deal with the loss of the generation which separates them from death, (2) makes sense of the experience, (3) anticipate shifts in the family formation, and (4) deal with their own feelings. Often these concerns get in the way of saying farewell in a direct and meaningful manner.

## Transitions Between Stages

It is important not to underestimate the effects of transitions between each of these developmental stages. Haley, Bowen, and other therapists observed that dysfunctional families have members who fail to make these transitions at the appropriate times in their lives. These members cause imbalance in their family systems by remaining at one developmental stage and not moving on. In these troubled families, they have observed a piling-up effect, with one or more members stuck at the same stage. Some of these same family members express external stresses (illness, separation, divorce) simultaneously with developmental changes and become unable to cope. However, functional families take these stages in stride and experience the transitions with temporary, but not permanent, stress.

This does not mean that marital satisfaction does not suffer during the family life cycle with consequent effects upon family communication. In a variety of studies which followed couples from the childless stage through the years of childbearing, adolescence, and stages beyond, results indicated a steady decline in satisfaction that did not level off until the children began to individuate and separate from their parents. Then, satisfaction increased in the postparental period when the children left and established their own families (Vaillant and Vaillant 1993; Giblin 1994; Schnittger and Bird 1990). Regarding cohesion and adaptability over the stages, Olson, McCubbin, and Associates (1983) found wives believed their families were more cohesive and adaptable than did their husbands. Adolescents consistently reported lower levels of cohesion and adaptability than either of their parents. In fact, cohesion and adaptability declined in the first five stages to the lowest points in the adolescent and launching stages and increased in the last two stages. Not only does this show differences in perceptions by family members but differences between stages that affect communication. It is interesting to note that families coped with these stresses by using the communication strategy of reframing their difficulties in ways they could manage. This required the communication skills of negotiation, problem-solving, and decision-making.

Nichols (1980) found that functional families experienced transitions as challenging and, at times, unpleasant events, but not as long-lasting negative influences. Transitions into marriage or birth of a child, for example, affected family functioning, but the family progressed through them as a normal maturation process. Transitions out of marriage, such as divorce, desertion, or death, had negative effects and cause higher stress over longer periods of time (Balsky et al. 1991). Steffensmeier (1982) studied the transition into parenthood and concluded that whether couples experienced difficulty with the stage depended on their views on parental responsibilities and the amount of gratification they received from the role and the quality of their intimacy and stability prior to and during the developmental stage. Importantly, Lavee and Olson (1991) found that the impact of transitions and intrafamily strain on the family system was not determined by either the levels of cohesion or adaptability alone but by the interaction of the two dimensions.

Lavee and Olson commented that some families become more crisis prone and others more adaptive moving through the life cycle stages. They discovered differences on cohesion and adaptability scales in the Circumplex Model of Family Systems related to a family's response to stress. Earlier research had indicated that families could be more accurately described on cohesion and adaptability scales as (1) flexible-separated (high on adaptability and low on cohesion) (2) flexible-connected (high on adaptability and cohesion) (3) structured-separated (low on both cohesion and adaptability) (4) structured-connected (high on cohesion and low on adaptability) (Olson, Lavee, and McCubbin 1988). Using this family system typology, Lavee and Olson (1991) discovered that marital adjustment to stress was an important predictor of adaptation, affecting perceived well-being directly or indirectly, for connected but not in separated families. Further, a direct effect of intrafamily strain on well-being was found in flexible but not in structured families. Other conclusions indicated that flexible, connected families were more affected by the pileup of stressful events but not by predictable transitions, while the structured, separated families had greater difficulty with transitional changes in the life cycle. The flexible, separated and structured, connected types experienced difficulties with both transitions and stressful events.

Throughout this chapter we have cited evidence that indicates the great variations in how families cope with stress. Some families experience a roller coaster effect with little relief, especially when multiple stressors accumulate (Burr, Klein, and Associates 1994).

As they struggle with change and transitions, most persons experience life in its moments, and often ignore the larger process. In short, the movement across the life span becomes lost in the moments. Carter and McGoldrick's (1988) comments serve to summarize this experience:

> Families characteristically lack time perspective when they are having problems. They tend generally to magnify the present moment, overwhelmed and immobilized by their immediate feelings; or they become fixed on a moment in the future that they dread or long for. They lose the awareness that life means continual motion from the past and into the future with a continual transformation of familial relationships. (10)

## CONCLUSION

This chapter provided an overview of the effects of developmental stresses on communication within families. After indicating how individuals move through a life cycle, the chapter focused on a stage model for intact American families. The stages included were (1) single young adults, (2) the couple, (3) families with young children, (4) families with adolescents, (5) launching children and moving on, and (6) families in later life. As families move through the years, each generation faces predictable developmental issues as couples marry, beget children, and live through stages of child development superimposed upon individual adult developmental changes. As children leave home to form new systems, the original couple, faces the middle years and adjustment issues. The cohesion-adaptability axis overlay each system's personal growth, while themes, images, and biosocial beliefs may be challenged as the years pass.

The entire family developmental process is extremely complex and challenging. Achieving the developmental tasks in each stage represents accomplishment and psychological growth for each family member. Stress gets expressed in the intrapersonal and interpresonal communication that follows as the family member struggles for balance in the dialectical tension between self needs and family system needs. Stamp (1994) succinctly summarized much of what we believe when he stated, "Couples do not become parents just by virtue of having a child: parenthood is constituted and maintained through conversation" (109). Coping effectively in each stage requires continual conversation.

## IN REVIEW

1. Reflecting upon your own family or one you know well, which stage of development seemed to have the greatest number of communication problems? Describe sample problems and hypothesize why this stage may have been so problematic.
2. Discuss what impact different cultural backgrounds have on the communication in various stages of development on children and parents. Does being Asian-American, Hispanic, African-American, etc. impact upon developmental issues?
3. Using your own family or a family you know well, give examples of verbal or nonverbal communication patterns that seemed commonplace at different developmental stages in the family life cycle.
4. Referring to your own family or a family you have observed, describe how a couple has dealt with the communication tasks of incorporating a child into their system and dealing with the following communication related issues: (1) renegotiating roles, (2) transmitting culture, (3) establishing a community of experiences, and (4) developing the child's communication competence.
5. What appears to characterize communication in families during the period when there are one or more adolescents living within the system?
6. How is communication affected by the moving out of young adults in the launching stage in two-parent systems?
7. Compare and contrast communication patterns you have observed in the interactions between middle-aged and older family members. To what extent were reminiscing, reflection, and sorting out important to members at these stages?

# 11

# Family Communication and Unpredictable Stress

"And the waters came!" In 1993 and 1995 in the Midwest thousands of families were wiped out by the raging waters of the Mississippi and Missouri Rivers. When these larger rivers failed to carry the runoff, the water backed up into the hundreds of smaller rivers and streams that fed into these larger rivers destroying more homes, businesses, and crops. "And the plane went down!" In 1994 outside Pittsburgh, a US Air flight suddenly crashed, killing all passengers and crew. In 1995, in Chicago, someone set fire to a home, burning to death the father and six of his children. These catastrophes represent only one kind of unpredictable stress that families fear. They can also live in dread of losing a father suddenly because of an artery blockage, a mother receiving a diagnosis of multiple sclerosis, or a young adult son diagnosed with leukemia. What happens to a family system when events occur that the family has had no preparation to cope with or warnings that this unpredictable crisis could occur? How does communication function in these circumstances?

In the previous chapter we focused more on a developmental life cycle approach explaining changes that cause predictable stress in two parent families from infancy to dissolution. The stages a family passed through had an overall timetable or temporal quality with expectancies as to when transitions would occur. The absence of "on time" movement through the cycle created stress. We included examples that indicated how critical role transitions became a part of developmental change, such as getting married, establishing careers, first parenthood, or having children leave home.

This chapter discusses those unpredictable events that cause great stress in families. In doing so we try to recognize the two perspectives on change in families: family development and life course. Aldous (1990) has pointed out that unpredictable family stress, "unlike family development, is largely concerned with *unexpected* events in the lives of families. Depending upon the resources they possess and their interpretation of the events, family members respond with varying degrees of stress" (572). The unpredictable stress in families caused by divorce, remarriage, and single unwed parenting leads to changes in the lives of family members, interrupting gradual family development processes. The suggested ages that family members move in or out of a life cycle show great fluctuations when major stresses occur. Later marriages, cohabitation, or stepfamily formation make it difficult to predict the points of stress family members experience going through life cycle changes. The later arrival of children, the greater number of years between children, and the decline in number of children all affect time in any life cycle stage. Unemployment and job shifts may affect timing of developmental cycles. Remember, in the family development approach, change is conceptualized as systematic shifts through a sequence of stages. A life course perspective suggests that when crises occur, a family member's education, income, occupation, value-structure, and satisfaction or dissatisfaction with life may cause more changes than timing in family stages. Issues of life state and life course simultaneously bear on how a family responds to unpredictable stress.

*Unpredictable stresses* are brought about by events or circumstances that disrupt life patterns but that cannot be foreseen from either a developmental or life course perspective. Such stresses may be positive, although more frequently they are perceived as negative. These are the "slings and arrows of outrageous fortune," or shocks to the system. Such stresses conjure up images of loss such as that involved in untimely death, divorce, economic reversal, or serious injury. Some positive events, such as a large inheritance, winning the lottery, a job promotion or transfer, or the rediscovery of long-lost relatives are also stresses for the system. These unpredictable stresses can maximize the dialectical tensions between individual family members and others or between the family and its environment. For example, the sudden death, long term illness, or severe injury of a parent or child can change a family from one that copes with ordinary stresses to one that cannot cope with a critical major stress.

Although we are dealing with unpredictable stress as distinct from the more predictable developmental or life course changes, there may be certain overlaps. Becoming pregnant or having a child may be considered a developmental event, but an unwanted pregnancy or the birth of a severely handicapped child may also be classified as an unpredictable stress. Death happens to all persons, but the untimely death of a family member is a severe crisis for the system. Whether the entire family or only certain members are initially affected by the event, the family system in its course will eventually reflect the tension created by the loss in its member's communication behaviors.

Crises occur when a family lacks the resources to cope with one or more stressful events. All families undergo some degree of strain or stress. Strain can be defined as that tension or difficulty sensed by family members which indicates that change is needed in their relationships and their family environment. Stressor events discussed in this chapter are characterized by unexpectedness, their greater intensity and longer duration, and their undesirability and serious effects (Lavee, McCubbin, and Olson 1987). Think about the stresses of a family dealing for over 20 years with what became a fatal illness for three members in the following example:

---

*There were nine children in our family, and three had muscular dystrophy. I remember how hard it was for Mom to accept their illness. She wouldn't talk about it within the family. Her rule was that it was better not discussed, yet I would find her alone in her room crying. We all learned from Marilyn, Dan, and Virginia. Communication reached a tense stage when Marilyn was the first to die. We sensed the fear and panic in Dan and Virginia. It took time to get them to talk about these fears and finally, near their own deaths, they would joke about who was going next. All of this was strictly with Dan and Virginia and myself. Mom, Dad, and the rest couldn't handle any humor on the subject. I feel they would like to have shared these feelings with all of us, but some of the living in our family put great distance between themselves and those who were dying.*

---

The previous chapter contains a model of family stressors (Figure 10.1) and a description of the developmental stresses a family faces. This chapter concentrates on the second type of horizontal stressors—the external, unpredictable stressors. It examines (1) coping with unpredictable stress (including the stressors), a model for coping, and the stages of crisis, and (2) communication patterns for coping with stresses such as death, illness, disability, and divorce.

## UNPREDICTABLE STRESS AND FAMILY COPING PATTERNS

Stress involves a physiological response to stressors, events, or situations that are viewed as powerful negative or positive forces. Individuals or families under stress reflect these physiological changes through their anxiety and attempts to cope.

Systems under stress tend to fall into predictable patterns, some functional, some dysfunctional, as the members try to handle the anxiety. As you might imagine, what is a major stressor to one family may be a minor concern to another. What one family does to reduce tension differs greatly from another family's strategies. In order to appreciate the process and the coping, the family stressors, models of coping, and stages of crisis must be examined.

### Stressors

Family researchers have examined stresses and crises for over forty years. In his early work, Hill (1949) identified family disruptions that

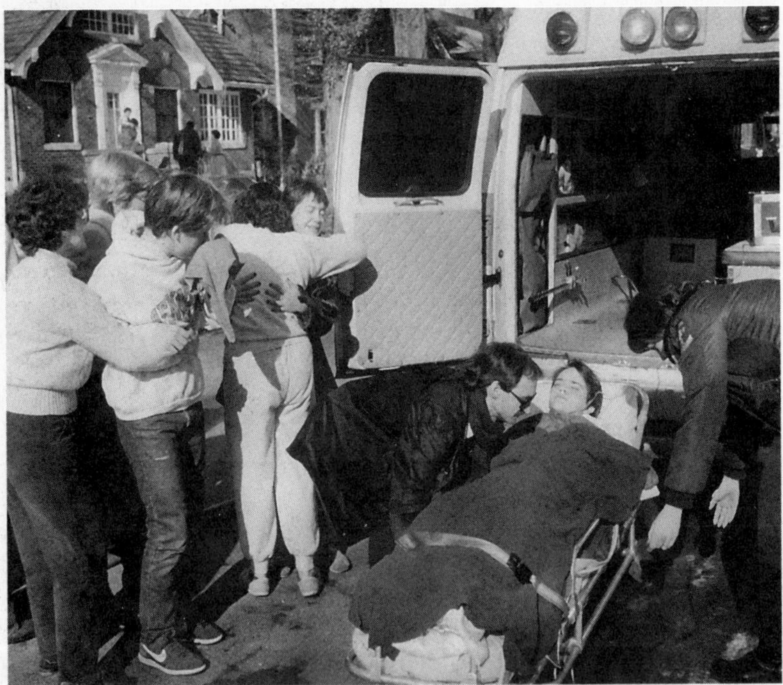

Family and community members need to support each other when one member is injured.

cause crises. These include (1) the coming apart of the family due to the death of a member; (2) the addition of new or returning family members; (3) the sense of disgrace, which may result from infidelity, alcoholism, or nonsupport; and (4) a combination of the above, which could include suicide, imprisonment, homicide, or mental illness. In their classic work on life stressors, Holmes and Rahe (1967) identified 43 events that cause stress. The top twelve reflected interruptions in strong family connections, such as death of a spouse, divorce, marriage, retirement, change in a family member's health, or pregnancy. In 1967, remarriage or stepparenting did not make the top twelve, but today they would. Addiction to drugs or alcohol might also be considered major stressors.

Bain (1978) provided important insights into a family's capacity to cope with stress. He found that a family's coping capacity was tied to four major factors: (1) the number of previous stressors the members had faced, (2) the degree of role change involved in the coping, (3) the social support available to members and (4) the institutional support available to members. As you might imagine, the severe illness of a child is likely to be very difficult for a family which has recently dealt with major financial or marital problems. It may cause greater strain if a parent has to change roles, such as giving up a career, to tend the child. A family with the social support of friends and relatives and the institutional support of doctors, teachers, and religious leaders is likely to cope better than a family left to its own resources. Yet, often a family has to ask for the support and not assume people will know what is needed or know how to respond. The observation by a teacher attests to the importance of support at the time of crisis in the following example:

---

*As a teacher, I watch a few students' families undergo divorce each year. The ones who seem to cope reasonably well with the pain are those that have some strengths or resources to bring to the process. Usually this is the family that has strong extended family or neighborhood friends and the family that tells the school or church what is going on. In short, this family lets people in on the pain—asks for some help.*

---

Research on family stress has examined concerns such as ongoing environmental stress, such as refugees or those living in dangerous inner city areas (McCubbin and Patterson 1983; Hines 1988). Throughout the family stress literature, writers emphasize the possible productive outcomes of dealing with stress as well as the difficulties inherent in such a process (Burr, Klein, and Associates 1994). McCubbin and McCubbin (1988) identified typologies of resilient families, taking into account factors of social class and ethnicity. They suggest the following:

> Resilient families appear to cultivate a commitment to ensuring stability by creating a sense of rhythm to family life through its rituals and routines ... [and] by a family emphasis on developing a sense of centeredness ... and confidence in its own ability to manage change. (253)

They suggest that resilient lower to low-middle income families have internal strengths complemented by community support, service, religious programs, and a sense of belonging to the community. In order to understand the coping process, you need to examine the process described in the Double ABCX model (Figure 11.1).

## Model

Each family exhibits unique coping behaviors. Coping implies "the central mechanism through which family stressors, demands, and strains are eliminated, managed, or adapted to" (McCubbin et al. 1983, 3). The primary models currently used to understand family crises have evolved from Hill's original model, which proposed that:

> A [the stressor event], interacting with B [the family's crisis-meeting resources], interacting with C [the family's definition of the event] produces X [the crisis]. (McCubbin and Patterson 1983, 6)

An explanation is as follows: the stressor, *a*, represents a life event or transition that has the potential to change a family's social system, indeed its life course. Such events as the loss of job, untimely death, serious illness, or good luck in the lottery may fall into this category. The *b* factor represents the resources a family can use to keep an event or change from creating a crisis, such as money, friends, time and space, or problem-solving skills. This factor ties into a family's levels of cohesion and adaptability in terms of how it has learned to deal with various crises over time.

The *c* factor represents the importance a family attaches to the stressor *a*. For example, in one family a diagnosis of a member's juvenile diabetes might overwhelm the entire system, whereas another family might cope well with that news, perceiving the diabetes as a manageable disease, one not likely to alter their lives drastically. The definitions of both the family and families-of-origin may come to bear on the perception of crises. For example, a three-generation family that has never experienced a divorce may define a young granddaughter's marital separation as a severe crisis. A multigenerational system with a history of divorce may not see the separation as a crisis. Together, *a*, *b*, and *c* contribute to the experience of stress that is unique to each family, depending on its background, resources, and interpretation of the event.

The *x* factor represents the amount of disruptiveness that occurs to the system. It is characterized by "the family's inability to restore stability and by the continuous pressure to make changes in the family structure and patterns of interaction" (McCubbin and Patterson, 10). In short, it is the family's total experienced anxiety and demands that the family can't assimilate.

McCubbin and Patterson have developed a Double ABCX model based on Hill's original work, but incorporate postcrisis variables (Figure 11.1), or the next stages of coping. Whereas Hill's ABCX model focused on pre-crisis areas, the Double ABCX model incorporates the family's efforts to recover over time. In this model, the *aA* factor includes not only the immediate stressor (e.g., death) but also the demands or changes that may emerge from individual system's members, a system as a whole, and the extended system. McCubbin and Patterson suggest that the *aA* factor includes: (1) the initial stressor or developmental stage issues, (2) normative transitions, (3) prior strains, (4) the consequences of the system's coping attempts, and (5) ambiguity. Imagine for example, the death of a man, age 36, in a family with a wife and three daughters, ages 6, 10 and 12. If a young father dies, the system must deal with the immediate loss as well as

**FIGURE 11.1**
**The Double ABCX Model**

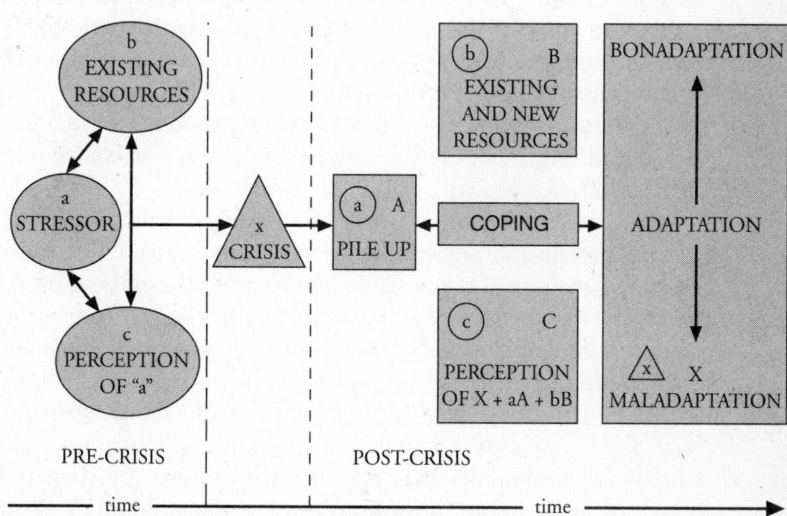

economic uncertainty and changes in the mother's role. In addition, the developmental stage of some children may soon require the family to cope with an adolescent's need for independence. This is compounded by any prior strains, such as in-law problems or mother-daughter conflicts. A consequence of the family's attempts to cope might be the mother's new job, which keeps her from meeting the children's needs for active parenting. Finally, ambiguity might be caused by the confusion of new roles now that the father has left the system. Boundaries shift as the life course changes later. Mother might consider remarriage. Changes become expected. Thus, *aA* is larger than the original conception of *a*.

The *bB* factor represents the family's ability to meet its needs. This factor includes family resources from an individual, system, and community point of view. A family may use existing and expanded resources. Existing resources are part of a family's background. In the case of death, these may include the ways in which a family coped in the past when the father was gone on business. The expanded family resources emerge from the crisis itself. A widow may create such resources by studying accounting, which leads to increased income, or by sharing in a widows' self-help group. The emerging social systems are a critical element in the *bB* factor.

The *cC* factor is the way in which a family interprets a crisis, including the meaning the family gives to the stressor event and to the added stressors caused by the original crisis, plus its perception of how to bring the family into balance. When a young father dies, a family must cope with that event and its meaning. If the widow comes to believe she has lost her only chance at happiness in life, her perceptions will strongly influence her attempts at recovery and those of her children. The members must also interpret the changes in finances, changes in the mother's role, and how the entire family is affected. Families who cope well can manage the situation through flexible changes in responsibilities and through support of one another. Families who have difficulty coping cannot see a sense of challenge and find themselves overwhelmed, with little sense of hope or opportunity for growth.

The *xX* factor is the effect of the family's adaptation on the individual system and community levels. Family adaptation is achieved "through reciprocal relationships where the demands of one of these units are met by the capabilities of another so as to achieve a 'balance' of interaction" (McCubbin and Patterson, 19). If members' demands are too great for the family's capabilities, there will be an imbalance. There will also be imbalance if the family demands more than the community is capable of providing. For example, the family and work community may create an imbalance by demanding too much of one parent. The positive end of the continuum of outcomes of a crisis, called *bonadaptation,* is characterized by balance between (1) member and family and (2) family and community. The negative end, or *maladaptation,* reflects imbalance or severe losses for the family. In some families, drastic changes allow members to renegotiate their relationships in positive ways. Thus, disruptions may be resolved in positive or negative ways.

Burr, Klein, and associates (1994) recognize that versions of the ABCX model have dominated and enriched family stress theory for about fifty years. However, they challenge the assumptions that support the model and some inconsistencies in the assumptions used to explain how the model operates. The intent of the ABCX Model is to identify causal relationships that specify recognizable patterns. What happens in *A, B,* and *C* factors causes or determines *X,* or the degree of crises in a family. The positivist assumptions inherent in the model are that the "variables operate in a relatively mechanistic, linear, cause and effect manner" (31). This approach doesn't provide adequately for the piling up of processes simultaneously and the fact that stress can come into a system at any time. To overcome this rigidity Burr et al. have added to the model their thinking about "rules of transformation," "boundary ambiguity," "stress piling," and "feedback loops" for alternative causes and effects, and recognizing different levels of "coping strategies" for individuals within families. Later in this chapter we will discuss these levels of coping.

Issues that affect stress relate to cohesion and adaptability as well as to boundaries, themes, images, and biosocial issues (Bain 1978). A family with a high capacity for adaptation and above average cohesion is likely to weather stressor events more easily than families who are rigid and fragmented. More adaptable families have the capacity to find alternative ways of relating and can adjust their communication behavior to encompass an event. During a crisis, family members often wish to rely on each other for comfort and support, a behavior that cannot suddenly occur if the family has a history of separateness. Families with rigid boundaries may be unable to cope adequately when severe external stresses occur. Boundary ambiguity increases stress. The term refers to the degree of uncertainty in family members' perceptions of who "belongs," who is expected to function in various roles, and how much openness there should be in the system to permit various outside resources to be used to deal with stress. By greatly limiting communication with such institutions as hospitals, courts, and schools, members deprive themselves of necessary information and possible emotional support. Additionally, boundaries that prevent a social network (friends or extended family) from knowing about the stressor eliminate sources of strength and comfort that might help "carry" a family through a critical period. The importance of such a network is shown in the following example:

*My mother, Aunt Maria, and her best friend, Aunt Elena, helped each other go through some terrible times. If the men were out of work at the steelmill, they still had to find ways of putting food on the table, help to keep the children feeling secure, and deal with their husbands who were depressed. Somehow I see these women as people who managed—sharing houses, food and clothes with each other, or simply talking about their troubles.*

Unlike the nurturing aunts in the previous example, families with themes of total self-sufficiency or images of boulder strength may find support from strong members. Yet such themes and images may prevent them from turning outward when the pain becomes too great for the family to handle functionally, resulting in severe conflict or separation. The number and magnitude of stresses may determine how functional these themes and images can be.

Seemingly positive events can create great stress. Newspapers contain accounts of the pressure put on lottery winners by the expectations of family and friends and the loss of a settled way of life. A long-wished-for promotion may be accompanied by the loss of a familiar co-worker, pressure to succeed at a new level of responsibility, and the possibility of a stressful family move to a new city or neighborhood. Family members may find it painful to cope with the marriage or the departure for college of a much-loved child. Great joys may be accompanied by great losses.

The picture is not entirely negative. On occasion, communication improves when the family deals with major crises. In a large study of a series of unpredictable crises, including bankruptcy, infertility, and muscular dystrophy, Burr, Klein, and Associates (1994) note 29 percent of the family members reported a lasting and definite increase in positive communication techniques. Another 21 percent related early increases in better communication with later variations, but not returning to the low levels experienced before the crises. Better communication included less conflict, more positive statements, and special remarks that nurtured and supported family members. The conclusion of the researchers was that most families under stress realize they need to communicate better and they listened more effectively to one another.

Because communication affects and is affected by all these behaviors, it plays a central role in the experiencing and eventual resolution of such stresses and contributes specifically to the family's movement through stages of stress reaction. In some families, members use direct verbal messages to explore options, negotiate needs, express feelings, and reduce tension. In other families, the members' stress may be apparent through the nonverbal messages that indicate their anxiety and other feelings. Members constantly interpret others' verbal and nonverbal messages as part of the coping pattern.

## Stages of Family Crisis

In any serious crisis situation, a family goes through a definite process in handling the grief or chaos that results. Depending upon the event, the stages may last from a few days to several months or years. These stages may be more pronounced in the case of a death, divorce, or news of an incurable illness, but in any crisis, family members experience a progression of feelings from denial to acceptance. Yet, since no two families accept crisis in the same way, and because family systems are characterized by equifinality, they will reach the final stages of the process in a variety of ways. The following stages approximate the general process of dealing with severe stress. Although the stages usually follow one another, they may overlap, and some may be repeated a number of times.

1. Shock resulting in numbness or disbelief, denial
2. Recoil stage resulting in anger, confusion, blaming, guilt, and bargaining
3. Depression
4. Reorganization resulting in acceptance and recovery (Kubler-Ross 1970; Parkes 1972; Feifel 1977; Mederer and Hill 1983)

The process of going through such stages after a serious life event usually results in transformation of the system. Persons may find themselves more separated from, or connected to, different members and may find a shift in adaptability patterns. Communication behavior reflects and aids progress through the stages. Understanding the process allows one to analyze others' progress through the stages or to be more understanding of one's own behavior and personal progress.

At the *shock stage*, family members tend to deny the event or its seriousness. Denying comments such as "It can't be true," "It's a mistake," or "It's temporary" are accompanied by nonverbal behavior, such as setting a dead person's place at the table, misplacing attempts at smiles and encouragement with a terminally ill person, or spending money lavishly when the paycheck has been cut off.

Most persons quickly move from this stage and exhibit behaviors that indicate a recognition of reality. Principal family members acknowledge their grief and feel the pain of the loss. Crying or sullen quietness for those who find it hard to cry characterizes communication. The truth of the crisis news begins to take on fuller meanings, such as "Mom will never get well" or "She has left and will never return." This kind of reasoning sends messages to the self that confirms the reality.

Denial is transformed into an intense desire to recapture what has been lost, especially in the case of a family death, desertion, or severe injury. This may lead to attempts to recapture memories, for example, "I keep expecting to see her in the kitchen."

After the initial blow, the family may move into the *recoil stage* of blaming, anger, and bargaining. Blaming often takes place as the grieving family members seek reasons for what has happened. This may include blaming the self ("I was too trusting; I should have watched closer" or "I never should have let her go") or blaming others ("It's his own fault" or "The doctors never told us the truth soon enough"). Such behavior may be interspersed with feelings of "It's not fair," "Why did this happen to us?" and "We don't deserve this." Anger may be directed at the event or person most directly involved or may be displaced onto others, such as family members, friends, or co-workers. Attempts at real or imagined bargains may occur. "If I take a cut in pay, they could hire me back." "If you come back I'll stop gambling forever."

Thoughts of the unfairness of the world, that God has been cruel to let this happen, that potentials of the members involved had never been realized and now never will be, fill the minds of family members and then are released to one another. Again, the pain of the loss comes out through strong feelings.

Usually, family members need to talk about what has happened. In fact, they often retell the crisis news over and over. This is a normal and healthy response for the family as they feel the intensity of the loss. This is especially necessary for families that will experience a long period of suffering because of death, incurable illness, permanent injuries, a long jail sentence, or mental breakdown. People outside the family often fail to understand the communication that goes on within and may attempt to avoid the people or the subject, not recognizing that support may only be possible from those not as directly affected. Families may allow their boundaries to become more flexible in order to gain this support. Often, family confusion and disorganization may be so great that outsiders tend to take over and guide decision making. This could easily have happened in the following example:

---

*I have never felt so much sorrow and stress as when my wife left with the children and I was without the daily company of my kids. Among other things life became totally unpredictable and I felt I lost my identity. For months I functioned in a total fog. I can compare the anger and despair to some of my experiences as a medic in Vietnam.*

---

Grief-stricken people normally pass through this stage to what they describe as a "turning point." Usually, a decision on their part marks the event. It may be a decision to take a trip, to sell a failing business, to get rid of mementos that serve as daily reminders, to register with a placement bureau, or to join Alcoholics Anonymous. Nonverbally, this decision signals that the individual has moved into the fourth crisis stage—acceptance and reorganization of events in his or her life to effect a recovery. This stage is characterized by family members' taking charge of their lives and making the necessary changes forced upon them by the crisis. They may not like the changes required, but they communicate an ability to cope in spite of the loss. Reorganization may require all sorts of adjustments, and the time required varies greatly with the type of crisis and the individuals involved. It may take six weeks for one family to recover from a job loss. It may take another family, suffering a death or divorce, anywhere from a year to eighteen months to achieve a semblance of balance in the system.

If emotions in crises could be diagrammed, the line would descend to the lowest point with depression. The descent begins with the impact of the news and continues the downward spiral with some rises in the recoil stages to descend again as reality returns (Figure 11.2).

Throughout this process, communication links members in sharing their reactions and links one or more to outside sources of institutional or social support, which can provide acceptance of the emotions which need to be expressed. If a family or member is cut off from support, the process may be incomplete—the family may remain stuck at some point, unable to complete the process and reach

**FIGURE 11.2**
**Linear Scale of Emotions During Crises**

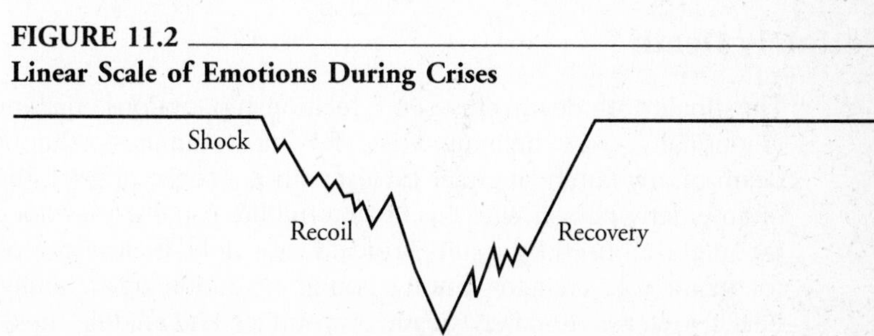

acceptance. The next section will consider some common types of family crises and communication issues involved with each.

## COMMUNICATION AND SPECIFIC FAMILY CRISES

Communication patterns and networks shift dramatically when members face major life crises (Brubaker and Roberto 1993). Interaction becomes unpredictable as individuals withdraw into silence, explode into anger, or move into constant talking as a way to handle the stress or grief. Although this section focuses on three major crises, death, illness, and divorce, remember that less dramatic events, such as moving, losing a job, or receiving a promotion or large inheritance also disrupt the family system. All of these events change the course of life events; they alter hopes and fantasies by introducing new tensions between family members and their environment. Any stress, particularly unpredictable, makes it difficult to maintain relationships, especially in any constant state. Crisis forces parents and their children to use different relationship maintenance strategies because frequently dialectical tensions change and what previously worked or could be labeled acceptable can no longer solve the problems (Baxter and Dindia 1990). Think how crisis impacts the dialectical issues. The crisis event can force openness and expose a family to public scrutiny, as for example in the case of a suicide, teenage pregnancy, or drug arrest. The event may create closeness and connection as the family attempts some sort of a united front to cope or to support one another. Autonomy issues may be set aside in the early stages of dealing with a crisis. Variations in the predictability-novelty dialectical dimension in individual family members' communication may be minimal as the crisis demands full attention and participation of each family member. The birth of a Down's Syndrome baby may lessen novelty or flexibility options in individual family member communication until the family has time to adjust.

### Untimely Death

The finality of death closes off relationship options, making it an emotionally overwhelming crisis for most families. Although the death of any family member carries with it a sense of grief, the death of an elderly person who has lived a full life usually does not contain the anger aroused by untimely death, nor does it carry the potential for major role changes among young or middle-aged family members. However, untimely death of younger and middle aged family members serves as a major unpredictable crisis for all families

(DiGiulio 1992). Surviving partners are not prepared to be called "widow" and "widower."

Untimely death throws a family into severe shock, allowing no chance for farewells or the resolution of relationship issues (Herz-Brown 1988). Prolonged illness, even though it interrupts the life course, provides the family with the opportunity to mourn, say farewells, and resolve relationship issues, if members can use the time in this manner.

Communication within families dealing with death ranges from the highly intense and emotional to the very superficial and denial-oriented. Variables to consider are how family rules impact communication about death; myths that sustain or create blocks to open communication on the subject; ethnic or religious differences such as attitudes toward death and mourning rituals; and the family's experience with previous losses (Brommel 1992). Persons who are dying and their family members often resort to verbal games to maintain a two-sided pretense that "Everything is going to be all right." Family members in their own grief may go into a denial of the information of a terminal illness. They shield the dying from such knowledge and begin a series of new communication rules around the dying person. Bowen (1976) calls death our chief taboo subject saying, "A high percentage of people die alone, locked into their own thoughts which they cannot communicate to others. People cannot communicate the thoughts they have lest they upset the family or others" (336). Triangles may form as two people draw in a third to relieve tension, or subgroups may collude to avoid any discussion of the impending death. This lack of communication about death is common even between marriage partners (Thompson 1989). Attempts to fool the patient can create tremendous stress for a rational, articulate human who has the capacity to cope with news of his or her own death, since the pretense frequently becomes apparent. Often, the dying member knows and then has to play the game of "not knowing" to protect the rest of the family. Such rules block the dying family member from dealing with all the interpersonal feelings, caring, and relationships, as well as with some of their immediate fears and loneliness. Some family members resent the dishonesty involved, as explained in the following example:

---

*I will never forget my uncle's complaining bitterly two days before he died about his family treating him like a helpless child and insisting he would recover whenever he started to talk about dying or his fear of never leaving the hospital. I was only fourteen and did not fully understand what he was trying to tell me at the time, but I never forgot his pain or*

(continued on page 330)

*anger as he tried to explain the feeling of dying without emotional support.*

---

Dunlop declares that "the dying person has his own grieving to do. We should remember too, that the dying person is not just losing himself (which is a considerable loss that other grievers are not having to deal with), but the dying person is also about to lose everything which is important and everyone who is significant to him and whom he loves" (2). Kubler-Ross suggests that death should be regarded as an "intrinsic part of life" and discussed openly like other events in family life, especially since almost all terminally ill patients are aware of it. The question should change from "Do I tell?" to "How do I share the information?" If a family confronts the issue openly, they can go through preparatory grief together, which facilitates the later bereavement process. According to Herz-Brown, "there is greater likelihood of emotional and/or physical symptom development when family members are unable to deal openly with one another about death" (473).

Reasons vary for not telling a family member that he or she has a terminal illness. Dunlop states, "Perhaps it is done out of the belief that if the dying person were told he was dying, he would become depressed and despondent, however, in time he will be both, and must be both if his dying is to have some psychological comfort to it" (5). In determining whether to tell a patient, Verwoerdt (1967) lists these criteria: (1) the dying member's emotional and intellectual resources to handle the news, (2) what the dying member already knows or has guessed, (3) the personal meaning the disease has for the dying based on his or her knowledge of others who had the same terminal illness, and (4) the degree to which the dying member wants to know his or her fate (10). The answer to the question of whether to tell the dying person requires considerable skill in assessing verbal and nonverbal communication from that person.

Even those persons who choose their own death through suicide find many of their preparatory messages are denied or ignored. In many cases, their attempts to communicate suicide plans go unrecognized until after the event. Parents of young people are advised to watch for such behaviors as talking of suicide, giving away possessions, acting abnormally cheerful after depression, and losing appetite (Shreve and Kunkel 1991). Those who deal with the elderly are advised to look for depression, withdrawal, isolation, changes in sleep patterns, lower self-image, and bereavement (Wass and Myers 1982). However, many refuse to interpret these messages as they are intended.

Kubler-Ross' classic five stages present one model for the process of dying: (1) denial, (2) anger, (3) bargaining, (4) depression, and (5) acceptance. The sequence of stages may vary, but eventually, the dying person will progress through all of them if he or she lives long enough and does not become stuck at a particular point, since the length of time one stays in a stage varies according to the individual. Persons may move back and forth through the stages, reworking certain issues.

Persons preparing for death need to express their denials—to articulate why such cannot be the case and to explore other remedies. They need to vent their anger at themselves, those they love, and possibly at God, science, medicine, or other institutions. Bargains must be struck or attempted—silently and openly. Finally, the loneliness, fears, and practical concerns must be unloaded, ranging from "What is really on the other side" to "How will they run the house without me?" Crying, praying, philosophizing, swearing, touching, worrying, and some joking contribute to the conversations.

Regardless of the phase, dying persons need an empathic listener who does not insist they will be better if they think about something else. Most dying people welcome an opportunity to talk about their deaths (Parkes). Bowen, who counseled dying patients for over thirty years, declares, "I have never seen a terminally ill person who was not strengthened by such a talk. This contradicts former beliefs about the ego being too fragile for this in certain situations" (1976, 337). Kubler-Ross agrees, "Dying persons will welcome someone who is willing to talk with them about their dying but will allow them to keep their defenses as long as they need them" (37). She further states that those patients who die comfortably have had a chance to rid themselves of guilt and were "encouraged to express their rage, to cry in preparatory grief, and to express their fears and fantasies to someone who can sit quietly and listen" (119). Although watching a person die can be devastating to the family members, "terminal illness of a family member (unlike sudden death) does allow the family, if the system remains open, to resolve relationship issues, reality issues, and to say the final goodbye before death" (Herz 1980, 228). What one couple experienced in the death of his partner is exemplified by the following example:

---

*We had been together for several years as partners-in-life. We knew that each of us cared for the other but we had intimacy issues because we found it difficult as two men to talk about what we really felt about one another, our relationship, and our kids from previous marriages. His AIDS diagnosis changed all that! His illness forced openness upon us. We began to have long talks late into the night, pouring out all the things we had never said, and trying to say what needed to be*

(continued on page 332)

> *said about a future I would face alone. He not only helped me to accept his leaving, but he reconnected with all his siblings and his mother, in deeper more meaningful ways. They all came for a weekend three weeks before he died and I made a two hour video of each of them reminiscing about happy and sad times in their lives. Each told him what his life had meant to them and he did the same. He wanted this tape to be his gift of remembrance. Never was communication better or easier for him and those he loved than in his last few months!*

---

From their study of caregiver communication with the dying, Miller and Knapp (1986) identified a number of commonly used communication strategies. The strategy labelled "being reflexive" was noted as the most appropriate at all time periods and across all emotional states. They describe this strategy as follows:

> The caregiver's presence is the primary force behind this strategy—not the initiation of specific words or behaviors. Here the caregiver allows the dying person to set the conversational agenda and adapts accordingly. Listening, "being there," and acting as a communicative reflector are the key elements of this strategy. (727)

After the death of a family member, the other members go through a bereavement process, from numbness to pining and depression to recovery (Parkes 1972 Thompson 1989). An unexpected death, either by accident or illness, forces a family into an initial state of shock. Eventually, the shock wears off and the bereavement process begins. The event traumatizes the family, even in cases where members know of an impending death. The survivors experience anger and depression. In the year after a death, widows and widowers had rates of depression ranging from 16 to 36 percent, compared to 8 percent for comparable married partners (Brown 1990, 436). There may be many regrets about unspoken issues. "If only I had told him how much I loved him." "If I had only taken time to listen to her." Survivors, too, need supportive listeners.

The death of an anticipated family member may have similar results. In recent years, studies of the devastating effect of experiencing stillbirth or newborn death indicates many parents experience tremendous loss and many couples report high levels of marital stress (Callan and Murray 1989). Friends and family members often are unaware of the impact of this loss.

It is important to recognize the process nature of grief and realize that people will be upset and irrational and communicate differently. If the death has been caused by a long terminal illness or injury, the bereaved may have been so occupied with the care of the individual and with maintaining a semblance of order in the family system that only the death frees them to get in touch with their feelings. Many bereaved persons report the sense of a continuing relationship with the deceased and a sense of being unfinished with the relationship because they wanted to do or say additional things.

Much also depends upon the place that the deceased had filled in the family system. The death of a parent of young children leaves many childrearing jobs and family role responsibilities to the remaining parent. "The loss of a husband, for instance, may or may not mean the loss of a sexual partner, companion, accountant, gardener, baby-minder, audience, bed warmer, and so on depending upon the particular roles normally performed by this husband" (Parkes, 7). The surviving spouse has additional burdens because he or she must learn new role functions and do so without the aid of the principal person that had been depended upon. Loneliness results from the desire for emotional intimacy. The survivor wants to interact with the partner who is not available and can't return (DiGiulio 1992). If the household contains young children, the remaining person has to help them through the crisis without allowing his or her own emotions to create distance from the child.

The death of a child carries with it the loss of parental images of their child graduating, marrying, and hopes for the future, creating extreme family pain. From her summary of the literature on childhood death, Herz-Brown suggests that family disruption is a common after effect, with divorce or separation occurring in a large number of the cases. Siblings may experience great stress and pressure (Bank and Kahn 1987).

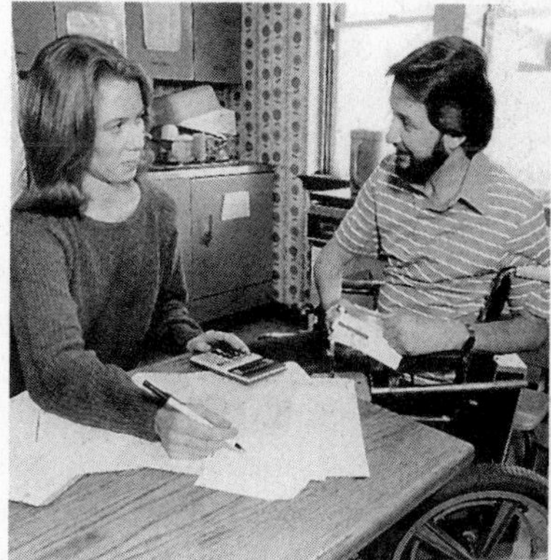

Death and disability are unpredictable stresses that strain a family's coping patterns.

Many families experience a return of sadness or distancing communication on anniversaries of deaths of family members. Such dates serve as markers of loss, forcing memories to surface with great force. Thus, the death of a family member alters the entire family system, requiring the other members to go through a grieving process with as open communication as possible in order to reintegrate the smaller system at a later point.

Family-of-origin plays a significant role in how a family deals with death (Herz-Brown). African American families, Irish families, and Italian families believe in a "good" send-off. White, Anglo-Saxon, Protestant families limit the emotions expressed. Puerto Rican families, especially the female members, suffer publicly. Jewish families, reflecting a tradition of shared suffering, tend to deal openly and directly with death. Chinese families believe a "good death" includes relatives surrounding the dying person. Rituals at the funeral service, including the burning of paper money and clothes, ensures a happy next life. Cultures which have rituals for dealing with death, a strong sense of community, and tolerance of verbal expressions provide members with greater support.

## Illness or Disability

A family with a seriously ill member, or one with a disability, goes through an important coping process before coming to terms with the problem. Using the Double ABCX Model in a research study, Bigbee (1992) discovered a strong relationship between family stress and family illnesses. Those families that demonstrated hardiness, a personality construct composed of control, challenge, and commitment, handled stress far better than those families that didn't possess it. Coping with a child's birth defect or the effects of a debilitating disease or accident requires major adjustments involving physical and emotional energy. The immediate disruption of the family in no way equals the long-term drain on family resources and energies required to help the injured family member deal with what may be a lifelong situation.

The mourning process that parents of affected children undergo parallels the stages of coping with death. Fortier and Wanlass (1984) propose a stage model describing the family process that follows the diagnosis of a child with a disability. Each of these stages has a communication component. The stages include: impact, denial, grief, focusing outward, and closure.

At the impact stage, the family learns, immediately or gradually, of a child's serious illness. Anxiety and tension characterize this period. Usually, the family responds in a frantic and disorganized manner. At first, the family can absorb very little information and has very limited responses. Usually, the denial state follows the initial impact, carrying with it a sense of disbelief and distorted expectations. Parents may reject the diagnosis, fictionally explain the child's failure to perform normally, and find themselves unable to hear what others are saying about the problem. It is a period of fear and isolation.

Anger and sadness characterize the grief. Parents question why this happened to them or to their child. They may blame each other for the difficulty, isolate themselves from interacting with usual friends and extended family, and prevent open and supportive communication. These parents experience great sadness. Often, sharing in support groups of parents with similarly affected children provides a sense of comfort.

Eventually, parents move toward the focusing outward stage, beginning a process of seeking information, discussing options, asking for help, and expressing feelings. Signs of relief are evident at this point as the family moves toward dealing with the issues. The closure stage represents a reconciliation with reality and sense of adaptation to the child's needs. The family pulls together and adjusts in ways that allow the member of the altered system to move forward and to communicate directly about their concerns.

A family working through the process experiences each of these stages. Some families may experience one stage very briefly and find themselves stuck in another for a long period of time. Some families block this mourning process by preventing the necessary communication at each stage. This is most likely to occur when individuals or systems operate according to such rules as "Keep a stiff upper lip" or "Solve your own problems." The family must support open communication for all members, including the patient, if the system is to move through the necessary stages. In a study of cancer patients, Gotcher (1993) found the communication of "emotional support was the most important predictor of effective adjustment" (176). Parents do not dream of giving birth to a child with a disability. The family must grieve the loss of a limb, health, or whatever before they can become fully attached to this child (Bristor 1984). In addition to the emotional stresses associated with handicapped family members, the financial demands can send a family into economic turmoil.

A serious illness affects the overall family system (Fagan and Jenkins 1989; Braithwaite 1991). As might be predicted following the onset of a chronic disease, it is typical for a patient to assume a central position in the family. This shift in focus, if continued over a longer period of time, affects marital and other parent-child relationships. In some families, adolescents may use illness to cross generational boundaries and regulate marital distance or parental conflict (Frey 1984). Parents who are forced to focus on a sick and demanding child have little time or energy to deal with each other. McCubbin et al. (1983) suggest that communication breakdowns occur between family members and between the family and relatives or neighbors due to a lack of leisure time and energy for these relationships. In a study of the coping patterns of parents with a child with cystic fibrosis, these same authors have found that both parents contribute to the coping process, but the mother's coping behavior focuses more on the interpersonal dimensions of family life—family cohesiveness and expressiveness. All family members are affected by unpredictable crises, as illustrated by the following example:

---

*A year and one half ago, my brother, Steve, suffered a paralyzing head injury when he swerved his motorcycle to miss a dog. He dreams of driving his Chevy pickup again but knows he might live the rest of his life in a nursing home. When asked when he expects to get out, his eyes go blank. "Never," he says. My father discourages such talk. "Now if you work real hard you might get your legs going again, right?" he says. Steve's eyes grow red. "OK," he replies and stares at the wall.*

---

Research on sibling response indicates siblings may have a surprising lack of information about the disability. This lack of information may confuse siblings in the following ways:

1. They may feel responsible for a particular condition.
2. They may wonder whether it can be transmitted or "caught" and whether they are susceptible to the same disorder.
3. They are confused about how they should communicate to family and friends about the handicap.
4. They wonder what implications a brother's or sister's handicap has for their future.
5. They may feel perplexed and overwhelmed by such discomforting feelings as anger, hurt, and guilt. (Seligman 1988, 168)

The disability puts stress on the marriage, usually in negative ways. For some couples, it limits their ability to have a family, or perhaps to add another child. Couples with families have reported their inability to go certain places or do certain things together. They may confront greater dialectical tension between predictability and novelty than before. Neither partner feels free to go places or begin new projects because duty compels each of them to be there for the other or their child. A severe illness or disability stresses a family system over a period of time. As in the Double ABCX model described earlier, the family organizes its current resources at the outset of the crisis and then attempts to develop new resources to carry them through the crisis. A study of persons with a disability indicated that they wanted to be acknowledged as persons first, especially with outsiders, and then hoped to keep the focus on the relationship, rather than the disability (Braithwaite 1991). The frustrations involved are revealed in the following example:

> *I certainly knew I had multiple sclerosis! I knew that if I started using a wheelchair, I would lose more than I would gain, including a feeling of control over my life and my disease. I had difficulty with steps, and not all buildings had friendly ramps. I left for classes a half hour early. I pulled myself up the steps slowly, using the railing for support. Too often I would be stopped and would have to listen to remarks that internally sounded like "Oh! Marilyn You poor thing"; I resented the intrusions—it may have been a beautiful day and I was thinking about the novel I read for my English literature class, and these clods had to remind me that I was a cripple!*

The ability of family members to communicate in a direct and supportive manner directly influences the coping process.

## Separation/Divorce

Divorce is a major disruption of the family life course and is characterized by loss, change, and complexity. According to Peck and Manocherian (1988), the normal life cycle tasks "interrupted and altered by the divorce process, continue with greater complexity due to the concomitant phase of the divorcing process" (335). Unlike death, which forces a family to adjust to a smaller number of members, the family in a divorce must adapt to an altered state (Bay and Braver 1990). In most cases, except total desertion, each parent remains somewhat involved with the children, thus continuing the parenting aspects of the original system (Dudley 1991; Cooper 1990).

Although divorce alters a family system, it does not end it, except in cases of total desertion or total distancing of partners without children. Even in these situations the extended family may maintain significant ties. When children are involved, a couple becomes divorced *to* each other rather than *from* each other. Family members remain linked around the children and must find ways to function as an ongoing altered system. Seltzer discovered fathers who paid child support, visited their children, and participated with their former wife in childrearing decisions had happier outcomes than other divorced persons (1991). Non-custodial father involvement plays a key part in communicating care and lessening children's feelings of abandonment. In the majority of cases, mothers are the custodial parents.

A systemic view of divorce acknowledges that both partners contribute to the dissolution of a marriage. When you think about the variety of issues in most divorces, it is often difficult to assign blame, since the immediate split may have been preceded by months or even years of dysfunctional communication.

The separation and divorce processes essentially follow the mourning pattern described earlier in this chapter. At some point, the spouses mourn the loss of the relationship, although one or the other may have mourned the "death" of the marriage years before the divorce became a reality. Initially, spouses may deny that anything is really wrong and communicate to children or others that "Our problems aren't all that serious" or "Daddy will be back soon, so don't tell anyone he's gone." As the reality takes hold, anger, bargaining, and depression intermingle. There may be attempts at reconciliation. "We had a great thing going once; we can have it again." Reconciliation does work for thirty percent of couples in a first marriage. Two factors that correlated highly with successful reconciliations were both partners having a religious similarity and cohabitation before marriage. Failed attempts may be met with such messages as "How can you leave after all I've done for you" and "What kind of a parent would move out on their children?" Painful accusations and negative conflict are often heightened by the adversarial positions required in legal divorce proceedings. Finally, depression reflects the sense of loss and/or rejection, often accompanied by great loneliness.

In terms of communication, the couple may experience a descent through the stages of development in the "social penetration model" described in an earlier chapter. Thus, they move from whatever stage they had reached, such as, affective exchange, back down toward the lower stages. As their relationship falls apart, partners gradually withdraw affect and intimate contact, and are likely to deal with one another to a lesser extent. Couples without children divorced much more amicably and had fewer conflicts after the divorce than if they had children (Masheter 1991).

According to Knapp and Vangelisti (1992), a relationship that is coming apart reflects: (1) a recognition of differences, (2) an experience of constricted communication, (3) a sense of stagnation, (4) a pattern of avoidance, and, finally, (5) the immediate or protracted experience of termination. Partners at these stages create messages that communicate an increasing physical and psychological distance and an increasing disassociation from the other person. Levels of cohesion drop to reflect the distancing, and little connectedness remains.

The amount of stress in the childhood of the parents influences the effect of separation and divorce. If the adults experienced losses in earlier periods of their lives, letting go of present relationships, starting a new single life, and assuming a single parenting role may be particularly difficult (Chiriboga, Catron, and Weiler 1987). These pressures are intensified by the predictable and problematic withdrawal of social supports. Divorce is the only major crisis in which social supports fall away (Wallerstein and Blakeslee 1989). Others are afraid to "take sides," or they act as if they believe divorce might be contagious. Fear of the loss of children haunts many fathers. In divorce, fathers receive custody of children less than 10 percent of the time (Arditti 1990). Although quite small in percentage terms, the number of "father only families" and "father with stepmother with custody of his children" families are among the fastest growing types (Johnson, D. 1993; Meyer and Garasky 1993). Interestingly there are more sons than daughters as well as older children in these father led families.

Studies have shown adverse effects of divorce on children (Hetherington 1987; Glenn and Kramer 1987; Wallerstein and Blakeslee 1989; Arditti 1990; Booth and Amato 1994). Some have indicated problems in the pre-divorce, transition, and early post-divorce periods, with children acting out their frustrations and rage. Certain adolescents experience accelerated parent-child separation, which promotes earlier individuation, ego maturity, and courtship activity. Children from divorced homes are more likely to rate their parents, especially fathers, less favorably than children from intact families. In fact, some make angry emotional cut-offs from the parent they like less (Lopez 1987). Many children witness intense verbal and physical anger acted out by parents in the acute stage of divorce (Kline et al. 1991). Over time the system recalibrates itself to deal with its altered course and its new communication dynamics. The presence of siblings makes the transition easier to manage for young people (Combrinck-Graham 1988) because they may protect each other from parents' attempts to hook them into the struggle, share the "care" of a distraught parent, or may support each other. Most children experience a sense of confusion and chaos when parents divorce. The following example illustrates what may happen if those fears are not addressed:

---

*When my parents divorced, although it was a relief from the fighting and constant tension, I experienced a sense of loss and many new fears about their future as well as my own. As a child who experienced divorce I was expected to "bounce back." I was just expected to adapt, but without being given time to express grief. As a result, I repressed these feelings and*

(continued on page 340)

*fears, and since they were never really addressed, they resurface now, years later, to haunt me.*

---

Although there is limited information on communication during the divorce process, current research indicates most couples do not discuss this decision in lengthy detail with all members. As a result of their longitudinal study of divorcing families, Wallerstein and Kelley (1980) expressed surprise at the limited communication between parents and children about the divorce, suggesting that the "telling is not a pronouncement but should initiate a gradual process" (40). In many cases, children are informed about the divorce but not encouraged to

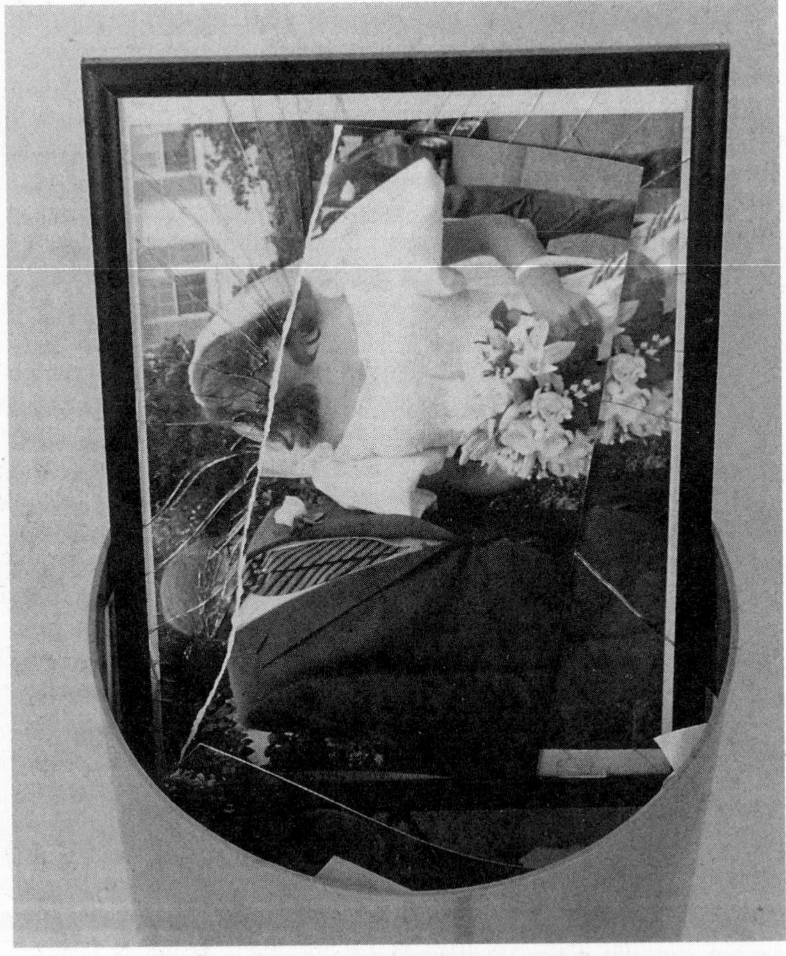

Sometimes former partners try to destroy all evidence of a powerful relationship.

discuss their concerns. Four-fifths of the youngest children in this study were not provided with either an adequate explanation or assurance of continued care. Because parents are so anxious about the discussion, many make it impossible for the children to express their feelings. Children may be told "You'll see more of Daddy now" or "You'll be able to get a dog," comments intended to make the child feel positive but which deny the child's distress. In their study of the long range effects of divorce, Wallerstein and Blakeslee (1989) suggest "nearly 50 percent of the families that we counsel waited until the day of the separation or afterward to tell their children that their familiar world is coming apart" (302). The abruptness of communication about the divorce often contributes to the children's inability to explore the issues and to release their feelings directly. Whereas loss through death involves a socially expected mourning period, there is no sanctioned mourning period for the loss of the "family that was," a situation that may prevent the use of resources available to the child. Just as there must be support systems available to the child at the time of divorce, there must also be resources available during the post-crisis period.

The amount of contact between divorced fathers and their children in the years following divorce determines the quality of relationship when the children reach adulthood (Booth and Amato 1994). Ninety percent of never divorced, older men have weekly contact with at least one adult child while only fifty percent of the divorced fathers have contact. One-third of the divorced fathers have lost contact. Divorced men were twice as likely as never divorced men not to expect any kind of help in times of crisis (Cooney and Uhlenberg 1990).

Usually communication between former spouses becomes less conflictual in the years following a divorce. Hetherington, Cox, and Cox (1976) found that two months after the divorce, 66 percent of the exchanges between partners involved conflicts over finances, support, visitation, childrearing, and relating to others in the system (423). The same study followed families over a two-year period and noted that conflicts and contacts with fathers diminished over time. Over this time period, the fathers went from being very permissive with the children when they were together to being increasingly restrictive. Mediation or counseling helps parents to work out their differences and lessen the stress on children (Grebe 1986; Brommel 1994). Many partners experience ambivalent feelings of love and hate in the divorce process. Children sense this, and talking about this conflict helps to sort out the entangled feelings. Children also can blame one parent or the other and take sides unfairly. Joint custody arrangements have been rapidly increasing (Ferreiro 1990). Both parents and children in joint custody arrangements report higher levels of satisfaction and fewer problems in parenting.

Although it is impossible in a divorce to remove all the negative aspects of stress upon children and their communication, parents can certainly reduce the stress (Buehler 1989). If neither parent uses the child as a go-between, nor encourages "tattletale" behavior, opportunities for conflict are reduced. If each supports the other's discipline, the child cannot play one against the other. According to Booth and Amato (1994), who completed a longitudinal study over twelve years, there is "evidence that divorce and low parental marital quality have long term negative consequences for child-parents relations" (32). In addition, when marital quality, including communication, deteriorate, children have difficulty in maintaining relationships with both parents and as a result develop closer ties to one parent. For all involved, divorce involves a sense of loss, especially for those who have lost their support systems as well as their current sense of family.

## Support and Communication

Throughout any of these crises—death, illness, disability, or divorce—the family's capacity for open communication, reflective of its levels of cohesion and adaptation and its images, themes, boundaries, and biosocial beliefs, determines how the system will weather the strain. A family with low cohesion may fragment under pressure, unless such pressure can link the unconnected members. A family with limited adaptability faces a painful time, since such crises force change upon the system and the lives of each member. A family whose images and themes allow outside involvement in family affairs may use its flexible boundaries to find institutional and social support. A family with rigid biosocial beliefs faces difficult challenges if key family figures are lost or injured and others are not permitted to assume some of the role responsibilities. Throughout this process, communication among family members either facilitates or hinders the revising of the system to meet the demands of the crisis.

***Coping*** Recent research by Burr, Klein, and Associates (1994) identifies an elaborate set of coping strategies. Their system will be briefly summarized. Every family undergoes periods of unpredictable stress. Many of these stresses are not as immediately critical as death, illness, or divorce, but they do eat away at members' resources.

Burr, Klein, and Associates (1994) view stress as a multifaceted phenomenon with multiple causes and coping strategies. Their research indicates families deal with stress in a sequential process, trying Level I coping strategies first and if these fail, move on to Level II and III strategies. (Table 11–1)

**Table 11-1**

| Level | Strategy |
|---|---|
| I | Change or adapt existing rules, ways of doing things, rearranging responsibilities to address the stress. |
| II | Change metarules (rules about rules) so that new areas of rules are created to address the stress. |
| III | Change the basic assumptions about life: reorder value structure to address stress. |

When a stress occurs, a family will first try to use a Level I process by perhaps changing the family rules or role expectations, modifying a family member's responsibilities, securing additional household help, trying to discipline a stubborn child differently, or agreeing to not use the credit cards. If any of these changes work, the family proceeds into a period of recovery and "has no need to try coping strategies that develop into Level II or III changes" (45). If changing the rules and more superficial aspects of the family's operation fails, then the family seeks more basic or metalevel changes at Level II.

Level II changes involve a middle level of abstraction, ones that change the system in fundamentally different ways. For example, at Level II the family may need to change metarules about how their rules are made and by whom. Level II strategies include talking about decisionmaking in the family; changing the way Mom as a single parent directs the family now that Dad has left; modifying the way the family makes and changes rules; and replacing the amount of competitive strategies with cooperative ones. If the family has a parent who gambles excessively, a Level II change would be giving up gambling and setting the money aside for a special family trip.

If Level II strategies fail to reduce the stresses to a comfortable point for the family's well being, the need arises for more abstract Level III coping strategies, ones that entail attempts to change the fundamental values or philosophies of life that governs the family (179). Changes at this level require communication about what being a member in a particular family means and how can members enhance one another's lives by participating more effectively or efficiently within the system they have created. Level III changes are the hardest to make, and desertion, divorce, and even violence happen when individual family members refuse to consider changes at this level of stress.

Level III refers to highly abstract processes that seek to make changes in the family beliefs, paradigms, and values to reduce stress. Recently an aged couple with strong views in their earlier years about their gay son using drugs discovered when he returned home dying from AIDS that he sometimes used marijuana to relieve some of the symptoms, especially eye problems and side effects from powerful drugs such as AZT, DDC, etc. At first they questioned their son's drug use, but when it seemed to relieve his pain and fears of dying, they relented and just ignored the drug use.

At Level III the family will question its basic beliefs and try and decide if they can change in any ways to accommodate the negative effects of stress. Examples of Level III changes might be a family changing religions or connecting to kinship networks after ignoring them for years.

Many of the predictable and unpredictable stresses will be handled easily by families with Level I coping strategies. Some significant stresses will force the family system to adopt new, creative, and possibly painful ways. Members have less experience in creating new coping strategies and thus creating Levels II and III strategies is difficult and requires trial and error.

The ways in which a family has established patterns of cohesion and adaptability have great bearing on its ability to cope with external stresses, especially at Level II and III. A family with a high capacity for adaptation and above average cohesion is likely to weather stressor events more easily than families who are rigid and fragmented. More adaptable families have the capacity to find alternative ways of relating and can adjust their communication behaviors to cope with a tragic or difficult situation.

***Support Groups*** Negative stresses, such as alcoholism, drug abuse, child abuse, economic reversals, job transfers, and suicides, take their toll on a family's emotional resources (Shreve and Kunkel 1991). Each of these issues has strong family systems implications (Lewis, Volk, and Duncan 1989). A stress, such as divorce, reduces the family's support systems at the same time that the family's pain is increasing. Without a strong communication network, the individuals—forced to rely on themselves—may become alienated or severely depressed. Even such seemingly positive experiences as raising a gifted child, getting a high-powered position, adopting a child, or receiving large sums of money can stress the system. In order to understand a family's coping capacity, a family's immediate and post-crisis resources, especially support networks, must be understood.

In recent years, self-help support groups have become increasingly large and visible (Wuthernow 1994). In a society characterized by mobility and smaller families, persons are finding interpersonal support from others who share similar experiences and pain. Chapters of groups such as Alcoholics Anonymous, Parents Without Partners, Candlelighters, Overeaters Anonymous, or groups for families with members who have AIDS, Alzheimers, Leukemia, Multiple Sclerosis, etc. are found within driving distance in most larger communities. The twelve-step program developed by AA has been adopted by related groups such as Al-Anon, Alateen, and CODA. In all cases, the self-help groups rely on members' communication and support as a healing process.

## CONCLUSION

This chapter examined communication and unpredictable life stresses. Specifically, it focused on (1) the process of dealing with unpredictable stresses and (2) communication during certain major stressful life events, such as death, illness, disability, and divorce. Over the years, every family system encounters external stress from crisis situations as well as stress from developmental change. The system's ability to cope effectively with stress depends on a number of factors such as the number of recent stresses, role changes, and social and institutional support. The Double ABCX model provides an effective explanation of family coping, because it focuses on pre-crisis and post-crisis variables. Death, illness, and divorce necessarily alter family systems over long periods of time. Communication may facilitate or restrict a family's coping procedures. In most families, sharing of information and feelings can lower the stress level. The family with flexible boundaries has the capacity to accept support and the potential for surviving crises more effectively than families who close themselves off from others. Many family members find support through membership in self-help organizations.

## IN REVIEW

1. Using a real or fictional family, analyze the effects on the family of a severe stress which impacted one member (e.g., drug problem, serious car accident, or severe illness).

2. Using the same example of family stress, compare and contrast an analysis of the problem according to the ABCX model and the Double ABCX model.

3. Describe how a "happy event" has brought high levels of stress to a family with which you are familiar.

4. Discuss how a family development or life cycle approach differs from a life course approach. What are the advantages and disadvantages of each. Cite examples from families you have known who faced crises.

5. How do different cultural and/or religious attitudes toward death aid or restrict the mourning process for surviving family members?
6. What guidelines for communication would you recommend to spouses who have children and are about to separate?
7. Using Baxter's concepts of dialectical tensions in relationships, discuss with examples how you think crises affect openness-closedness, predictability-novelty, and autonomy-connectedness in a family system.
8. Give examples of Level I, II, and III coping strategies that reflect how families cope with crises.

# 12

# Communication Within Various Family Forms

As you listen to everyday conversation, read the newspapers, or watch television, you are confronted with discussions of "the breakdown of the American family." Such terminology is misleading and potentially destructive. Our culture appears to have an idealized view of the family, vividly depicted in holiday television advertising, that involves a middle-class, blood related family with smiling parents and grandparents eating an elaborate traditional turkey dinner. In reality, this image represents only one family form, and a life experienced by a segment of today's American families at any given time.

*The* American family does not exist. Family historian Harevan (1982) suggests that American families have always represented great diversity and that our nostalgia is for a lost family tradition that never really existed. Historically, the American family has fulfilled its members' economic, socialization, education, and emotional needs. Harevan expresses her concern with the idealized two-parent, middle-class family, claiming, "American society has contained within it great diversities in family types and family behavior that were associated with the recurring entrance of new immigrant groups into American society. Ethnic, racial, cultural, and class differences have also resulted in diversity in family behavior" (461). More recently, another family historian, (Coontz 1992) wrote:

> Most Americans move in and out of a variety of family types over the course of their lives—families headed by a divorced parent, couples raising children out of wedlock, two-earner families, same-sex couples, families with no spouse in the labor force, blended families, and empty-nest families. (183)

Over time family descriptors have shifted from ethnic terms, to social class terms, to the current focus on marital status, new family forms, or sexual preference (Sporakowski 1988). Diversity is acknowledged in a more forthright manner. The family is understood as having many forms (Cheal 1993; Lewis, J. 1993).

This chapter will explore some of the specific communication issues related to various family forms, focusing specifically on (1) single or primary parent families, (2) stepfamilies, (3) gay male and lesbian partners and parents, and (4) co-habitating relationships.

## SINGLE OR PRIMARY PARENT SYSTEMS

An increasing number of families consist of one parent and one or more children. This formation may include: An unmarried woman or man and his or her offspring; men or women who lost spouses through death, divorce, or desertion and their children; single parents with adopted or foster children. Currently a normal childhood experience in America is for 61 percent of young people to live with only one parent before reaching age 18. At the present time, 24 percent of all children live in one parent homes. Twenty-one percent live in mother headed homes. Divorce accounts for about 46 percent, and out-of-wedlock births account for 26 percent of one-parent households. The other percentages reflect parental separation or death (Single Parents 1992). In 1990, a quarter of all births were out of wedlock; in half of those there was no identified father (Coontz 1992). Therefore, approximately one-fourth of all families with children are single parent families; most are formed through divorce or separation, yet over one-quarter are systems in which the parent never married. Among African-American single-parent families, over 50 percent involve a never-married mother (Demo 1992). This combined with the fact that African-American women have higher divorce rates and lower remarriage rates than whites means African-American children in single parent homes remain in them longer than white children (Coontz 1992). Yet African-American children are more likely to live a part of an extended family household than white children. Although most single parent households are headed by a female, single father households are the fastest growing family type today. For many children, the experience in a single-parent system is temporary until the parent remarries. However, approximately one-third of custodial mothers will not remarry.

Although the term *single parent* is commonly used, we will alternate the term with primary parent occasionally, recognizing Walsh's

(1993) point that single parent describes one parent carrying out all parental obligations while ongoing involvement with the other parent is precluded. This occurs most frequently in cases of death and abandonment. When two parents take some, usually unequal, responsibility for children, the custodial parent is referred to as the primary parent. Both adults may be referred to as co-parents.

Single-parent families face task overload and emotional overload, most evident in the life cycle of single mothers with young children. Social isolation, increased anxiety, depression, loneliness, and economic worries affect the single parent (Walsh 1993; Kissman and Allen 1993). Single parents frequently find themselves emotionally cut off from extended family relationships and social networks (Beal 1980). As noted in the last chapter, divorced persons find themselves separated from their spouse's extended family as the boundaries are tightened against them. Friends frequently withdraw social support from both parties during and after a divorce (Wallerstein and Blakeslee 1989).

A one-parent system creates special issues related to power and roles. The "two-against-one" triad in the two-parent home may force children to abide by parental wishes. When one parent leaves the system, some power may be removed from the parental image. There is strong evidence that single parents tend to make fewer demands on children and utilize less effective disciplinary strategies than married parents (Simons et al. 1993). A troubled parent-child relationship cannot be adequately balanced by the other parent. When one parent leaves the system, the other may attempt to co-opt a child into the emotional role of confidant or household helper. "You're the man of the house now" typifies this lowering of boundaries between parent and child subsystems and often results in communication breakdowns. This may place great pressure on the child, alienate the child from other siblings, and eventually interfere with the normal process of separating from the family at the appropriate developmental point. In a description of his adolescent life in a single-parent home, Goldberg (1983) remembers life in a primary-parent household and his personal worries about support checks, the parental date who might appear at breakfast, and the younger siblings who could not remember a two-parent household. He indicates the difficulty of trying to give advice on dating, giving support on childcare, and staying in the middle between warring parents. Such experiences are not rare as some single parents rely heavily on children as their support systems.

Pressured single or primary parents function more effectively when they experience consistent social support systems. Friends may aid an individual going through a loss as he or she attempts to change self-perceptions, experimenting with new behaviors, and move into a broader social world (Eggert 1987). Unmarried women with children may find more support within their extended families, particularly in matriarchical systems. Single mothers with little education have limited support from social networks. Those under severe economic pressure have exposure to negative events and social support. Such circumstances are associated with psychological distress and poor parenting practices (Simons et al. 1993). Because they do not have a partner to share problems or joys and decision making, single parents need to function within strong communication networks. They need other adults to talk with about pressures and specific parenting issues. Such network support keeps single parents from relying too heavily on one child for emotional support, a situation described in the following example:

---

*My best friend and I rely on each other for so many big and little things. If I'm having a bad day, I call her. If she has a fight with her boyfriend, she calls me. We share childcare responsibilities and often travel together with the kids. I turned down a new job because it meant moving too far away from her.*

---

Most single-parent systems face economic pressures. The economic status of women is likely to decline 30 percent during the first year after a divorce (Glick 1989). Single-parent families generally experience a lower standard of living than two-parent systems. Over one-quarter of mothers receive no support—many others get only limited support. Economic concerns in the single-parent family have direct bearing on communication patterns. When a single mother's income is low and the father fails to pay for child support, many children become pawns in the battle. Communication with their father may be restricted, or they may become part of a chain network relaying requests for, and responses about, the money. In either situation, the children experience great stress. In their landmark study, Wallerstein and Blakeslee (1989) found that one in four children experienced a severe and lasting drop in their standard of living and observed a major discrepancy between their mother's and father's homes. "They grew up with their noses pressed against the glass, looking at a way of life that by all rights should have been theirs" (298).

Poverty does not automatically mean less interpersonal attention. Coontz reports results of a national study demonstrating that in poor African-American families, officially absent fathers actually had more contact with their children and gave them more informal support than did white, middle-class absent fathers. When the economic pressure escalates the stress within the single-parent system, it may be played out in excessive conflict or depression as one woman reports in the following example:

---

*Although I try not to put my kids in the middle, I resent their father's lifestyle. We worry about buying school clothes and he's buying a $700 dog! The kids live like royalty six days a month—and then there's "life with Mom." I know they hear me badmouth their father but I just can't help it.*

---

Numerous researchers have debated the effects of the single-parent family, especially upon children. These studies have importance because they relate to family communication. In measuring self-concept, which also includes assessment of social and personal adjustment, Raschke and Raschke found that children were "not adversely affected by living in a single parent families but that family conflict and/or parental unhappiness can be detrimental" (373). After comparing intact families with single-parent families, they discovered that in both types, there was a high correlation between perceived happiness and children's healthy self-concepts. Beal (1980) stresses the importance of distinguishing between life in conflict-laden, intact families and life in well-functioning, single-parent homes, concluding that the latter leads to better adjustment. Hetherington (1988) in comparing adaptation in divorced and non-divorced families finds children fare poorest in dysfunctional families that remain together. Walsh concludes: "Of all the research on divorce, the most significant is the clear and consistent finding that children adjust best when both parents can remain involved with them and cooperate in child rearing" (527).

In her summary of research findings on single-parent homes, Gongla (1982) indicates the following: (1) children can develop normally in warm, non-conflict-ridden families; (2) children gain responsibility and power by performing some of the volume of tasks which cannot be performed by one parent; (3) initially, the mother may be restrictive and the children may be aggressive, but this changes over time if support exists; and (4) interdependence of family members grows (11). The role of the father in the family after divorce, separation, or out-of-marriage birth is important. Researchers suggest that maintaining supportive contact on important child-related matters has beneficial consequences for the mother and children (Gongla, 20). Children who are not forced to choose between parents suffer less stress than those who are discouraged, directly or indirectly, from such contact. Other work questions some of these assumptions about adjustment. After studying long term effects of divorce on children,

Wallerstein and Blakeslee report that whereas divorced parents may have found their second chances, many of the children found conditions in the post-divorce family more stressful and less supportive than conditions in the failing marriage. Some of the children in their study "literally brought themselves up, while others were responsible for the welfare of a troubled parent as well" (299).

Although the research on divorce indicates an initial decline in the capacity to parent from a surprising number of families, the diminished parenting continues permanently, disrupting the childrearing functions of the family. In contrast to earlier work, Wallerstein and Blakeslee suggest parental happiness does not necessarily result in more effective parenting. Another study reports that when other adults live in the home, children are described more positively by their parents (Risman and Park 1988). This finding may indicate a lessening of emotional and/or financial pressure on the single parent. The results of a major study on divorced parents with an adolescent child (Simons et al. 1994) raise issues about quantity of contact with non-residential fathers versus quality of the contact. In addition, the study looks at the extent to which variations in control by single mothers relates to adjustment of adolescent children. Findings include: The quality of fathers' and mothers' parenting is related to externalizing problems (fighting, poor school performance) for boys and girls. Mother's parenting is also related to boys internalizing problems (emotional distress). Parental conflict is associated with boys' emotional distress. Externalizing problems reduces the quality of mothers' parenting for boys and girls and fathers' parenting of boys.

The long range effects of divorce or single parenting on children need further research. The type of communication possible within single-parent families created reflects the ability of the family to adjust to the new systemic arrangement, whether through the permanent or partial loss of a member. As conflicts diminish, increased cohesion may develop among members. Families with high adaptability can create new and functional communication networks. In almost all cases, boundaries are adjusted to reflect the system's need or desire for outside influence. Themes, images, and biosocial beliefs may also experience adjustment. No matter what, a family with low adaptability will face a more painful time than a family with high adaptability, as evidenced by the following family's inability to adapt to a new identity as a single-parent system. Changing family systems necessitate continual negotiation, as indicated by the mother in the following example:

---

*I have to negotiate with my own two children regularly. We all lived with my parents after my divorce. While living with my parents, my children started to view and treat me as a friend or older sibling. Now in our own home, I am trying desperately to find a point in where I am respected as an authority, but more of a teacher or guide than a threatening policewoman. I would like our rules to be made and agreed upon by all of us together.*

Hanson (1986) found physical and psychological health in single-parent families was related to good communication and problem-solving ability of the parents and adolescents. Richards and Schmiege (1993) identify the following strengths of single parenting as: (1) parenting skills, (2) managing a family, (3) growing personally, (4) providing financial support and (5) communicating. Good communication includes building a sense of honesty and trust and conveying ideas clearly to family and friends (280).

Any single-parent family, whether formed through the loss of a parent or addition of a child, needs support from its community of extended family and friends. Functional stability must exist or all the family energy will be devoted to issues of basic life necessities, concerns that often evoke conflict. Eventually, many single parents marry and form stepfamilies. At that time, they must alter the single-parent system to create a stepfamily, which includes children from one or both parents. This transition brings new stress and communication concerns.

## STEPFAMILY SYSTEMS

The stepfamily has been compared to a challenging and complex chess game, to a delicate and intricate spider's web, and to a chaotic and confusing toddler's birthday party (Einstein 1982). No matter what the analogy, the stepfamily is a complex, growing, and little-understood segment of American family life. At the start of the 1980s, 35 million adults were stepparents. In 1988, one-eighth of children living with two parents are stepchildren (Glick). Probably a third of all children growing up today will be part of a stepfamily before they reach adulthood (Furstenberg 1987). Many other adult children will see their parents divorce after twenty to fifty years of marriage. Demographers estimate that over one half of today's young persons may be stepchildren by the turn of the century (Larson 1992). Nearly two-thirds of children living in stepfamily situations live with their biological mother-stepfather. Stepfamilies are more likely to be white than African-American and more often poor than rich (Larson 1992). Recent census data indicates approximately half the children in blended families had a half-brother or half-sister.

The term "stepfamily" refers to many types of family forms, which can be created as two adults and the children of one or both come together. These systems, although similar to other two-parent forms, have ten characteristics:

1. A history of loss emerges for those who were previously in a two-parent system.

2. Some or all members bring past family history from a relationship that has changed or ended.

3. The couple does not begin as a dyad but, rather, the parent-child relationship predates the spousal bond.

4. One or two biological parents (living or dead) influence the stepfamily, often through triangulation.

5. Some or all members come with a set of rituals, patterns, and stories established in the former family.

6. Children may function as members of two households.

7. The family has a complex extended family network.

8. No legal relationship exists between the stepparent and the stepchildren.

9. The family may have to deal with complicated sexual secondary issues.

10. Many of these family relationships began as not-so-freely-chosen, or involuntary, relationships. (Visher and Visher 1982; Mills 1984; Pasley and Ihninger-Tallman 1987; Papernow 1993; Galvin 1993)

A stepfamily reflects ties to former systems. Death or divorce represents the end of a marital relationship, but not the termination of a parental relationship. When children are involved, the death or divorce alters, rather than ends, the family system. After a death, the remaining family members are faced with the necessity of restructuring themselves into a smaller system. The hole must be closed, because the family cannot continue limping indefinitely due to the "missing" member. After a divorce, the members may exist for a long period of time in an altered system of the same size in which ex-spouses still communicate around issues related to children or money. Eventually the altered system may expand into one or two stepfamilies.

These stepfamilies continue to be influenced by the original marital system. In their discussion of forming a remarried family, McGoldrick and Carter (1988) suggest that the emotions connected with the breakup of the first marriage can be visualized as a "roller coaster" graph with peaks of intensity at the points of:

1. Decision to separate
2. Actual separation
3. Legal divorce
4. Remarriage of either spouse
5. Shift in custody of any of the children
6. Moves of either spouse
7. Illness or death of either ex-spouse
8. Life cycle transitions of children (graduations, marriage, illness, etc.) (408)

In a divorce involving children, each of these points causes disruption or distress for the original system members. Many counselors consider that divorce and remarriage expand rather than end a family system saying: "When children are involved, a couple gets divorced *to* each other, not *from* each other." Thus, a system is reconstituted. For example, a family system may expand to include a woman, two children, her current husband, and her former husband who has remarried and has a stepson. The diagram in Figure 12.1 demonstrates how the original marital system of Peggy and Seth has grown and altered. Although Seth does not live with his children and former wife,

**FIGURE 12.1**
**Reconstituted Family System**

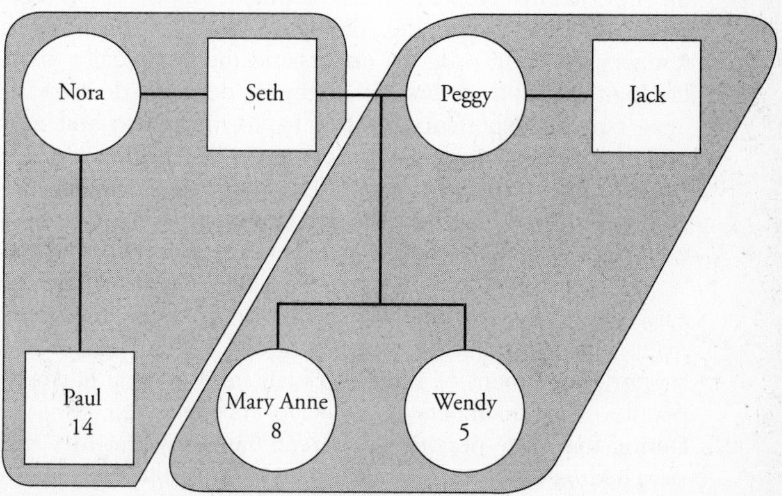

there are emotional, economic, and practical ties which bind all these people to each other. If Mary Anne has difficulty in school, her biological mother, biological father, and stepparents may all be affected by the problem.

## Stepfamily Development

How often have you heard comments such as "I wish Dad would leave Sally home during my wedding" or "My mother's husband thinks he can tell me what to do."? The stepfamily represents a family form frequently created on the basis of the voluntary positive relationship between the spouses as well some involuntary, conflictual relationships between the stepparent and stepchildren.

In Chapter 5, literature on adult romantic relationship development was presented that emphasized voluntary, romantic involvements. Parent-child communication literature presumes biological or voluntary connections between these persons which date from the arrival of the child. In contrast, many individuals involved in stepfamily relationships, specifically as a stepparent or as a stepchild, enter involuntarily into a so-called familial relationship with implied parent-child status and the intense involvement of a third party, the biological parent. In short, many stepfamilies are formed from a conflictual and complicated beginning because: (1) One or both parties may resist the relationship. (2) A third party, the biological parent, serves as the reason for this relationship. (3) Society provides expectations for how people should relate within a "family." (4) The instant family may force a type of intimacy through shared time and space. (5) Some stepfamily members may not have resolved their losses from the first family. Stepfamily development must be viewed through models distinct from the biological family model (Ahrons and Rodgers 1987). In order to understand the complexity of stepfamily life, particularly in its first years, the model must describe the stages most families experience as they try to blend two systems, at least one of which reflects a previous parent-child relationship.

In Table 12–1 Papernow (1993) describes seven stages of stepparent development and places them within a developmental framework for stepfamilies, which includes early, middle, and later stages.

Family structure remains biologically organized throughout the early stages (Papernow 1993). In the *fantasy* stage, the stepfamily remains divided primarily along previous system lines of emotional support, agreement of rules or rituals, and general alliances among people. Some members continue to confront their previous losses. During this early period, stepparents fantasize that they will rescue stepchildren from inadequate situations and that they will create a

**Table 12-1** Stages in Stepfamily Development

| | |
|---|---|
| Early | 1. Fantasy |
| | 2. Immersion |
| | 3. Awareness |
| Middle | 4. Mobilization |
| | 5. Action |
| Later | 6. Contact |
| | 7. Resolution |

loving, nurturing, devoted new family. Most new stepparents report a high level of fantasies and hopes as well as high expectations of gratitude from the stepchildren (Turnbull and Turnbull 1983). On the other hand, the children are more likely to fantasize about the departure of the stepparents and the reunion of their biological family, unless one of the biological parents is dead or has deserted the family.

At the *immersion* stage, members become acutely aware of their different rhythms, rules, relational currencies, and everyday behaviors and recognize the difficulty in blending them. Confusion and distress mount. Stepchildren experience tremendous clashes of loyalty as they try to sort out how to deal with a stepparent without being disloyal to the same-sex biological parent. Often, this is exhibited through anger or indifference. The biological parent, pleased to have an adult partner, is frightened by that partner's inability to establish satisfactory relationships with his or her children. Most stepfamilies encounter a persisting inequality of the biological parent-child relationship; therefore, truly shared parenting functions seldom become reality (Mills 1984). It becomes clear that something is not working, but due to fear of repeated failure, it is too frightening to address the issue directly.

The confusion of this early stage affects the extended family members who have to negotiate their relationship with this new family. The extended family might include four sets of grandparents as well as large numbers of relatives and fictive kin. These members provide feedback to the family on how they are seen, either by emphasizing the differences (giving expensive toys to biological grandchildren and token gifts to a stepgrandchild) or by supporting the newly formed system by treating all children equally. It is hard for the adults involved to share what is going on; shame or blame may interfere. Their fantasies are hard to forego since reality implies conflict. Therefore, for newly formed stepfamilies, boundaries may be biologically, legally and spatially unclear. Members may be confused about family membership and norms for behavior (Pasley 1987).

As the early stages conclude, awareness of their situation emerges and members start to make sense out of what is happening to them. The *awareness* stage is most critical because clarity and self-acceptance begin to replace confusion. According to Papernow (1984), "While the pain doesn't go away, the picture of where it comes from and why it hurts so much gets clearer" (358). The biological parent may be feeling great stress as a central figure trying to protect the children and mollify the spouse. Although some families remain stuck in the early stages for many years, most systems move on to the middle stages.

During the *mobilization* stage, spouses are more likely to address their differences directly, expressing feelings, needs and perceptions about life in the stepfamily. Such directness leads to important conflicts. At the time, some of the issues may appear trivial, but the conflicts represent the underlying issues of the family's structure. Such comments as "You're too tired to go to the grocery store but when Jill calls, you are awake enough to pick her up from work!" address the alliances and strengths of certain boundaries within the system. A stepfather may claim that he needs time alone with his wife, upsetting his children but strengthening the marital boundary. The struggles of this period are captured in a student's comments in the following example:

---

*I think our family's divorce ended up with a long recovery period because the divorce initially created such upheaval. The house was sold, I went off to college, my brother, Josh, changed schools, and my father got a new wife, all in the period of about two months. Because these drastic changes were extremely sudden, I think the wounds have taken longer to heal. Josh's reactions were typical for a 6 year old. His insecurity and fears exposed themselves through his sudden hyperactivity and inability to concentrate. He became quite the bully and a well-practiced liar. Even now, two years later, he causes chaos at my father's house, constantly forcing my father to choose between him and Dad's wife. I hate being there with Josh.*

---

As the middle period continues, the family moves into an *action* stage that marks the beginning of truly working together. Papernow (1993) calls this "going into business together." Members share the former dreams and expectations while remaining connected enough to engage in active problem solving around past and current issues. Some solutions may reflect former ways of doing things for certain members, while others involve creative attempts to represent the desires of the blended system. The process is called creating the "middle ground" (Papernow 1987). For example, a family may decide to adopt certain holiday rituals that one part of the system experienced before, while creating new ones reflecting the new system. Although the time when a stepfamily identity is being built is a perfect time to establish new traditions (Einstein 1982), many families never discuss expectations; all members assume that old ways will be carried on. Yet the middle ground is strengthened through stepfamily rituals (Whiteside 1989). Such silence only deepens the pain as members feel misunderstood or disconfirmed. Most families at this stage renegotiate rules for everyday events and discuss acceptable ways of handling anger and affection within the system. Members may begin to create an identity for themselves in a positive light, instead of working from a sense of deficiency. This action period reflects a sense of "we-ness."

This sense of "we-ness" comes very gradually. For example, in the first two years of a remarriage, stepfathers reported themselves low on "felt" or "expressed" affection for stepchildren. Compared to biological fathers, stepfathers express less positive affection and fewer negative or critical responses (Hetherington 1987). This cautiousness reflects the tentative nature of building new, and sometimes undesired, relationships. But when it develops, the middle grounds gives a stepfamily its sense of identity.

As families enter the later stages, members experience greater intimacy and authenticity; the biological ties have loosened and a new group identity is emerging. In the *contact* stage "the couple relationship, previously polarized by step issues, is now more often felt as an intimate sanctuary in which to share these issues, including painful or difficult feelings" (Papernow 1984, 360). The triangles that had consumed the couple's attention and energy have diminished, allowing them to function more adequately in all areas of family life.

Eventually, the question of how biological parents and stepparents are to be integrated into the children's lives is resolved. Papernow (1984) ascribes the quality of the stepparent role in this way:

> (a) The role does not usurp or compete with the biological parent of the same sex; (b) The role includes an intergenerational boundary between stepparent and child; (c) The role is sanctioned by the rest of the stepfamily, particularly the spouse; (d) The role incorporates the special qualities this stepparent brings to this family. (361)

Family members experience a sense of clarity and security. Confusion about language for referring to family members has passed; discussion of the stepfamily is comfortable. Levels of openness once considered impossible may now exist. The original fantasies have been explored in the light of reality.

At the *resolution* stage, family relationships not only provide a sense of satisfaction but also feel reliable. Outsider and insider roles shift easily. Family members have developed dyadic relationships characterized by personal interaction, not just by marital merger. Wallerstein and Blakeslee suggest an "independent relationship between a stepparent and stepchild is made of countless transactions and responses through which the child learns why this person cares about me. I have a claim separate from my mom. When a stepparent brings this feeling about, it is a magical moment created by sweat and tears" (252). All experience a strong sense of family.

Present situations move into the foreground, while past struggles and issues become part of the background. This does not imply permanent resolution of all issues, because certain concerns reappear indefinitely—the later phases of the "roller coaster" graph described earlier. Clearly, well functioning stepfamilies don't just "happen."

Stepfamily development involves great effort and sensitivity.

## Communication in Stepfamilies

The complexity of stepfamily formation is reflected in members' communication concerns and patterns. As a remarried system forms, partners bring communication patterns from: (1) families-of-origin, (2) the first marriage, and (3) the period between marriages. Children bring patterns from the second and third situations. Forming such a system requires extensive initial adaptation if functional cohesion and adaptability levels are to be established. Family members are cast instantly into multiple roles. A single man may become husband and stepfather. A woman may become wife, stepmother, or even stepgrandmother with a simple "I do." The results of research on stepparent and stepchildren relationships indicate areas where problems in communication can develop (Cissna, Cox, and Bochner 1990; Galvin and Cooper 1990).

A stepfamily's initial communication may reflect the directness or indirectness of communication surrounding the divorce. If children were not prepared for the divorce, and assured that all major changes would be discussed with them, then the same pattern may influence remarriage. Many children learn about their stepfamily status through announcements such as, "I'm getting married next week," or "Guess what we did last weekend!" (Galvin 1989). Few adults give children time and opportunities to discuss how the new family will be created and work. In certain cases future stepsiblings are given opportunities to meet and encouraged to identify similarities and possible rewards of such a relationship.

If they are to communicate openly with both parents, children need to understand that they did not cause the divorce. Both parents need to assure children that it's acceptable to love the other parent. Often, one parent says little, but children sense the nonverbal disdain when the other's name is mentioned. Divorced parents need to remember that as children grieve, they may act out their own feelings of loss and alternately blame one parent for the divorce, or they may take out their anger on a stepparent (Luepnitz 1979).

Each member of a remarried system must participate in the creation of new family themes, images, boundaries, and biosocial beliefs. These negotiations should result in new stepfamily rituals (Whiteside 1989). Disparate backgrounds and negative feelings about the remarriage will result in intense periods of conflict, reflected verbally and nonverbally, as family members jockey for position and power. The former oldest child may fight against the role of middle daughter. A child used to great freedom and autonomy may rebel against themes that push for strong cohesion and similarity among family members. Each new system must negotiate such boundaries issues as:

1. Membership (Who are the "real" members of the family?)

2. Space (What is mine? Where do I really belong?)

3. Authority (Who is really in charge ... Of discipline? Of money? Decisions?)

4. Time (Who gets how much of my time and how much do I get of theirs?) (McGoldrick and Carter 1988, 406–407)

The boundary issue of membership is resolved more easily "when members interact on a regular basis (physical presence) and come to see one another as belonging to the existing family unit (psychological presence)" (Pasley 1987, 210). Discussions need to be held addressing who is "in" the family. This may be less evident than it first appears. In a study of stepfamily membership, 15 percent of stepparents did not list stepchildren who lived in their households. Thirty-one percent of stepchildren excluded a residential stepparent and 41 percent of children excluded a residential stepsibling (Furstenberg 1987, 50). Wallerstein and Blakeslee found that half the children whose mother remarried did not feel welcome in the new family (239). Space may be physical or psychological. For many stepchildren, a physical space indicates acceptance and a "place" in the family. In addition, participation in family tasks may strengthen a feeling of being a member rather than being a visitor.

New authority patterns emerge in stepfamilies. Both sons and daughters in divorced families are allowed more responsibility, independence, and power in decisions than are children in non-divorced families (Hetherington 1987). This freedom affects life in remarried families. Stepfathers initially tend to allow the mother to exert most of the authority. In fact, stepfathers make significantly fewer control attempts and are less successful in gaining control with both sons and daughters than are biological fathers. Over time their control of stepsons is better. Stepdaughters tend to be more resistant. Mothers and stepmothers both tend to exert authority. The biological parent may be caught between discipline beliefs of a spouse and ex-spouse.

A typical example of covert struggle is described in the following example:

---

*One morning when I was 10 I was late so I had breakfast and ran to catch the school bus without washing my dishes. When*

*I got home that afternoon, I discovered my stepfather had stuck my plate, complete with jam and toast crumbs, under my pillow. We rarely confronted each other directly because fighting was too scary, but we expressed our feelings, often in trivial ways.*

---

Time is a highly valued currency in stepfamilies, particularly for dyads such as spouses or biological parent and child. Such pressure often leaves a stepchild or stepparent feeling "left out" and a biological parent feeling "pulled between two worlds." "Visiting" often feels awkward and creates depression in non-custodial fathers because of the lack of daily routines.

Communication networks must expand to encompass new members and possibly to maintain ties with first marriage members, as children and former spouses and extended family members attempt to maintain necessary contacts. Negative remarks or overt conflict between members of former systems create pressures. Children may feel "pulled to one side." Each group may establish communication rules to keep information from the other. "Don't tell your mother about my trip to Mexico" or "Don't mention that I'm dating someone." Children may be filled with secrets and resentments, which they cannot divulge. A difficult situation arises as former spouses criticize each other in front of the children. An area of great stress for children was experiencing one natural parent's talking negatively about the other natural parent (Lutz 1983). Amato and Rezac (1994) found high conflict between the non- residential parent and custodial parent is associated with child behavior problems. If members of the extended family take sides, the children suffer additional pressures.

Stepfamiles are becoming a common part of the American way of life, but the issues of living in such a system remain varied and complex. To date, society's vocabulary has not even developed words to deal with the roles and relationships involved. For example, a child has no names for her stepgrandparents, no way to communicate easily about her relationship to the son of her father's second former wife, and no name for the first stepfather who is now divorced from her mother. Such difficulties make contact with outsiders and institutions more difficult and sometimes more painful. The amazing power of language is described in the following example:

---

*The power of language in the family is amazing. Over the past eight years my stepdaughter and I have struggled mightily to create a working relationship. We have come a long*

(continued on page 364)

*way. Yet it's always been clear that I am "Jean, my stepmother" and her mother is "Mom." That's been okay. Now that her mother is about to remarry I hear my stepdaughter referring to "my other father" and it really hurts. The first time I heard that it felt like a knife went into my stomach since I have never been "my other mother."*

---

There is still much to be learned about communication within a stepfamily, a form that usually involves nonvoluntary relationships. Limited research points to similarities in parent- child adjustment between African-American and white stepfamilies (Fine et al. 1992). A growing body of literature indicates slightly lower levels of school performance for certain stepchildren (Zill 1988). At the same time, school administrators are attempting to adapt to a child's life in a stepfamily, especially if it involves multiple residences. Recent legislation indicates that courts and government bodies are becoming more sensitive to the possibly enduring nature of stepparent-stepchild relations (Fine and Fine 1992). Yet, this growing segment of family life presents challenges that have yet to be fully appreciated from a communication perspective.

## GAY AND LESBIAN COUPLES AND FAMILIES

Gay and lesbian families are formed "from lovers, friends, biological and adopted children, blood relatives, stepchildren, and even ex-lovers" (Laird 1993, 294). These are families that do not necessarily share a common household. In describing the recognition of various family forms, Harevan suggests that an alternative, such as same-sex couples or gay and lesbian families, is not necessarily a new family form but rather a form that is becoming more visible. Although census figures on gay male couples and lesbian couples are not available and little hard data exist on homosexual parents, there is growing interest in and awareness of these family forms. Golanty and Harris (1982) estimate that 5 to 10 percent of the population maintains sexual and emotional involvements exclusively with members of the same sex. Patterson (1992) estimates the number of lesbian mothers ranges from 1–5 million; gay father estimates fluctuate between 1–3 million. Because some of these couples and families are in many ways invisible and maintained in silence, they are harder to study; the existing research has focused on white middle class subjects (Laird).

This text is concerned primarily with homosexual persons who have formed couple attachments in which they consider each other as family or with those who are functioning as parents. In their work on homosexual relationships, Bell and Weinberg identified what they called the "close couple," or the homosexual relationship most similar to heterosexual marriage. In the 1970s, Bell and Weinberg (1978) found strong support among lesbians for being in a permanent relationship (45). In the classic study, *American Couples*, by Blumstein and Schwartz (1983) included same sex couples as a significant part of their population. They found that 71 percent of their sample of gay men between ages 36 and 45 were living with a partner. When questioned about their sense of family, both males and females counted lovers as family. The other persons listed were primarily, though not exclusively, lesbians and gay men (Weston 1993).

Until the 1970s, gay men and lesbians were a real but fairly invisible part of the American population (Blumstein and Schwartz). Yet, the authors suggest "couplehood," either as a reality or as an aspiration, is as strong among homosexuals as it is among heterosexuals (44). In this relationship, partners are sexually exclusive and rely on each other for interpersonal satisfaction. Other studies point toward the desire for couple relationships within the gay and lesbian community (McWhirter and Mattison 1984; Johnson 1984; Zacks, Green, and Marrow 1988; Weston 1993; Fitzpatrick et al. 1994). The AIDS crisis of the 1980s created a climate which supports more monogamous, long-term relationships.

"There are many similarities between gay and lesbian, and heterosexual familial relationships. Gay and lesbian families must be viewed intergenerationally since each partner, child, and other family member is influenced by and must come to terms with the specific history and culture of his or her own family-of-origin in its sociocultural context" (Laird, 283). They must negotiate roles, struggle with dialectical tensions of autonomy and connectedness or novelty and predictability, and develop problem solving strategies. They must negotiate boundaries between members as well as between their unit and, extended family and the outside world.

Same sex couples display many similarities to heterosexual couples. When Fitzpatrick's marital typology was used with homosexual couples as well as heterosexual couples, the types were applicable across groups. For gay males there are approximately the same proportion of traditionals, yet significantly fewer independents and more separates than in the random heterosexual sample. Lesbian respondents reported more traditionals, fewer independents, and fewer separates than the random heterosexual sample (Fitzpatrick et al.).

Although many similarities exist between heterosexual and homosexual couples, important differences also exist. Some of the differences occur in areas of relationship development, sources of recognition/support, and ways of dealing with money, sex, and power (Blumstein and Schwartz). In most cases, young homosexuals are denied role models and positive images of long-term, same-sex relationships. Such a lack of role models forces a more pressured trial and error discovery in relationship development and maintenance.

The lack of interpersonal and institutional support creates great pressure for homosexual partners and parents. For example, Tanner (1978) suggests in a lesbian relationship many partners face the following problems: not being able to express affection or acknowledge their partner in public; a lack of language for talking about partnership; a lack of a full support network. Many individuals cannot tell even their own families about their lifestyle. In fact, the family is often the last group to know due to fear of rejection (Brown 1989). Others feel comfortable sharing their relationship with only very close friends. In certain urban areas, the large recognized gay community has provided support for couples or families, but in other areas, persons live in secretive isolation.

Even when partners are recognized as a couple, the interpersonal support remains different. Current language does not contain socially approved terms for gay and lesbian couple and family relationships. For example, there is no appropriate descriptive term for two men who have been together for ten or twenty years. DeVito (1979) captures this frustration saying, "In gay parlance they are 'lovers' but as popularly used and understood the term is too general and does not include the years of commitment, the permanency of the relationship, and a host of other dimensions that are included in both the denotative and connotative meanings of the term marriage" (8). Children struggle with vocabulary for addressing a co-parent or for discussing the adult parental relationship or the co-parents' extended family.

Gay and lesbian couples and families experience fewer socially recognized rituals than other family types. There is no legal marriage ceremony, and secrecy may limit such rituals as engagement, marriage, christenings, and birth announcements. Less public rituals such as exchanging rings and sending anniversary gifts or cards are more common (Baptiste 1987). Some homosexual couples live together openly after going through a "unity" service or marriage celebration similar to heterosexual rites, but such community celebrations are rare (Stinnett, Walters, and Kay 1984). Due to the lack of public rituals, partners tended to see offers of assistance, commitment to working through conflict, and a common history as signs of kinship (Weston).

The concern for secrecy forces most couples to rely more on each other to meet interpersonal needs—less than their heterosexual counterparts experience. Laird suggests that secrecy for lesbians fosters a common language and tradition but this may also isolate the relationship as this respondent notes:

> *One of the most difficult parts of our lifestyle is the intense dependence we have to have on each other because we cannot discuss our relationship or certain other serious aspects of our lives with many other people. We experience an isolation as we function among friends who live a heterosexual lifestyle and can be more open about the good and the bad parts of their lives. I value the closeness of our relationship, but I recognize the strains caused by the need to depend so totally on each other.*

In addition to limited social support, homosexual partners and parents receive almost no societal support. Whereas spouses in heterosexual partnerships become immediately eligible for health insurance and other organizational benefits, most institutions do not cover long-term homosexual unions; frequently a partner or child of a partner is entitled to nothing. These examples highlight the pressures placed on long-term, same-sex relationships that heterosexual couples do not experience.

From the perspectives of money and work, Blumstein and Schwartz uncovered many differences between heterosexual couples and same-sex couples and also between gay male and lesbian couples. Money establishes the balance of power in most relationships, except among lesbians. Whereas in heterosexual couples the greater the amount of money the wife earns, the freer she is to spend the money as she sees fit, in lesbian couples the balance of power appears unrelated to income. "They make a conscious effort to keep their relationships free of any form of domination, especially if it derives from something as impersonal as money" (55). In gay male couples, income is an extremely important force in determining which partner is dominant. When partners are disappointed with the amount of money the couple has, they find their entire relationship less satisfying, except among lesbians. The majority of same-sex couples believe that both should work, although lesbians are more likely to feel obligated to support a partner than are gay males.

Same-sex couples, due to a lack of traditional marital role models, tend to negotiate each conflict rather than rely on societal expectations or previous gender role models for their answers. In a study of relationship quality for child-free lesbian couples and those with children, Koepke et al. (1992) found solid and happy relationships existed for the total sample. No differences in disclosure or longevity were found. Couples with children scored higher in relationship satisfaction and on sexual relationship satisfaction. Couples with children had been together longer. Kurdek (1994) found gay and lesbian respondents rated their partners as using positive problem solving more frequently than married mothers who ranked their spouses. For all couples, frequent use of positive problem solving was linked to increased relational satisfaction.

In dealing with the issue of "work versus the relationship," same-sex couples tended to be relationship-oriented. Lesbians of all ages cannot seem to find enough time to share together. Fusion is a primary quality in lesbian relationships (Laird) which emphasizes the "autonomy – connection" dialectical struggle as key movements. In some cases, fusion is blamed for diminishing sexual interest. A study of cohesion and adaptability in lesbian relationships confirms previous findings of high cohesion in female couples, a reality which may help them function more successfully in a primarily heterosexual world. This is consistent with Day and Morse's (1981) conclusion that lesbian pairs appear to be equalitarian in style.

Gay men appear more satisfied with the time they have available to them. Blumstein and Schwartz speculate that one reason same-sex couples are so relationship-oriented may be their capacity to spend their leisure time together, having been socialized to enjoy many of the same activities and interests, as in the situation described in the following example:

---

*There's a comfort just being in the same room together. We can sit and be quiet and feel very comfortable for hours. We often find ourselves doing the same things, buying the same cards, planning the same meals, starting to say the same things. We are very much alike and share the same interests. We can leave a great deal unsaid and still understand each other.*

---

Blumstein and Schwartz report that sexual frequency varies among the couple types. Gay men have sex more often in the early part of their relationship than any other type of couple. But after ten years, they have sex together far less frequently than do married couples. Lesbians have sex less frequently than any other type of couple. The quality of sexuality is important to all couples. In same-sex couples, it is the more emotionally expressive partner who initiates sex most frequently. As a distinction between same-sex couples types, gay men value physical attractiveness of a partner more highly than do lesbians.

The pressure of high cohesion and limited social support creates serious stress and violence in some relationships. Recent studies have explored abuse in same-sex couples. Like heterosexual couples, gay male and lesbian couples may use physically aggressive, or occasionally, violent tactics to resolve relationship conflicts (Kelly and Warshafsky 1987). Hart (1986) explains lesbian battering as a pattern of violence or coercive behaviors "whereby a lesbian seeks to control the thoughts, beliefs, or conduct of her intimate partner or to punish the intimate for resisting the perpetrator's control" (173). Although the patterns of conflict may be similar between heterosexual and same-sex couples, the stigmatization of such couples may affect their willingness to seek help and the responses of those called on to help (Renzetti 1989). Thus, conflict and abuse plague same-sex as well as heterosexual couples.

Parenting involves a small but growing number of same-sex couples. Baptiste (1987) argues that all families that are parented by gay or lesbian couples "are by virtue of their role and relationship to the partner's children, stepparents" (114). Historically most gay families were formed with the biological children of one previously married partner. Currently a growing number are formed with a known or unknown donor or adoption; over 10,000 lesbians have formed families in this manner (Coontz 1992). These families frequently create strong boundaries to protect the family within the larger community. Yet the children often help to soften the extended family's concerns as they link the family of blood to the family of choice (Laird). Lesbian mothers face an "inappropriate mother" stereotype (DiLapi 1989) due to outsider fear that the child will be homosexual or not given enough parental attention. Partners often find it difficult to create a viable shared parenting situation for a child. Language does not easily include the non-biological parent. There are few legal rights available to this parent figure.

These families find boundaries difficult to manage. According to Ross (1988), the homosexual family in middle class American communities struggles to maintain the level of secrecy needed to prevent negative consequences while the children bring the family into contact with numerous school and community groups. Schools are a site of great controversy dealing with issues of homosexual families (Richardson 1993; Celis 1993). Thus these families face boundary management challenges unknown to other groups. Sometimes children exert social control to protect their image with friends using strategies such as limiting father's access, using misleading language to refer to the co-parent. On occasion a child may "prepare" a friend (Bozett 1989a) for entering the family system.

Discussing one's own homosexuality with a child creates special concerns. In one of the few studies in this area, Miller (1979) found that gay men feared it would lessen the children's respect and affection for their fathers. Of the men who had told their children, all found the children more positive than had been anticipated (548). The children reported that their father's honesty had relieved some family tension and helped to strengthen the parent-child relationship. Father disclosure strategies may be direct, such as open discussion, or indirect, such as taking a child to gay social events (Bozett 1987). Children who showed the greatest acceptance of their fathers were those who were gradually introduced to the subject of homosexuality through printed material, discussion, and meeting gay family friends before the full parental disclosure.

Adolescence provides special challenges. Many parents who are homosexual can present problems to adolescents who are trying to fit into a peer group and come to grips with their own sexuality. In a study of gay male stepfamilies, the adolescents were the most likely to be secretive about living in a gay family (Crosbie-Burnett and Helmbrecht 1993).

Same-sex couples with children face many struggles similar to heterosexual couples. For example, in her study of lesbian partner abuse, Renzetti found that in 35 couples who lived with children, one third of these children were sometimes abused by the violent partner as well.

Lesbian and gay male partners and parents are becoming a more visible family form. They, like any kinship group, must develop a set of communication patterns and rituals by which to create and maintain their relationships.

## COHABITATION

If you live with a boyfriend or girlfriend for two months, are you a cohabitor? If you keep two apartments but sleep together in one or the other, are you a cohabitor? Although definitions abound, cohabitating generally refers to the lifestyle created by two unrelated and unmarried adults of the opposite sex living together, with or without children, over a period of time. Cohabiting implies an indefinite agreement to share living quarters and a life; it is not a convenient response to a college schedule or apartment shortage. Most cohabitors are presumed to care deeply about each other; a recognition of each other as a "family" is often implied. This conception limits the number of couples or families to be considered.

Accurately estimating the population of cohabitors is difficult. Coontz (1992) estimates there are almost 3 million cohabitating couples in America, an increase of 80 percent since 1980. Three quarters of a million cohabitors are raising children together. Whereas some cohabitors have never been married, others have experienced one or more marriages. Wallerstein and Blakeslee found 10 percent of divorcing parents eventually moved to long term cohabitation arrangements. They report that usually one of the partners in long term cohabitation does not want marriage, leaving the other powerless to force the issue, as a respondent describes in the following example:

---

*We are as married as any of our "legal" friends but, having been through a terrible divorce, I cannot see marrying again. The children on both sides treat us as a couple and since we don't plan to add to that population, I see no need to marry. In fact, I think we do so well because we don't take each other for granted.*

---

Statistical estimates of the number of couples who cohabit and eventually marry vary from one in four to one in eight; Schoen and Weincik (1993) estimate 50 to 60 percent of first cohabitations lead to marriage. The median life of cohabitating is 1.3 years (Kingsbury and Sanzoni 1991). In addition, these authors state perseverance is devalued in cohabitation and suggest the option of cohabitation appears to append the clause "must make a decision—either marry or terminate" (207). Yet, Macklin (1987) refers to cohabitation as "informal marriage" since there are few differences except for degree of commitment. On the other hand, Schoen and Weinick report cohabiting couples are more dissimilar in religion and age compared to married couples. Cohabiting couples are most similar with respect to education; they see cohabiting as living by a "looser bond."

Some partners may fear that their relationship will not last. Popenoe (1993) sees a growing body of evidence that premarital cohabitation is associated with proneness for divorce saying:

> Cohabitation does not seem to serve very well the function of a trial marriage, or of a system that leads to stronger marriages through weeding out those who find that, after living together, they are unsuitable for each other. More likely, a lack of commitment at the beginning may signal a lack of commitment at the end. (534)

Cohabiting does not necessarily predict future marital satisfaction. According to DeMaris and MacDonald (1993):

> Despite a widespread public faith in premarital cohabitation as a testing ground for marital incompatibility, research to

> date indicates that cohabitors' marriages are less satisfactory and more unstable than those of non-cohabitors. (399)

One study of cohabiting couples who married reports that in the year after the marriage, wives perceived a significantly lower quality of communication, and both spouses reported significantly lower marital satisfaction (DeMaris and Leslie 1984, 77). In another study, couples who had not cohabited had higher marital adjustment scores one year after marriage than did those who had cohabited (Watson 1983). Yet, when DeMaris and MacDonald distinguished between "single-instance cohabitors"—those married persons who had lived with their current marital partner and "serial cohabitors," only the latter group was significantly associated with marital instability.

Communication differs in some respects between cohabiting and married couples. Without the legal ties and ceremonial rituals that publicly announce the relationship as a long-term commitment, partners may have difficulty communicating to friends and relatives that their living together, especially in the beginning, represents love more than sexual needs. Their couple social support system may be more fragile.

Loose bonds can influence patterns of conflict and decision making. In his study of communication of married and cohabiting couples of various ages, Yelsma (1986) found that older couples in both married and cohabiting states were less likely to discuss sexual interests, disagreements, and personal problems than were younger couples.

Although the impact of the critical decision to marry or terminate a relationship is not totally clear, such an issue would overshadow many smaller decision making moments. Communication differences between cohabitators and marital pairs may result in role performance issues. As you remember, role performance may differ greatly from original expectations. Becoming a wife or husband may bring with it a set of pressures from the spouse or outside persons that cause the role to be played out differently than expected. In his classic book *Becoming Partners*, Carl Rogers (1972) records poignant statements about this process from two young people who married after living together for a lengthy period of time:

> DICK: *"When Gail and I were living together, we were sort of equal partners in making the living, and if we were broke, nobody really took the blame for it; but when we moved back and came into such close proximity with our respective in-laws, all of a sudden it became my fault when we weren't making any money, and I was the bum who wasn't going out and looking for work."*

> GAIL: *"I sort of had expectations like he did, you fall into a role even if you don't want to ... of a husband who is supposed to be this way and a wife who is supposed to be this way ... So it put me into a big conflict because I'm thinking, 'Well, I've got to be like this, I'm married and I'm supposed to do this." (43)*

In this case, both personal expectations of both "husband and wife" and family pressure forced individuals to view their roles differently than they expected.

The lack of clear definition of cohabiting roles may increase the partners' sense of individual freedom. Blumstein and Schwartz found that cohabiting couples regard money, work, and sex differently than do other couples. These varying perceptions influence the ways cohabiting couples negotiate differences and establish patterns and rules affecting their interaction. Cohabiting couples reported a stronger sense than married couples of each partner's contributing his or her share.

Cohabiting women view money as a way to achieve equality, and thus, they seek independence and want to avoid economic dependence. The cohabiting men expect economic equality more than married men. The cohabiting partner with the greater income determines more of the couple's recreational activities, including vacations. Cohabiting couples usually maintain separate checking accounts and when they do, they fight less about finances than do married couples.

These same researchers found that cohabitors believe that both partners should work and share housework. Yet, women do more of this work than men. Male cohabitors, more than married men, rank the relationship as more important than their job. Male cohabitors are more competitive with their partners, although the partners' success or lack of it has less effect on the relationship. Cohabitors more frequently spend time on their own.

Sexual communication also differs, since cohabitors report having sex more frequently than married couples. Cohabiting women more readily express an interest in sex by initiating it, but in a long-standing relationship, the male cohabitor usually resents it. In a summary of cohabiting couples experiences, Pearson (1989) concludes that (1) cohabiting couples appear to be more egalitarian, (2) more independent of each other, and (3) more loving toward each other than married couples (106–107).

Noller and Fitzpatrick (1993) report on an Australian study of 600 married and cohabitating couples saying there was more conflict in cohabitating couples, particularly violent conflict, saying, "conflict seemed to come from the cohabiting lifestyle and to involve feelings of anxiety, guilt, and isolation from family and other sources of social support" (229).

Cohabitation affects the pairs relationships to extended family and community. Many parents of cohabiting children have difficulty accepting their children's wishes to live together in a trial marriage. Frequently, communication in the family network becomes quite complicated, with certain members or subsystems knowing the "secret" and others kept uninformed. Cohabitation represents a small but growing type of family form with certain unique communication concerns.

Because of the more limited range of role models for some of the family forms discussed in this chapter, the successful development of an operating family system requires extensive effort and mutual understanding on the part of the members involved. Without the ability to share information and feelings and to negotiate constructively, the stress may lead to dissolution. Maintenance of the system depends heavily on the communication between and among the system members.

## CONCLUSION

This chapter develops a position stated earlier in this text—there is no one right way to be a family—and its corollary, there is no one right way to communicate in a family. Single parent systems, an increasingly common form, may experience destructive pressure without appropriate economic, emotional, and social supports. Single parents fare better when strong communication networks are in place for them. Creating stepfamilies, the process of blending two systems, and the communication tasks inherent in this process, reflect a highly complex type of family formation. A system created out of loss, with voluntary and involuntary relationships, presents a host of communication challenges. Same-sex partners, who may also function as parents, function with limited support systems both interpersonally and legally. The AIDS crisis, forcing more gay men and lesbians into monogamous relationships, is predicted to increase this type of system. Finally, family systems formed through cohabitation carry with them unique communication demands. Each of these family forms requires the conscious effort of members to communicate their needs and feelings during the development and maintenance of the family. In short, remember the effort it takes to create a family of any form that works.

## IN REVIEW

1. What language changes have you encountered which support the emerging and growing family forms?
2. What do you see as some communication-related differences between a single-parent system with three children and a two-parent system with three children?
3. Apply Papernow's model of stepfamily development to a real or fictional stepfamily, indicating: (1) experiences similar to or different from the model and (2) communication patterns indicative of certain stages.
4. Take a position and discuss: When children are involved, ex-spouses are divorced "to" each other rather than "from" each other.
5. In what ways might unrelated persons communicate to outsiders that they consider each other to be family?

# 13

# Contextual Dimensions of Family Communication

All family interaction occurs within a specific context. Social relationships cannot be separated from their social, physical, and cultural contexts. More concretely, family interaction occurs in a particular place, at a particular time, and within a particular social setting. Just as it is important to understand the individual within families context, so too, the family must be understood within environmental and social context. Decontexted individuals do not exist; decontexted families do not exist. Therefore, to fully understand familial interaction, one needs to explore family relationships through the dual lenses of space and time within the physical and psychological context of "home," as in the following example:

---

*We have always been part of a strong extended family and lived with my parents since the divorce four years ago. Although my children are eight and five, we have, until now, been connected with the overall family so we adapted to that household and acted as they did. This week we moved into our own apartment and realized that a lot had changed. We looked at each other around the small kitchen table which seemed so incomplete with just the three of us. Here we were, alone, in our own space, and a little scared. We sat in uneasy silence for a while before we began the tentative discussion about how we would live in this new world.*

---

The following questions may stimulate your initial thinking about family relationships as they are affected by environmental context:

1. What was the best place and time to talk to a parent about personal problems when you were younger? Did these talks involve food, walking, or driving around?

2. When having dinner, did all family members eat at the same time while sitting in specific places, or did you eat when you felt like it anywhere you chose? Were there certain rituals connected with particular meals?

3. Could family members shut the door to rooms to be alone? If doors were closed, did you knock first or did you just open them and walk in? Did family members have any spaces which were theirs?

4. How were holidays celebrated in your home? Who was included? How did your home, neighborhood, or community reflect these events?

5. As a small child, what were the safety boundaries surrounding your home that you could not cross? A neighbor's yard? The apartment hallway? A main street? How did this change as you grew older?

6. How did the cultural, regional, or religious nature of your community affect your family's interaction? Did your family reflect the surrounding community or differ from the community? How did that affect your interaction?

These are some of the issues that will be explored further as you investigate the interaction between environmental factors and the interpersonal relationships within a family.

Advances in environmental psychology have led architects, designers, and social scientists to focus more directly on the environment as a context for, as well as a type of, communication. Professionals involved in social service have developed ecological approaches to understanding human behavior by examining interaction between people and their environment (deHoyos 1989). The environmental context creates a system of communication that is learned, socially understood, and structured like language (DeLong 1974). Persons learn to react appropriately within particular dimensions of space and time because the messages received from the physical and social environment provide cues about appropriate behavior. In addition, the environment contains cultural expectations for interaction which become routine for persons familiar with it.

Relationships and context are inseparable. Werner, Altman, and Brown (1992) suggest "relationships cannot be understood outside the cultural norms and psychological processes that bind people together (300). Just as relationships are embedded in families, friendships, and groups, relationships are also embedded in homes with their spaces and objects. Finally, relationships are embedded in time. Psychologist Scheflen (1971) suggests that hierarchical levels of social relationships, including parent-child and family relationships, are organized both spatially and temporally. Reiss et al. (1981) refer to space and time as two fundamental resources a family requires for conducting its day-to-day life. They propose that families are "strikingly different in their management of these two resources," and that these differences are crucial in how a family defines itself (233).

Contextual issues create boundaries that limit and define a family's experience and, hence, communication. Places, objects, routines, and cultural traditions are as embedded in the relationship as are feelings and other aspects of relationships (Brown, Werner, and Altman, 1994). Structural design, arrangement of furniture and objects within the structure, and time of day or year can influence: (1) who interacts with whom, (2) where, (3) when, (4) for how long, and (5) the style or tone of the interaction and the kinds of things about which they can communicate. In more concrete terms, certain family members are more likely to have greater interactions because they share a room, play basketball in the backyard, or sit up together for an evening cup of coffee. Whereas basketball games do not foster intense, deep conversations but provide shared experiences, talking on the porch or at the kitchen table may lead to special conversations which increase closeness; it may encourage the airing of conflicts that result in greater distance, or possibly, resolution. Ritualistic patterns of behavior, past encounters, and cultural norms influence the style of interaction.

Relational life and its physical, cultural, and social contexts are interdependent. Failure to respect this intrinsic wholeness may result in overlooking the interrelations which support the stability of the entire system. Although spatial or temporal factors do not determine the kinds of family interactions that take place, they do influence interactions that occur both within and outside the home. Thus, a transactional viewpoint recognizes the mutual influence of context and family interaction through the process of placemaking. This is the lifelong process of constructing, altering, embellishing, and assigning meaning to places (Brown, Werner, and Altman).

## FACTORS OF FAMILY CONTEXT

The environment and the people in it combine to form a communication system. This section will examine the environmental factors of space and time from a physical and psychological perspective and then demonstrate how these interrelate with each other and may affect communication within family systems across cultures.

## Space

Space may be viewed from the perspective of distance regulation. It affects the issues of closeness, distance, coming together, or separating. Space may be understood as physical—an actual place, or as psychological—the sense of intimacy or privacy.

***Proxemics*** The study of distances as a function of communication, or proxemics, is based on an understanding of how people use space. Early work by anthropologist Hall (1966) conceptualized the ways humans use space as fixed feature space, semi-fixed feature space, and informal space (103–12). *Fixed feature space* refers to that physical space organized by unmoving boundaries, such as walls in a room or the invisible line dividing space that is recognized by those who use it. The latter may be called a nonphysical, or psychological, boundary. Each type serves as a "real" boundary to which inhabitants must adapt. The actual wall between the kitchen and the dining room may keep the cook out of the conversation. Such boundaries are obvious and often culturally designed. According to Brown, Werner, and Altman:

> In the US … the walls of a household help to create what we think of as natural separation between the household and the larger community … Inside the home the separate bedrooms for parents and children corresponds to our way of thinking of these relationships as having a certain degree of separation (350).

Yet, if you shared a room with a brother or sister, you may remember the times that your side of the room and his or her side became separate territories, and you did not cross the line.

*Semi-fixed feature space* refers to flexible space created by the arrangement of furniture and/or other moveable objects over which the inhabitants have control. You probably remember rearranging your room according to your moods or having to help rearrange the living room when one of your parents wanted to encourage conversation at a party.

*Informal space* refers to the way people position their bodies as they relate to others. Hall has divided the distances at which a person relates into four major levels: intimate space, ranging from zero to eighteen inches; personal space, ranging from eighteen inches to four feet; social space, including four to twelve feet; and public space, which encompasses interaction at distances over twelve feet.

Whereas *intimate space* encourages the nonverbal expression of such emotions and behaviors as hugging, kissing, tickling, lovemaking, wrestling, hitting, and whispering, *personal space* supports interpersonal discussions, decision making, and the sharing of emotions with limited physical contact. Within *social space,* small groups may engage in social or business conversations. *Public space* encourages short discussions or waves and greetings from a distance. Touch is not possible, but unique communication signs, such as a wink or a disapproving look, may travel between persons who know each other well.

Extensions of Hall's work in proxemics has found practical applications in areas such as family therapy. Therapists have written about observing family seating patterns for clues to a family's hierarchy and affiliation patterns (Haley 1976; Minuchin 1974). In addition, the area of proxemics has yielded some interesting and consistent variations across age, gender, and culture (McGoldrick, Pearce, and Giordano 1982; McGoldrick, Anderson, and Walsh 1989).

***Territory*** Territoriality, a basic concept in the study of animal behavior, involves behavior by which an animal lays claim to an area and defends it against members of its own species. Territoriality for people is concerned with places for "doing" things: places to learn, places to play, and safe places to hide. Hall relates territory to the concepts of fixed feature space when he suggests,

> The boundaries of the territories remain reasonably constant, the territory is in every sense of the word an extension of the organism which is marked by visual, vocal, and olfactory signs and, therefore, it is relatively "fixed" (9).

Family territory may be understood as an area that a member of a close-knit group in joint tenancy claims and will "defend." Individual family members may claim territory within the system. In other words, a family or a person stakes out real or imagined space and lays personal claim to it.

Those who own a territory or others who recognize the territory, behave in particular ways as they approach the boundary, even if it is not marked by fences, walls, or other barriers. Scheflen suggests that small territories may be marked by postural behavior, such as an arm that defends a space, or by the placement of a possession. People defend their territory through verbal and nonverbal communication strategies, such as aggression or dominance.

Territory in a home may be as real as "my parents' room," or as nonphysical as "Mike's part of the yard." Places may be recognized as belonging to someone by decrees ("This is my chair"), by tenure ("I always sat there"), by markers ("We left our books here because we were coming back"), or by agreement ("We each have one drawer"). If you think about your own home, you should be able to identify numerous territorial behaviors by which members declare their spatial demands and their desire for privacy within certain space. Yet, without mutual agreement among those who believe the territory is "theirs" and other potential users, the concept of limited use may eventually disappear or conflicts about the use will arise.

***Privacy*** may be viewed as the "claims of individuals, groups, or institutions to determine for themselves when, how, and to what extent information about them is communicated to others" (Westin 1967, 10). Privacy maintains an individual's need for personal autonomy, through which he or she can control the environment, including the ability to choose to be alone or to have private communication with another. Privacy regulation refers to how people manage the psychological and physical boundaries between themselves and others (Werner, Altman, and Brown 1992). The ability to regulate privacy varies with socioeconomic status since poor families often live in crowded dwellings and have litte power to regulate their space:

---

*In our family, there seems to be a careful balance between allowing someone to have total personal control of space, and allowing everyone to go wherever they please. A rule is that when a door is shut, a person wants to be left alone and nobody should enter the room without knocking and getting permission first. Friends frequently enter our home at various hours and often unannounced without disruption or question. The only exceptions to this rule occur when family members have set aside time to be home alone together, and such visits seem to be intrusions. Then we try to cut the visit short so we can enjoy our time alone with each other.*

---

Some dwellings encourage such privacy while others cannot or do not. If you share a home with nine others and a bedroom with three others, privacy may be a luxury attained only outside the home. Yet, in certain households with ample physical space, privacy is restricted by family rules or one's own perceptions. Privacy and territory interrelate to provide the means of protective communication, such as the sharing of confidences, problems, and affection.

As with spatial distance, territory and privacy are relative within and between cultures. In certain types of homes, personal places and possessions are held in high regard, whereas in others, total sharing is the norm. One gains privacy in some cultures by isolation, whereas in other cultures, psychological withdrawal permits privacy within a group. In his study of urban families, Scheflen asked women, "What do you do when you want to be alone?" and discovered that one half of the Puerto Rican wives "did not comprehend the implication of the question in American middle-class terms. They said they never wanted to be alone ... the other half said they went home to see family" (437). The concept did not have the same meaning across cultures.

## Time

Familial relationships are influenced by cultural and historical patterns, and unfold in temporal routines and rhythms involving mundane daily events and occasional important ceremonies (Brown, Werner, and Altman; Werner and Baxter 1993). The way in which a family lives in time interacts with how it lives in space. Kantor and Lehr (1976) discuss families' use of time as orientation, clocking and synchronization. Families or individuals may experience an *orientation* toward the past or future, which supersedes life in the present. Each individual also has a time orientation. Some people live in the "good old days" and their communication reflects a respect for, or delight in, yesterday. A present orientation reflects a concern for the "here and now." Current relationships are valued and current joys and sorrows take top priority; less time is spent reminiscing or planning than is spent on daily issues. A future orientation emphasizes what is to come. Planning, dreaming, or scheming characterize such a mind set and have typified many American families on their way to "the good life." Such orientations may be reflected in household furnishings, contacts with kin, patterns of friendship, attitudes toward money, and career planning (Reiss et al.). Time is a commodity, the use of which indicates much about a family's view of the world.

*Clocking* refers to the daily use of time. It regulates the order, frequency, length, and pace of immediate events. Certain family rules, such as who talks first in certain situations or who gets the last word, may be part of a subtle sequencing pattern. On a more obvious level, some families must establish functional rituals for moving into a day:

---

*In our attempt to maintain a two-career family with two small children, we have become very organized with specific morning patterns so we can get out of the house on time and in a good frame of mind. I get up and start to make coffee. My wife then gets out of bed, dresses, and starts to wake our*

(continued on page 384)

*daughters. When they come into the kitchen, I dress while Helen fixes the rest of breakfast. During the week, no one eats breakfast until they are dressed and ready to go. This way we can have a semi-peaceful morning, talk a little, and minimize the conflict.*

---

Families clock how often and for how long things may be done such as time with friends or length of disagreements. All families need some built-in repetition and guidelines to keep their lives functional. Clocking also refers to the speed with which a day is lived. Do you do fifty-two things and call it a "good day," or do you like to take things easy and maintain a slower pace? Pacing varies with age, health, and mental state. Large variations in pacing patterns often lead to conflict among family members.

*Synchronization* is the process of maintaining a program for regulating the overall and day-to-day life of a family. Often, this is done through discussing how things are going and setting or reaffirming plans and priorities. Family members integrate individual schedules to create an overall approach to spending time. A spouse may turn down a position that requires a great deal of travel because it would take time away from the family. A couple may agree to a long-term separation because a commuter marriage would establish each partner's career. Werner and Baxter suggest synchrony refers to "the willingness and ability of two partners to coordinate their individual cycles into an overall rhythm" (333). Partners and family members are most satisfied when there is a "fit" in rhythms. Family discontent may lead to a reorganization of original priorities. Some families may establish respect for individual "clocks," whereas others may dictate a "family clock" to which everyone must adhere. The use of time varies according to culture; Northern European families may stress punctuality, whereas Latin-American families may not recognize this as a value.

Space and time are synchronized to some degree in families as members go about the patterned routines of their lives. There may be appropriate times for being alone and times when togetherness is important. Children may be allowed to play in adult spaces until an adult indicates that the space is taken. Holidays may require the presence of all family members in a particular space for a specified time, particularly if their themes and images stress togetherness. Gender beliefs influence how time may be spent "legitimately" by males or females. The degree of synchronization may distinguish well-functioning families from those experiencing conflict and/or change. Listen to the metaphors people use for time. Do they see time in economic terms, as something to save, buy, or spend, or do they see it as a gift to be enjoyed, made the most of, or shared? Underlying beliefs about time are played out in family discussions and in the messages members receive about "using" time. Space and time are important dimensions of a family's communication context influencing their sense of home and their relations with each other.

## THE HOME WORLD: OUTSIDE AND INSIDE

Sometimes the terms "home" and "house" (or apartment) are used synonymously, although the words may carry different meanings. Not all houses or apartments qualify as "homes." Many environment scholars believe that a "person's concept of home is better understood as a *relationship* to such an environment, rather than the environment itself" (Horwitz and Tognoli 1982, 335). A house has strong psychological and social meaning since "It is part of the experience of dwelling—something we so, a way of weaving up a life in particular geographical spaces" (Saegert 1985, 287). Brown, Werner, and Altman discuss creating a home as a type of placemaking and suggest placemaking activities include particular patterns of territoriality, privacy regulations, rituals, use of objects, and ongoing maintenance that contribute to a sense of identity and meaning in the world. The physical dwelling is an important factor in the development of a sense of home, which must be examined in conjunction with related community factors. Thus, we will examine the home within its environment to understand how it influences the family.

A home influences the interactions that occur within it, and around it since its structure, design, and location affect the development of relationships with oneself and between family members, friends, and strangers (Lawrence 1987; Werner 1987). In his work on environment and interaction, psychologist Osmond (1970) distinguished between sociofugal and sociopetal space. *Sociofugal space* discourages human interaction; *sociopetal space* supports it. "Sociopetality is that quality which encourages, fosters, and even enforces the development of stable interpersonal relationships and which may be found in small face-to-face groups, in home or circular wards" (576). Both the exterior and interior of a house contributes to the creation of relational experiences for the family members. In addition, the design and use of home interiors and their external appearance reflect cultural and social values (Lawrence 1987).

### Exterior Arrangements

A dwelling's exterior may affect the interactions of family members with the community at large and specifically with neighbors. Some studies of homogeneous populations indicate that housing planned for easy social interaction (such as doors opening on a common court or homes built around a cul-de-sac) promote neighborliness (Chilman 1978). Yet some homogeneous populations are living in neighborhoods of violence where the external environment reflects continual danger and homes attempt to function as fortresses. The exterior of a dwelling may be understood by examining its placement, the surrounding community, and the management of boundaries.

***Housing Placement*** Housing placement influences with whom you interact and therefore, to some extent, with whom you develop friendships. In a famous study, researchers Festinger, Schachter, and Back (1950) examined the development of friendships in a new housing project for married students. This development consisted of apartment structures arranged in U-shaped courts with the two end-structures facing the street. They were able to demonstrate that the distance between apartments and the direction in which an apartment faced affected friendships. Friendships developed more frequently between next-door neighbors and less frequently between persons who lived in apartments separated by more than four or five other apartments. In addition, those who lived near the mailboxes, stairways, entrances, and exits tended to make more friends because they encountered other residents regularly. Such findings remain current even today. If your front or back door leads into a heavily trafficked area, you have a greater chance of developing neighborhood relationships and becoming a central part of the communication network. Yet perception of similarity with neighbors also affects contacts. In a study of a multicultural urban apartment housing community, Silverman (1992) found where neighbors were of different cultures, jurisdictional problems, such as shared patio space or noise levels, were magnified. Residents who were afraid to voice complaints over minor issues remained frustrated by them. They did not know how to disagree with diverse neighbors and resolve problems.

***The Neighborhood*** The surrounding territory partially dictates a family's way of relating to the outside world. A planned community may expect certain social responses from its individual households; those who choose to live another life-style may find themselves ostracized. Particular communities may set expectations for attendance at coffee klatches or participation in the local Fourth of July parade—activities that require space and time commitments. As families move from one home to another, a new community influences their interactions with each other and with the neighbors.

Planned communities continue to expand, ranging from such highly structured communities as Reston, Virginia, to more informal communities developed by an individual planner. Some individuals and families are establishing long-term commitments to build community and share space such as the Casatos or "Cheesecake" project. The Casatos project involves eleven partners, 4 married couples and 3 women (Louie 1994) who have made a commitment to share their later years together in a carefully designed space believing that activity and strong friendships will make aging more productive. Co-housing communities are homes and neighborhoods created by a group who agree to share tasks such as cooking, child care, and yard maintenance (Dreyfous 1994). These may be an oversized home, a small neighborhood, or a set of apartments (McCarmant and Durrett 1994). Such lifestyles imply that boundaries and expectation must be negotiated through regular discussion. Even some high-rise buildings attempt to foster a sense of community through the integration of stores, athletic facilities, and movie theaters into their overall construction plans. The current aging of the U.S. population points toward continued growth of retirement communities, such as Sun City, Arizona (Baker 1984). Most of these communal opportunities are available only to those of mid-to-high socioeconomic status.

In contrast, certain communities may prevent attempts at socialization or communication because the territory is "unsafe." Scheflen conducted a classic study of 1,200 African-American, Puerto Rican, and Eastern European families living in the East Tremont urban ghetto in upper Manhattan. He reported:

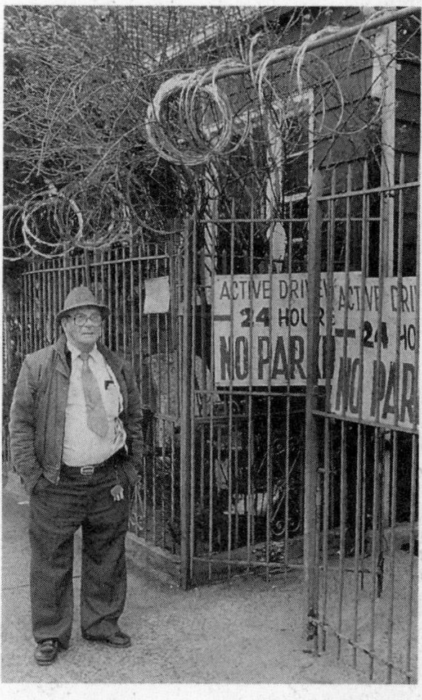

A home's exterior affects interactions of family members with the community.

> [Within this area] a black teenager can often go out for the evening. But the Puerto Rican child may not even be allowed to go out of the apartment let alone the street or to a neighbor's house. The mother may consider any area outside the apartment to be dangerous, and often she is right. (437)

In St. Louis, Missouri, urban high-rise buildings in the Pruitt Igoe housing project were leveled because of the dangerous conditions created by this type of housing. Life in "unsafe" territory is accompanied by many rules about whom not to talk to in order to be safe. The architecture reflects this fear. Gonzalez (1993) suggests fear affects a range of the less well- off neighborhoods, from working class to the most hard pressed, saying:

> The architecture of fear has transformed the landscape with urban fortifications along bunkerlike blocks where a frontier mentality guides the daily routine. .... Front porches once used for socializing have given way to caged-in entry ways; bricked up windows keep out both intruders and sunlight, and miles of razor ribbon lace more and more gates. (2,18)

Life in such an environment creates a mental state captured by one resident who reported "When I come home I feel like I'm entering a jail, and psychologically I am." Children in urban inner city areas may encounter violence regularly and randomly. In a recent study of Cleveland and Denver, large numbers of adolescents witnessed knife attacks, stabbings, and shootings (Goldberg 1994).

Certain territories encourage or permit particular behaviors. For example, a single family home may not encourage romantic behavior in teenagers due to the presence of other family members, but the car or a secluded hallway may provide the environment for such behavior:

---

*I observed a difference in the socialization process in my housing complex and the project building. My peers in the project stayed out much later and had more freedom to go places than those in the housing complex. They began to have sexual intercourse and children at an earlier age. I observed intimate behavior when I visited my friends, while on the elevator or walking up the stairs. The parents knew what their kids were doing and acknowledged the fact by trying to get them to use some type of birth control. They had boyfriends before my friends from the housing complex and I did and they began kissing early in grammar school.*

---

The growing multiculturalism of United States society is reflected in changing neighborhoods, yet such change may be difficult. In some cases communities are slow to support members who represent differences. For example, African-American families in suburbia often found themselves rejected and isolated by their new neighbors. They also felt estranged from the friends, relations, and associates they left behind in the city (Billingsley 1988).

An increasing architectural concern is the development of appropriate housing for the aged. A growing awareness exists of the need for elder housing that (1) encourages interaction and (2) stimulates participation in new activities (Jordan 1984). Thus, buildings designed for senior citizens may have carefully designed eating or recreation areas and programs ranging from drama and exercise classes to intergenerational day care experiences. Many communities are developing day care centers for elderly citizens in order to expand their network of regular contacts.

## Boundary Management

One purpose of home design is to distinguish between public and private domains (Lawrence 1987). Each family engages in managing its boundaries to regulate physical traffic across its borders. Kantor and Lehr (1976) call this process *bounding*. Through bounding a family sets a perimeter and defends its territory. It says, "This is ours, we are safe here" (68). It may defend these territorial borders through the use of devices to regulate entrance to the home. Buzzers, shades, peepholes, bushes, and double locks all provide some privacy and control. At the extreme, razor ribbon or high fences are used. Children may experience a designated territory, which is permitted for safe exploration. In housing projects, there may be no safety beyond the front door, so the boundary may be synonymous with the apartment doorway. In other areas, a neighbor's yard or the road in front may be the limits. A family can create boundaries by turning off the phone, establishing rules or hours for visiting, and appearing not to have the time for interaction. Lack of availability sends a temporal message about the desire for limited interaction.

A family with flexible boundaries in a safe territory may indicate a desire for interaction by using the openings of a house to invite in the outside world. Neighborhood children may run through unlocked doors or friends may shout through the window. In some urban communities, an apartment may overflow to a porch, steps, or the street below where folding chairs extend the living room to the sidewalk. A less-scheduled, flexible family can make time for these distractions more easily than a family that runs on a tight clock.

## Interior Arrangement

Home interiors are organized spatially and temporally. The fixed and semi-fixed feature spaces stand as supports for, or as barriers to, interpersonal communication. The interior design influences how much privacy can be attained and how easily members can come together, whereas the furnishings and decor contain messages about how to relate and what is valued. Each of these factors reflect cultural values.

***Rooms and Floor Plan*** One way to view a house spatially is to start with the floor plan and determine the possible relationships that may or may not occur based on space arrangement. Interpersonal communication and general living activities may be seen in relation to the public and private zones of a home (Kennedy 1953; Werner 1987). The more public zones provide great possibilities for social interaction, whereas the more private zones exclude persons from some or all interpersonal contact. Different areas of the home may be associated with specific family functions and, hence, to the system and subsystem boundaries. Various levels and types of interactions are acceptable in different spaces, reflected in the range of highly interpersonal to highly private spaces. As you move through a home, the spaces may become more highly private to members, while persons outside the system or subsystem may be excluded from certain spaces. In many homes, there are spaces for interpersonal interactions with guests, close friends, and other family members. For example, in one family, visitors may have access to living, dining, and kitchen areas but may not enter the bedrooms. In another family, there may be a formal living area for socializing with guests and a family room for relaxing and talking with family members. Some families establish clear spatial boundaries for nonmembers; others do not.

---

*If I have friends I'm close with over, we don't go into the dining room. We sit in the kitchen, talk, and drink coffee. If it's someone I don't know well, we go into the living room.*

---

Member boundaries may vary. Some families set rigid standards for privacy. In such cases, bathrooms and bedrooms are locked, and special possessions are concealed (Reiss). On the other hand, you may come from a family where one brother may be showering, the next brushing his teeth, and another urinating in the same small bathroom. Such variables as age, gender, culture, and family size all interact with the spatial dimension.

The actual floor plan can dictate which persons will have the greatest contact and, potentially, the greatest communication. If you share adjoining territories with your sister, you are more likely to communicate with her than with some other family members. If your mother spends more time in a central place, such as the kitchen, she is more likely to serve as a network hub, as in the following example:

---

*When my mother remarried, she married a widower with eight children, which meant that our family suddenly had twelve children, ten of whom lived at home. This led Mom and Grant to remodel the attic as a dormer, where they created more bedrooms on the second floor. This really determined the way relationships developed in the family. I didn't see much of the boys who stayed upstairs or who were out playing sports. Because we were on the same floor and always were in and out of each other's rooms, all the girls became really close, and some of us would sit up until 2:00 in the morning talking about people and things.*

---

Becker (1994) maintains a home should be viewed as a "nesting ground" or place of refuge which brings people together. He suggest family fragmentation can be presented by a "communications system of architecture" which opens up living areas so people cannot retreat from each other.

The size of a dwelling affects the distances between the people in it. Small apartments force greater contact than do larger houses. Yet, even when space is held constant, families differ in their use of informal space. Crane et al. (1987) report spatial distance is an indicator of conflicted marital relationships since distressed couples tended to converse at greater distances than non-distressed ones. A study of the daily experiences of couples showed that happy couples spent more time together at home, especially for leisure activities, than unhappy couples (Kirchler 1988).

Space, in some houses, may discourage communication among family members. Although in previous generations, children shared beds and rooms; many children today have separate rooms equipped for autonomous living. This may lead to limited experience in certain interpersonal encounters. If each child has a room and even a television set and stereo, there may be little reason to learn sharing and problem solving skills. Thus, two children do not have to decide together, for example, which television show to watch, rather "You watch your show, I'll watch mine." Similarly, if the child and parent are at odds, the child can easily say, "I'm going to my room." That room then becomes an escape hatch when personal relationships falter. In large homes, no one may know if the others are home or what they are doing.

Yet, in many cases, small, cramped quarters result in difficulties or pressure. For example, a study of 200 families suggests that there is a marked difference in stress levels between families with one bathroom and families with a small half-bath in addition to the bathroom (Guenther 1984). A new set of stresses befalls a divorced parent when children visit, and the space adequate for one or two adults does not comfortably hold four or five. Families experiencing the "refilling nest" syndrome report stress as adult children return to live at home. Many of today's families are attempting to integrate home and occupational spheres. Just as multiple simultaneous roles have been thought to be stress-producing for farm wives (Berkowitz and Perkings 1984), the new rise of cottage industries and part-time work at home adds stress to family interaction. The rise in telecommuting has forced many families to renegotiate the use of space and time since Mom or Dad are "there but really not there." Families are confronted with managing an ever present work/home boundary issue.

Countless immigrant and poor families experience severe family stress due to crowding. Many Asian immigrants choose to sacrifice short-term needs for adequate shelter in hopes of providing professional career education for their children. Yet, the self-sacrifices can be great. The loss of familiar environmental and social support networks makes the family's functioning more difficult (Shon and Davis 1983). Large families in Scheflen's East Tremont study lived in small apartments, and most of the time, everyone functioned in the living room. In the Puerto Rican families, all members remained in the living room either bundled together or divided between the TV area and conversational area. Few secrets or personal conversations occurred within these systems. African-American women attempted to keep the living room as a parlor, although children usually had to be allowed access to it. If company arrived, the children were likely to be sent to play in a bedroom. Conversations were more likely to be separated for "appropriate ears." Often, an overlapping of space occurred in these cramped quarters so that space was scheduled to be used according to the time of day. As Scheflen states:

> In one Puerto Rican family, breakfast occurred at a fixed time every day. Then Father went to work, the children settled down to watch television, and Mother began a highly regular schedule of chores. In the afternoon, a single visitor came, sat in a particular chair and talked with the mother. At noon each day, the older children were allowed to go out for an hour (These observations were made in the summer

> when school was not in session). Then at a fixed time, the mother cooked dinner, and the children ate in the living room. An hour later the father came home from work, sat at a small table in an alcove and had his supper served to him. Then mother cleaned up and the family settled down for an evening in the living room before the television set. In this case the same sites were used by the same people each day, according to a regular schedule of household activities. (444)

Personal and cultural traditions for use of the environment also suggest connections and separations between people and help define relationships. Rules suggest what types of people have what types of access to each other (Brown, Werner, and Altman). Individuals or subsystems may have to plan for time and space to be alone. Sometimes it may be very structured, or sometimes it seems to occur naturally, as noted in the following contrasting situations:

---

*Growing up, there was a rule in our house that no one bothered our parents before 11:00 a.m. on Saturday. Their bedroom door was locked, and it was understood they were not to be disturbed.*

---

---

*My parents still manage to have some privacy, although I don't know how, because their bedroom door has always been open to us day and night, and many times it serves as a place to go if you cannot sleep.*

---

In each family, rules evolve for having visitors locking doors, opening drawers, reading mail, or using another's things. Frequently repeated statements such as "always knock," "call before you visit," or "never open another's mail" evolve into operating rules. Sometimes status or liking can be conveyed through rule functioning. Parents may have the right to invade privacy; babies may have access to places that are off limits to teenagers or vice-versa; a favorite sibling may be able to use a special place.

For many families, mealtime has specific rituals and is a communication event that takes place in a very specific spatial and temporal setting. A study of dinner time in middle-class families with small children revealed that dinner occurred in a dining room, dining area, or kitchen at a dinner table that was almost always rectangular. The formal eating territories were distinct. Patterns guided the interaction since:

> Within families, the members sat in the same places at the table every evening. Among families, the only invariable positioning of family members at the dinner table was that the father occupied one side (the head of the table by himself). Mother's position could be either opposite him, or on his right or left. In about half of the families observed, the mother and father sat opposite each other at the table ... In over two thirds of our families the mother sat next to the youngest child in the family. (Dreyer and Dreyer 1973, 294–95)

Yet, in different socioeconomic settings, things are done differently. Scheflen found that the average ghetto kitchen measured nine by twelve feet and held cabinets, closets, sink, stove, and refrigerator. If a table existed, it was small with two or three chairs pushed against the wall. Because there were no dining rooms, all the members of large families could not physically eat together, resulting in two major adapting patterns. Some members carried their plates to the living room and ate off their laps; some of the children were fed from a small children's table in the kitchen. In the middle-class family, mothers welcomed others into their domain, but in cramped quarters, a mother usually staked out the kitchen as her territory and would not welcome "intruders."

Home life shifts as families undergo unpredictable changes such as divorce. For example, these changes are likely to involve negotiation between new partners and children about the design and management of spaces (Brown, Werner, and Altman). A key stepfamily issue involves creating a space which adequately supports the newly configured system. Divorce may force a woman and her children to move to a lower income area or to small quarters.

Finally, the home interior serves to bring people together or separate them appropriately. Kantor and Lehr capture the regulation of distance within a house with their concept of "linking." For example, a large dining room table may encourage people to come together and may set up some interaction networks. Or, because an apartment is so small that everyone needs to eat and interact in the living room, members may retreat to their rooms to study or to "regain a sunny disposition." At a family party, teenagers may be sent to the yard and basement while adults converse. Everyone may interact together, or a variety of patterns may develop. Homes are traditionally sites of family or cultural celebrations which serve to support identity and create identification. Through the linking process, family members regulate their contact within the home environment.

***Furnishings and Decor*** A home's furniture and decorations carry strong messages about how persons should communicate within that space. Some homes contain arrangements of chairs or couches in the family room conducive to relaxed conversations. Perhaps you and your best friend are allowed the privacy and time to talk for hours in your bedroom. On the other hand, you have probably seen a cavernous living room with plastic furniture covers and realized this was not the place for relaxed conversation. In his study of interpersonal discussions in living rooms, Scott found that "both the topic and the indicated relationship of the person in the other chair were significantly related to distance between chosen chairs" (35). Thus, distance may not determine, but it does affect, communication.

Additionally, the quality of communication in a home may be enhanced by artifacts that either stimulate conversation or represent an integral part of the family, which allow you to understand the inhabitants and talk about appropriate topics. Throughout the home the artifacts may reflect both individual and communal aspects of identify (Brown, Werner, and Altman). Past memories, present experiences, and future dreams of each person are linked to the objects in the environment (Csikszentmihalyi and Rochberg-Halton 1981). Intriguing pieces of art, rock collections, matchbooks, family pictures, hunting rifles, or plants may provide the stimulus for good interaction. Certain items may lead you to the "core" of the family. Symbols of religion, ethnic heritage, hobbies, and family life may indicate what is important. In their study of the meaning of things to people, Csikszentmihalyi and Rochberg-Halton found that objects such as furniture, visual art, and photographs carried special meaning reflecting ties to past events, family members, and other people (61). Eighty-two percent of the respondents cherished at least one object because it reminded them of a close relation. For example, photographs were valued as the prime vehicle for preserving the memory of family members. Women were more likely to decorate with objects that symbolize relationships and treasure those objects. Such treasured objects frequently serve as a stimulus for family stories. The childhood photographs, an old farm implement, or an elegant vase may be the repository of powerful memories. Asking a home's resident about an object may unleash a series of stories that would never have been told told without such a stimulus.

The lack of significant objects may also make a statement. One home designer indicates, "People have begun to reexamine the role of possessions in their lives—the energies they take to maintain, the ways they may restrict one's freedom—and out of this there's been a certain paring down, rather than a building up" (Murphy 1984, 98D). This may also reflect a family's low income level or signal the inability to retain anything of value in an area where stealing is a way of life.

In some cases prized possessions become the "spoils of war" since "in the last gasp of a marriage two people who failed to save a relationship may try to salvage their belongings instead" (Landis 1988). Many divorce proceedings have been delayed for months or years over key household objects or family photographs.

The aesthetic design of a room, lighting, and acoustics also play a part in influencing communication. In the often-replicated beautiful-ugly room study by Maslow and Mintz, the ugly room was variously described as producing "monotony, fatigue, headaches, discomfort, sleep, irritability, and hostility." In contrast, the beautiful room produced feelings of "pleasure, comfort, enjoyment, importance, energy, and desire to continue activity" (Knapp 1972, 31). This correlates with Mehrabian's early finding (1971) that people tend to be more pleasant in pleasant settings rather than in unpleasant settings. This does not mean to imply that effective communication depends on surroundings. Pleasant surroundings can enhance relationships if they help people become comfortable and relaxed, but so many other factors intervene that environment cannot be seen as the single influencing factor. Some researchers go so far as to say that the quality of relationships is not really affected by the quality of habitat, except in extremely adverse conditions but that "high satisfaction with home and community may ameliorate high dissatisfaction with mate or parent-child relationships" (Chilman 1978, 106).

Every family engages in "centering" behavior, or regulating space according to its values and beliefs. Thus, space reflects the family's view of itself and supports the values held by its members. There are family rules for how space is used (when one may go outside, who may be allowed in). There also may be specific ways of using things to keep the family in touch with each other. Blackboards, memo boards, and notes can keep a family in touch. Objects that remind a family of its identity and values, such as crucifixes, travel posters, or trophies, serve a centering function. Celebrations are essentially centering functions. For example, According to Brown, Werner, and Altman, "United States Christmas celebrations involve intricate weaving together of particular artifacts and practices to draw kin together." Highly cohesive families may have stronger rules about family togetherness and how to achieve it within the home than families characterized by low cohesion. Family placemaking activities impact the ability of members to relate to each other and to persons in the surrounding community. Such experiences directly tie to ethnicity, gender, and socioeconomic status, giving meaning to a family's everyday life.

## Family Fit and Environment

An ecological approach to group interaction focuses on the way human beings and their environment accommodate each other. "Good-

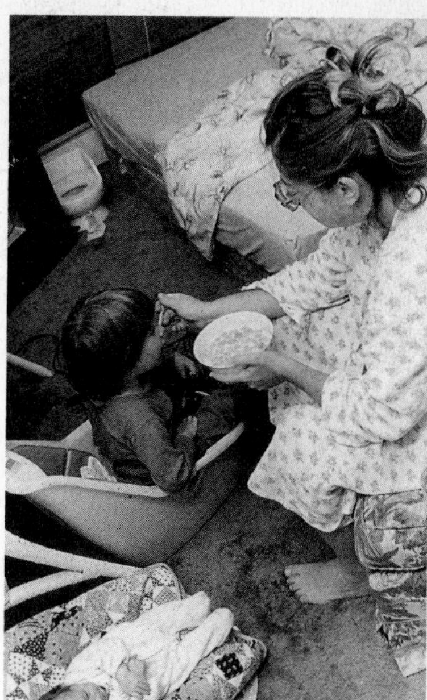

When families add members, their space needs are altered.

ness of fit" is reflected in mutual interaction, negotiation, and compromise (deHoyos 1989). The concept of "fit" has been applied to people and their home environments. Lennard and Lennard (1977) describe the "fit" between the style of family interaction and the home environment as: the isomorphic fit, complementary fit, and non-fit (58).

*Isomorphic fit* implies congruence between the family and its environment. It occurs when aspects of the environment are clear expressions of the family's identity, the way the members relate, and the way they see the outside world. Let us use the Cameron family as an example. The Camerons could be characterized as a generally cohesive and highly adaptable family with few intrafamily boundaries, who live by such themes as "We work hard and play hard" and "We stick together in hard times." The Camerons (mother, father, four boys, and one girl) bought a large, old farmhouse and have torn out some of the walls on the first floor to create more open space. The Camerons engage in outdoor activities together and exhibit a rough-and-tumble style of interpersonal interaction. The farmhouse contains a large "mudroom" for skis and assorted sporting equipment. The large kitchen provides a place where the family can congregate when someone is cooking, or a number of people can be involved in a cooking operation at once. The family room is a place that invites informality and occasional wrestling matches and storytelling evenings.

The house does not have a formal living room. The bedrooms are small, but since no one seems to spend time alone, it does not matter. The Camerons and their home are well matched.

*Complementary fit* implies a balance of opposites among two or more aspects of a family's interaction and home environment. This kind of fit can reflect the contrasting elements that exist within the family, or it can be consciously selected by a family in order to balance or counteract a special feature of family life. For example, the Muellers are a blended family with four teenagers (two from each former system) who tried their best to avoid one another when they first began their new life together. At that point in their development, interaction was difficult. The family was characterized by low cohesion and limited adaptability. Themes at this period reflected the lack of connectedness, such as "We don't get involved." In the former family homes, each child had a large, well-equipped room to which he or she retreated whenever discomfort arose. When the families merged, the parents purposefully invested in a townhouse with fewer, smaller bedrooms. This forced the two boys to room together and all four young people to spend time in common areas, such as the attractively furnished family room. The parents consciously selected a home-style that was complementary to the life-style that had evolved in their former homes.

The *non-fit* category includes those homes that are unsuited to the family's interaction pattern. Obviously, most lower-income housing falls into this category, since many families are trying to fit large numbers of people into a few tiny rooms that cannot hold them comfortably. Yet, this style need not apply solely to families economically unable to afford larger housing. When the Morris' married, they decided not to have children. During their early thirties, they built their "dream house," a wood and glass structure with such features as cathedral ceilings, open walkways and staircases, a small kitchen with a breakfast bar for all their meals, and two loft bedrooms. Their life was characterized by a belief that "We are complete as a couple"; as their energies were directed toward cultural and educational pursuits. As they approached forty, they rethought their decision and, at age thirty-nine, Sharon Morris brought twins, a boy and a girl, home to the "dream house." During the next few years, the Morris family and the house entered a non-fit stage. The unrailed walkway across the living room became a dangerous bridge, and their children could never be left alone on the second floor. Both children fell off the stairs. The lack of a regular dining area and a third bedroom became a problem. Eventually the dream house included gates, railings, plexiglass panels, and other odd additions.

The concept of fit also applies to how families use time. An isomorphic fit characterizes a family that functions according to a particular orientation and clocking pattern, which reflects that family's values. The Breznehan family consists of a father and three school-age children. Their world involves, among other things, swimming, baseball, and soccer, along with orthodontist visits and newspaper routes. This is a present- and future- oriented group of people who can adapt to tight schedules and fast pacing. Gus Breznehan's schedule is flexible, and he can adjust it relatively easily. Since family priorities include getting ahead and self-improvement, this life-style is consistent with group goals.

Grant and Jean Foster are a couple whose jobs take them to exciting places, and whose pace of life never slows down. They place great priority on their marriage and value a connected interpersonal relationship, believing that "Together we can cope with whatever life deals us." Yet, they became afraid that this hectic, work-orientated lifestyle could destroy their relationship unless they created a retreat for being together. Scorning a fashionable high-rise condominium, they bought a large, old farmhouse in a growing suburban area and dedicated themselves to redoing the home in precise historic fashion and to cultivating large flower and vegetable gardens. Except when Jean travels, they spend most of their personal time at a slower pace and in a past-orientation to consciously counteract the hectic, present-oriented pace of their daily lives. They have created a complementary style of living with time for their personal hours.

A small baby has thrown the McConnell family into a temporary non-fit situation. As a two-career, sociable couple with good positions, they had planned a lifestyle in which they would take equal responsibility for the baby, whom they expected to take to many social functions. Five months into parenthood, they became totally frustrated trying to share responsibilities, because Frank's job requires that he stay late for meetings and Myra's real-estate position requires her to drop everything and run when a potential buyer wants to talk. Although Charmaine is a healthy baby, she gets fussy and seldom sleeps through the night. She cannot be taken easily into adult situations. Thus, each parent needs more ability to live in the present and according to the baby's schedule. Each also needs time to do more around the house.

Although the examples of spatial and temporal fit have been developed separately, you can see the need for an integration of the spatial and temporal needs of a family with each other. Some people can integrate these with their levels of cohesion and adaptability for a comfortable fit, while others have real difficulty. No matter how carefully families plan, an unforseen crisis may affect their living arrangements as this salesman found in the following example:

---

*We had both looked forward to buying our first home. What we could afford was a two bedroom townhouse. This was big enough for us and for a first child when the time came. Very quickly I started to use the second bedroom as a home office and the closet filled up with computer stuff. Then my wife's mother began to suffer from Alzheimers so we took her into our home. She goes to a day care center but at night the space is tight. We try to share the room but it gets complicated. Our starter home isn't large enough and now we are saving to buy more room.*

---

Sometimes, people have to make significant changes in order to overcome their spatial and temporal situations. A big new house may lessen but not solve all of a family's conflictual problems unless new negotiating behaviors also accompany the move. Slowing down the pace by eliminating activities may have a limited effect on relationships unless the new lifestyle includes positive interpersonal messages and activities for people to share within the less frantic world. Large families in small apartments have the capacity to develop strong nurturing relationships, just as a co-parenting situation does not mean that the quality of a parent-child relationship is cut by 50 percent. Unlimited time together has the potential to enhance a relationship, but the quality of the interactions will finally determine the nature of the relationship. For example, in his study of geographically separated premarital partners, Stephen (1986) found such couples could overcome the separation and the restricted verbal/vocal means of communication via the telephone. Members of these couples worked to overcome the handicap, perhaps by focusing their talk on topics significant to the relationship or by deemphasizing the importance of talk. Lennard and Lennard explain this issue as one of choice and control: "To the extent that the interrelationships between a family and the environment are made explicit, the family's area of freedom and control is enlarged" (49–50).

Finally, a family's living experience is tied to culture. Csikzentmihalyi and Rochberg-Halton capture this point, stating "Although we live in physical environments we create cultural environments within them. Persons continually personalize and humanize the given environment as a way of both adapting to it and creating order and significance. Thus, the importance that the home has … also depends on values" (122). Spatial and temporal factors can only create an atmosphere conducive to nurturing family communication. The rest is up to the family.

## CONCLUSION

This chapter examined the family environment as a context for communication. Each family's use of space and time affects who interacts with whom, where, when, for how long, about what and in what way. A consideration of family environment indicated that a relationship exists between family members' communication and the spatial/temporal world in which the family functions.

To understand the family context you must examine spatial issues, including spatial distance, territory and privacy, and the issue of time. A family's physical dwelling must be considered within the context of its exterior arrangements including its community and the actual physical surroundings as well as its interior arrangements. The room arrangements, plus furnishings and decor play a role in establishing a communication conflict. Finally the "fit" between the family and the dimensions of time and space was explored. This chapter is based on the assumption that a way of life and its context are interdependent; environmental patterns do not determine but they do influence family interaction.

## IN REVIEW

1. Take a position and discuss: How significantly does the physical environment affect family interaction patterns?
2. Describe how the cultural dimensions of space and/or time has affected the communication patterns in a real or fictional family.
3. Using the floor plan of a home found in a magazine or newspaper ad, predict how this floor plan might affect the interaction patterns of a family who lived there.
4. Using a real or fictional family, describe the spatial and temporal "fit" between the family and its environment. If possible, cite implications for the family's communication patterns.
5. Take a position and discuss: To what extent should communities support the development of restrictive housing, i.e., housing excluding children or designed for senior citizens only? What are the communication implications of such decisions?

# 14

# Improving Family Communication

How do members of functional families live, grow, and relate to each other year after year? How do they cope with problems and changes? To what extent can family members create new communication patterns, develop different ways of loving, fighting, or making decisions? Up to this point, you have encountered a descriptive view of family interaction, indicating the role of communication in the development of family relationships. This chapter will focus on functional families and how people make choices to reach or keep satisfying family relationships by relying on their communication knowledge and skills.

Many people believe that life happens *to* them, giving them no sense of control or ability to improve on human relationships. Thus these people become reactors, taking no responsibility for their part in the problem or for change in relationships. Other persons serve as actors, believing they can make personal changes and co-create constructive changes within their relationships. The differences between a reactor and an actor are captured in the following example:

---

*"That's the way I am. Take me or leave me" was the common comment of my first husband. He believed that if you had to work on a relationship there was something wrong with it. Needless to say after a few years we dissolved the marriage. Now I am engaged to a man who wants to talk and think about how to keep a relationship growing over a lifetime. We have even had some premarital counseling to explore important issues before the marriage. Life is very different when both people are open to change.*

---

As human systems, families have the potential to grow in chosen directions, although such growth may require great risk, effort, and pain. The systems perspective implies that whenever change is attempted by some members, it may be resisted by the other members who wish to keep their system in balance no matter how dysfunctional that balance is. It is difficult, although not impossible, for an individual to initiate change in the system. Change is more easily accomplished when most or all members are committed to an alternative way of relating. Also, it is difficult for members of the system to recognize certain patterns they are caught in. It may take a third party or clearheaded objective analysis to recognize a destructive pattern. From a transactional or symbolic interaction perspective, change depends on one's ability to understand the other, to discover the meanings underlying one's own actions, and that of other family members.

There is no "one right way" for all families to behave—the members of each family have to discover what works well for their system. A family's unique membership, family-of-origin patterns, ethnic heritage, and developmental stage influences this process. Communication may be considered the cornerstone for changing family systems but the outcome is that functional communication will appear different across families.

This book has focused on healthy, or functional families, rather than severely troubled or dysfunctional ones, recognizing that every functional family experiences alternating periods of ease and stress. Yet, distinguishing between healthy/unhealthy in an either-or manner does not reflect reality. Families must be considered on a continuum ranging from severely dysfunctional to optimally functional.

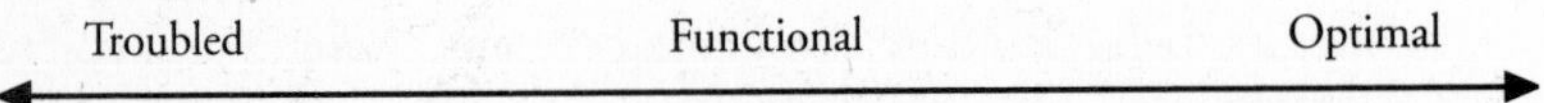


As you might imagine, few families remain at the optimal end extreme indefinitely because of tension caused by developmental or unpredictable stress, yet many do function within the functional to optional range over long periods of time. The question is: How do they do it? This chapter will attempt to answer that question by exploring: (1) factors that characterize functional to optimal families with an emphasis on communication and (2) personal, educational, and therapeutic approaches for creating and maintaining effective communication within families.

As you have lived in and observed families over the years you must have found some that appeared to work well. People probably seemed to "have it all together." Yet, each of these functional families probably reflected differences as well as similarities in the ways members related to each other. Each family shares the systems characteristic of equifinality demonstrating many ways to achieve the same end. Therefore highly functional families exhibit both similarities and differences in all areas of living, including their communication.

## PERSPECTIVES OF THE HIGHLY FUNCTIONING FAMILY

In recent years much attention has been given to family strengths and well-family functioning both in professional circles and through the popular media. The following sections highlight representative views of academic and therapeutic experts as well as more popular advice. As you read these consider the decade in which some of the views were expressed and remember most experts were not taking family types or cultural variations into consideration. Thus, you may recognize limitations of the perspectives.

### Academic/Therapeutic Views

Just as there is no one right way to be a family, there is no one family scholar who has all the answers. Each reflects his or her own professional and personal orientation to family life, as evidenced by the emphasis given to varied areas of concern. Henry (1973), in his classic work on family functioning studied five dysfunctional families intensively identifying the following characteristics of family psychopathology: (1) interactions are highly complex, (2) there is more cruelty and less compassion, (3) one person, usually a child, is viewed as an "enemy" and treated as a scapegoat, (4) members do not know how to restrain their reactions appropriately, (5) means of satisfaction are distorted so boundaries may be blurred, (6) life is taken too seriously, and (7) misperceptions govern interactions as sick members are treated as if well, or young members treated as if old (Bochner and Eisenberg 1987).

In contrast, one may reverse Henry's findings and hypothesize that functional families may exhibit the following characteristics: (1) interactions are patterned and meaningful, (2) there is more compassion and less cruelty, (3) persons are not scapegoats because problems are identified with the appropriate persons, (4) members exhibit appropriate self restraint, (5) boundaries are clear, (6) life includes joy and humor, and (7) misperceptions are minimal.

Virginia Satir (1988) maintains that untroubled and nurturing families demonstrate the following patterns: "self-worth is high; communication is direct, clear, specific, and honest; rules are flexible, human, appropriate, and subject to change; and the linking to society is open and hopeful" (4). In other words, she sees that untroubled families contain people who feel good about themselves, level with each other, function within a flexible system of rules, and whose boundaries are flexible enough to permit extensive contact with new people and ideas. Walsh (1993) echoes these ideas, maintaining clarity, consistency, and predictability in patterns of interaction, open communication, effective problem solving and conflict resolution processes are important in family functioning. Walsh and Satir's ideas may need to be adapted across cultures since such open communication may not be possible or desirable for every family.

Yet Satir's call for directness and clarity is critical as indicated by the following:

---

*My grandmother has always sworn that my sister looked just like her daughter, Lorraine, who died at sixteen. She has tried to replace her daughter with her first granddaughter in the hopes of reviving a communication pattern that once existed but now is gone. Yet, my sister Lori has had to fight this distorted perception all her life, and her communication with Grandma is very confused.*

---

In his early research on family competence, Beavers (1976) viewed families on a continuum of functioning, ranging from severely disturbed to mid-range to healthy. He details each of these continuum locations in terms of five major areas: power structure, degree of individuation, acceptance of separation and loss, perception of reality, and affect. His data suggests that families with adaptive, well functioning offspring have a structure of shared power, great appreciation and encouragement of individuation, and ability to accept separation and loss realistically. Additionally, they have a "family mythology consistent with the reality as seen by outside observers, a strong sense of the passage of time and the inevitability of change, and a warm and expressive feeling tone"(80). Beavers describes healthy families as "skillful interpersonally" and with members who can participate in and enjoy negotiation, respect views of others, share openly about themselves, see anger as symptomatic of necessary changes, view sexual interest as positive, and establish meaningful encounters outside the family system. He found that the most effective families use humor, tenderness, warmth, and hopefulness to relate. Family members make negative feelings known but do so with a keen awareness of whom or what they dislike. Also, they are supportive while doing so. Effective families more readily recognize their conflicts, deal with them promptly, and find solutions quickly.

In his later work, Beavers (1982) holds that well-functioning families consciously operate from a systems orientation, characterized by a flexible position on human behavior. In short, family members intuitively adopt a systems perspective. This does not mean the family members know technical systems terminology. Rather, it means family members maintain a flexible position on human behavior.

Beavers describes the four basic intuitive assumptions of families with a flexible systems orientation as follows:

> 1. An individual needs a group, a human system, for identity and satisfaction.
>
> 2. Causes and effects are interchangeable.
>
> 3. Any human behavior is the result of many variables rather than one "cause." Therefore, simplistic solutions are questioned.
>
> 4. Human beings are limited and finite. No one is absolutely helpless or absolutely powerful in a relationship (45).

In families holding the first assumption, members presume that people do not exist in vacuums but that human needs are met through relationships. Even after children from these families are grown they seek a sense of human community in new family systems or social networks. Holding the second assumption reflects an understanding of mutual influence. Family members see actions as both responses and as stimuli to other actions. For example, anger in one person promotes withdrawal in another and that withdrawal promotes anger and so on.

The third assumption recognizes that human behavior reflects many influences. Beavers describes this clearly by listing some possible familial explanations for why a three-year-old's spilled his or her milk. Possible explanations include (1) accident—no motive, (2) interpersonal meaning—child is angry with mother, (3) child is tired, (4) glass is too heavy or large for child's hand (145). Whereas a dysfunctional family may always attribute spilled milk to one set explanation, e.g., child is angry, an optimally functioning family's responses vary according to each situation. Holding the final assumption implies an awareness that humans are fallible and that self-esteem comes from relative competence. Total control over one's own life or the lives of others is impossible, but one should aim to be responsible. Striving for goals in a realistic way is desirable. In the following description of a stepparent, the speaker captures Beaver's ideas:

---

*My stepfather represents the kind of parent I would like to become. He seems to operate from a basic belief of optimism and faith in people. He usually can see both sides of an issue, can see both parties' points of view and tries to create solutions without dumping blame on one person. He says "You do your best and go on."*

---

In their recent summary of work on family process Bochner and Eisenberg (1987) summarize the following features as characteristic of optimal family functioning: (1) Strong sense of trust. Members rarely take oppositional attitudes and avoid blaming each other. (2) Enjoyment. Optimal families are spontaneous, witty, and humorous. (3) Lack of preoccupation with themselves. They do not over analyze their problems looking for hidden motives. Life is not taken too seriously. (4) Maintenance of conventional boundaries reflecting a strong parental coalition, and clear sense of hierarchy (559).

Although he does not list specific desirable characteristics, Gottman (1994) describes a relatively constant 5:1 ratio of positive to negative interactions saying, "Marriages seem to thrive on, proportionately, a little negativity and a lot of positivity" (45). He speculates that conflict and negativity are normal but suggests that in stable marriages the positive experience are significantly higher than the negative ones. Such a ratio concept could well be applied to entire families. Similarly, Notarius and Markman (1993) report the ability to manage conflict is a key factor in couple functioning. Many other experts attempt to describe well functioning families with similar conclusions (Barnhill 1979; Gantman 1980; Ammons and Stinnett 1980; Visher and Visher 1993; Foster 1993).

Almost all experts, such as those cited, speak to the centrality of effective communication in well functioning family systems. Fitzpatrick (1987) suggests the strong correlations between marital satisfaction and self-reports of communication behavior may constitute evidence for strongly held beliefs about the role of communication in marriage, that is, the happily married believe that they have remarkably good communication with their spouses. The same beliefs may be held by those in well functioning family systems.

## Popular Advice

Just enter any bookstore, video store, or shopping mall and you will be surrounded by books, magazines, audio tapes, and videotapes, all addressing the issues of "How to Have a Healthy Marriage," "How to Create a Happy Family." Most of the more popular advice literature, based on expert opinion and research, supports the positions of more academic experts but presents the ideas in more readable and prescriptive language. Some popular material directly reflects particular religious or moral positions, or reflects the life changing experience of the author.

In her groundbreaking book *Families*, journalist Howard (1978) presented another conception of functioning families. The author traveled across the country, interviewing the members of various types of family systems (two-percent biological, blended, single-parent, and extended, including social, racial, and sexual variations) in an attempt to understand what makes them work well. In her conclusion, she listed the general characteristics of what she calls "good" families (241–45):

1. Good families have a chief, heroine, or founder—someone around whom others cluster. Such a person may appear in different generations, but somehow this figure set an achievement level and inspired stories that influenced others.

2. Good families have a switchboard operator someone who keeps track of what the others are up to. This person also may be the archivist who tells stories or keeps photographs or albums that document the family's continuity.

3. Good families are much to all of their members but everything to none. Links to the outside are strong, and boundaries are not so tight that people cannot become passionately involved in nonfamily activities.

4. Good families are hospitable—there are surrounding rings of relatives and friends who are cared about and supported, just as they serve as the family's support system and as extended family members in many cases.

5. Good families deal directly with problems. Problems and pains are not avoided in hopes they will disappear. Communication is open, and any topic may be addressed.

6. Good families prize their rituals. These may be the formal traditions of Passover, Christmas, birthdays, funerals, or the informal ones unique to the individual family or clan—the annual Fourth of July picnic—that becomes a unifying ritual.

---

*I have come to realize the importance of traditions and rituals in families. When my father married my stepmother she spent a great deal of time and energy creating ways to celebrate holidays. We had celebrations for Valentine's Day, Halloween, as well as the usual big ones. At first it seemed rather silly but over the years I have come to look forward to seeing the decorations and participating in the preparations since these*

(continued on page 410)

*events seem to bind us together. They are part of our identity as a family and give me a sense of place and belonging.*

---

7. Good families are affectionate and willing to demonstrate and share that affection with other family members. Children learn this pattern of affection from their first moments.

8. Good families have a sense of place—a sense of belonging that may be tied to a specific geographic location or to the mementos that make a house a home for specific individuals—the old dining room table, the Precious Moments figurines, or the photographs that declare "This is home." You may find comfort in being a Bostonian or an Iowan, or you may carry with you important objects that symbolize roots and family connectedness.

9. Good families find a way to connect to posterity. For many, this involves having children; for others, it means becoming involved in a sense of the generation—connecting to the children in some way.

10. Good families honor their elders. The wider the age range, the stronger the clan. This may involve biological or "adopted" grandparents and vice versa, but strong families have a sense of generations (241–245).

In addition to many journalistic views, key family counselors and researchers have produced more popular works for a general audience. In a survey of professionals in family-related areas, Curran (1983) found "the ability to communicate and listen" selected most frequently as an indicator of family health. She lists these hallmarks of healthy families:

1. Parents demonstrate a close relationship.
2. Parents have control over TV.
3. All family members can listen and respond.
4. Family recognizes and values nonverbal messages.
5. Family respects individual feelings and independent thinking.
6. Family avoids turn-off and put-down phrases.
7. Family members interrupt, but equally.
8. Family processes disputes into reconciliations (55).

After studying more than 3,000 families, family researchers, DeFrain and Stinnett (1985) listed six crucial traits of strong families.

1. Family members are committed to each other. Family unity is valued.

2. Family members spend a good deal of time—quality time—together.

3. Family members show appreciation for each other.

4. Family members have good communication skills and spend a lot of time talking to each other.

5. Family members view crises and stresses as opportunities for growth.

6. Family members reflect spiritual wellness, a sense of a greater power which gives them strength or purpose.

In a more specifically directed work, *Second Marriage*, Stuart and Jacobson (1985) discuss issues common to remarriage and suggest beliefs, attitudes which characterized a workable second marriage:

1. Realistic expectations that every marriage has good and bad times.

2. The willingness to examine your role in every positive and negative exchange in the relationship.

3. The willingness to consider everything negotiable, with no demands that your partner accept your way of doing things without fair consideration of alternatives.

4. The willingness to consistently learn to understand your partner's point of view.

5. A commitment to try different ways of doing things long enough to see if the new way works.

6. The maturity to forgive your partner for mistakes made in good faith efforts to make your marriage better.

As the members of stepfamilies increase exponentially, popular advice to such families does the same (Berman 1986; Bernstein 1989; Einstein and Albert 1986; Visher and Visher 1993; Bloomfield 1993). Each of these contain suggestions which might apply to any family form, plus special issues unique to stepfamilies.

You can find thousands of pages of prose detailing how happy or functional families live, or how they should live. Yet, what is good for a relationships cannot be considered apart from what people think is good for a relationship. These creative relational standards are the products of member negotiation and represent belief in structures. As you read these descriptive and prescriptive views on well-family functioning, what is your personal reaction? Are these views too idealistic? Too culture specific? What characteristics would you defend as critical to well-family functioning according to your creative relational standard?

## Author Views

Your authors hold strong beliefs about the healthy family, based on our concern for communication within such a system reflecting many of the issues introduced in earlier chapters. Our beliefs may be stated as follows:

> A healthy family recognizes the interdependence of all members of the system and attempts to provide for growth of the system as a whole, as well as the individual members involved. Such families develop a capacity for adaptation and cohesion that avoids the extremes of the continuum; it welcomes each life stage, tries to find some joy in the present, and creates a personal network to provide support during crises. Such families exhibit levels of cohesion which allow members to feel cared for but not smothered. Family members make an effort to understand the underlying meanings of messages expressed by other members. All members find a sense of connections in the family's stories and rituals.

We have been influenced by our counseling experiences where we repeatedly see families who lack the necessary communication skills to negotiate their difficulties and an inability to understand another member's perspective. Recurring themes, boundaries, and rules from partners' family-of-origin interfere with present relationships. Basic parenting skills may be missing. Often, our task involves helping family members sort out both the values and weaknesses of past experiences and learn how they can use these in combination with the resources in their own family.

Family systems need constant and consistent nurturing. In most families, day-to-day routines overwhelm members' lives, resulting in primarily functional rather than nurturing communication patterns. Families can profit from taking time to ask, "How are we doing as a family?" and "How can we improve our communication?" Well-functioning families are able to engage in metacommunication—able to talk about how members relate to each other and how, if necessary, the current communication patterns could be strengthened.

We happen to appreciate the jazz ensemble metaphor (Wilkinson 1995) which captures the dynamics of well-functioning family.

> I like to think of the family as a jazz ensemble, where members move with the flow of what's happening around them, looking for a harmony of sorts, playing off one another, going solo at times, always respecting the talents and surprises surrounding them. Standards, yes. Expectations, always. But everyone moving with the "feel" of the moment and one another. Anyone at anytime can say or shout, "This isn't working!" and can challenge other members toward a different beat or movement or settle into a silence that regenerates spontaneous creativity and energy. We do know "family" isn't a lonely drum in the distance or a plaintive flute with hearing. Family is found in the creative energy and interplay of its members.

Strong families have learned the values of communication,, commitment, caring, and change. The following section will describe some specific strategies couples and families have used to strengthen their relationship.

## APPROACHES FOR IMPROVING FAMILY COMMUNICATION

If you believed that communication in your family should be improved, what would you do about it? Would you be willing to talk about the difficulties with other family members or to participate in a structured improvement program? As you saw in the recent chapters, a family goes through predictable developmental stresses and unpredictable external stresses, which affect the system's well-being, but often, members do not know how to help themselves deal with the difficulties.

Approaches to family change may be viewed on a continuum ranging from personal through instructional to therapeutic approaches.

Personal ←——— Instructional ———→ Therapeutic

Most of the personal and instructional approaches are designed for functional couples or families who wish to change some aspect of their relationship or wish to find ways to deal with a particular stressful situation. Some instructional and most therapeutic approaches are designed to aid a couple or family cope with a particular problem or repair a troubled relationship.

## Personal Approaches

Personal approaches include (1) seeking personal education, such as that found through books or the media, (2) engaging in conscious negotiation with partners or family members, (3) creating ongoing programs or meetings for the family members, and (4) obtaining help from friends or members of a support network.

Do you believe that a couple or family can deal with their communication problems on their own? Many individuals, couples or whole family systems have tried to change old, dysfunctional communication patterns. Frequently, these endeavors reflect a personal approach in which system members embark on the process without significant active outside support.

***Personal Education*** Concern for family issues appears widespread in all areas of society, resulting in the growth of preventive approaches designed to aid family members before things really fall apart. A walk through a local bookstore or video store reveals many books and magazine articles and ideas on improving your marital and family life, parenting skills, and adjusting to relational change. There are checklists, rules, and prescriptions for family meetings, sexual relations, and constructive conflict. Most of these prescriptions contain some directives about improving communication among family members.

Family related self-help resources continue to expand with materials developed for every type of family form. Readers or viewers find relief in discovering their problems are normal for a family or couple in a particular situation. For example, bibliotherapy has become a common tool to educate new stepfamily members and normalize their intense emotional experiences.

The "checkup" stands as an important concept in a personal negotiation approach to improving marital or family communication. In their classic work *Mirages of Marriage,* Lederer and Jackson (1968) created the concept for marital checkups, saying, "It seems to us that marriages deserve the same care and attention given our bodies, or our automobiles" (358–59). Couples or families may call for a conversation on the question: "How are we doing?"—the equivalent of the preventive medical annual physical.

***Personal Negotiation*** Family members may discuss and plan new ways to communicate or to solve problems. Based on information or instruction partners attempt to identify recurring "trouble spots" in their relationship and plan how to avoid them. They may learn to recognize times when intimacy or conflict is too threatening and find ways to acknowledge this.

Other couples create and practice their own rules for fair fighting. They may agree to avoid gunnysacking and physical abuse, or struggle to restate the other's position and to find areas of compromise. Parents may develop new vocabulary when dealing with children, reflected in their use of "I" statements rather than the blaming "you" messages. Parents and children may try to share feelings when silence or sulking would be more comfortable but less effective. Such negotiations involve a process. One meeting seldom results in permanent change, as demonstrated in the following example:

---

*In my own marriage, my wife and I have been using two mechanisms to serve as a kind of check-up on our marital relations. First, we have learned to communicate both the negative and the positive feelings we have. Second, we sit down together with no outside distractions and, while maintaining eye contact, express our innermost feelings or our current concerns. We each try very hard to listen rather than judge the other. This ritual is a special part of our relationship.*

---

Members may create quality time together to eat, sing, ride bikes, or just talk. A couple may attempt a second honeymoon. Father and son may try to find a mutual hobby or topic of mutual interest. Sometimes members wish for changes that are impossible due to lack of money, difficult schedules or illness.

You may wonder "How do these conversations actually start?" In some families, one or more members have nagging feelings that things could be different. They compare themselves to other families and see something lacking. They may encounter new ideas or models for relationships through the media, friends, or religious and educational experiences. Then, they take the risk of trying out new behaviors and evaluating their effectiveness. Such approaches take mutual cooperation. If only one member attempts to make the efforts, changes will occur more slowly and may be met with strong resistance.

***On-Going Commitments*** Long-term patterned approaches involve family members in experiences such as "couple time," or "family meetings." Couple time or family meetings occur when persons come together regularly to solve problems or improve relationships. This can be done at formal times or as part of other family rituals, as described in the following example:

---

*Sunday morning breakfasts are our sacred family time to check in and see how everyone is doing. Sometimes we eat in and other times we head for a local coffee shop, but all times we talk about family concerns. We may check practical things, like member's schedules, or we may air gripes, fears, or joys. Without these breakfasts our family conflicts might have been much greater.*

---

Many couples find their fast-paced life provides few obvious interludes for personal exploration and discussion unless that time is built into their weekly schedules. Partners, at all stages of family development and representing varied types of family forms, are carving out predictable times to be together and to "really talk." Some find their topics emerge easily and directly; others prefer to use a guidebook which prescribes topics or provides questions or evaluation material. For example, Dinkmeyer and Carlson (1984) prescribe couple time commitments, plus daily dialogues.

Family meetings or family councils provide opportunities for all family members to address mutual concerns. Rudolf Dreikurs (1964), founder of the family council movement recommends that councils be established formally as an ongoing part of family life. A definite hour on a definite day of the week should be set aside for this purpose; it should become part of family routine. Every member is expected to be present. The principles of family councils include:

> Each member has the right to bring up a problem. Each one has the right to be heard. Together, all seek for a solution to the problem, and the majority opinion is upheld. In the Family Council, the parents' voices are no higher or stronger than that of each child. The decision made at a given meeting holds for a week. (301)

Such experiences provide children with practice in discussion and decision making, which may prove extremely valuable in later family life. This approach undergirds the ideas of the STEP Program, or *Systematic Training for Effective Parenting Program* and the Stepping ahead Program.

Many religious groups recommend this approach. The Mormons' Family Home Evening is probably the most well-known family meeting program. Established in the late 1950s, the program requests Mormons to set aside an evening each week for family group meetings or activities centered around the annual guidebook *Family Home Evening,* which contains weekly lessons. These often contain ideas appropriate for improving interpersonal communication. Many of the ideas suggested for sharing require the family to use positive modes of communication. Other religious and community groups operate similar programs.

***Support Networks*** In an era when the extended family is increasingly inaccessible, individuals, couples, and families are creating informal or formal support systems to help them face family problems.

Informal support networks, such as friends and neighbors, provide adequate support for some persons. Talking to a good friend may help put things into perspective or just serve as a point of emotional release. Sometimes the support groups become a kind of extended network of friends to provide the caring their biological families cannot or will not provide (Weston 1993). In other cases a more structured support system has advantages. Currently, four out of ten Americans belong to a small group that meets regularly and provides caring and support for its members (Wuthnow 1994). Some of these take the form of an ongoing couples group in which problems are discussed and solutions shared within a context of privacy and confirmation. Many persons, such as the following speaker, attest to the importance of such groups in their lives:

---

*For eight months I have participated in a divorce recovery group through our church and it has helped me with parenting my three sons and with coping with my ex-husband's remarriage. This group has saved my sanity more than once and I have reached some important insights about loss and change.*

---

Occasionally whole families form a support network. One such approach is known as the *Family Cluster*, best described as a group of four or five families which agree to meet together periodically over an extended period of time to serve as an extended family network (Sawin 1979). The designer suggests, "when starting a new family cluster, it is usually helpful to begin with a unit of communication … communication is a vital force for group building, as well as a crucial element in the family system"(47). Today school districts are creating home-school partnership programs which include parent network support groups as well as parenting classes stressing communication skills (Kaplan 1992; Prodicano and Fisher 1992).

The previously discussed approaches are only a few of the many ways of involving individuals, families, and groups of families in enriching their relationships. Would you be willing to make the effort required to participate fully in a structured family council meeting or a support network? In addition to personal approaches, couples or individuals may attempt to improve family communication through direct instruction.

## Instructional Approaches

---

*My husband and I are team leaders for the Jewish Marriage Encounter, and we keep trying to tell our friends that every marriage should have an "annual checkup." People spend thousands of dollars on "preventative maintenance" for their cars, teeth, bodies, and homes, but how much do we spend either in dollars, effort, or time to have a marital examination? Too often in attempting to get couples to attend an Encounter weekend, I am told, "Our marriage is OK" or "We don't need to go on any weekend, as we have no problems." I am both angry and sad at such blindness, stupidity, and fear. There is not a marriage existing that does not have some problems, and if they are not attended to, they will get bigger."*

---

This statement captures the underlying philosophy of one instructional approach. The past four decades witnessed a tremendous growth in marital and family enrichment programs designed to instruct individuals, couples, and whole family systems. Generally their purposes are educational, not therapeutic; they are oriented toward enrichment, not counseling.

Cole and Cole (1993) define marriage and family enrichment programs as:

> The process of assisting couples and families who have relatively healthy relationships in the development of interpersonal skills that will enable them to enhance and add to individual couple and family strengths, develop more effective strategies for dealing with difficulties, and learn to view their relationships as growing and changing rather than static. (525)

Morgaine (1992) sees instructional programs as "innoculating" functional families with facts, skills and information to help prevent disasters.

Most persons who attend enrichment programs are self-referred and self-screened. Potential participants receive the message "If your marriage or family life is in serious trouble, our program is not for you. We are designed to help good relationships become better." If identified before the program, couples contemplating divorce or families experiencing problems are referred to therapy or to enrichment programs that use trained counselor-facilitators (Hof and Miller 1981).

***Marital Enrichment Programs*** At least twenty-five national organizations offer marriage enrichment programs (Mace 1987). These programs are designed to enhance couple growth. Family growth may result in an extension of change in the marital pair. Most programs insist that the couple attend together in order to affect the system.

Communication skills appear as the core of most of these marital enrichment programs. These programs break the "intermarital taboo," or the strong reluctance of married people to talk about their relationships (Mace 1985).

Although there are numerous systems-oriented marital and family enrichment programs that stress communication, only a few representative ones will be noted. The most well-known and frequently attended marital enrichment programs include the religion-based Marriage Enrichment, Marriage Encounter, and Marriage Communication Lab programs and the privately developed Couples Communication Program, Training in Marriage Enrichment Program (T.I.M.E.) Relationship Enhancement, and the Prevention and Relationship Enhancement Program (PREP) (Otto 1975; Hof and Miller; Guerney 1977; Garland 1983; Dinkmeyer and Carlson 1987; Renick, Blumberg,

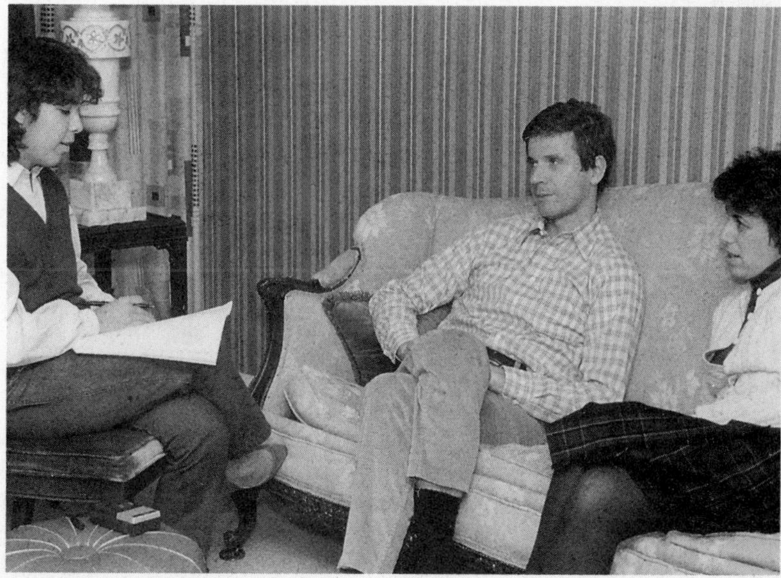

Engaged and married couples may attend couple enrichment programs where they share experiences and feelings.

and Markman 1992). Each places a heavy emphasis on communication. As you read the following brief descriptions, remember that there may be some variations depending on sponsoring groups and specific leaders.

One of the Marriage Enrichment programs sponsored by the Methodist church is a small-group experience conducted by a leader or leader-couple who works with four other couples through a structured weekend. After having been prepared by leader modeling, reflecting, and role playing, each couple engages in a series of interactions within the small group framework. Couples prepare for this through guided rehearsal sessions with nonspouses. Group members also give feedback to each couple. Some of the weekend experiences include sharing the qualities one admires in his or her spouse and discussing wished-for behaviors from the spouse. Thus, intimacy receives great focus. The actual sharing and discussion behavior is constantly monitored and corrected by the team leader, who is trying to teach communication skills. The small group functions as a powerful support system for trying new behaviors.

Marriage Encounter is a weekend program conducted by three couples and a religious leader. The format follows a simple pattern. Each husband and wife "give" each other the Encounter, with the team members merely providing the information and modeling to facilitate each couple's private dialogue. Through a series of nine talks, team members reveal personal and intimate information to encourage participants to do the same when alone. After the talks, each husband and wife separate and write individual responses to the issues raised in each talk. Specific questions to be considered may be provided, or the individual may write his or her feelings about the topic. The couple then comes together for private dialogue using each other's written responses as a starting point. The Marriage Encounter process involves exposition, reflection, encounter, and mutual understanding. Dialogue topics include understanding of the self, relationship with the partner, and the couple's relationship with God, their children, and the world. Although the program began within the Catholic church, the past years have witnessed the growth of Jewish and Protestant Marriage Encounters.

The Couples Communication program involves a small group experience with five to seven couples meeting one night a week for four consecutive weeks with an instructor. The "couples" may be spouses, friends, or work teams. This program serves as an educational experience in which couples identify, practice, and experiment with communication skills around topics of their choice. Each couple receives feedback on their skills from the leader and other couples. No attempt is made to deal with the content of an interaction. The focus remains solely on skills accomplishment. Practice sessions are held with non-partners, but the final demonstration of skills occurs with one's partner. The approach in Couples Communication is to have the couple do exercises so they can experience new ideas and approaches to relating to one another, not just learn about them (Garland 21).

The Prevention and Relationship Enhancement Program (PREP) is an empirically based approach to prevention and treatment of marital distress. The program may take place over a weekend or over 12 sessions. Dickson and Markman (1993) summarize the content as follows: Session one involves a description of the program. Session two describes the skills for effective speaking and listening. The third session covers destructive and constructive styles of communication. Hidden agendas and expectations are covered in sessions four and five. Session six focuses on fun in relationship maintenance while session seven is on problem solving. Team-building occurs in session eight. Sessions nine and ten deal with spiritual values and beliefs. The eleventh session focuses on sexual and sensual communication. The last session deals with integrating and applying the skills (587–588).

Personal Reflections is a program uniquely focused on remarried partners (Kaplan and Hennon 1992). The program focuses on role expectation and role strain as partners bring scripts from earlier marriages into the new one. There is a strong communication component focussing on self-disclosure, sharing differences, and negotiation.

Finally, the PREPARE/ENRICH materials and programs should be noted since they serve as a bridge between instructional and therapeutic approaches. Developed by Olson and colleagues, the PREPARE/ENRICH program is grounded in the circumplex model of family functioning and consists of three inventories and guidelines for counselor/leader training. PREPARE and PREPARE-MC (Married with Children) are designed for couples entering marriage either as two adults or adults with children. ENRICH is designed for use in marriage enrichment programs or marriage counseling. After couples complete the inventories and receive their computerized results they may discuss the findings with a religious leader as part of a premarital program, within a marriage enrichment program or with a therapist. Recent research supports the predictive validity of these instruments which are being used widely by professionals in religious and academic circles (Larsen and Olson 1989). A number of the programs have variations for engaged couples, although, according to Mace (1985) giving information to engaged pairs is like "pouring water on a duck's back" since emotionally they cannot imagine being headed for trouble. Instead he recommends guiding newly married couples through the first year.

Sometimes, variations of weekend programs are offered over eight to fifteen weeks in two- to four-hour sessions. The advantages include spaced learning and the opportunity to do homework and practice new skills, but such disadvantages as fights, irregular attendance, and the routines of daily life weaken the communication focus (Hof and Miller).

As you read the descriptions of these major marital enrichment programs, it becomes clear that communication assumes a central place within each. Desirable interpersonal behavior may be taught differently through modeling, role playing, lecture, guided feedback, and readings, but it is incorporated into each program. The unique feature of such programs is the learning context—you learn and practice communications skills with people with whom you have a relationship.

In a summary of communication training within overall marital enrichment programs, Cleaver (1987) reports the following three aspects receive major focus: (1) listening skills, (2) speaking skills, and (3) negotiating or problem-solving skills. Almost every national program has a communication component. Many churches and private organizations run unique marital communication programs for their own congregations or specific constituents such as remarried couples, engaged couples, or senior couples.

***Family Enrichment Programs*** Although programs for families have developed more slowly, many marital programs have fostered familial counterparts, encouraging entire families to examine and improve their relationships. The Marriage Encounter Program now offers the Family Weekend Experience. As in Marriage Encounter, the family members "give" each other the weekend. Parents and school age children spend their waking weekend hours in a local facility engaging in activities, listening to short talks, seeing films, and holding family discussions. Members examine their everyday lives, as background for discussing nine "blocks" to family relationships, such as fighting, criticism, or indifference, and the skills for overcoming such blocks, including listening, acceptance, and respect. Family members experience personal reconciliation with each other and plan ways to maintain the newfound feelings of closeness.

One of the most widely accepted family-oriented educational programs has been PET, Parent Effectiveness Training (Gordon 1975), through which parents spend eight evenings attempting to learn more effective parenting skills, relying heavily on communication strategies. This program, based on Rogerian psychology, encourages parents to examine their own self-concepts, to re-evaluate their verbal and nonverbal messages, and to find new approaches to deal with old problems, primarily through the communication skills of "active listening" and sending I-messages, which reveal how one is feeling as a result of the other's behavior.

Another widely known program is STEP, Systematic Training for Effective Parenting, developed by the American Guidance Service

(AGS). Based on Adlerian psychology, STEP focuses on the goals of children's behavior, the natural and logical consequence of the behavior, and good versus responsible parenting. The program stresses active listening, I-messages, and family meetings.

Relationship Enhancement, or RE (Guerney 1977), includes a skills approach which may be taught to all family members. In describing her experience with this model, Kirk (1989) declares RE is based on a family systems perspective, focusing on the improvement of interpersonal communication and problem-solving skills. The skills are implemented through a set of specific techniques such as the expresser mode, empathic responder mode, problem/conflict resolution mode, and the generalization/ maintenance mode. Kirk describes the results of her teaching saying:

> The family learned the skills and were able to both share their feelings and also resolve their conflicts. The parents had originally felt uncomfortable when they disciplined their stepchildren, and the children felt resentful when they adhered to their stepparents. Their communication climate eventually become one of silence and hostility until they were able to communicate in a skilled manner. (20–21)

In recent years, specialized programs for stepfamilies have emerged aimed at normalizing the stepfamily experience and developing communication skills of stepfamily members (Einstein and Albert 1986). The Stepfamily Association of America promotes local support groups and educational programs for stepfamily members, particularly the Stepping Ahead Program (Visher 1989). Family programs are stressing caregiver and parenting needs of fathers (Meyers 1993). There are even programs, for divorcing parents designed to help families manage the stresses of separation and family dissolution (Buehler et al. 1992).

Many self-help groups are oriented toward specific topics that also provide a family or relational focus and formal or informal instruction in communication skills for their members. Such groups include Al-Anon, Parents Anonymous, Families Anonymous, Parents Without Partners, Parents of Gays, Families Who Have Adopted Children of Every Skin, Compassionate Friends, and Candlelighters. Such groups are part of a cultural realignment and a source of American cultural transformation (Wuthnow).

***Appraisal of Enrichment Programs*** Although these programs sound intriguing, we need to raise some questions in considering their effectiveness focusing primarily on the marital programs. There are difficulties in attempting to teach communication principles and skills without the mutual commitment of both partners. If such mutual commitment does not exist, the results may be contrary to the expected outcomes. Additionally, the skills must be combined with a desire or spirit of good will to motivate partners to use them appropriately (Davis et al. 1982; Stevens 1984; Renick, Blumberg, and Markman 1992). Concerns include long-range effects, skill maintenance, and nature of participants.

The research on these programs does not attribute undisputed success to their efforts. In 1977, 29 studies on the impact of marriage enrichment programs concluded that although positive results were found in a majority of the measures, most studies used questionnaires or interviews administered immediately after the program. Few studies had follow-up procedures (Gurman and Kniskern). Hof and Miller (1981) reported more positive changes in the treatment group than control group across 27 of 34 studies.

In her follow-up study of Marriage Enrichment couples, Ellis (1982) reported that participants talked more freely about their feelings to spouses and to other persons than they had before their involvement. Former participants are able to express negative feelings more constructively. Yet, some participants reported that although they were emotionally expressive during the weekend, they could not sustain this later. Thus, few changes in behavior or long-range effects could be documented.

Although the programs are designed to help couples with satisfactory marriages, Powell and Wampler (1982) found that this was not always the case. Many couples entered such workshops because they felt a need for help. They suggested more stringent controls and measures to determine each partner's commitment to the enrichment experience and also examinations of the makeup of the control groups. Witteman and Fitzpatrick (1987) examined marital enrichment programs and compared them unfavorably to therapy, particularly due to lack of skills orientation.

In their admittedly critical appraisal of the Marriage Encounter, Doherty, McCabe, and Ryder (1978) suggest that the program can create illusions through emotional "highs," deny the importance of differences between people, and lead to a kind of ritual dependency and guilt if the couple does not engage in the follow-up, and other possible difficulties. A content analysis of interview and essay data from couples who attended Marriage Encounter revealed those who were highly positive or highly negative about the experience were likely to report experiencing serious marital distress prior to the weekend (Doherty, Lester, and Leigh 1986). The authors suggest that distressed couples who attend are likely to suffer greater marital deterioration, a situation which leads them to recommend more careful screening of the potential participants, changes in the program structure to encourage more leader-participant interactions, and specific crisis training for leaders.

Couple Communication is the most extensively documented instructional program ever developed. Since 1971, 31 studies have been published in professional journals or as doctoral dissertations. More are in progress. Most of the research has been conducted at major universities throughout the U.S. in cooperation with CC Instructors in a variety of community contexts. The findings indicate: (1) An extremely positive impact on behavior immediately after the program with most studies finding partial decline at follow up; (2) Increases in relationship satisfaction with some decline at follow up; and (3) No documented negative effects. (Thirty-one …, 1988). The primary concern is the long term maintenance of skills.

In similar findings, the Relationship Enhancement Program was reported to have positive effects in short-term increases in self disclosure, empathy relationship adjustment, and intimacy, but long-term effects were not studied (Ridley et al. 1982).

In their research on PREP program, Renick, Blumberg, and Workman (1992) report on a ten year longitudinal study involving 83 of the original 135 couples. PREP couples showed increases in overall positive communication as well as problem solving and support-validation. Gender differences appeared on several measures, including higher male dedication to the relationship. At the five year followup, PREP husbands showed greater relationship satisfaction than control husbands. Nineteen percent of control group couples divorced or separated; eight percent of PREP couples had done so. Currently this program is under review in numerous other studies.

Even the structure of a program may affect the outcome. In a study comparing psychological changes in couples who attended a weekend program with couples who were involved in a five-week program, the latter group gained more improvement in their marital adjustment scores. In both groups, wives changed in more positive ways than did their husbands (Davis et al., 89).

A key consideration in evaluating enrichment programs lies in the extent of skill training provided. Witteman and Fitzpatrick (1986) maintain that behavior changes in marital communication are tied to some type of skills training and not the discussion of communication, an approach frequently found in church related enrichment programs. Information without skills does not provide enough basis for change.

Most research on marital enrichment examines outcome criteria of marital satisfaction, relationship skill development, and individual personality variables. In their summary of such, Dinkmeyer and Carlson (1986) report positive change is usually demonstrated on approximately 60 percent of the criterion tests in these general categories following completion of the enrichment experience. Yet this research is based primarily on self-reported measures. Giblin, Sprenkle, and Sheehan (1985) report generally positive gains for couples involved in marital enrichment, especially for those in Relationship Enhancement programs for couples followed by those in the Couple Communication Program and Marriage Encounter.

In their review of parenting programs, Noller and Fitzpatrick (1993) conclude, "There has been little systematic research that has evaluated the effectiveness of parenting program." They report that studies which compare one parent training program with another had far from conclusive results. Many of the individual program evaluation programs are methodologically weak. There are significant difficulties in balancing the desire for certain types of measurement with understanding the clientele who choose to enroll in certain family programs (Buehler et al. 1992).

Additional critiques of programs note positive and negative effects (L'Abate 1981; De Young 1979; Wampler and Sprenkle 1980; Witteman and Fitzpatrick 1986; Renick, Blumberg, and Markman 1992). The growing care with which professionals recommend such programs is reflected in the following example:

---

*As a minister I used to suggest to all couples I worked with that they become involved in a marriage enrichment program. It seemed like a cure-all for my congregation members because of the emphasis on communication skills. Yet, over time, I've learned more about the program and am more discriminating in my recommendations since I no longer see them as a panacea but as a valuable resource for many couples. I no longer refer severely troubled couples to this resource because the time is too limited and they do not have a high enough trust level to practice the communication skills effectively.*

---

Research on the long term effectiveness of marital and family enrichment programs is too limited to draw secure conclusions. Yet, in recent years, new approaches to marital enrichment have been developed to reflect recent research and to include a research component, thus ensuring a more systematic approach to evaluation (Worthington, Buston, and Hammonds 1989; Cleaver 1987; L'Abate 1984; Renick, Blumberg, and Markman 1992).

The important questions about the impact of such programs include: Do the programs result in changes in communication that last for a reasonable period of time? And in positive changes relationships? Do the marriage programs result in changes that generalize to dealing with children? How does evaluation reflect a balance of external and internal validity, especially in community based settings?

What are the major factors in these programs that create the impacts that occur, such as skills or format and design (Wackman; Garland 1983; Buehler et al. 1992)?

## Therapeutic Approaches

The families in relational pain or crisis are most effectively served by therapeutic approaches. Because this text is concerned with communication issues of functional families, marital and family therapy is presented only in order to extend the continuum of options for improving relationships. There is a vast body of literature that explores these approaches in detail (Gurman and Kniskern 1991); this section highlights only some relevant issues. Individual therapy has long been an established approach to dealing with personal problems or illnesses. This counselor-client situation remains one valid therapeutic approach for certain issues. In certain cases this is not the most appropriate approach.

For those families experiencing a severe crisis or living in long-term dysfunctional patterns, therapeutic interventions may be warranted. In contrast to previous eras when the "identified patient" or "problem person" was shipped off to be "fixed" by a counselor, many family-related problems are addressed through family therapy, sometimes called systems therapy. Family therapists created the following definition:

A couples group provides therapeutic support to work through specific difficulties and improve communication.

> Family Therapy is a psychotherapeutic approach that focusses on altering interactions between a couple, within a nuclear (biological) family or extended family, or between a family and other interpersonal systems, with the goal of alleviating problems presented by individual family members, family subsystems, the family as a whole or other referral sources. (Wynne 1988, 9)

Family therapists look at system patterns as this comment indicates:

---

*Two years ago, my family went into therapy because my younger brother was flunking school and shoplifting and his treatment center required the entire family to become involved in the treatment program. Over about a year we were able to understand the patterns of family interaction that "fed" Chris's problem. The therapist kept stressing that Chris's acting out was a family problem, not just Chris's problem. The therapy forced my mother and stepfather to deal with some problems in their marriage that they had been ignoring and allowed us to make enough changes that Chris could return to high school and control the shoplifting.*

---

The family therapy movement's roots are found in the research and clinical developments of the 1950s, including hospital psychiatry, group dynamics, interpersonal psychiatry, the child guidance movement, research in communication and schizophrenia, and marriage counseling. Persons such as Nathan Ackerman, Gregory Bateson, John Bell, Ivan Boszormenyinagy, Murray Bowen, James Framo, Jay Haley, Don Jackson, Christian Midelfort, Salvador Minuchin, Virginia Satir, Carl Whitaker, Theodore Widz, Lyman Wynne, and Gerald Zuk were significant pioneers in the "first wave" family treatment (Broderick and Schrader 1991).

Communication issues emerged as a key feature of the family therapy movement since many of these pioneers, most notably Satir, focused explicit attention on communication patterns. In his description of the roots of the family therapy movement, Nichols (1984) noted how communication was an integral part of early methods. Family therapy as a treatment method began when clinicians first brought families together for observation. Doing so forced a shift in focus from intrapsychic content to interpersonal process. Instead of trying to understand what was going on inside people, family therapists began to manipulate what goes on between them. Clarifying communication, and issuing tasks and directives were the first methods used to outwit resistance and to help families change. Even in the early days of family therapy, however, different practitioners developed alternate strategies and tactics of change.

The family therapy approach is rooted in a systems perspective, reflecting assumptions about change and context reflecting systems theory. Napier and Whitaker (1978) describe the initial signals which forced therapists to consider system approaches.

> Some therapists discovered the family system by being bruised by it ... working with an individual and being totally defeated by the family's power over the patient; or seeing the client "recover," only to witness all the progress undermined by the family; or treating the scapegoat child "successfully," only to find another child in the family dragged into the role; or working with an individual patient and feeling the fury of the family's sudden explosion just as the patient improved. (52–53)

In many cases, once therapists examined a whole family system, they realized that the "problem" member, or symptom bearer, reflected the rest of the system's dynamics. Thus, events in families must be examined in the context in which they happen and attention given to how communication among family members affects connections and relationships (Papp 1983, 7).

After explaining the overlap of systems theory and family therapy, Doherty and Baptiste (1993) list the six core working assumptions: (1) family relationships are a principal source of mental health and psychopathology for individuals, (2) family interaction patterns tend to repeat across generations, (3) family health requires a balance of conviction and individuation, (4) family flexibility is a core trait that prevents family dysfunction, (5) the triad is the minimum unit for a complex understanding of family interactions, and (6) individuals' symptoms frequently have meaning within the family's interaction patterns or worldview (511–512).

After interviewing counselors about couples' communication problems, Vangelisti (1994) reported the most frequently voted communication problems involved failing to take the other's perspective when listening, blaming the other for negative occurences and criticizing the other. Counselors felt communication problems were the result of patterns taught in individuals by their family of origin. A majority of counselors saw communication frequently as a manifestation of more fundamental difficulties. Only one-quarter saw communication as a central issue.

Family therapy looks at the family unit as the client to be treated; the focus shifts from the individuals to the entire unit and the relationships among people. Ackerman (1966) describes family therapy as "the therapy of a natural living unit; the sphere of the therapeutic intervention is not a single individual but the whole family unit"(209). Attempts are made to change the system, not just the "problem" person, since this person's "acting out" may be thought of as symptomatic of the system's problems (Satir 1988; Gurman and Kniskern 1991; Nichols 1984).

The primary goal of family therapy is to affect changes in family members' interpersonal relationships but there are many schools of thought regarding the most effective ways to alter family systems. Therapeutic approaches may be classified in numerous ways. Kaslow (1987) identifies the major recognized theories of family therapy in her classification system which includes: (1) psychoanalytic, (2) Bowenian, (3) contextual-relational, (4) experiential, (5) problem-solving, (6) communicational-interactional, (7) structural, (8) strategic-systemic, (9) behavioral, and (10) integrative, dialectic, or multimodal. She suggests that each theory offers a different view of the "reality" of the family. Gurman and Krieskern (1991) address 14 models of family therapy.

Many therapists borrow freely across the approaches. In a survey of family therapists, Rait (1988) reported that 34 percent of therapists reported they used eclectic family-oriented approaches, 18 percent classified their approach as structural and 12 percent saw themselves as systemic/strategic. The rest reflected diverse general approaches. Family therapists may work with individuals, couples, families, or entire social networks, a therapeutic range which necessitates flexibility. Whereas one therapist may value an examination of family history to uncover family of origin or transgenerational patterns, another may focus exclusively on the "here-and now" interaction patterns. Currently many therapists are focusing on personal narratives or family stories with the belief that therapy can be described as the process of transforming a family's dominant stories to include new meanings (Sluzki 1992). Over time, a family's needs and issues may change as indicated in the following statement:

---

*Over the sixteen years of our marriage we have experienced marital or family therapy two times, each a very different experience. Early in our marriage we had trouble separating from my original family so we worked a lot on couple identity, family-of-origin issues using genograms. During our daughter's lengthy hospitalization for kidney disease the other four of us went into therapy to keep us functioning and to release our feelings. Now I would be comfortable going again if an issue arose that we could not handle.*

---

Family therapy has influenced approaches to treatment for drug and alcohol abuse, eating disorders, major illness, sexual abuse, and related areas.

Currently, American family therapists are grappling with critical issues of culture and gender as they affect the treatment process. The growing number of families, representing varied cultures who need the services of family therapists has led to extensive interest in cross cultural family norms and treatment approaches and a move away from ethnocentric approaches (McGoldrick et al. 1991; Boynton 1987; Markowitz 1994). Research investigating communication in intercultural marriages reveals the continuing salience of cultural background of the partners and the unique problems encountered in these relationships (Martin, Hecht, and Larkey 1994). Cross cultural family relationships frequently encounter differences in areas of attitudes toward marriage, male/female roles and the significance of extended family. Although no therapist can demonstrate expertise in communication patterns of multiple cultures, it is essential for therapists "to develop an attitude of openness to cultural variability and to the relativity of their own values" (McGoldrick et al. 1991).

Recent accusations of gender-blindness by major figures in the field has led to consideration of gender as a fundamental organizing principle of families and a significant area for future concern (Goldner 1989; Walsh and Scheinkman 1989; Rampage 1992). According to Doherty and Boss (1991) feminism in family therapy has raised questions of equity and justice. They recommend that all therapists must examine myths such as: women need to be taken care of; women are nurturers, men are not; men must be instrumental, women must be expressive; women should meet men's sexual needs but not reveal their own. Rampage clearly depicts difficulty with systems therapy in certain circular problems such as wife beating, rape and incest saying:

> Circular causality subtly removes responsibility for his behavior from the man, while implying the woman is co-responsible and in some way 'asks for it' by participating in the interactional patterns which results in violence and abuse. (4)

The past two decades witnessed an increase in research addressing the overall effectiveness of family therapy and specific issues of unique approaches (Gurman and Kniskern 1981; Barton et al. 1985; Beach and O'Leary 1985; Johnson and Greenberg 1988; Kaslow 1987). The effectiveness of family therapy has been investigated primarily through an analysis of family improvement through treatment, treatment results compared to no treatment, and comparison of family treatment to other forms. Traditional research in family therapy indicates 65 to 75 percent of the families seen in family therapy improve (Kniskern 1983). Behavioral marital therapy appears effective for mildly or moderately distressed couples (Hahlweg and Markman 1988).

The complexity of family dynamics and the relative youth of the field is reflected in debates as to the methods of studying the field. In a published debate on research methods, Kniskern argues that traditional research methods have been effective and yielded data "supporting the conclusion that family therapies are valid and effective methods of intervening in family and individual problems" (38). An opponent, Tomm (1983) argues against studies using experimental design due to their linear approach, calling instead for more holistic approaches. Even as researchers uncover some answers to key questions, there is more to be examined since, according to Nichols (1984), "There are many studies that verify the overall effectiveness of family therapy, but too few that deal with specific questions about which methods work with which patients and in what circumstances" (119). Current issues in family therapy research are informed consent, confidentiality and benefits versus risk (Doherty and Boss 1991). Yet, there is much left to learn. Gottman (1994) argues that marital therapy remains relatively uninformed by empirical research relying instead on clinical history. The need continues for longitudinal, large sample, well-controlled studies.

For many families, the systemic orientation of family therapy has provided the basis for their eventual change. The emphasis on patterns, rather than individual blame, has permitted all members to accept some responsibility for their family's current state and has given them keys to future change. Yet, in certain situations this orientation may not provide equity.

As you change the current communication patterns within your family system, many options are open to you, ranging from individual approaches to efforts on the part of the system. The most exciting aspect is the possibility of change. Communication can be improved; families can grow through effort, time, and struggle. Relationships take work to maintain, and communication stands at the core of that process.

## CONCLUSION

This chapter attempts to explore (1) factors that characterize functional to optimally functional families, with an emphasis on communication, and (2) approaches for creating and maintaining effective communication within families. Historically, academic and therapeutic experts have emphasized effective communication as a central factor in well family functioning. Although there is no absolute agreement on definitions and terminology one may hypothesize that functional families may exhibit the following characteristics. Some or all of the

1. Interactions are patterned and meaningful
2. There is more compassion and less cruelty
3. Persons are not scapegoated as problems are identified with the appropriate persons
4. Family members exhibit appropriate self restraint
5. Boundaries are clear
6. Life includes joy and humor
7. Misperceptions are minimal
8. Positive interactions outweigh negative ones

Popular literature espouses similar ideas in a prescriptive mode.

Approaches to improving marital and family communication include personal actions, instructional programs and therapeutic interventions. Such approaches can be helpful because they require a level of commitment and openness to change and, by forcing the participants to move beyond the daily maintenance issues and provide a chance to reflect on family experience. These opportunities provide a chance for individual and system self-examination. Each approach reflects a strong communication component. More research is needed to establish the effectiveness of these approaches.

## A FINAL WORD

As authors we have grown from the process of writing this book and hope that you have developed new insights about families in general, and your family in particular. We close with our belief, shared with Beavers (1976), that a healthy family may be viewed as a "phoenix." It grows in an atmosphere of flexibility and intimacy. It accepts conflicts, change, and loss. It declines—to rise again in another well-functioning generation, which, in turn, produces well-functioning family members.

## IN REVIEW

1. How would you describe communication in a well-functioning family? Answer within a context of a specific developmental stage, culture, and family form.
2. Analyze the prescriptions for marital or parent-child communication found in a popular book or magazine article and evaluate their effectiveness based on your understanding of family systems and communication patterns.
3. What goals and criteria would you establish for a successful marriage or family enrichment program with a communication focus?
4. Take a position: To what extent should couples be required by religious or civic institutions to engage in marital workshops or therapy?
5. In what ways would you predict family therapy would differ across two ethnic groups?

# BIBLIOGRAPHY

Abelman, A. (1975). *The relationship between family self-disclosure, adolescent adjustment, family satisfaction, and family congruence*. Unpublished dissertation. Northwestern University.

Ackerman, N. (1966). Family therapy. In S. Arieti (Ed.), *American handbook of psychiatry.* New York: Basic Books.

Ackerman, N.J. (1980). The family with adolescents. In E. Carter and M. McGoldrich (Eds.) *The family life cycle: A framework for family therapy*, New York: Gardner Press.

Acock, A.C., and W.S. Yang (1984). Parental power and adolescents' parental identification. *Journal of Marriage and the Family,* 46: 487-494.

Adelman, M. (1988). *Sustaining passion: Eroticism and safe sex talk.* Paper presented at the Speech Communication Association Convention, New Orleans.

Ahrons, O., and R. Rodgers (1987). *Divorced families.* New York: W. W. Norton.

Aida, Y., and T. Falbo (1991). Relationships between marital satisfaction, resources & power strategies. *Sex roles* 41: 43-50.

Ainslie, J., and K.M. Feltry (1991). Definitions and dynamics of motherhood and family in lesbian communities. *Marriage and the Family Review,* 17: 1-2, 63-85.

Alberts, J. (1988). Analysis of couples' conversational complaints. *Communication Monographs,* 55: 184-197.

Aldous, J. (1990). Family development and the life course: Two perspectives on family change. *Journal of Marriage and the Family,* 52: 571-583.

Aldous, J., and D. Klein (1991). Sentiment and services: Models of intergenerational relationships in mid-Life. *Journal of Marriage and the Family,* 53: 585-608.

Allen, C. M., and M. A. Straus (1979). Resources, power, and husband-wife violence. In M. A. Straus & G. T. Hotaling (Eds.), *The social causes of husband-wife violence.* Minneapolis: University of Minnesota Press. Also reference to article in *Journal of Marriage and the Family,* 41: (1979) 85.

Altman, I., and D. Taylor (1973). *Social penetration.* New York: Holt, Rinehart & Winston

Altman, I. (1993). Dialectics, physical environments, and personal relationships. *Communication Monographs,* 60: 26-34.

Amato, P. (1986). Marital conflict, the parent-child relationship and child self-esteem. *Family Relations,* 35 (3): 403-409.

Amato, P. R., and S. Rezacs (1994). Contact with nonresident parents, interpersonal conflict, and children's behavior. *Journal of Family Issues,* 15: 191-207.

Ambry, M. K. (1993). Receipts from marriage. *American Demographics,* 15: 30-38.

Ammons, P., and N. Stinnett (1980). The vital marriage: A closer look. *Family Relations,* 30: 37-42.

Anderson, C. (1982). The community connection: The impact of social networks on family and individual functioning. In F. Walsh (Ed.), *Normal family processes* (pp. 425-621). New York: Guilford Press.

Aquilino, W. (1991). Family structure & home-leaving: A further specification of the relationship." *Journal of Marriage and the Family,* 53: 999-1010.

Aquilino, W., and K. R. Supple (1991). Parent-child relations and parent's satisfaction with living arrangements when adult children live at home. *Journal of Marriage and the Family,* 53: 13–27.

Arditti, J. (1990). Noncustodial fathers: An overview of policy & resources. *Family Relations,* 39: 460–465.

Arntson, P., and L. Turner (1989). Sex role socialization: Children's enactment of their parents' behaviors in a regulative and interpersonal context. *Western Journal of Speech Communication,* 51 (3): 304–315.

Avery, C. (1989). How do you build intimacy in an age of divorce? *Psychology Today*, 23: 27–31.

Aylmer, R. (1988). The launching of the single young adult. In B. Carter & M. McGoldrick (Eds.), *The changing family life cycle: A framework for family therapy* (2nd ed., pp. 191–208). New York: Gardner Press.

Bahr, K. S. (1990). Student responses to genogram and family chronology. *Family Relations,* 39: 243–249.

Bahr, S., C. Chappell,C. Bradford, and G. Leigh (1983). Age at marriage, role enactment, role consensus, and marital satisfaction. *Journal of Marriage and the Family,* 46: 795–803.

Bain, A. (1978). The capacity of families to cope with transitions: A theoretical essay. *Human Relations,* 31: 675–688.

Baker, M. (1984). Arizona retirement communities and the changing needs of an aging population. *Arizona Review*: 14–22.

Balsky, J., L. Youngblade, M. Rovine, and E. B. Volling. (1991). Patterns of marital change & parent-child interaction. *Journal of Marriage and the Family,* 59: 486–497.

Balswick, J., and C. Averett (1977). Differences in expressiveness: gender, interpersonal orientation, and perceived parental expressiveness as contributing factors. *Journal of Marriage and the Family,* 39: 121–127.

Bank, S. P., and M.D. Kahn (1987). Formulations of self and family systems. *Family Process,* 26: 185–202.

Baptiste, D. (1987). The gay and lesbian stepparent family. In F. Bozett (Ed). *Gay and lesbian parents*. pp. 112–137. New York: Praeger.

Barber, B. K. (1994). Cultural, family, and personal contexts of parent-adolescent conflict. *Journal of Marriage and the Family,* 56: 375–386.

Barber, B., B. Chadwick, and R. Oerter (1992). Parental behaviors and adolescent self-esteem in the U.S. & Germany. *Journal of Marriage and the Family,* 54: 128–141.

Barbour, A., and A. Goldberg (1974). *Interpersonal communication: teaching strategies and resources*. ERIC/RCS. Speech Communication Association.

Barge, K. (1984). A power primer: A review and critique of conceptions of power. Paper presented at Central States Speech Association, Chicago.

Barnett, R.C., and N. Marshall. The relationship between women's work and family roles and subjective well-being and psychological distress (1991). In M. Frankenhaeuser, U. Lumberg and M. Chesney (Eds.) *Women, Work and Health: Stress and Opportunities*: 111–136. New York: Plenum.

Barnett, R.C., N. Marshall, and J. Pleck (1992). Men's mutliple roles and their relationship to men's psychological distress. *Journal of Marriage and the Family*, 54: 358–367.

Barnett, R.C., R.T. Brennan, and N. Marshall (1994). Gender & the relationship between parent role and psychological distress *Journal of Family Issues,* 15: 229–252.

Barnett, R.G., N. Kibria, G.K. Baruch, and J.H. Pleck (1991). Adult daughter-parent relationships and their associations with daughters: Subjective well-deing and psychology distress. *Journal of Marriage and the Family,* 53: 29–42.

Barnhill, L. R. (1979). Healthy family system. *Family Coordinator,* 28: 94–100.

Barranti-Ramirez, C. (1985). The grandparent/grandchildren relationship: Family resource in an era of voluntary bonds. *Family Relation,s* 34 (3): 343-355.

Barton, C., J. Alexander, H. Waldron, C. Turner, and J. Warburton (1988). Generalizing treatment effects of functional family therapy: Three applications. *The American Journal of Family Therapy,* 13: 16-26.

Bavelas, J., and L. Segal (1982). Family systems theory: Background and implications. *Journal of Communication,* 32: 99-107.

Baxter, L.A. (1991) Bakhtin's ghost: dialectical communication in relationships. Paper presented at Speech Communication Association Convention, Atlanta.

Baxter, L.A.(1987). Symbols of relationship identity in relationship cultures. *Journal of Social and Personal Relationships,* 4: 261-280.

Baxter, L.A. (1990). Dialectical contradictions in relationship development. *Journal of Social and Personal Relationships,* 7: 69-88.

Baxter, L.A. (1993). Talking things through and putting it in writing. *Journal of Applied Communication Research,* 21: 313-326.

Baxter, L.A., and K. Dindia (1990), Marital partners' perceptions of marital maintenance strategies, *Journal of Social and Personal Relationships,* 7: 187-208.

Baxter, L., and E.P. Simon (1993). Relational maintenance strategies and dialectical contradictions in personal relationships. *Journal of Social and Personal Relationships,,* 10: 225-242.

Bay, C.R., and S.L. Braver (1990). Perceived control of the divorce settlement process & intraparental conflict. *Family Relations,* 39: 362-387.

Beach, S., and D. O'Leary (1985). Current status of outcome research in marital therapy. In L. L'Abate (Ed.), *Handbook of family psychology and therapy* (Vol.2). Homewood, IL: Dorsey Press.

Beal, E. W. (1980). Separation, divorce, and single-parent families. In E. A. Carter & M. McGoldrick (Eds.), The family life cycle: *A framework for family therapy* (pp. 241-264). New York: Gardner Press.

Bearison, D.J., and T.Z. Cassel (1975). Cognitive decentration and social codes: Communication effectiveness in young children from differing family contexts. *Developmental Psychology*: 29-36.

Beavers, R.W. (1976). A theoretical basis for family evaluation. *In J. M. Lewis, W. R. Beavers, J. T. Grossett & V. A. Philips (Eds.), No single thread: Psychological health in family systems.* (pp. 46-82). New York: Brunner/Mazel.

Beavers, R.W. (1982). Healthy midrange, and severely dysfunctional families. In F. Walsh (Ed.), *Normal family processes.* New York: Guilford Press.

Beavers, W. and M. Voeller (1983).Family models: Comparing and contrasting. the olson circumplex model with the beavers systems model. *Family Process* 22: 85-97.

Becker, T.J. (1994). 90s homes try to match the way we really live. *Chicago Tribune,* February 19, sec. 4, 1-2.

Beier, E.G., and D.P. Sternberg (1977). Marital communication: Subtle cues between newlyweds. *Journal of Communication,* 27: 92-103.

Bell, A.P., and M.S. Weinberg (1978). *Homosexualities: A study of diversity among men and women.* New York: Simon and Schuster.

Bell, R., N. L. Buerkel-Rothfuss, and K. E. Gore (1987). Did you bring the yarmulke for the cabbage patch kid?: The idiomatic communication of young lovers. *Human Communication Research,* 14: 47-67.

Bellak, L. (1970). *The Porcupine dilemma: reflections on the human condition.* N.Y.: Citadel Press.

Belsky, J., and L. Youngblade, M. Rovine, and B. Volling (1991). Patterns of marital change & parent-child interaction. *Journal of Marriage and Family,* 53: 488-497.

Benin, M. H., and D. A. Edwards (1990). Adolescent's chores: The difference between dual- and single-earner families. *Journal of Marriage and the Family*, 52: 361-373.

Benjamin, B. (1988). Aging and normal changes in speech-language- hearing. In C.W. Carmichael, C.H. Botan & R. Hawkins (Eds.), *Human communication and the aging process* (pp. 45-56). Prospect Heights, IL: Waveland Press.

Berger, C. R., and J.J. Bradac (1982). *Language and social knowledge*. London: Edward Arnold.

Berger, C.R. (1980). Power and the family. In M. Roloff G. Miller (Eds.), *Persuasion: New direction in theory and research* (pp. 174-224). Beverly Hills: Sage Publication.

Berger, P. and Kellner, H. (1964). Marriage and the construction of reality: An exercise in the microconstruction of knowledge. *Diogenes*, 46: 1-25.

Berkowitz, A. and H.W. Perkins (1984). Stress among farm women: Work and family as interacting systems. *Journal of Marriage and the Family*, 46: 161-166.

Berman (1986). Making it as a stepparent: *New roles/new rules* (2nd ed). New York: Harper & Row.

Bernstein, A. (1989). *Yours, mine, and ours*. New York: Charles Scribner's Sons.

Bernstein, Basil. A sociological approach to socialization: With some references to educability. In F. Williams (Ed.), *Language and poverty*. Chicago, Markham, 1970.

Beutler, I., W. Burr, K. Bahr, and D. Herrin (1988). The family realm: Theoretical contributions for understanding its uniqueness. *Journal of Marriage and the Family*, 51, (3): 805-815.

Bigbee, J.L. (1992). Family stress, hardiness and illness: A pilot study." *Family relations* 41: 212-217.

Billingsley, A. (1988). The impact of technology on afro-american families. *Family relations*, 37: 420-425.

Bios, P. (1979). *The adolescent passage*, New York: International Universities Press.

Blieszner, R. Close relationship over time, (1994). In A. Weber and J. Harvey (Eds.) *Perspectives on close relationships*, (pp. 1-17). Needham Heights, MA: Allyn & Bacon.

Blood, T.O., and D.M. Wolfe (1960). *Husbands and wives: The dynamics of married living*. New York: The Free Press.

Bloomfield, H. (1993). Making peace with your stepfamily. NY: Hyperion.

Blos, P. (1979) *The adolescent passage*. New York: International Universities Press.

Blumstein, P., and P. Schwartz (1983). *American couples*. New York: William Morrow and Co.

Bochner, A., and E. Eisenberg (1987). Family process: System perspectives. In C. Berger & S. Chaffee (Eds.), *Handbook of communication science*, (pp. 540-563). Beverly Hills: Sage Publications.

Booth, A., and P.R. Amato (1994). Parental marital quality, parental divorce ... *Journal of Marriage and the Family* 56: 21-34.

Boss, P., and B. Thorne (1989). Family sociology and family therapy: A feminist linkage. In M. McGoldrick, C. Anderson & F. Walsh (Eds.) *Women in families*: (pp. 78-96). New York: W.W. Norton.

Bowen, M. (1976). Family reaction to death. In P. H. Guerin (Ed.), *Family therapy: Theory & practice:* (pp. 335-349). New York: Halsted Press.

Bowen, M. (1978). *Family therapy in clinical practice*. New York: Aronson.

Bowen, S., and P. Michal-Johnson (1989). The crisis of communicating in relationships: Confronting the threat of AIDS. *AIDS and Public Policy Journal*, 4: 10-19.

Boynton, G. (1987). Cross-cultural family therapy: An escape model. *The American Journal of Family Therapy*, 15: 123-130.

Bozett, F. (1987). Gay fathers. In F. Bozett (Ed.). Gay and lesbian parents. (pp 3-22) New York: Praeger.

Bozett, F. and M. Sussman (1989). Homosexuality and family relations: Views and research issues. *Marriage and the Family Review,* 14: 1-8.

Bozett, F. (1985). Male development & fathering throughout the life cycle. *American behavioral scientist* 29: 41-52.

Bozett, F. (1987). (Ed.) *Gay and lesbian parents.* New York: Praeger.

Bradac, J., and A. Mulac (1984). Attributional consequences of powerful and powerless speech styles in a crises intervention context. *Journal of Language and Social Psychology,* 3: 1-19.

Bradt, J. (1988). Becoming parents: Families with young children. In B. Carter & M. McGoldrick (Eds.), *The Changing family life cycle: A framework for family therapy* (2nd Ed., pp. 237-253). New York: Gardner Press.

Braithwaite, D. (1991). Just how much did that wheelchair cost? Management of privacy boundaries by persons with disabilities. *Western Journal of Speech Comm,* 55: 254-274.

Breines, W., and L. Gordon (1983). The new scholarship on family violence. *Signs,* 8: 490-531.

Brighton-Cleghorn, J. (1987). Formulations of self and family systems. *Family Process,* 26: 198-201.

Bristor, M. (1984). The birth of a handicapped child—A wholistic model for grieving. *Family Relations,* 33 (1): 25-32.

Brock, L., and G. Jennings (1993). What daughters in their 30s wish their mothers had told them. *Family Relations,* 42: 61-65.

Broderick, C. (1975) Power in the governance of families." In R.E. Cromwell and D. H. Olson (Eds.) *Power in Families.* New York: Halsted Press: 117-128.

Broderick, C. (1993). *Understanding family process,* Newbury Park, CA, Sage Publications.

Broderick, C., and S. Schroder (1991). A History of professional marriage and family therapy. In Gurman, A. and D. Kriskern (Eds), *Handbook of Family Therapy,* Vol. II. New York: Brunner/Mazel.

Brommel, B. J. (1992). Teaching about death and dying in family communication, Central States Communication Association Conference, Chicago.

Brommel, B. J. (1993, November). Family communication patterns in "Star Trek: The Next Generation." Speech Communication Association National Convention, Miami.

Brommel, B. J. (1994, November). Therapeutic issues affecting custody, Speech Communication Association Convention, New Orleans, LA.

Bronstein, P., J. Clauson, J.M.F. Stoll, and C.L. Abrams (1993). Parenting behavior and children's social, psychological and academic adjustment in diverse family structures, *Family Relations* 42: 268-276.

Brown, B., I. Altman, and C. Werner (1994). Close relationships in environmental context, pp. 340-358. In A. Weber and J. Harvey (Eds.) *Perspectives on Close Relationships.* Boston: Allyn and Bacon.

Brown, J.E. and L. Mann (1990). The relationship between family structure and process variables and adolescent decision making. *Journal of Adolescence,* 13: 25-37.

Brown, James C. Loss and grief: An overview & guided imagery intervention model. (1990) *Journal of Mental Health Counseling,* 12: 434-445.

Brown, L. (1989). Lesbians, gay men, and their families: Common clinical issues. *Journal of Gay and Lesbian Psychotherapy,* 1 (1), 65-77.

Brubaker, T. and K. Roberto (1993). Family life education for the later years. *Family Relations,* 42: 212-221.

Buehler, C., P. Betz, C. Ryan, and B. Trotter (1992). Description and evaluation of the orientation for divorcing parents: Implications for past divorce prevention programs. *Family Relations,* 41: 2: 154–162.

Buehler, C. (1989). Influential factors and equity issues in divorce settlements. *Family Relations,* 389: 76–82.

Burgess, E. W. (1926) The family as a unit of interacting personalities. *The Family*, 7: 3–9.

Burgess, E.W., H.J. Locke and M.M. Thomas (1963). *The family: From institution to companionship*. New York: American Book Company.

Burgess, R.L., and R.D. Conger (1979). Family interaction in abusive, neglectful, and normal families. *Journal of Youth and Adolescence*, 8: 1163–1178.

Burgoon, M., J. Dillard, and N. Doran (1984). Friendly or unfriendly persuasion: The effects of violations of expectancy by males and females. *Human Communication Research*, 10: 283–294.

Burke, R., T. Weir, and D. Harrison (1976). Disclosure of problems and tensions experienced by marital partners. *Psychological Reports*, 38: 531–542.

Burleson, B.R., J. Delia, and J. Applegate (1992). Effects of maternal communication and children's social-cognitive and communication skills on children's acceptance by the peer group. *Family Relations,* 41: 264–272.

Burnett, E., and J. Daniels (1985). The impact of family-of-origin and stress on interpersonal conflict resolution skills in young men. *American Mental Health Counselors Association Journal*: 162–171.

Burr, Wesley R., and Shirley Klein & Associates (1994). *Reexamining family stress*. Thousand Oaks, CA: Sage.

Cahn, D. (1987) Male/female communication and relationship development: Communication characteristics of mateship stages. Paper presented at Speech Communication Association Convention, Boston.

Cain, B. (Feb. 18, 1990). Older children and divorce. *New York Times magazine*, 26, 50–55.

Callan, V.J., and J. Murray (1989). The role of therapists in helping couples cope with stillbirth and newborth death. *Family Relations,* 38: 248–253.

Canary, D., H. Weger, and L. Stafford (1991). Couples' argument sequences & their associations with relational characteristics. *Western Journal of Speech Communication,* 55: 159–179.

Canary, D.J. and L. Stafford (1992). Relational maintenance strategies and equity in marriage. *Communication monographs* 3: 243–267.

Carter, B., and M. McGoldrick (1988). Overview, the changing family life cycle: A framework for family therapy. In Carter, B. & McGoldrick, M. (Eds.), *The Changing family life cycle* (2nd. ed., pp. 3–28). New York: Gardner Press.

Celis, W. (1993). Schools across the U.S. cautiously adding lessons on gay Life. *The New York Times*. (Ed.) 1-6-93. (A7).

Cheal, D. (1993). Unity and difference in postmodern families. *Journal of Family Issues* 14, 1: 5–19.

Cherlin, A.J. (1992). *Marriage, divorce, and remarriage*. Cambridge, MA: Harvard University Press.

Chilman, C. (1978). Habitat and american families: A social-psychological overview. *The Family Coordinator*, 27 (2), 105–111.

Chiriboga, D., L. Catron, and P. Weiler (1987). Childhood stress and adult functioning during marital separation. *Family Relations*, 36, (2): 163–166.

Cissna, K.H., D.E. Cox, and A. P. Bochner (1990). The dialectic of marital & parental relationships within the stepfamily. *Communication. Monographs,* 57: 45–61.

Cleaver, G. (1987). Marriage enrichment by means of a structured communication program. *Family Relations*, 36: 49-54.

Clements, M. (1994, August 7). Sex in America today. *Parade*: 4-6.

Cline, K. (1989). The politics of intimacy: Costs and benefits determining disclosure intimacy in male-female dyads. *Journal of Social & Personal Relationships*, *6*: 5-20.

Cloven, D. H., and M.l Roloff (1993). The chilling effect of aggressive potential on the expression of complaints in intimate relationships. *Communication Monograph*, 60, 660: 199-219.

Cohen, S. (1993). *Tender power*, Reading, MA; Addison Wesley.

Cole, C., and A. Cole (1993). Family therapy theory implications for marriage and family enrichment. In P. Boss et al. (Eds.) *Source Book for Family Theories and Methods*. (pp. 525-529). New York: Plenum Press.

Coleman, D. (1992, Dec. 2). Gay parents called no disadvantage. New York Times (Health), p. 31.

Coleman, D. (1992, Dec. 6). Attending to the children of all the world's war zones. *New York Times* (E), p. 7.

Coleman, L., T. Antonucci, P. Adelmann, and S. Crohan (1987). Social roles in the lives of middle-aged and older black women. *Journal of Marriage and the Family*, *49*, (4): 761-771.

Coltrane, Scott, and M. Ishii-Kuntz (1992). Men's housework: A life course perspective. *Journal of Marriage and the Family,* 54: 43-57.

Combrinck-Graham, L. (1988). When parents separate or divorce: The sibling system. In Kahn, M. & Lewis, K. (Eds.), *Siblings in Therapy* (pp. 190-208). New York: W.W. Norton.

Constantine, L. (1986). *Family paradignms: The practice of theory in family therapy*. New York: Guilford Press.

Cooney, T. M., and P. Uhlenberg. The role of divorce in men's relations with their adult children after mid-life. *Journal of Marriage and the Family,* 52, 1990: 677-688.

Coontz, S. (1992). *The way we never were: American families and the nostalgia trap*. New York: Harper Collins.

Cooper, P. (1990, April). Stepmothers-stepdaughters: Gender issues in stepfamily communication. *Central States Communication Association Convention*, Detroit, MI.

Corrales, R.G. (1975). Power and satisfaction in early marriage. In R.E. Cromwell & D.H. Olson (Eds.), *Power in families* (pp. 197-216). New York: John Wiley & Sons.

Coser, L.A. (1967). *Continuities in the study of social conflict*. New York: The Free Press.

Courtright, J.A., F.E. Millar, and L.E. Rogers-Miller (1979). Domineeringness and dominance: Replication and expansion. *Communication Monographs*, 46: 179-192.

Cowan, C.P., P.A. Cowan, H. Heming, E. Garrett, W. Coysh, H. Curtis-Boles, and A.J. Boles. (1985). Transitions to parenthood: His, hers, theirs. *Journal of Family Issues,* 6: 451-481.

Crane, D. R.,D. Dollahite,W. Griffin, and K. Taylor (1987). Diagnosing relationships with spatial distance: An empirical test of a clinical principle. *Journal of Marital and Family Therapy*, 13: 307-310.

Cromwell, R.E., and D.H. Olson (Eds.). (1975). *Power in families.* New York: Halsted Press.

Cronen, V., W.B. Pearce, and L. Harris. (1979). The logic of the coordinated management of meaning: A rules-based approach to the first course in inter-personal communication. *Communication Education*, 23: 22-38.

Crosbie-Burnett, M., and L. Helmbrecht (1993). A descriptive empirical study of gay male stepfamilies. *Family Relations,* 42: 256-262.

Cryer–Downs, V. (1989). The grandparent–grandchild relationship. In J. Nussbaum (Ed.), *Life-span communication: Normative processes* (pp. 257–281). Hillsdale, NJ: Erlbaum.

Csikszentmihalyi, M., and E. Rochberg-Halton (1981). *The meaning of things: Domestic symbols and the self*. Cambridge UK: Cambridge University Press.

Curran, D. (1983). *Traits of healthy family*. Minneapolis: Winston Press.

Current Population Reports. (1992). U.S. Department of Commerce, Bureau of Census.

Cushman, D. and R.T. Craig (1976). Communication systems, interpersonal implications. In G. R. Miller (Ed), *Explorations in interpersonal communications*. Beverly Hills: Sage.

Cutler, B.R., and W.G. Dyer (1973). Initial adjustment processes in young married couples. In M.E. Lasswell and T.E. Lasswell (Eds.), *Love, marriage, family: A developmental approach* (pp. 290–296). Glenview, IL.: Scott, Foresman and Co.

Davis, E.C., A.H. Hovestadt, F.P Piercy, and S.W. Cochran (1982). Effects of weekend and weekly marriage enrichment program formats. *Family Relations*, 31: 85–90.

Day, C., L., and B.W. Morse (1981). Communication patterns in established lesbian relationships. In J. W. Chesebro (Ed.), *Gayspeak: Gay male and lesbian communication*. New York: Pilgrim Press.

DeFrain, J. (1979). Androgynous parents tell who they are and what they need. *Family Coordinator*, 28: 237–43.

DeFrain, J., and N. Stinnett (1985). *Secrets of strong families*. Boston: Little, Brown & Company.

deHoyos, G. (1989). Person in environment: A tri-level practice model. *Social Casework*, 70 (3): 131–138.

Dell, P. (1989). Violence and the systemic view: The problem of power. *Family Process*, 28: 1–14.

Dell, P.F. (1982). Beyond homeostasis: Toward a concept of coherence. *Family Process*, 21: 21–42.

DeLong, A. (1974). Environments for the elderly. *Journal of Communication*, 24 (4): 101–112.

Demaris, A., and G.R. Leslie (1984). Cohabitation with future spouse: Its influence upon marital satisfaction and communication. *Journal of Marriage and the Family*, 46: 79–84.

Demaris, A., and W. MacDonald (1993). Premarital cohabitation and marital instability: A test of the unconventionality hypothesis. *Journal of Marriage and the Family* 55, No. 2: 399–407.

Demo, D., S. Small, and R. Savin-Williams (1987). Family relations and the self-esteem of adolescents and their parents. *Journal of Marriage and the Family*, 49 (4): 705–715.

Demo, D. (1992). Parent-child relations: Assessing recent changes. *Journal of Marriage and the Family*, 54: 104–117.

deTurck, M., and G. Miller (1986). The effects of husbands' and wives' social cognition on their marital adjustment, conjugal power, and self-esteem. *Journal of Marriage and the Family*, 48 (4): 714–724.

DeVito, J. A (1993). *Messages: Building interpersonal communication skills*, New York. Harper-Collins.

De Vito, J. (1979). Education responsibilities to the gay and lesbian student. Paper presented at the Speech Communication Association Convention.

de Young, A. J. (1979). Marriage encounter: A critical examination. *Journal of Marital and Family Therapy*, 5: 27–41.

Dickson, P. (1988). *Family words*. Reading MA: Addison-Wesley.

Dickson-Markman, F., and H. Markman (1993). The benefits of communication research. Intervention programs for couples and families. In P. Boss et al. (Eds). *Source book of family theories and methods.* (pp. 525-529). New York: Plenum Press.

DiGiullio, J. F. (1992). Early widowhood: An atypical transition. *Journal of Mental Health Counseling,* 14: 97-109.

DiLapi, E. (1989). Lesbian mothers and the motherhood hierarchy. *Journal of Homosexuality,* 18, 1-2: 101-121.

Dilworth-Anderson, P., L.M. Burton, and W.L. Turner (1993). The importance of values in the study of culturally diverse families. *Family Relations,* 42: 238-242.

Dilworth-Anderson, P., and H. P. McAdoo (1988). The study of ethnic minority families: Implications of practitioners and policymakers. *Family Relations,* 37: 265-267.

Dinkmeyer, D., and J. Carlson (1984). *Time for a better marriage.* Circle Pines, MN: American Guidance Service.

Dinkmeyer, D., and J. Carlson (1984). *Training in marriage enrichment.* (T.I.M.E.) Circle Pines, MN: American Guidance Service.

Dinkmeyer, D., and J. Carlson (1986). A systematic approach to marital enrichment. *The American Journal of Family Therapy,* 14: 139-144.

Doherty, W. (1981). Locus of control differences and marital dissatisfaction. *Journal of Marriage and the Family,* 43: 369-377.

Doherty, W. (1987). Have yourself a merry little Christmas ... or else. *Family Networker,* 11:6: 53-56.

Doherty, W., and J. Baptiste (1993). Theories emerging from family therapy. In P. Boss et al. (Eds). *Sourcebook of Family Theories and Methods.* (pp. 525-524). New York: Plenum Press.

Doherty, W., and P. Boss (1991). Values and ethics in family therapy. In Gurman, A., and D. Kniskern (Eds). *Handbook of Family Therapy,* Vol. II. (pp. 606-637) New York: Brunner/Mazel.

Doherty, W., M. Lester, and G. Leigh (1986). Marriage encounter weekends: Couples who win and couples who lose. *Journal of Marital & Family Therapy,* 12: 49-62.

Doherty, W.J., P. McCabe, and R.G. Ryder (1978). Marriage encounter: A critical appraisal. *Journal of Marriage and the Family Counseling,* 4: 99-106.

Dornbusch, S. M., J. M. Carlsmith, S. Bushwall, P. Ritter, H. Leiderman, A. Hastorf, and R. T. Gross (1985). Single parents, extended households and the control of adolescents. *Child Development Journal,* 56: 326-341.

Dornbusch, S. M., P. L. Ritter, R. Mont-Reynaud, Z.-Y. Chen (1990). Family decision making and academic performance in a diverse high school population. *Journal of Adolescent Research,* 5: 143-160.

Douglas, S.R., and Y. Wind (1978). Examining family role and authority patterns: Two methodological issues. *Journal of Marriage and the Family,* 40: 35-47.

Douvan, E. (1983) Commentary: theoretical perspectives on peer association. In J.L. Epstein and N. Karweit (Eds.) *Friends in school: Patterns of selection and influence in secondary schools.* New York: Academic Press: 63-69.

Dreikurs, T. (1964). *Children: The challenge.* New York: Hawthorn Books.

Dreyer, C. and A. Dreyer (1984). Family dinner times as unique behavior habitat. *Family Process.* 12,: 291-302.

Dreyfous, L. (1994). Cohousing: A new way of living. *Chicago Tribune.* sec 16, : 5.

Duck, S. (1993). *Learning about relationships.* Newbury Park: Sage.

Duck, S. (1994). General perspectives on the multidisciplinary field of personal relationships. *Perspectives in close relationships,* (pp. 359_371). Ann L. Weber and John H. Harvey (Eds.), Needham Heights, MA: Allyn & Bacon.

Duck, S. (Ed.). (1984). *Personal relationships: Repairing personal relationships*. New York: Academic Press.

Duck, S., D. Rutt, M. Hoy Hurst, and H. Strejc (1991). Some evident truths about conversations in everyday relationships: All communications are not created equal. *Human Communication Research,* 18: 228–267.

Duck, S., D. Miell, and D. Miell (1984). Relationship growth and decline. In H. Sypher & J. Applegate (Eds.), *Communication by children and adults* (pp. 292–312). Beverly Hills: Sage Publications.

Dudley, J. (1991). Increasing our understanding of divorced fathers who have infrequent contact with their children. *Family Relations,* 40: 279–285.

Duncan, B.L., and J.W. Rock (1993). Saving relationships: The power of the unpredictable." *Psychology Today*. January/February. 46-51, 86, 95.

Dunlop, R.S. (1978). *Helping the bereaved*. Bowie, MD: Charles Press.

Durrett, M.E., P. Richards, M. Otoki, J. W. Pennebaker, and L. Nyquist (1986). Mothers' involvement with infant and her perception of spousal support, Japan and America." *Journal of Marriage and the Family,* 48: 187–194.

Duvall, E. (1988). Family development's first forty years. *Family Relations, 37*: 127–134.

Eggert, L. (1987). Support in family ties: Stress, coping and adaptation. In T. Albrecht & M. Adelman, (Eds.), *Communicating Social Support* (pp. 80–104). Newbury Park CA: Sage.

Einstein, E. (1982). Stepfamily: Chaotic, complex, challenging. *Stepfamily Bulletin*, 1: 1–2.

Einstein, E., and L. Albert (1986). *Strengthening your stepfamily*. Circle Pines, MN: American Guidance Service.

Ellis, T. (1982). *The marriage enrichment weekend: A qualitative study of a particular weekend experience*. Unpublished dissertation, Northwestern University.

Epstein, N.B., D.S. Bishop, and L.M. Baldwin (1982). McMaster model of family functioning. In F. Walsh (Ed.), *Normal family processes* (pp. 115–141). New York: Guilford Press.

Erickson, E.H. (1968). *Identity, youth, and crisis*. New York: W.W. Norton & Co.

Evans, N. (1987). A framework for assisting student affairs staff in fostering moral development. *Journal of Counseling & Development*, 60: 191–193.

Fagan, T. K., and W. M. Jenkins (1989). People with disabilities: An update. *Journal of Counseling and Development,* 68: 140–144.

Falicov, C., and B. Karrer (1980). Cultural variations in the family life cycle: The Mexican-American family. In E. Carter & M. McGoldrick (Eds.), *The Family Life Cycle: A Framework for Family Therapy* (pp. 383–425). New York: Gardner Press.

*Family Home Evening: Love Makes Our House a Home*. (1974). Salt Lake City: The Church of Jesus Christ Of Latter–day Saints press.

*Family Hone Evening Resource Book*. (1983). Salt Lake City: The Church of Jesus Christ of Latter-day Saints.

Farrell, M. P., and G. M. Barnes (1993). Family systems and social support: A test of the effects of cohesion and adaptability on the functioning of parents and adolescents. *Journal of Marriage and the Family,* 55: 119–132.

Feifel, H. (1977). *New meaning of death*. New York: McGraw-Hill Book Co.

Feist, S. (1993). Marriage and family: Understanding the changing family. *The Advocate*.

Feldman, L.B. (1979). Marital conflict and marital intimacy: An integrative psychodynamic-behavioral systemic model. *Family Process,* 18: 69–78.

Feldman, L.B. (1982). Sex roles and family dynamics. In F. Walsh (Ed.), *Normal Family Process* (pp. 345-382). New York: Guilford Press.

Ferreiro, B. (1990). Presumption of joint custody: A family policy dilemma. *Family Relations,* 39: 420–426.

Festinger, L., S. Schacter, and K. Beck (1950). *Social pressure in informal groups: A study of human factors in housing*. New York: Harper & Row.

Fiese, B. H., Karen A. Hooker, L. Kotary, and J. Schwagen (1993). Family rituals in the early stages of parenthood. *Journal of Marriage and the Family,* 55: 633-642.

Filley, A.C. (1975). *Interpersonal conflict resolution*. Glenview, IL: Scott, Foresman and Co.

Fine, M. and D. Fine (1992). Recent changes in laws affecting stepfamilies: Suggestions for legal reforms. *Family Relations,* 41: 334-340.

Fine, M. A. (1989). A social science perspective on stepfamily law: Suggestions for legal reform. *Family Relations,* 38: 53-58.

Fine, M., P. C. McKenry, B. W. Donnelly, and P. Voydanoff (1992). Perceived adjustment of parents and xhildren: Variations by family structure, race and gender. *Journal of Marriage and the Family,* 54: 118-127.

Fine, M., and J. Norris (1989). Intergenerational relations & family therapy research: What we can learn from other disciplines. *Family Process,* 28: 301-315.

Fitzpatrick, M. (1988). *Between husbands and wives*. Beverly Hills: Sage.

Fitzpatrick, M. A. (1987). Marital interaction. In C. Berger & S. Chaffee (Eds.), *Handbook of communication science* (pp.564-618). Newbury Park, CA: Sage.

Fitzpatrick, M.A. (1977). A typological approach to communication in relationships. In B. Rubin (Ed.), *Communication Yearbook I* (pp. 263-275). New Brunswick, NJ: Transaction Press.

Fitzpatrick, M.A., and D.M. Badzinski (1985). All in the family: Interpersonal communication in kin relationships. In M. L. Knapp & G. R. Miller (Eds.), *Handbook of Interpersonal Communication*, (pp. 687-736). Beverly Hills, CA: Sage.

Fitzpatrick, M. A. and D. Badzinski (1994). All in the family: Interpersonal communication in kin relationships. In M. L. Knapp & G. R. Miller (Eds), Handbook of Interpersonal Communication, 2nd ed. (pp. 726-771). Thousand Oaks, CA: Sage.

Fitzpatrick, M.A., and P. Best (1979). Dyadic adjustment in relational types: Consensus, cohesion, affectional expression, and satisfaction in enduring relationships. *Communication Monographs,* 46: 165-178.

Fitzpatrick, M.A., F. Jandt, F. Myrick, and T. Edgar (1994). Gay and lesbian couple erelationships. In R. Jeffrey Ringer (Ed.) *Queer words, queer images*: 265-276. NY: New York University Press.

Fitzpatrick, M.A., S. Fallis, and L. Vance (1982). Multifunctional coding of conflict resolution strategies in marital dyads. *Family Relations*: 31, 61-70.

Floyd, F. (1988). Couples' cognitive/affective reactions to communication behaviors. *Journal of Marriage and the Family*, 50: 523-532.

Ford, D.A. (1983). Wife battery and criminal justice: A study of victim decision making. *Family Relations*, 32: 463-476.

Forehand, R., A. McCombs, N. Long, G. Brady, and R. Fauber (1988). Early adolescent adjustment to recent parental divorce: The role of interparental conflict and adolescent sex as mediating variables. *Journal of Consulting and Clinical Psychology*, 56, (4): 624-627.

Forgatch, M. (1989). Patterns and outcomes in family problem solving: The disrupting effect of negative emotion. *Journal of Marriage and the Family*, 51: 115-124.

Fortier, L., and R. Wanlass (1984). Family crisis following the diagnosis of a handicapped child. *Family Relations*, 33: 13-24.

Fossett, M., and J. K. Kiecolt (1991). A methodological review of the sex ratio: Alternatives for comparative research. *Journal of Marriage and the Family,* 53: 941-957.

Foster, C. (1993). *The family patterns workshop*. New York: Tarcher-Perigee.

French, J.R.P., Jr., and B.H. Raven (1962). The bases of social power. In D. Cartwright and A. Zander (Eds.). *Group Dynamics*, (pp. 607–623) Evanston, IL: Row Peterson: (Republished 1975).

Frey, J. (1984). A family/system approach to illness-maintaining behaviors in chronically ill adolescents. *Family Process*, 23: 251–260.

Friedan, B. (1993). *The fountain of age*. New York: Simon and Schuster.

Furstenberg, F. (1987). The new extended family: The experience of parents and children after remarriage. In K. Pasley & M. Ihinger-Tallman (Eds.), *Remarriage and stepparenting: Current research* (pp. 42–61). New York: Guilford Press.

Gage, G. M., and D. Christensen (1991). Parental role socialization & the transition to parenthood. *Family Relations,* 40: 332–337.

Gagnon, J. (1977). *Human sexuality*. Glenview, IL: Scott, Foresman and Co.

Galvin, K. (1989). Stepfamily identity development. Speech presented at annual Van Zelst Lecture. Northwestern University.

Galvin, K.M. (1993, April). Family forms and interaction patterns: Impact on home–school communication. Paper presented at International Reading Association, Orlando.

Galvin, K.M. (1982). Pishogues and paddywhackery: Transmission of communication patterns and values through three generations of an extended Irish-American family. Paper presented at the Speech Communication Association Convention, Minneapolis.

Galvin, K.M. (1993). First marriage families: Gender and communication. In L. Arliss and D. Borisoff (Eds.) *Men and Women Communicating*: (pp. 86–101). Fort Worth, TX: Harcourt Brace Jovanovich.

Galvin, K.M. (1990). Developing stepfamily identity through boundary management: Potential communication components. *Central States Communication Association*, Detroit, MI.

Galvin, K., and Cooper, P. (1990). Development of involuntary relationships: The stepparent/stepchild relationship. Paper delivered at the International Communication Association Conference. Dublin, Ireland.

Ganong, L., and M. Coleman (1989). Preparing for remarriage: Anticipating the issues, seeking solutions. *Family Relations* 38: 28–33.

Gantman, C. (1980). A closer look at families that work well. *International Journal of Family Therapy*, 2: 106–119.

Garcia-Preto, Hill, N. (1988). Transformation of the family system in adolescence. In B. Carter & M. McGoldrick (Eds.), *The changing family life cycle: A framework for family therapy* (2nd. ed., pp. 255–283). New York: Gardner Press.

Garland, D.S. (1983). *Working with couples for marriage enrichment*. San Francisco: Jossey–Bass.

Garrett, P., J. Ferron, N. Ng'Andu, D. Bryant, and G. Harbin (1994). A structural model for the developmental status of young children. *Journal of Marriage and the Family,* 56: 147–163.

Gecas, V., and M. Schwalbe (1986). Parental behavior and adolescent self esteem. *Journal of Marriage and the Family*, *48*: 37–46.

Gerber, G. (1991). Under stereotypes & power: Perceptions of roles in violent marriages. *Sex Roles* 24: 439–455.

Giblin, P., D. Sprenkle, and R. Sheehan (1985). Enrichment of outcome research: A meta-analysis of premarital, marital and family interventions. *Journal of Marital and Family Therapy*, 11: 257–271.

Giblin, P. (1993). Marriage and marital therapy. *The Family Journal,* 1: 339–341.

Giblin, Paul (1994). "Marital Satisfaction." *Family Journal,* 2: 48–50.

Gilbert, L.A., G.R. Hanson, and B. Davis (1982). Perceptions of parental role responsibilities: Differences between mothers and fathers. *Family Relations*, 31: 261–270.

Gilbert, S. (1976). Self-Disclosure, intimacy, and communication in families. *Family Coordinator*, 25: 221-229.

Giles, H., and J. Wiemann (1987). Language, social comparison, and power. In C. Bergerand and S. Chafee (Eds.) *Handbook of communication science* (pp. 619-650). Beverly Hills: Sage Publications.

Gilligan, C. (1982). *In a different voice*. Cambridge, MA: Harvard University Press.

Gilligan, C., P. Lyons, and T. Hammer (Eds.). (1989). *Making conversations: Interpreting the interpersonal world of adolescent girls at Emma Willard School*. Troy, New York: Emma Willard School.

Giordano, J. (1988). Parents of the baby boomers: A new generation of young-old. *Family Relations*, 37: 411-414.

Glenn, N., and K. Kramer (1987). The marriages and divorces of the children of divorce. *Journal of Marriage and the Family*, 49: 811-826.

Glick, P. (1989). American families: As they are and were (realities in fact). Paper presented at the Florida Conference on Family Development. Jacksonville, FL.

Glick, P. (1990). Marriage and family trends. In D. Olson & M. K. Hanson (Eds.), *2001: Preparing families for the future:* (pp. 2-3). Minneapolis: National Council on Family Relations.

Golanty, E., and B.B. Harris (1982). *Marriage and family life*. Boston: Houghton Mifflin.

Goldberg, J. (1994, August). Rescuing children and adolescents from the coming crime storm. *Family Theory News* 14-15: 23-25.

Goldberg, L. (March 1983). They stole our childhood. *Newsweek*: 32.

Goldner, V. (1989). Generation and gender: Normative and covert hierarchies, In M. McGoldrick, C. Anderson & F. Walsh (Eds.) *Women in families*: (pp. 42-60). New York: W.W. Norton.

Goldner, V., P. Penn, M. Sheinberg, and G. Walker (1990). Love & violence: Gender paradoxes in volatile attachments. *Family Process* 29: 343-364.

Goldner, V. Generation and gender, normative and covert hierarchies. In M. McGoldrick, C. Anderson, Froma Walsh (Eds.) *Women in Families*, pp. 42-60. New York: W.W. Norton.

Gongla, P. (1982). Single parent families: A look at families of mothers and children. *Marriage and the Family Review* 5: 2, New York: Haworth Press.

Gonzalez, D. (1993, Jan 17). Seeking security, man retreat behind bars and razor wire. *New York Times*, sec. 1: pp. 1, 18.

Gordon, T. (1975). *Parent effectiveness training*. New York: New American Library.

Gotcher, J. Michael (1993). The effects of family communication on psychological adjustment of cancer patients. *Journal of Applied Communication Research* 21: 176-188.

Gottlieb, B. (1994). "Social support. In A Weber and J. Harvey (Eds). *Perspective on Close Relationships* (pp. 307-324). Boston: Allyn and Bacon.

Gottman, J. (1993). The roles of conflict engagement, escalation of avoidance in marital interaction: A longitudinal view of five types of couples. *Journal of Consulting and Clinical Psychology*. 61 6-15.

Gottman, J. M., H. Markham, and C. Notarius (1977). The topography of marital conflict: A sequential analysis of verbal and nonverbal behavior. *Journal of Marriage and the Family*, 39 461-477.

Gottman, J.M. (1979). *Marital interaction: Experimental investigations*. New York: Academic Press.

Gottman, J.M. (1982). Emotional responsiveness in marital conversations. *Journal of Communication* 32: 103-120.

Gottman, J. M. and L. J. Krokoff (1989). Marital interaction and satisfaction: A longitudinal view. *Journal of Consulting and Clinical Psychology* 57: 47-52.

Gottman, J. M. and L. J. Krokoff (1990). Complex statistics are not always clearer than simple statistics: A reply to Woody and Costenzo. *Journal of Consulting and Clinical Psychology,* 58: 502-505.

Gottman, J. Why marriages fail. *Family Therapy Networker*, May/June 94: 41-48.

Grebe, S. (1986). Mediation in separation and divorce. *Journal of Counseling & Development*, 64: 379-382.

Green, B. (1970). *A clinical approach to marital problems*. Springfield, IL: Charles C. Thomas.

Grimm-Thomas, K., and M. Perry-Jenkins (1993). All in a day's work: job experiences, self-esteem and fathering in working-class families. *Family Relations,* 42: 174-181.

Gudykunst, W., Y.C. Yoon, and T. Nishida (1986). The developmental tasks of siblingship over the life cycle. *Journal of Marriage and the Family*, 48, (4): 703-714.

Guelzow, M., G.W. Bird, and E. Koball (1991). An exploratory path analysis of the stress process for dual-career men and women. *Journal of Marriage and the Family,* 53: 151-164.

Guenther, R. (1984, April 11). Real estate column. *The Wall Street Journal,* p 1.

Guerney, B. G. (1977). *Relationship enhancement: Skill training programs for therapy, problem prevention, and enrichment*. San Francisco: Jossey-Bass.

Gunter, N., and B.G. Gunter (1990). Domestic division of labor among working couples. *Psychology of Women Quarterly,* 14: 355-370.

Gurman, A. and D. Kniskern (Eds.) (1991). *Handbook of family therapy*, Vol. II. New York: Brunner/Mazel.

Gurman, A., and D. Kniskern (1977). Enriching research on marital enrichment programs. *Journal of Marriage and the Family Counseling*, 3: 3-10.

Gurman, A., and D. Kniskern (1981). *Handbook of family therapy*. New York: Brunner-Mazel.

Gurman, A., and D. Kriskern (1978). Research on marital and family therapy: Progress, perspective and prospect. In S. Garfield & A. Bergen (Eds.), *Handbook of psychotherapy and behavior change*, (2nd Ed.,) New York: Wiley.

Hagestad, G. (1985). Continuity and convertedness. In V. Bengtson & J. Robertson (Eds.), *Grandparenthood* (pp.31-48). Beverly Hills, CA: Sage.

Hahlweg, K., and H. Markman (1988). The effectiveness of behavioral marital therapy: Empirical status of behavioral techniques in preventing and alleviating marital distress. *Journal of Consulting and Clinical Psychology,* 56: 440-447.

Haley, J. (1974). Establishment of an interpersonal relationship. In B. R. Patton & K. Griffin, (Eds.), *Interpersonal communication: Basic text and readings* (pp.368-373). New York: Harper and Row.

Haley, J. (1976). *Problem-solving psychotherapy*. San Francisco: Jossey-Bass.

Hall, E. T. (1966). *The hidden dimension.* Golden City, NY: Doubleday.

Handel, G., and G. Whitchurch (Eds.) (1994). *The psychological interior of the family*. Hawthorne, NY: Aldine de Gruyter.

Hansen, G. (1991). Balancing work & family: A literature & resource review. *Family Relations,* 40: 348-353.

Hanson, S. (1986). Healthy single parent families. *Family Relations* 35: 125-132.

Hare-Mustin, R. (1989). The problem of gender in family therapy theory. In M. McGoldrick, C. Anderson and F. Walsh, (Eds.), *Women in families,* (pp. 61-77). New York: W.W. Norton.

Harevan, T. (1982). American families in transition: Historical perspective on change. In F. Walsh (Ed.), *Normal Family Processes*. (pp 446-465). New York: Guilford Press.

Harris, L., & Associates. (1987). *The Philip Morris family survey*. New York.

Harrison, C. (1993). Here's baby. dad stays home. dad gets antsy. *New York Times*, August 31.

Hart, B. (1986). Lesbian battering: An examination. In K. Lobel (Ed.), *Naming the violence* (pp. 173-189). Seattle: Seal Press.

Haslett, B., and S. Perlmutter-Bowen (1989). Children's strategies in initiating interaction with peers. In J. Nussbaum (Ed.), *Life-Span Communication: Normative Processes*: 27-52, Hillside, NJ: Lawrence Erlbaum.

Hatfield, E., and R. Rapson (1993). *Love, sex and intimacy.* New York: Harper Collins.

Hawkins, A. J., S. L. Christiansen, K. P. Sargent, and E. J. Hill (1993). Rethinking father's involvement in child care: A developmental perspective. *Journal of Family Issues,* 14: 531-549.

Hawkins, A., and J. Belsky (1989). The role of father involvement in personality change in men across the transition to parenthood. *Family Relations,* 38: 378-383.

Hayes, R. L. (1994). The legacy of Lawrence Kohlberg: Implications for counseling and human development. *Journal of Counseling/Development,* 72: 261-267.

Heaton, T. B., and C. K. Jacobson (1994). Race differences in changing family demographics in the 1980s. *Journal of Family Issues,* 15: 290-308.

Heiss, J. (1968). An introduction to the elements of role theory. In J. Heiss, (Ed.), *Family Roles and Interaction* (pp. 3-27). Chicago: Rand McNally.

Herz, F. (1980). The impact of death and serious illness on the family life cycle. In E. Carter & M. McGoldrick (Eds.), *The family life cycle: A framework for family therapy* (pp. 223-240). New York: Gardner Press.

Herz, F., and E. Rosen (1982). Jewish families. In M. McGoldrick, J. Pearce & J. Giordano (Eds.), *Ethnicity and family therapy* (pp. 364-392) New York: Guilford.

Herz-Brown, H. (1988). The post divorce family. In B. Carter & M. McGoldrick (Eds.), *The changing family life cycle: A framework for therapy*. (2nd ed., pp. 371-398). New York: Gardner Press.

Hess, R., and G. Handel (1959). *Family worlds*. Chicago: University of Chicago Press.

Hetherington, E. (1987). Family relations six years after divorce. In K. Pasley & M. Inhinger-Tallman (Eds.), *Remarriage and stepparenting: Current Research* (pp. 185-205). New York: Guilford Press.

Hetherington, E. M., M. Cox, and R. Cox (1976). Divorced fathers. *The family coordinator*, 25: 417-428.

Hey, R., and G. Neubeck (1990). Family life education. In Dolson & M. K. Hanson (Eds.), *2001: Preparing families for the future* (pp.7-25). Hillsdale, NJ: Laurence Erlbaum.

Hill, R. (1949). *Families under stress*. New York: Harper & Brothers.

Hill, R. (1986). Life cycle stages for types of single parent families: Of family development theory. *Family Relations*, 35: 19-29.

Hill, W., and J. Scanzoni (1982). An approach for assessing marital decision-making processes. *Journal of Marriage and the Family*, 44: 927-940.

Hines, P.M. (1988). The family life cycle of poor black families. In B. Carter and M. McGoldrick (Eds.) *The changing family life cycle: A framework for family therapy* (2nd Ed.) (pp. 513-544). New York: Gardner Press.

Hobart, C. (1988). The family system in remarriage: An exploratory study. *Journal of Marriage and the Family*, 50: 649-661.

Hochschild, A. (1989). *The second shift*, New York: Avon Books.

Hocker, J. L, and W. Wilmot (1991). *Interpersonal conflict*, Dubuque, Iowa: Wm. C. Brown & Co.

Hof, L., and W.R. Miller (1983). *Marriage enrichment*. Bowie, MD: Brady/Prentice-Hall.

Hoffman, L. (1980). The family life cycle and discontinuous change. In E. Carter & M. McGoldrick (Eds.), *The family life cycle: A framework for family therapy* (pp. 53–68). New York: Gardner Press.

Hoffman, L. (1990). Constructing realities: The art of lenses. *Family Process,* 29: 1: 1–12.

Hohn, C. (1987). The family life cycle: Needed extension of the concept. In T. K. Burch & K. W. Wachter (Eds.), (pp. 156–180). *Family demography: Methods and their application.* New York: Oxford University Press.

Holmes, T. H., and R.H. Rahe (1967). The social readjustment rating scale. *Journal of Psychosomatic Research*, 2: 213–218.

Hood, J. (1986). The provider role: Its meaning and measurement. *Journal of Marriage and the Family*, 48: 349–359.

Hoopes, M. (1987). Multigererational systems: Basic assumptions. *American Journal of Family Therapy*, 15: 195–205.

Hoopes, M. M., and J.M. Harper (1987). *Birth order roles and sibling patterns in individual and family therapy*. Rockville, MD: Aspen Publishers.

Hopper, R., M.L. Knapp, and S. Lorel (1981). Couples' personal idioms: Exploring intimate talk. *Journal of Communication*, 31: 23–33.

Horwitz, J., and J. Tognoli (1982). Role of home in adult development: Women and men living alone describe their residential histories. *Family Relations*, 31: 335–341.

Howard, J. (1978). *Families.* New York: Simon & Schuster.

Hurvitz, N., and M. Komarovsky (1977). Husbands and wives: Middle class and working class. *The marriage game*, (2nd ed.) Cathy Greenblatt et al., eds. New York: Random House.

Huston, T. L., S.M. McHale and A.C. Crouter (1986). When the honeymoon's over: Changes in the marriage relationship over the first year. In R. Gilmore & S. Duck (Eds.), *The emerging field of personal relationships* (pp. 109–132). Hillsdale, NJ: Laurence Erlbaum.

Invik, J., and M. A. Fitzpatrick (1982). If you could read my mind love … Understanding misunderstanding in the marital dyads. *Family Relations,* 31: 43–52.

Ishii-Kuntz, M. (1994). Paternal involvement and perception toward fathers' roles: A comparison. *Journal of Family Issues* 15: 30–48.

Issod, J. (1987). A comparison of 'on-time' and 'delayed' parenthood. *American Mental Health Counselors Association Journal, 92.*

Jackson, A. W., and D. W. Hornbeck (1989). Educating young adolescents why we must restructure middle grade schools. *American Psychologist,* 44: 831–836.

Jaramillo, P., and J. Zapata (1987). Roles and alliances within Mexican-American & Anglo families. *Journal of Marriage and the Family*, 49, (4): 727–735.

Johnson, C., and L. Vinson (1990). Placement and frequency of powerless talk and impression formation. *Communication Quarterly,* 28: 325–333.

Johnson, D. (1993, Aug. 31). More and more, the single parent is dad. *New York Times*, 31: 24.

Johnson, R. (1984). Conflict management in established gay male dyads: A qualitative study. Paper presented at the Speech Communication Association Convention, Chicago.

Johnson, S., and L. Greenberg (1988). Relating process to outcome in marital therapy. *Journal of Marital and Family Therapy*, 14: 175–183.

Jones, E., and C. Gallois (1989). Spouses impressions of rules for communication in public and private marital conflicts. *Journal of Marriage and the Family*, 51: 957–967.

Jones, J. (1993). Historical perspectives on families and justice in distressed communities. *Speech at National Council of Family Relations Convention*, Minneapolis.

Jones, T. (November, 1982). Analysis of family metaphor: Methodological and theoretical implications. Paper presented at Speech Communication Association, Louisville, KY.

Jordon, J. (Dec. 1983-Jan. 1984). The challenge: Designing buildings for older Americans. *Aging*, 342: 18-21.

Jourard, S. (1971). *The transparent self*. New York: Van Nostrand Reinhold Co.

Julian, T., P. McKenry, and M.W. McKelvey (1994). Cultural variations in parenting—perceptions of Caucasian, African-American, and Asian parents. *Family Relations* 43: 30-37.

Kalmuss, D. S. (1984). The intergenerational transmission of marital aggression. *Journal of Marriage and the Family*, 46: 11-19.

Kalmuss, D., A. Davidson, and L. Cushman (1992). Parenting expectations, experiences and adjustments to parenthood: A test of the violated expectations framework *Journal of Marriage and the Family*, 54: 516-526.

Kantor, D., and W. Lehr (1976). *Inside the family*. San Francisco: Jossey-Bass.

Kaplan, L. (Ed.) (1992). *Education and the family*. Needham Heights, MA: Allyn and Bacon.

Kaplan, L., and C. Hennon (1992). Remarriage education: Reflections program. *Family Relations*, 41: 127-134.

Kaslow, F. (1987). Marital and family therapy. In M. B. Sussman & S. K. Steinmetz (Eds.), *Handbook of marriage and the family* (pp. 835-860). New York: Plenum Press.

Kelley, D. (1988). Privacy in marital relationships. *The Southern Speech Communication Journal*, 53: 441-456.

Kelly, D., and L. Warshafsky (1987). Partner abuse in gay male and lesbian couples. Paper presented at the Third National Conference for Family Violence Researchers, Durham, N.C.

Kennedy, R. W. (1953). *The house and the art of its design*. New York: Reinhold Publishing Co.

Killmann, R., and K. Thomas (1975). Interpersonal conflict handling behavior as reflections of Jungian personality dimensions. *Psychological Reports*, 37: 971-980.

Kingsbury, N., and J. Scanzoni (1993). Structural-functionalism. In Pauline Boss, et al. (Eds.), *Sourcebook of family theories and methods*, (pp. 195-221). New York: Plenum Press.

Kirchler, E. (1988). "Marital Happiness and Interaction in Everyday Surroundings." *Journal of Social and Personal Relationships*, 5: 375-82.

Kirk, L. (1989). Contemporary family scripts and intergenerational communication. Paper delivered at Speech Communication Association Convention, San Francisco.

Kissman, K., and J.A. Allen (1993). *Single parent families*. Newbury Park, CA: Sage.

Kivett, R. V. (1993). Racial comparisons of the grandmother role. *Family Relations*, 42: 165-172.

Kline, M., et al. (1991). The long shadow of marital conflict: A model of children's post-divorce adjustment. *Journal of Marriage and the Family*, 53: 297-309.

Knapp, M. L. (1972). *Nonverbal communication in human interaction*. New York: Holt, Rinehart & Winston.

Knapp, M., and A. L. Vangelisti (1992). *Interpersonal communication and human relationships*, 2nd ed. Needham Heights, MA.

Knapp, M., and E. Taylor (1994). Commitment and its communication in romantic relationships. In A. Weber, J. Harvey (Ed.) *Perspectives on close relationships*: pp. 153, 175. Boston: Allyn & Bacon.

Kniskern, D. (1983). The new wave is all wet. *The Family Therapy Networker*, 7: 39-41.

Koepke, L., J. Mare, P. Moran (1992). Relationship quality in a sample of lesbian couples with children and child free. *Family Relations*, April '92.

Kohlberg, L. (1964). Development of moral character and moral ideology. In M. L. Hoffman & L. W. Hoffman (Eds.), *Review of child development research 1* (pp. 383-431). New York: Russell Sage Foundation.

Kohlberg, L. (1969). Stage and sequence. The cognitive developmental approach to socialization. In D. Goshen (Ed.) *Handbook of socialization theory and research*, (347–480). Chicago: Rand McNally.

Kohlberg, L. (1973). Continuities in childhood and adult moral development revisited. In P. Baltes & K. W. Schaie (Eds.), *Life-span developmental psychology: Personality and socialization*. New York: Academic Press.

Kolb, T. M., and M.A. Straus (1974). Marital power and marital happiness in relation to problem solving ability. *Journal of Marriage and the Family*, 36: 756–766.

Kraemer, S. The origins of fatherhood: An ancient family process. *Family Process*, 1991: 377–390.

Kramer, C. H. (1980). *Becoming a family therapist*. New York: Human Sciences Press.

Kramer, J. (1985). *Family interfaces: Transgenerational patterns*. New York: Brunner-Mazel.

Krueger, D. L. (1983). Pragmatics of dyadic decision making: A sequential analysis of communication patterns. *Western Journal of Speech Communication*, 47: 99–117.

Kubler-Ross, E. (1970). *On death and dying*. New York: Macmillan.

Kurdek, L. (1994). Conflict resolution styles in gay, lesbian, heterosexual nonparent and heterosexual parent couples. *Journal of Marriage and the Family,* 56, 3: 705–722.

Kurdek, L. A. (1991). The relations between reported well-being and divorce history, availability of a proximate adult, and gender. *Journal of Marriage and the Family,* 53: 71–78.

Kurdick, L. (1989). Relationship quality in gay and lesbian cohabiting couples: A 1-year follow-up study. *Journal of Social and Personal Relationships*, *6*: 39–60.

L'Abate, L. (1981). Skill training programs for couples and families. In A. Gurman & D. Kniskern, (Eds.), *Handbook of family therapy,* (pp. 631–661). New York: Brunner-Mazel.

L'Abate, L. (1984). Structured enrichment (SE) with couples and families. *Family Relations*, 34 (2): 169–175.

Laing, R. D. (1972). *The politics of the family*. New York: Vintage Books.

Laird, J. (1993). Lesbian and gay families. In F. Walsh (Ed.) *Normal family processes*, (2nd Ed.), (pp. 282–328). New York: Guilford Press.

Landis, D. (1988, January 10). Yours, mine, but no longer ours: Dividing the spoils after divorce. *Chicago Tribune*, sec. 15. pp. 1,5.

Langhinrichsen-Rohling, J., N. Smutzler, and D. Vivian (1994). Positivity in marriage: The role of discord and physical aggression against wives. *Journal of Marriage and the Family,* 56: 69–79.

LaRossa, R., and D. Reitzes (1993). Symbolic interactionism and family studies. In P. Boss, et al. (Eds.) *Sourcebook of family theory and methods*, pp. 135–163. New York: Plenum Press.

Larsen, A., and D. Olsen (1989). Predicting marital satisfaction using PREPARE: A replication study. *Journal of Marital and Family Therapy*, 15: 311–322.

Larson, J., S.M. Wilson, and R. Beley (1994). The impact of job insecurity on marital and family relationships. *Family Relations,* 43: 138–143.

Larson, J. (1992, July). Understanding stepfamilies. *American demographics,* 14, 7: 36–40.

Lavee, Y., H. McCubbin, and D. Olson (1987). The effect of stressful life events & transitions on family functioning and well-being. *Journal of Marriage and the Family*, 49 (4): 857–873.

Lavee, Y., and D. Olson (1991). Family types and response to stress. *Journal of Marriage and the Family,* 53: 786–798.

Lawrence, R. (1987). What makes a house a home? *Environment and behavior*, 19 (2): 154–158.

Lederer, W., and D.D. Jackson (1968). *The mirages of marriage*. New York: W. W. Norton and Co.

Lederhaus, M. A., and S. K. Paulson (1986). An analysis of dyadic dominance in family decision making among older adults. *Sociological spectrum*, 6: 161-177.

Lee, C. (1988). Meta-commentary: On synthesis and fractionation in family theory and research. *Family process*, 27: 93-97.

Lee, G. (1988). Marital satisfaction in later life: The effects of nonmarital roles. *Journal of Marriage and the Family*, 50: 775-783.

Lennard, S. and H. Lennard (1977). Architecture: Effect of territory, boundary, and orientation on family functioning. *Family Process*, 16: 49-66.

Leonard, L. (1982). *The wounded woman*. Boston: Shambala Publishers.

Lerner, H. (1989). *The dance of intimacy*. New York: Harper and Row.

Levinson, D. (1978). *The seasons of a man's life*. New York: Ballantine Books.

Lewis, J. (1986). Family structure and stress. *Family Process*, 25: 235-247.

Lewis, J. M., W.R. Beavers, J.T. Gossett, and V.A. Phillips (1976). *No single thread: Psychological health in family systems.* New York: Brunner/Mazel.

Lewis, Judith A. (1993). Farewell to motherhood and applie pie: Families in the postmodern era. *The Family Journal* 1: 337-338.

Lewis, R., R.J. Volk, and S.F. Duncan (1989). Stresses on fathers and family relationships related to rural youth leaving and returning home. *Family Relations,* 38: 174-181.

Lewis, Robert (1993). These are not the best of times: Poverty on rise among elderly as economy drags. *AARP Bulletin* 35:7.

Littlejohn, S. (1983). *Theories of human communication*. (2nd ed) Belmont, Ca: Wadsworth Publishing.

Littlejohn, S. (1992). *Theories of human communication* (4th Ed.) Belmont, CA: Wadsworth.

Lopez, F. (1987). The impact of parental divorce on college student development. *Journal of Counseling & Development*, 65: 484-486.

Louie, E. (1994, Jan. 6). Retirement? For 11 friends it's off to campus. *New York Times* (B1) 1, 4.

Luepnitz, D. A. (1979). Which aspects of divorce affect children? *Family Coordinator*, 28: 79-85.

Lutz, P. L. (1983). The stepfamily: An adolescent perspective. *Family Relations*, 32: 367-376.

Lyson, T. (1985). Husband and wife work roles and the organization and operation of family farms. *Journal of Marriage and the Family*, 47: 759-764.

MacDermid, S., T. Huston, and S. McHale (1990). Changes in marriage associated with the transition to parenthood: Individual differences as a function of sex-role attitudes and changes in the division of household labor. *Journal of Marriage and the Family,* 52: 475-486.

Mace, D. (1985). The coming revolution in human relationships. *Journal of Social and Personal Relationships,* 2: 81-94.

Macklin, E. (1980). Nontraditional family forms: A decade of research. *Journal of Marriage and the Family*, 42: 905-922.

Macklin, E. (1987). Nontraditional family forms. In M.B. Sussman and S.K. Steinmetz (Eds.) *Handbook of marriage and the family*, (pp. 317-353). New York: Plenum.

Maddock, J. (1989). Healthy family sexuality: Positive principles for educators and clinicians. *Family Relations*, 38: 130- 136.

Malone, T. and P. Malone (1987). *The art of intimacy*. New York: Prentice Hall.

Markowitz, L. (1994). The cross-currents of multiculturalism. *The family therapy networker* 18, 4: 18–27, 69.

Married with Children (1992). *American demographics.* (Desk Reference Series), 3: 6–9.

Marshall, L., and P. Rose (1988). Family-of-origin violence and courtship abuse. *Journal of Counseling and Development*, 66: 414–418.

Martin, J., M. Hecht, and L. Larkey (1994). Conversational improvement strategies for inter-ethnic communication: African-American and European American perspectives." *Communication monographs,* 61, 3: 237–255.

Masheter, C. (1991). Postdivorce relationships between ex-spouses: The roles of attachment & interpersonal conflict. *Journal of Marriage and the Family,* 53: 103–110.

Maxwell, C., and D. Weider-Hatfield (1987). Level of marital satisfaction as it relates to verbal and paralinguistic cues in discussion of conflict topics. Paper presented at the Speech Communication Association Convention, Boston.

McAdams, D. (1985). *Power, intimacy, and the life story*. Homewood, IL: Dorsey Press.

McAdams, D. (1993). *Stories we live by: Personal myths and the making of the self.* New York: William Morrow.

McCarmant, K., and C. Durrett (1994, August). Co-housing American style. *New Age Journal*: 67–71.

McClelland, R., and S. Caroll (1984). Applying social epidemiology to child abuse. *Social casework*, 65: 214–218.

McCubbin, H. I., and B. Dahl (1985). *Marriage and family: Individuals and life cycles.* New York: John Wiley and Sons.

McCubbin, H. I., and J.M. Patterson (1983). Family transitions: adaptation to stress. In H. I. McCubbin & C. R. Figley (Eds.), *Coping with normative transitions*, (Vol. I) (pp. 5–25). New York: Brunner/ Mazel.

McCubbin, H. I., J.M. Patterson, A.E. Cauble, W.R. Wilson, and W. Warwick (1983). CHIP-coping health inventory for parents: An assessment of parental coping patterns in the case of the chronically ill. *Journal of Marriage and the Family*, 45: 359–370.

McCubbin, H., and M. A. McCubbin. Typologies of resilient families: Emerging roles of social class and ethnicity. *Family Relations,* 37: 247–254.

McCullough, P. G., and S.K. Rutenberg (1988). Launching children and moving on. In B. Carter & M. McGoldrick (Eds.), *The changing family life cycle*, (2nd. ed., pp. 285–309). New York: Gardner Press.

McDermott, J., J. Waldron, W. Char, J. Ching, S. Izutsu, E. Mann, D. Ponce, and C. Fukunaga (1987). New female perceptions of parental power. *American Journal of Psychiatry,* 144: 1086–1087.

McDonald, G. W. (1980). Parental power and adolescents parental identification: A reexamination. *Journal of Marriage and the Family*, 42: 289–296.

McDonald, G. W. (1980A). Family power: The assessment of a decade of theory and research, 1970–1979. *Journal of Marriage and the Family*, 42: 841–852.

McDonald, G. W. (1981). Structural exchange and marital interaction. *Journal of Marriage and the Family*, 43: 825–840.

McGoldrick, M. (1982). Irish families. In M. McGoldrick, J. Pearce & J. Giordano (Eds.), *Ethnicity and family therapy*. (pp. 310–339) New York: Guilford Press.

McGoldrick, M. (1982). Normal families: An ethnic perspective. In F. Walsh (Ed.), *Normal family processes* (pp.399–424). New York: Guilford Press.

McGoldrick, M. (1993). Ethnicity, cultural diversity and normality. In F. Walsh. *Normal family processes* (2nd ed.) (pp. 331–36). New York: Guilford Press.

McGoldrick, M. (1993, October). You can go home again. Lecture at Family Institute, Northwestern University, Chicago, October 12.

McGoldrick, M. (1994). The ache for home. *The family therapy networker,* 18, 4: 38–45.

McGoldrick, M., C. Anderson, and F. Walsh (Eds.) (1989). *Women in families*. New York: W. W. Norton.

McGoldrick, M., and B. Carter (1988). Forming a remarried family. In B. Carter & M. McGoldrick (Eds.), *The changing family life cycle: A framework for family therapy*, (2nd ed., pp. 399-429). New York: Gardner Press.

McGoldrick, M., and R. Gerson (1985). *Genograms in family assessment*. New York: W. W. Norton.

McGoldrick, M., J. Pearce, and J. Giordano (Eds). (1982). *Ethnicity and family therapy*. New York: Guilford Press.

McGoldrick, M., N. Garcia Preto, P.M. Hines, and E. Lee (1991). Ethnicity and family therapy. In German, A. and D. Kniskern (Eds) (1991). *Handbook of family therapy*. (Vol. II.) (pp. 546-582) New York: Brunner/Mazel.

McLanahan, S. and L. Bumpass (1989). Intergenerational consequences of family disruption. *American Journal of Sociology*. 94 (1): 130-152.

McWhirter, D. P., and A.M. Mattison (1984). *The male couple*. Englewood Cliffs, NJ: Prentice-Hall.

Mederer, H., and R. Hill (1983). Cultural transitions over the family span: Theory and research. In H. McCubbin, et al., (Eds.), *Social stress and the family* (pp. 39-60). New York: Hayworth Press.

Mehrabian, A. (1971). *Silent messages*. Belmont, CA: Wadsworth.

Menaghan, G., and T.L. Parcel (1991). Determining children's home environments: The impact of maternal characteristics and current occupational and family conditions. *Journal of Marriage and the Family* 53: 417-431.

Meyer, D. R., and S. Garasky (1993). Custodial fathers: Myths, realities, and child support policy. *Journal of Marriage and the Family*, 55: 73-89.

Meyer, S. (1993). Adapting parent education programs to meet the needs of fathers: An ecological perspective. *Family Relations*, 42: 4, 447-452.

Michall-Johnson, P., and S. Bowen (1989). AIDS and communication: Matter of influence. *AIDS and Public Policy Journal*, 4: 1-3.

Midelfort, C. F., and H.C. Midelfort (1982). Norweigian families. In M. McGoldrick, J. Pearce and J. Giordano (Eds.) Ethnicity and family therapy (pp. 438-456). New York: Guilford Press.

Millar, F., Rogers-Millar, L. E., and K. Villard (1978). A proposed model of relational communication and family functioning. Paper presented at the Central States Speech Association Convention, April.

Miller, B. (1979). Gay fathers and their children. *Family Coordinator*, 28: 544-552.

Miller, S., R. Corrales, and D.B. Wackman (1975). Recent progress in understanding and facilitating marital communication. *The Family Coordinator*, 24: 143-151.

Miller, V., and M. Knapp (1986). The *post nuntio* dilemma: Approaches to communicating with the dying. In M. McLaughlin (Ed.), *Communication Yearbook* (Vol. 9, pp. 723-738), Beverly Hills, CA: Sage Publications.

Mills, D. (1984). A model for stepfamily development. *Family Relations*, 33: 365-372.

Minuchin, S. (1974). *Families and family therapy*. Cambridge, MA: Harvard University Press.

Minuchin, S. (1984). *Family kaleidoscope*. Cambridge, MA: Harvard University Press.

Minuchin, S., et al. (1967). *Families of the slums*. New York: Basic Books.

Moen, P., and D. Dempster-McClain (1987). Employed parents: Role strain, work time, and preferences for working less. *Journal of Marriage and the Family*, 49: 579-590.

Montgomery, B. (1988). Quality communication in personal relationships. In S. Duck (Ed). *Handbook of personal relationships*. (pp. 343-359). New York: John Wiley.

Montgomery, B. (1993). Relational maintenance versus relational change: A dialectical dilemma. *Journal of Social and Personal Relationships*, 10: 205-223.

Montgomery, B. M. (1981). The form and function of quality communication in marriage. *Family Relations*, 30: 21-30.

Montgomery, B. M. (1992). Communication as the interface between couples and culture. *Communications Yearbook,* 15, Newbury Park, CA: Sage: 475-507.

Montgomery, B. M. (1994). Communication in close relationships. In A. Weber and J. Harvey (Eds.) *Perspectives on close relationships*. (pp.67-87). Needham Heights, MA: Allyn & Bacon.

Montgomery, M., E.M. Hetherington, and W.G. Clingempeel (1992). Pattern of courtship for remarriage: Implications for child adjustment & parent-child relationships. *Journal of Marriage and the Family,* 54: 686-698.

Mooney, L., and S. Brabant, (1988). Birthday cards, love, and communication. *Social Science Research*, 72: 106-109.

Morgaine, C. (1992). Alternative paradigms for helping families change themselves. *Family Relations,* 41: 12-17.

Moss, B., and A. Schwebel (1993). Defining intimacy in romantic relationships. *Family Relations,* 42: 31-37.

Mott, F. L. (1994). Sons, daughters and fathers' absence: Differentials in father-leaving probabilities and in home environments. *Journal of Family Issues,* 15: 97-128.

Murphy, W. (1984). Albert Hadley—the search for right clues. *Architectural Digest*, 41: 98-98J.

Napier, A. with C. Whitaker (1978). *The family crucible*. New York: Harper and Row.

Neugarten, B., and K.K. Weinstein (1964). The changing American grandparent. *Journal of Marriage and the Family,* 26: 199-204.

Nichols, M. (1984). *Family therapy: Concepts and methods*. New York: Gardner Press.

Noller, P., and M. A. Fitzpatrick (1993). *Communication in family relationships*. Englewood Cliffs, NJ, Prentice-Hall.

Noone, R. (1989). Systems thinking and differentiation of self. *Center for family communication consultation review*. 1 (1).

Notarius, C., and H. Markman (1993). *We can work it out*. New York: G.P. Putman's Sons.

Nussbaum, J.F. (1983). Relational closeness of elderly interaction: Implications for life satisfaction. *Western Journal of Speech Communication,* 47: 229-243.

Offer, D., and M. Sabshin (1984). *Normality and the life cycle*. New York: Basic Books.

Olson, D. H., and H. McCubbin and Associates (1983). *Families: What makes them work*. Beverly Hills: Sage.

Olson, D., C. Russell, and D. Sprenkle. (Eds). (1983). *Circumplex model: Systematic assessment and treatment of families*. New York: Haworth Press.

Olson, D., C. Russell, and D. Sprenkle (1979). Circumplex model of marital and family systems: Cohesion and adaptability dimensions, family types, and clinical applications. *Family Process*, 18: 3-28.

Olson, D., Y. Lavee, and H. McCubbin (1988). Types of families and family response to stress across the family life cycle. In J. Aldous and D. Klein (Eds.) *Social stress and family development*. New York: Guilford Press, 16-43.

Orbuch, T., J. Veroff, and D. Holmberg (1993). Becoming a married couple: The emergence of the meaning in the first year of marriage. *Journal of Marriage and the Family,* 55: 815-826.

Osmond, H. (1970). Function as the basis of psychiatric ward design. In H. Proshansky, W. Ittleson & L. Rivlin (Eds.), *Environmental Psychology*. (pp. 560-588). New York: Holt, Rinehart & Winston.

Otto, H. (1975). Marriage and family enrichment programs in North America: Report and analysis. *The family coordinator*, 24: 137-142.

Papernow, P. (1984). The stepfamily cycle: An experiential model of stepfamily development. *Family Relations*, 33: 335-363.

Papernow, P. (1987). Thickening the middle ground: Dilemma and vulnerabilities of remarried couples. *Psychotherapy*, 24: 630-639.

Papernow, P. (1993). *Becoming A stepfamily*. San Francisco: Jossey-Bass.

Papp, P. (1983). *The process of change*. New York: Guilford Press.

Parkes, C.M. (1972). *Bereavement*. New York: International Universities Press.

Pasley, K. (1987). Family boundary ambiguity: Perceptions of adult stepfamily members. In K. Pasley & M. Ihninger-Tallman (Eds.), *Remarriage and stepparenting: Current research* (pp. 206-224). New York: Guilford Press.

Patterson, C. (1992). Children of lesbian and gay parents. *Child Development,* 63: 1025-1043.

Patterson, J. M., and H.I. McCubbin (1984). Gender roles and coping. *Journal of Marriage and the Family*, 46: 95-104.

Pearce, W. B., and S.M. Sharp (1973). Self-disclosing communication. *Journal of Communication*, 23: 409-425.

Pearson, J. (1989). *Communication in the family*. New York: Harper & Row.

Pearson, J. (1992). *Lasting love*. Dubuque: Wm. Brown.

Peck, J., and J. Manocherian (1988). Divorce in the changing family life cycle. In B. Carter & M. McGoldrick (Eds.), *The changing family life cycle*. (2nd. Ed., pp. 335-369). New York: Gardner.

Perlmutter, M. (1988). Enchantment of siblings: Effects of birth order on family myth. In M. Kahn & K. Lewis, *Siblings in therapy*. (pp. 25-45). New York: W. W. Norton.

Perry-Jenkins, M., and K. Folk (1994). Class, couples, and conflict: Effects of the division of labor on assessments of marriage in dual-earner families. *Journal Marriage and the Family,* 56: 165-180.

Pilkington, C., and D. Richardson (1988). Perceptions of risk in intimacy. *Journal of Social & Personal Relationships*, 5: 503-508.

Pittman, J. and S. Lloyd (1988). Quality of family life, social support and stress. *Journal of Marriage and the Family,* 50: 53-67.

Pleck, Joseph H. (1992). Pleck discusses work—family issues. *National Council on Family Relations Report,* 37: 1-4.

Pleck, Joseph H. (1993). Are "family supportive" employer policies relevant to men? In J.C. Hood (Ed.) *Men, work and families*: 217-237. Newbury Park, CA: Sage.

Popenoe, D. (1993). American family decline, 1960: A review and appraisal. *Journal of Marriage and the Family,* 55, 3: 527-542.

Powell, G. S., and K.S. Wampler (1982). Marriage enrichment participants: Levels of marital satisfaction. *Family Relations, 31*: 389-394.

Prodicano, M., and C. Fisher (Eds.) (1992). *Contemporary families: A handbook for school professionals*. New York: Teachers College Press.

Rait, D. (1988). Seeing results. *Family therapy networker*, 12: 52-56.

Rampage, C. (1992). Family therapy and violence toward women: A feminist perspective. *The family institute news,* 1, 1: 4-5.

Ranney, E. C., and R. R. Cottone (1989). Emotional abuse in the family: The need for awareness & treatment. *Journal of Mental Health Counse,l* 13: 435-448.

Raschke, H. J., and V.J. Raschke (1979). Family conflict and children's self-concepts: A comparison of intact and single-parent families. *Journal of Marriage and the Family*, 41: 367-374.

Raush, H. L., W.A. Barry, R.K. Hertel, R.K., and M.A. Swain (1974). *Communication conflict and marriage*. San Francisco: Jossey-Bass.

Raven, B., C. Centers, and A. Rodriges (1975). The bases of conjugal power. In R. E. Cromwell & D. H. Olson (Eds.), *Power in families* (pp. 217–234). New York: Halsted Press.

Rawlins, W.K. (1989). Rehearsing the margins of adulthood: The communication management of adolescent friendships. In J. Nussbasum (Ed.), *Life-span communication: Normative processes* (pp. 137–154). Hillsdale, NJ: Lawrence Erlbaum.

Rawlins, W.K. (1992). *Friendship matters*. New York: Aldine de Guyter.

Reilly, T., D. Entwisle, D., and S. Doering (1987). Socialization into parenthood: A longitudinal study of the development of self-evaluation. *Journal of Marriage and the Family*, 49 (2): 295–309.

Reiss, D. (1981). *The family's construction of reality*. Cambridge, MA: Harvard University Press.

Reiss, D., and M.E. Oliveri (1980). Family paradigm and family coping: A proposal for linking the family's intrinsic adaptive capacities to its responses to stress. *Family Relations*, 29: 431–444.

Remer, R. (1984). The effects of interpersonal confrontation on males. *American Mental Health Association Journal*, 6: 81–90.

Renick, M., S.L. Blumberg, and H.J. Markman (1992). The prevention and relationship enhancement program (PREP): An empirically based preventive intervention program for couples. *Family Relations,* 41: 141–147.

Renzetti, C. (1989). Building a second closet: Third party responses to victims of lesbian partner abuse. *Family Relations*, 38: 157–163.

Richards, L. N., and C. Schmiege (1993). Problems and strengths of single-parent families. *Family Relations,* 42: 277–285.

Richardson, J. (1993). Lesbian parents' school visit sparks a clash of cultures in Boise suburbs. *Education Week,* 12, 20 (Feb. 10): 117.

Richardson, R., R. Abramowitz, C. Asp, and A. Petersen (1986). Parent-child relationships in early adolescence: Effects of family structure. *Journal of Marriage and the Family*, 48 (4): 805–811.

Ridley, C. A. Peterman, D. J., and A.W. Avery (1978). Cohabitation: Does it make for a better marriage? *The family coordinator*, 27: 129–136.

Risman, B., and K. Park (1988). Just the two of us: Parent-child relationships in single-parent homes. *Journal of Marriage and the Family*, 50: 1049–1062.

Ritter, E. (1979). Social perspective-taking ability, cognitive complexity and listener-adopted communication in early and late adolescence. *Communication Monographs*, 46: 42–50.

Roberts, L., and L. Krokoff (1990). A time-series analysis of withdrawal, hostility and displeasure in satisfied & dissatisfied marriages *Journal of Marriage and the Family,* 52: 95–105.

Robinson, L, and P. Blanton (1993). Marital strengths in enduring marriages. *Family Relations,* 42: 38–45.

Rogers, C. R. (1972). *Becoming partners: Marriage and its alternatives*. New York: Delta Books.

Rogers, E. (1984). Potentials in family communication research. Paper presented at the SCA/Northwestern University Research Conference on Family Communication.

Rogers-Millar, L. E., and F.E. Miller (1979). Domineeringness and dominance: A transactional view. *Human Communication Research*, 5: 238–246.

Rogler, S., and M. Procidano (1986). The effect of social networks on marital roles: A test of a Bott Hypothesis in an intergenerational context. *Journal of Marriage and the Family*, 48: 714–724.

Roloff, M. (1987). Communication conflict. In C. Berger and S. Chaffee (Eds.) *Handbook of communication science*, (pp. 484-534). Beverly Hills: Sage.

Rosenblatt, P. C., S.L. Titus, and M.R. Cunningham (1979). Disrespect, tension, and togetherness-apartness in marriage. *Journal of Marital and Family Therapy*, 5: 47-54.

Rosenfeld, R. (1986). U.S. farm women: Their participation in farm work and decision making. *Work & Occupations*, 13: 179-202.

Ross, C. (1991). Marriage & the sense of control. *Journal of Marriage and the Family,* 53: 831-838.

Ross, J. (1988). Challenging boundaries: An adolescent in the homosexual family. *Journal of Psychology,* 2, 2: 227-240.

Rotunno, M. and M. McGoldrick (1982). Italian families. In M. McGoldrick, J. Giordano and J. Pearce (Eds). *Ethnicity and family therapy.* (pp 340-363) New York: Guilford Press.

Roxema, H.J. (1986). Defensive communiation climate as a barrier to sex education in the home. *Family Relations,* 35: 531-537.

Rubin, J. Z., and B.R. Brown (1975). *The social psychology of bargaining and negotiation.* New York: Academic Press.

Rubin, L. (1979). *Women of a certain age: The midlife search for self.* New York: Harper & Row.

Rubin, L. (1983). *Intimate strangers.* New York: Harper and Row.

Russell, C. S. (1979). Circumplex model of marital and family systems: III. Empirical evaluation with families. *Family Process*, 18: 29-45.

Ryan, K., and M. Ryan (1982). *Making a marriage*. New York: St. Martin's Press.

Sabourin, T.C. (1992, October). Dialectical tensions in family life: A comparison of abusive and nonabusive families. Paper presented at SCA National Meeting; Chicago.

Sabourin, T.C., D. Infante, and J. Rudd (1990, November). Argumentativeness and verbal aggression in interspousal violence: A test of the argumentative skill deficiency model using couple data. Paper presented at SCA National Meeting; Chicago.

Saegert, S. (1985). The role of housing in the experience of dwelling. In I. Altman & C. Werner (Eds.), *Home environments: Human behavior and environment* (Vol. 8, pp. 287-309). New York: Plenum Press.

Safilios-Rothschild, C. (1970). The study of family power structure: 1960-1969. *Journal of Marriage and the Family*, 32: 539-552.

Sanderson, B., and L. A. Kurdek (1993). Race and gender as moderator variables in predicting relationship satisfaction and relationship commitment in a sample of dating heterosexual couples. *Family Relations,* 42: 263-267.

Sandor, G. (1994, June). The "other" Americans. *American demographics* 16: 36-42.

Santi, L. (1987). Change in the structure and size of American households: 1970-1985. *Journal of Marriage and the Family*, 49 (4): 833-837.

Satir, V. (1967). *Conjoint family therapy*. Palo Alto, CA: Science & Behavior books.

Satir, V. (1972). *Peoplemaking*. Palo Alto, CA: Science & Behavior Books.

Satir, V. (1988). *The new peoplemaking*. Mountain View CA: Science and Behavior Books.

Sawin, D. B., and R.D. Parke (1979). Fathers' affectionate stimulation and caregiving behaviors with newborn infants. *Family Coordinator*, 28: 509-519.

Sawin, M. (1979). *Family enrichment with family clusters*. Valley Forge, PA: Judson Press.

Scanzoni, J. (1972). *Sexual bargaining*. Englewood Cliffs, NJ: Prentice-Hall.

Scanzoni, J., and K. Polonko (1980). A conceptual approach to explicit marital negotiation. *Journal of Marriage and the Family*, 42: 31-44.

Scanzoni, J., and M. Szinovacz (1980). *Family decision making: A developmental sex role model*. Beverly Hills: Sage.

Schaap, C., B. Buunk, and A. Kenkstra (1987). Marital conflict resolution. In P. Noller & M. A. Fitzpatrick (Eds.), *Perspectives on marital interaction* (pp. 203-244). Philadelphia: Multilingual Matters.

Schaefer, R. B., and P.M. Keith (1981). Equity in marital roles across the family life cycle. *Journal of Marriage and the Family*, 43: 359-367.

Schaeffer, N. C. (1989). The frequency and intensity of parental conflict: Choosing response dimensions. *Journal of Marriage and the Family*, 51: 759-766.

Schaninger, C. M., and W. C. Buss (1986). A longitudinal comparison of consumption and finance handling between happily married and divorced couples. *Journal of Marriage and the Family,* 48: 129-136.

Scheflen, A. (1971). Living space in an urban ghetto. *Family Process*, 10: 429-449.

Scheiner, L. C., A.P. Musetto, and D.M. Cordier (1982). Custody and visitation counseling: A report of an innovative program. *Family Relations*, 31: 99-108.

Schnittger, M., and G. Bird (1990). Coping among dual-career men and women across the family life cycle. *Family Relations*: 199-205.

Schoen, R., and R. Weineck (1993). Partner choice in marriage and cohabitations. *Journal of Marriage and the Family,* 55: 408-414.

Schwartz, P. (1994). *Peer marriage*, New York: Free Press.

Scoresby, A. L. (1977). *The marriage dialogue*. Reading, MA: Addison-Wesley.

Scott, J. (1984). Comfort and seating distance in living rooms. The relationship of interactants and topic for conversation. *Environment and behavior*, 16: 35-54.

Seligman, M. (1988). Psychotherapy with siblings of disabled children. In M. Kahn & L. Lewis (Eds.), *Siblings in therapy: Life span and clinical issues* (pp. 167-189). New York: W. W. Norton.

Seltzer, Judith (1991). Relationships between fathers & children who live apart: The father's role after separation. *Journal of Marriage and the Family,* 53: 79-98.

Shamir, B. (1986). Unemployment and household division of labor. *Journal of Marriage and the Family*, 48: 195-206.

Shepard, W. (1980). Mothers and fathers, sons and daughters: Perceptions of young adults. *Sex Roles*, 6: 421-433.

Shimanoff, S.B. (1983). The role of gender in linguistic references to emotive states. *Communication Quarterly,* 30: 174-177.

Shon, S., and J. Davis (1983). Asian families. In M. McGoldrick, J. Giordano and J. Pearce. (Eds). *Ethnicity and family therapy* (pp 208-228). New York: Guilford Press.

Shreve, B., and M. Kunkel (1991). Self-psychology, shame and adolescent suicide: Theoretical and practical considerations. *Journal of Counseling & Development,* 69: 305-312.

Shumm, W., H. Barnes, S. Bollman, A. Jurick and M. Bugaighis (1987). Self-disclosure and marital satisfaction revisited. *Family Relations*, 34: 241-247.

Shweder, R. A. (1994, Jan. 9). What do men want? A reading list for the male identity crisis. *The New York Times Book Review*, Jan. 9, 1994.

Sieburg, E. (1973). Interpersonal confirmation: A paradigm for conceptualization and measurement. Paper presented at International Communication Association, Montreal, Quebec. ERIC document No. ED 098 634 1975.

Sillars, A. L. et al. (1983). Communication and conflict in marriage. In R. Bostrom (Ed.), *Communication Yearbook* (Vol. 7, pp. 414-429). Beverly Hills: Sage.

Sillars, A., and W. Wilmot (1989). Marital communication across the life span. In J. Nussbaum (Ed.), *Life-span communication: Narrative processes*. (pp. 225-254). Hillsdale, NJ: Laurence Erlbaum.

Sillars, A., J. Weisberg, C. Burggraf, and E. Wilson (1987). Content themes in marital conversations. *Human Communication Research*, 13: 495-528.

Silverberg, S., and L. Steinberg (1987). Adolescent autonomy, parent-adolescent conflict and parental well-being. *Journal of Youth & Adolescence*, 16: 293-312.

Silverman, C. (1992). Neighborhood life, communication and the metropolis. *Asia Journal of Communication,* 2, 3: 92-105.

Simon, R. (1982). Reflections on the one-way mirror: An interview with Jay Haley, part II. *Family Therapy Networker,* 6: 32-36.

Simons, R., L. Whitbeck, R. Conger, and J. Melby (1990). Husband and wife differences in determinants of parenting: A social learning and exchange model of parental behavior. *Journal of Marriage and the Family,* 52: 375-392.

Simons, R; J. Beaman; R. Conger; and W. Chao (1993). Stress, support, and antisocial behavior trait as determinants of emotional well-being and parenting practices among single mothers. *Journal of Marriage and the Family*, 55: 385-398.

Simons, R. L., L. B. Whitbeck, J. Beman, and R. D. Conger (1994). The impact of mothers' parenting, involvement by nonresidential fathers, and parental conflict on the adjustment of adolescent children (1994). *Journal of Marriage and the Family,* 56: 356-374.

Single Parents. (1992). *American demographics.* (Desk Reference Series), 3: 14-15, 24

Slevin, K. F., and Balswick, J. (1980). Children's perceptions of parental expressiveness. *Sex roles*, *6*: 293-299.

Sluzki, C. (1992). Transformations: A blueprint for narrative changes in therapy. *Family process,* 31, 3: 217-230.

Small, S., and D. Riley (1990). Toward a multidimensional assessment of work spillover into family life. *Journal of Marriage and the Family,* 52: 51-61.

Spitze, G. (1988). Women's employment and family relations. *Journal of Marriage and the Family*, 5:, 595-618.

Spooner, S. (1982). Intimacy in adults: A developmental model for counselors and helpers. *The Personnel and Guidance Journal*, 60: 168-170.

Sporakowski, M. (October 1988). A therapist's views on the consequences of change for the contemporary family. *Family Relations*, 37: 373-378.

Sporakowski, M. J., and G. Hughston (1978). Prescriptions for happy marriage: Adjustments and satisfactions of couples married 50 or more years. *The Family Coordinator*, 27: 321-328.

Sprecher, S. and K. McKinney (1994). Sexuality in close relationships. In A. Weber & J. Harvey (Eds). *Perspectives in close relationships*. (pp. 193-216). Needham Heights, MA: Allyn and Bacon.

Stamp, G. H. (1994). The appropriation of the parental role through communication during the transition to parenthood. *Communication Monographs* 61: 89-112.

Status of African American children under three living in poverty. (Fall 1992). National Center for Children in Poverty. News & Issues (Fall, 1992).

Steffenmeier, R. H. (1982). A role model of the transition to parenthood. *Journal of Marriage and the Family*, 44: 319-334.

Steinberg, L., and S. Silverberg (1987). Influences on marital satisfaction during the middle stages of the family life cycle. *Journal of Marriage and the Family*, 49: 751-761.

Steinmetz, S. K. (1977). The use of force for resolving family conflict: The training ground for abuse. *Family Coordinator*, 26: 19-26.

Steinor, C. (1978). Problems of power. Lecture at National Group Leaders Conference, Chicago.

Stephen, T. and D. Enholm (1987). On linguistic and social forms: Correspondences between metaphoric and intimate relationships. *The Western Journal of Speech Communication*, 51: 329-344.

Stephen, T. (1984). A symbolic exchange framework for the development of intimate relationships. *Human Relations*, 37: 393–408.

Stephen, T. (1986). Communication and interdependence in geographically separated relationships. *Human communication research*, 13: 2, 191–210.

Stephen, T. D. (1984). A symbolic exchange framework for the development of intimate relationships. *Human Relations*, 37: 393–408.

Stevens, J. H., Jr. (1984). Child development knowledge and parenting skills. *Family Relations*, 33: 237–244.

Stier, F. (1989). Toward a radical and ecological constructivist approach to family communication. *Journal of Applied Communication Research*, 17:1-26.

Stinnett, N., & J. De Frain (1985). *Secrets of strong families*. Boston: Little Brown.

Stinnett, N., J. Walters, and E. Kay (1984). *Relationships in marriage and the family* (2nd ed.). New York: Macmillan.

Stone, E. (1988). *Black sheep and kissing cousins*. New York: Penguin Books.

Straus, M. A. (1974). Leveling, civility, and violence in the family. *Journal of Marriage and the Family*, 36: 13–29, and "Addendum" 36 (Aug.): 442–445.

Straus, M.A. (1979). Measuring intrafamily conflict and violence. The conflict tactics (C.T. Scales. *Journal of Marriage and the Family*, 41: 75–88.

Straus, M. A., and R. Gelles (Eds.) (1990). *Physical violence in 8145 families: Risk factors and adaptations to violence*. New Brunswick, NJ. Transaction Publishers.

Straus, M. A., and S. Sweet (1992). Verbal/symbolic aggression in couples ... *Journal of Marriage and the Family*, 54: 346–357.

Stuart, R., and B. Jacobson (1985). *Second marriage*. New York: W. W. Norton.

Suitor, J., and K. Pillemar (1987). The presence of adult children: A source of stress for elderly couples' marriages? *Journal of Marriage and the Family*, 49, 717–725.

Swanson, John L. (1992). Sexism strikes men. *American counselor*: 10–13.

Tanner, D. (1978). *The lesbian couple*. Lexington, MA: DC Health & Co.

Tardy, C., L. Hosman, and J. Bradac (1981). Disclosing self to friends and family: A reexamining of initial questions. *Communication Quarterly*, 29: 263–268.

Tein, J.Y., M. Roosa, and M. Michaels (1994). Agreement between parent & child reports on parental behaviors. *Journal of Marriage and the Family*, 56: 341–355.

Terkelsen, K.G. (1980). Towards a theory of the family life cycle. In E. Carter and M. McGoldrick (Eds.) *The family life cycle: A framework for family therapy*. (pp. 21–52). New York: Gardner Press.

"The Challenge of Change: What the 1990 Census Tells Us About Children" (1992). *Population reference bureau of the center for the study of social policy*, Washington, DC, CSSP.

Thirty-One studies published on couple communication. (March 1989). *Relationship building*, 3 (1), 1-5.

Thomas, V. (1990). Determinants of global life happiness & marital happiness in dual-career black couples. *Family Relations*: 174–178.

Thomas, V., and D. H. Olson (1994). Circumplex model: Curvilinearity using clinical rating scale (CRS) and FACES III." *Family Journal*, 2: 36–44.

Thompson, T. (1989). Communication and dying: The end of the life-span. In J. Nussbaum (Ed.), *Life-span communication: Normative processes* (pp. 339–359). Hillsdale, NJ: Laurence Erlbaum.

Thompson, T., and J. Nussbaum (1988). Interpersonal communication: Intimate relationships and aging. In C. W. Carmichael, C. H. Botan & R. Hawkins (Eds.), *Human communication and the aging process* (pp. 95–110). Prospect Heights, IL.: Waveland Press.

Toman, W. T. (1969). *Family constellations* (2nd ed.). New York: Springer.

Tomm, K. (1983). The old hat doesn't fit. *The family therapy networker*, 7: 39-41.

Troll, L. E. (1975). *Early and middle adulthood.* Monterey, CA: Brooks-Cole Publishing Co.

Troll, L. E., S. Miller, and R. Atchley (1979). *Families in later life*. Belmont, CA: Wadsworth Publishing Co.

Tschann. J. (1988). Self-disclosure in adult friendship: Gender and marital status differences. *Journal of Social and Personal Relationships*, 5: 65-81.

Turk, J.L., and N.W. Bell (1972). Measuring power in families. *Journal of Marriage and the Family,* 34: 215-222.

Turnbull, S. K., and J.M. Turnbull (1983). To dream the impossible dream: An agenda for discussion with stepparents. *Family Relations*, 32: 277-230.

Turner, R.H. (1970). Conflict and harmony. *Family interaction*. New York: John Wiley & Sons. 135-163.

U.S. Census (1992). Washington, D.C., Government Printing Office.

Vaillant, C. O., and G. E. Vaillant (1993). Is the U-Curve of marital satisfaction an illusion? A 40-year study of marriage. *Journal of Marriage and the Family,* 55: 230-239.

Vangelisti, A. L. (1993). Communication in the family: The influence of time, relational prototypes and irrationality. *Communication Monographs,* 60: 42-54.

Vangelisti, A. L. (1994). Couples' communication problems: The counselor's perspective. *Journal of Applied Communication Research,* 22: 106-126.

Vangelisti, A. L and M. A. Banski (1993). Couples debriefing conversations, the impact of gender, occupation and demographic characteristics. *Family Relations,* 42: 149-157.

Vermoert, A. (1967). Comments on communicating with the fatally ill. *Omega*: 10-11.

Villard, K., and L. Whipple (1976). *Beginnings in relational communication*. New York: John Wiley and Sons.

Visher, E. (1989). The stepping ahead program. *Stepfamilies stepping ahead.* (pp. 57-89). Lincoln: NE: Stepfamilies Press.

Visher, E., and J. Visher (1979). *Stepfamilies: A guide to working with stepparents and stepchildren*. New York: Brunner/ Mazel.

Visher, E., and J. Visher (1988). *Old loyalties, new ties: Therapeutic strategies and stepfamilies*. New York: Brunner/ Mazel.

Visher, E., and J. Visher (1993). *Stepfamilies: Myths and realities*. New York: Citadel Press.

Visher, J., and E. Visher (1982). Stepfamilies and stepparenting. In F. Walsh (Ed.), *Normal family processes*. (pp 331-353). New York: Guilford Press.

Vuchinich, S. (1987). Starting and stopping spontaneous family conflicts. *Journal of Marriage and the Family*, 49 (3): 591-601.

Vuchinich, S., J. Teachman, and L. Crosby (1991). Families and hazard rates that change over time: Some methodological issues in analyzing transitions. *Journal of Marriage and the Family,* 53: 898-912.

Wackman, D. (1978). Communication training in marriage and family living. Paper presented at Speech Communication Association Convention. Minneapolis.

Waite, L. (1987). Nest-leaving patterns and the transition to marriage for young men and women. *Journal of Marriage and the Family*, 49 (3): 507-516.

Walker, A. J. (1993). Teaching about race, gender, and class diversity in U.S. families. *Family Relations,* 42: 342-350.

Waller, W., and A. Jennings (1990). On the possibility of a feminist economics: The convergence of institutional & feminist methodology. *Journal of Economic Issues,* 24: 613-620.

Wallerstein, J., and S. Blakeslee (1989). *Second chances*. New York: Ticknor and Fields.

Wallerstein, J., and J. Kelly (1980). *Surviving the breakup*. New York: Basic Books.

Walsh, F. (1982). *Normal family processes*. New York: The Guilford Press.

Walsh, F. (1985). Social change, disequilibrium, and adaptation in developing countries: A Moroccan example. In J. Schwartzman (Ed.), *Families and other systems*. New York: Guilford Press.

Walsh, F. (1989). The family in later life. In B. Carter & M. McGoldrick (Eds.), *The changing family life cycle: A framework for family therapy*. (2nd. ed., pp. 311-332). New York: Gardner Press.

Walsh, F. (1991). Promoting healthy functioning in divorced and remarried families. In A. German, and D. Kniskern (Eds) (1991). *Handbook of family therapy*. Vol. II. (pp. 525-545). New York: Brunner/Mazel.

Walsh, F. (1993). Conceptualization of normal family processes. In F. Walsh (Ed). *Normal Family Processes*. (2nd ed.) (pp. 3-69). New York: The Guilford Press.

Walsh, F., and M. Scheinkman (1989). (Fe)male: The hidden gender dimension in models of family therapy. In M. McGoldrick, C. Anderson & F. Walsh (Eds.), *Women in families* (pp. 16-41). New York: W. W. Norton.

Wamboldt, Frederick, and David Reiss (1989). Defining a f amily heritage and a new relationship identity: Two central tasks in the making of a marriage. *Family Process,* 2: 317-335.

Wampler, K. S., and D.H. Sprenkle (1980). The Minnesota couple communication program. *Journal of Marriage and the Family*, 42: 577-584.

Warner, R.M. (1991a). Incorporating time. In B.M. Montgomery and S. Duck (Eds.), *Studying interpersonal interaction*: 82-102, New York: Guilford.

Warner, R. (1991b). Does the sex of your children matter? Support for feminism among women and men in the U.S. & Canada. *Journal of Marriage and the Family,* 53: 1051-1056.

Warner, R. L., R. G. Lee and J. Lee (1989). Social organization, spousal resources, and marital power: A Cross-Cultural Study (1986). *Journal of Marriage and the Family,* 48: 121-128.

Warner, R. L., G. R. Lee, and J. Lee. Social relations: View and research issues. *Marriage and the Family Review,* 12: (3-4) 1-8.

Wass, H., and J.E. Myers (1982). Psychosocial aspects of death among the elderly: A review of the literature. *The Personnel and Guidance Journal*, 60: 131-145.

Waterman, J. (1979). Family patterns of self-disclosure. In G. Chelune and Associates (eds.), *Self-disclosure* (pp. 225-242). San Francisco: Jossey-Bass.

Watson, J.J., and R. Remer (1984). The effects of interpersonal confrontation on females. *Personnel and Guidance Journal,* 62: 607-611.

Watson, R. E. (1983). Premarital cohabitation vs. traditional courtship: Their effects on subsequent marital adjustment. *Family Relations*, 32: 139-148.

Watzlawick, P., J. Beavin, and D.D. Jackson (1967). *Pragmatics of human communication*. New York: W. W. Norton & Co.

Webster-Stratton, C. (1989). The relationship of marital support, conflict, and divorce to parent perceptions, behaviors, and childhood conduct problems. *Journal of Marriage and the Family*, 51: 417-430.

Weiss, R. L. (1984). Cognitive and strategic intervention in behavioral marital therapy. In K. Hohlweg & N. S. Jacobson (Eds.), *Marital interaction: Analysis and modification* (pp. 337-355). New York: Guilford Press.

Wells, B. (1986). *The meaning makers*. Portsmouth, NH: Heineman.

Wenk, D. A., C. L. Hardesty, C. S. Morgan, and S. L. Blair (1994). The influence of parental involvement on the well-being of sons and daughters. *Journal of Marriage and the Family,* 56: 229-234.

Werner, C. (1987). Home interiors: A time and place for interpersonal relationships. *Environment and behavior*, 19 (2): 169–179.

Werner, C.M. and L. A. Baxter (1994). Temporal qualities of relationships: Organisimic, transactional and dialectical. In Mark L. Knapp and Gerald R. Miller (Eds.), *Handbook of interpersonal communication*, Thousand Oaks, CA: Sage Publications: 323–379.

Werner, C; I. Altman; and B. Brown (1992). A transactional approach to interpersonal relations: Physical environment, social context and temporal qualities. *Journal of Social and Personal Relationships,* 9: 287–323.

West, J., J. Zarski, and R. Harvil (1988). The influence of the family triangle on intimacy. *American Mental Health Counselors Association Journal*: 166–174.

Westin, A. (1967). *Privacy and freedom*. New York: Atheneum.

Weston, K. (1993). *Families we choose*. New York: Columbia University Press.

Whitchurch, G. and L. Constantine (1993). Systems theory. In P. Boss, et al. (Eds) *Sourcebook of family theories and methods*. 325–352. New York: Plenum Press.

White, B. (1989). Gender differences in marital communication patterns. *Family Process*, 28: 89–106.

Whitehead, E. E., and J. Whitehead (1981). *Marrying well: Possibilities in Christian marriage today*. New York: Doubleday.

Whiteside, M. F. (1989). Family rituals as a key to kinship connections in remarried families. *Family Relations* 38: 34–39.

Wietig, S.G., and A. McLaren (1975). Power in various family structures. In R.E. Cromwell and D.H. Olson (Eds.) *Power in families*. New York: John Wiley and Sons, 95–116.

Wilkinson, C. (1989). Family first. In *Emphasis*, Mental Health Association of Evanston, 24: 1–2.

Wilkinson, C. (1990). Family communication: Developing the marital partnership. Speech presented at Community Church of Wilmette.

Wilkinson, C. (1995). Family images and metaphors. Speech presented at Northbrook Court Speakers Series. Northbrook, IL.

Wilmot, J., and W. Wilmot (1981). *Interpersonal conflict*. Dubuque, IA: William C. Brown.

Wilmot, W. W. (1987). *Dyadic communication* (3rd ed.). New York: Random House.

Winter, W.D., A.J. Ferreira, and N. Bowers. Decision making in married and unrelated couples. *Family Process* 12: 83–94.

Witteman, H., and M.A. Fitzpatrick (1987). A social scientific view of marriage encounter. *Journal of Clinical and Social Psychology*.

Wolff, Leanne O. (1993, November). Family narrative: How our stories shape us. Paper presented at SCA Conference: Miami, FL.

Wood B., and M. Talmon (1983). Family boundaries in transition: A search for alternatives. *Family Process*, 22: 347–357.

Wood, J. (1982). Communication and relational cultures: Bases for the study of human relationships. *Communication Quarterly,* 30: 75–83.

Wood, J. T., and C. C. Inman (1993). In a different mode: Masculine styles of communicating closeness. *Journal of Applied Communication Research,* 21: 279–295.

Worobey, J. (1989). Mother-infant interaction: *Proto* communication in the developing dyad. In J. Nussbaum (Ed.), *Life-span communication: Normative process* (7–25). Hillsdale, N.J.: Laurence Erlbaum.

Worthington, E. Jr., G. Buston, and T. Hammonds (1989). A component analysis of marriage enrichment: Information and treatment modality. *Journal of Counseling and Development,* 67: 555–560.

Wuthnow, R. (1994). *Sharing the Journey*. New York: The Free Press.

Wynne, L. (Ed). (1988). The state of the art in family therapy research: Controversies and recommendations. New York: Family Process Press.

Wynne, L. C., and A. R. Wynne (1986). The quest for intimacy. *Journal of Marital and Family Therapy,* 12: 383-394.

Yelsma, P. (1984). Functional conflict management in effective marital adjustment. *Communication Quarterly*, 32: 56-62.

Yelsma, P. (1986). Marriage vs. cohabitation: Couples communication practices and satisfaction. *Journal of Communication*, 36: 94-107.

Yep, G. A. (1993, November). Disclosure of HIV infections to significant others: A communication boundary management perspective. Paper presented at SCA Annual Meeting: Miami, FL.

Yerby, J. (1993). Co-constructing alternative stories: Narrative approaches in the family therapy literature. Paper presented at Speech Communication Association, Miami.

Yerby, J., and N.L. Buerkel-Rothfuss (1982). Communication patterns, contradictions, and family functions. Paper presented at the Speech Communication Association Convention, New York.

Yerby J., Buerkel-Rothfuss, N., and A. Bochner (1990). *Understanding family communication*. Scottsdale, Az: Gorsuch Scarisbrick

Yerby, Janet. (November, 1992). Family systems theory reconsidered: Integrating social construction theory and dialectical process into a systems perspective of family communication. Paper presented at Speech Communication Association, Chicago.

Youniss, J., & Smollar, J. (1985). *Adolescent relations with mothers, fathers and friends*. Chicago: University of Chicago Press.

Zacks, E., R. Green, and J. Marrow (1988). Comparing lesbian and heterosexual couples on the circumplex model: An initial investigation. In *Family Process*, 27: 471-484.

Zill, N. (1988). Behavior, achievement, and health problems among children in stepfamilies: Findings from a national survey of child health. In E.M. Hetherington and J. Arasteh (Eds.), *The impact of divorce, single-parenting and step-parenting on children*, (pp. 325-368). Hillsdale, NJ: Lawrence Erlbaum.

Zvonkovic, A., C. Schmiege, and L. Hall (1994). Influence strategies used when couples make work-family decisions and their importance for marital satisfaction. *Family Relations,* 43: 182-188.

# ACKNOWLEDGMENTS

## Text Credits

The following works, from which substantial portions are quoted in this book, are protected by the copyright law of the United States and international copyright laws.

Altman I., and D. A. Taylor. *Social Penetration*. Copyright © 1973 by I. Altman and D. A. Taylor. Reprinted by permission of Holt, Rinehart & Winston.

Carter. B., and McGoldrick M. *The Changing Family Life Cycle: A Framework for Family Therapy,* 2ed. Copyright ©1989 Allyn & Bacon. Reprinted by permission.

Hess, R. D., and G. Handel. *Family Worlds*. Copyright © 1959 by University of Chicago Press. Reprinted by permission.

Howard, J. *Families*. Copyright © 1978 by Simon & Schuster. Reprinted by permission.

Kantor, D., and W. Lehr. *Inside the Family*. Copyright © 1976 by Jossey-Bass, Inc. Reprinted by permission.

Knapp, M., and A. Vangelisti, "A Model of Interaction Stages," in *Interpersonal Communications and Human Relationships*. Copyright © 1984 by Allyn & Bacon. Reprinted by permission.

Lerner, H. G. *The Dance of Intimacy*. Copyright © 1989 by HarperCollins, Inc. Reprinted by permission.

Littlejohn, S. W. *Theories of Human Communication,* 3 ed. Copyright © 1989 by Wadsworth Publishing. Reprinted by permission.

McDonald, G. W., "Family Power: The Assessment of a Decade of Theory and Research, 1970-1979," in *Journal of Marriage and the Family,* Vol. 42. Copyright © 1980 by National Council of Family Relations.

Noone, R, "Systems Thinking and Differentiation of Self," in Center for Family Consultation Review, Vol. 1. Copyright © 1989 by *Center for Family Consultation Review*. Reprinted by permission.

Olson, D. H., Sprenkle, D. H., and C. Russell, "Circumplex Model of Marital and Family Systems," in *Family Process,* Vol. 18. Copyright © 1979 by Family Process, Inc. Reprinted by permission.

Papernow, Patricia, "The Stepfamily Cycle: An Experiential Model of Stepfamily Development," in *Family Relations,* Vol. 33. Copyright © 1984 by National Council on Family Relations and P. Papernow. Reprinted by permission.

Rogers, C. *Becoming Partners*. Copyright © 1972 by Delacorte Press. Reprinted by permission.

Scanzoni, J., and K. Polonko, "A Conceptual Approach to Explicit Marital Negotiation," in *Journal of Family and Marriage,* Vol. 42. Copyright © 1980 by National Council of Family Relations and J. Scanzoni.

Scheflen, A., "Living Space in an Urban Ghetto," in *Family Process*. Vol. 10. Copyright © 1971 by Family Process, Inc. Reprinted by permission.

Scoresby, L. *The Marriage Dialogue*. Copyright © 1977 by McGraw-Hill, Inc. Reprinted by permission.

Stuart, R. B., and B. Johnson. *Second Marriage*. Copyright © 1985 by W. W. Norton. Reprinted by permission.

Walsh, F. *Family Interfaces*. Copyright © 1982 by Brunner/Mazel. Reprinted by permission.

Walsh, F. *Normal Family Processes*. Copyright © 1982 by the Guilford Press. Reprinted by permission.

## Photo Credits

**Cover Photo:** Comstock, Inc. **Pages** 4, **52(L), 104(L), 104(R), 156, 283, 307(R), 333(L)** Jean-Claude LeJeune; **6, 146(R)** Laimute Druskis/StockBoston; **22, 187, 246(R)** Elizabeth Crews/Stock Boston; **52(R)** michael Grecco/Stock Boston; **75, 333(R)** Bob Daemmrich/Stock Boston; **80(L), 80(R)** Kelly Davis/PhotoEdit; **107(L), 307(L)** Hazel Hankin/Stock Boston; **107(R), 397(L)** Spencer Grant/Stock Boston; **125** Jim Bradshaw; **146(L), 340, 360, 419** Judy Gelles/Stock Boston; **207** Michael Weisbiot/Stock Boston; **277** Comstock, Inc.; **318** Michael Hayman/Stock Boston; **387(L)** Fredrik Bodin/Stock Boston; **387(R)** Angel Franco/NYT Pictures; **397(R)** Francis M. Cox/Stock Boston; **427** Michael Newman/PhotoEdit.

# AUTHOR INDEX

# SUBJECT INDEX